I dedicate this book to my mother and father, Donna and A. J. "Jim" Giametta. Your positive influence throughout my childhood and into adulthood, and the life lessons you provided, made me the man I am today. What you have taught me has carried on into my family, allowing me to raise my children with respect, high character standards, and a strong work ethic. I am proud to have you as parents. I also won't forget the times you watched me mow the lawn while drinking lemonade, Buddy. Or the famous phrase, "I can do it." I think that old Johnson outboard motor is still rusting at the bottom of Meril's Lake in East Texas.

Pro Flex on Spring

Chris Giametta

Apress®

Pro Flex on Spring

Copyright © 2009 by Chris Giametta

ISBN-13 (pbk): 978-1-4302-1835-7

ISBN-13 (electronic): 978-1-4302-1836-4

9 8 7 6 5 4 3 2 1

Lead Editors: Steve Anglin, Tom Welsh
Technical Reviewer: Bradford Taylor
Editorial Board: Clay Andres, Steve Anglin, Mark Beckner, Ewan Buckingham, Tony Campbell,
    Gary Cornell, Jonathan Gennick, Jonathan Hassell, Michelle Lowman, Matthew Moodie,
    Duncan Parkes, Jeffrey Pepper, Frank Pohlmann, Ben Renow-Clarke, Dominic Shakeshaft,
    Matt Wade, Tom Welsh
Project Manager: Kylie Johnston
Copy Editor: Marilyn Smith
Associate Production Director: Kari Brooks-Copony
Production Editor: Laura Esterman
Compositor: Susan Glinert Stevens
Proofreader: Nancy Sixsmith
Indexer: Carol Burbo
Artist: April Milne
Cover Designer: Kurt Krames
Manufacturing Director: Tom Debolski

Distributed to the book trade worldwide by Springer-Verlag New York, Inc., 233 Spring Street, 6th Floor, New York, NY 10013. Phone 1-800-SPRINGER, fax 201-348-4505, e-mail orders-ny@springer-sbm.com, or visit http://www.springeronline.com.

For information on translations, please contact Apress directly at 2855 Telegraph Avenue, Suite 600, Berkeley, CA 94705. Phone 510-549-5930, fax 510-549-5939, e-mail info@apress.com, or visit http://www.apress.com.

Apress and friends of ED books may be purchased in bulk for academic, corporate, or promotional use. eBook versions and licenses are also available for most titles. For more information, reference our Special Bulk Sales–eBook Licensing web page at http://www.apress.com/info/bulksales.

The source code for this book is available to readers at http://www.apress.com.

Contents at a Glance

Contents

▰APPENDIX   **Installing the RIA Tools Platform** 435

▰INDEX

About the Author

 **CHRIS GIAMETTA** has been a principal architect for Miller & Associates for the past five years, overseeing application development primarily with Adobe Flex and Spring. Of course, being an architect involves much more than just programming languages and software frameworks. Over his career, Chris has developed systems that require a complete knowledge of hardware and software architecture at the systems and enterprise level. In those years, he has helped Miller & Associates to become one of the premier RIA consulting companies in the Dallas/Fort Worth area of Texas, through thought leadership and innovation.

Chris is an Adobe Certified Expert in Adobe Flex. He was been working with Flex and Spring since 2004. Before learning Flex and Spring, he cut his teeth developing customer relationship management (CRM) systems integrated with Java on the front end and a C++ ORB implementation on the server side.

Chris graduated from the University of Southern Mississippi and now resides in the Dallas area with his wife and two children.

About the Technical Reviewer

BRADFORD TAYLOR is a software architect at Credera, a business and technology consulting firm based in Dallas, Texas. Bradford has been implementing Java solutions for ten years. He has implemented and developed Flex, Spring, and J2EE solutions for major telecommunications companies, retail companies, and small businesses.

In his spare time, Bradford enjoys spending time with his family.

Acknowledgments

I'd like to thank my wife, Kristi, for picking up my slack while I worked on this book, as it took a considerable amount of after-hours time to complete.

Additionally, I'd like to thank Apress for giving me the opportunity to write this book, and the following individuals who were instrumental in helping the book come together.

Steve Anglin, my acquisitions editor, for giving me a shot at writing about the book's topic, for helping me work the table of contents into a formal piece of work, and for organizing the team who dedicated themselves to making this a great book.

Tom Welsh, my book editor, who provided literary and technical support throughout the writing process. Tom always kept me pointed in the right direction when it came to keeping on topic and delivering the chapter content in good form.

Kylie Johnston, my project manager, who did a great job juggling the project plan and working with me and my timetables. She was critical in keeping me on task, while being flexible enough to accommodate project scope modifications.

Marilyn Smith, my copy editor, for providing flow and organization to the chapters, as well as improving grammar throughout the book.

Laura Esterman, my production editor, who made the book look great by organizing the page proofs and allowing me to make last-minute changes where necessary.

Chris Jennings, graphic artist, for using his artistic talents to create the nice, clean icons for the AF – Client Manager application, as well as giving me insight on my web site (www.appfoundation.com).

Paul Kuzan, from SpringSource, who technically reviewed the first few chapters on Spring and Flex. He did a great job pointing out improvements in areas that lead to using best practices when delivering code.

Bradford Taylor, who technically reviewed the entire book, for giving me his professional expertise on Flex, Spring, and integration architecture considerations that made every technical example and description better.

Mark Miller and Randy Barker, at Miller & Associates, for supporting my efforts to deliver this book and allowing me to use company experience to support content in the book.

Introduction

Pro *Flex on Spring* is about building rich Internet applications (RIAs) that combine the interactive user experiences of Adobe Flex with the delivery of back-end services through the Spring Framework. You'll find all the details you'll need to integrate these two technologies, ranging from building custom reusable Flex components to using an object-relational mapping (ORM) implementation to manage database connectivity. The examples in this book are taken from real-world applications, culminating with a practical, large-scale, complete application that applies all the main concepts covered in the book.

The ultimate goal of this book is to make you a more efficient developer using Flex and Spring to deliver RIAs with a robust server-side implementation. I also detail how to achieve reusability (via components) throughout your Flex applications. I focus on two key ideas: keep it simple and keep it consistent. Along the way, you'll learn best practices for architecting large-scale RIAs with Flex and Spring.

The topics covered include persisting data using Flex's three protocols (HTTPService, WebService, and RemoteObject), using Spring BlazeDS Integration (SBI), implementing Spring Security, using ORM solutions with Spring (iBATIS and Hibernate), and working with solid developer frameworks in Flex, such as Cairngorm and PureMVC. You'll learn how to bring all of the technology together to build integrated applications.

Who This Book Is For

This book is for Java, Flex, and Flash developers who want to get hands-on experience in integrating Flex on the Spring Framework. This book is well suited for those with some experience with Flex and Spring, who are looking for development design patterns and practical RIA architecture integration techniques.

How This Book Is Structured

This book covers Spring 2.5 and Flex 3, from the fundamentals to advanced concepts that become important when you integrate them. Chapters 1 through 9 focus on the core concepts needed to deliver large-scale RIAs with Flex and Spring. These chapters give you a good understanding of Flex and Spring through solid examples. Chapters 10 through 14 walk you through the architecture and development processes needed to build a large-scale RIA called AF – Client Manager, based on the concepts covered in the preceding chapters.

Here's a chapter-by-chapter rundown of this book's contents:

Chapter 1, Rich Internet Applications with Flex and Spring: This chapter serves as an introduction to RIAs, Adobe Flex, and the Spring Framework.

Chapter 2, Project Planning for Flex and Spring: This chapter provides the project planning for the book's main example (the AF – Client Manager application) and gives you a look into real-world project management for large-scale RIAs integrated with Spring. The concepts in this chapter can be applied to any technical project.

Chapter 3, The Tools for the Job: This chapter discusses the tools you can use to build Flex and Spring solutions. They include Eclipse, Flex Builder, and command-line options.

Chapter 4, Introduction to Flex Applications: This chapter focuses on core concepts for Flex and gives you a solid understanding of Flex application development.

Chapter 5, Introduction to Spring: This chapter shows how Spring combines its building blocks (classes and objects) for building robust server-side solutions through its framework components. You see how to wire Spring beans, use Spring MVC with Flex, create bean factories, and test your Spring code.

Chapter 6, Flex and Spring Integration Architecture: This chapter covers the basic architecture for Flex and Spring integration, with an emphasis on the Flex and Spring communication layers. You get an introduction to `SpringFactory` and the Spring BlazeDS Integration (SBI) project from SpringSource.

Chapter 7, Architecting the View: Cairngorm and PureMVC: Here, you learn the purpose of using a development framework when building Flex applications. This chapter provides solid examples for implementing Cairngorm and PureMVC in your Flex applications.

Chapter 8, Data Persistence: This chapter introduces popular ORM components that help you to persist data in databases when working with Spring.

Chapter 9, Security: This is a broad chapter that covers security in Flash Player, Flex, and Spring Security. You see how authentication and authorization play primary roles in security, and how to integrate Spring Security with the BlazeDS server context.

Chapter 10, Flex, Spring, Cairngorm, Hibernate: Bringing It All Together: This chapter defines the three projects needed to code the sample AF – Client Manager application: Flex, Flex Library, and Spring projects.

Chapter 11, Building the Database: This chapter introduces the database schema used to build the AF – Client Manager application. The database of choice is MySQL, although you can use another database.

Chapter 12, Building the Spring Services: This chapter demonstrates how to engineer robust Spring services that can support large-scale RIAs. You use Hibernate to map query results to Spring domain objects, and annotations to make your Spring methods transactional.

Chapter 13, Building the Flex User Interface: This chapter shows how to build the AF – Client Manager user interface with Flex. You see the benefits of using Cairngorm to deliver the transport architecture for the Flex application that uses RemoteObjects to call Spring services running on a BlazeDS server.

Chapter 14, Porting the Flex Application to AIR: This chapter is an introduction to the Adobe Integrated Runtime (AIR) framework for building desktop applications. It shows you how to take the AF – Client Manager Flex application and port it to AIR.

This book also has an appendix, which explains how to install the tools necessary to develop RIAs and Spring applications.

Downloading the Code

This book was written using Java 1.5, Spring 2.5, and Flex 3. The source code for this book is available online from the Apress web site (http://www.apress.com). You can access it from this book's details page or from the Source Code section. The source code is organized in chapter order. Each chapter has its own project or projects to support its content.

Contacting the Author

I would like to hear from you. Please contact me if you have any questions, comments, or suggestions regarding this book's content. You can send messages directly to flexonspring@appfoundation.com, and can access book discussion and RIA goodies at http://www.appfoundation.com/flexonspring.

CHAPTER 1

■ ■ ■

Rich Internet Applications with Flex and Spring

More than ever, organizations are turning to data-driven communications to increase their productivity. Internet-based applications such as eBay and Facebook have delivered new directions to businesses and consumers alike through e-commerce and social networking. Some of these applications have left much to be desired in usability and consistency when compared with the best desktop applications.

The lack of richness and usability in Internet-based applications has led to the development of Web 2.0 and the marriage of desktop applications with Internet-based applications. Many people may be skeptical of what Web 2.0 means from a technology standpoint. Web 2.0 describes changing trends in Internet usage that have led to technology that enhances information sharing, web application functionality, and collaboration. It is important to point out that Web 2.0 has not changed technical specifications in the infrastructure of the World Wide Web.

Rich Internet applications (RIAs) combine characteristics of desktop applications and Internet-based applications. RIAs have a rich new look and feel. They can increase user productivity and seamlessly present aggregated data. Advanced data visualization through corporate dashboards, business intelligence tools, and web-based RIAs are helping organizations quickly integrate legacy data streams with dynamic, rich user interfaces.

The production of a strong framework to work with RIAs is important to the delivery of business applications. As you'll see, RIAs offer an exciting new way to craft the user interface, and they work exceptionally well if complemented by a robust, flexible server-side application framework. Spring is an excellent choice for this purpose. It offers many integration options when combined with Adobe Flex.

The goal of this book is to present a solid road map for integrating Flex and Spring applications. To get you started, this chapter introduces RIAs, Adobe Flex, and the Spring Framework.

What Are Rich Internet Applications?

RIAs are a cross between traditional desktop applications and Internet-based applications. They blend together the best attributes of both application types. Internet-based applications, since the 1990s, have brought us e-commerce sites, along with the ability to book airline tickets online, check e-mail, trade stocks, submit tax forms, and more. These types of web application functions are being merged with traditional desktop application functionality to provide richer user experiences (including audio, video, and communications), online and offline support, and more responsive applications. And, unlike standard web pages, RIAs do not require page reloading.

RIAs provide the following benefits:

Improved server performance: RIAs generally employ a no-page-refresh model that loads the application into the client's memory, so page refreshes are not required unless the user navigates away from the web application entirely. With the RIA framework enabling more client-side processing and a no-page-refresh model, less work is required of server hardware to load RIAs. This creates a stateful application with data as well as the application components. The long-term added value is a lower cost of ownership for corporate hardware to support RIAs.

Richer user experience: User interfaces in RIAs offer behaviors not available using plain HTML. These include drag-and-drop functionality, heavy application functions calculated on the client side, and the use of components to change data dynamically.

Increased developer productivity: RIA development is based on reusable component development methodologies that are easy to learn. Development patterns such as the model-view-controller (MVC) pattern, command pattern, and observer pattern are easy to implement in RIA projects.

A Short Introduction to RIAs

Remote scripting, *X Internet*, *rich web clients*, and *rich web applications* are all terms that apply to what are today called *rich Internet applications*, or *RIAs*. X Internet is the evolution of the current state of the Internet, where there are static web pages with heavy mechanisms to deliver content and business functionality. X Internet will embrace what RIAs have to offer by delivering executable software code to the client's user interface.

Note The term *rich Internet application* was coined by Macromedia (now part of Adobe) in 2001, although similar ideas had been discussed years earlier.

Since the inception of the first RIAs, demand for these types of applications has exploded. Consider the following prediction, published in "Management Update: Rich Internet Applications Are the Next Evolution of the Web" by Mark Driver, Ray Valdez, and Gene Phifer (Gartner, Inc., May 11, 2005):

By 2010, at least 60 percent of new application development projects will include RIA technology, and at least 25 percent of those will rely primarily on RIA (0.7 probability).

Application modernization with RIAs is moving away from traditional client/server architecture with a thin client that displays static HTML pages to a thick client, with a more distributed computing architecture based on using web services to obtain data.

Thin client refers to a client/server architecture that relies on a central server for data processing and maintains the state of the data at the server layer instead of the client. The thin client is geared toward input and output between the user and external server.

In contrast, a *thick client* processes as much data on the client's machine as possible. The thick client maintains the state of the data and passes data only to communicate the state of the data to the remote server for storage.

Traditional web applications require the user to refresh each page while moving through the application. This causes more load on the web and application servers associated with the web application. Figure 1-1 illustrates HTML page refreshing versus RIA refreshing.

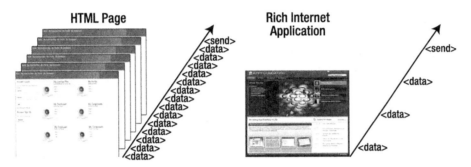

Figure 1-1. *A representation of HTML page refreshing versus RIA refreshing*

Since RIAs are stateful, they can limit the amount of data refreshes to a minimum. The client engine does the heavy lifting for the user. The client engine is downloaded to the client when the application is run for the first time. It retains the context or state of the application on the user's workstation, where the application makes asynchronous communications to distributed servers. Retaining state within the client application instead of on a centralized server allows developers to code more logic—like sorting, filtering, data management, and caching—to create a thicker client. The application does not need to requery servers for data or to display content. This creates a compelling development model for building large-scale enterprise web applications, which require a considerable amount of bandwidth.

Advances in Internet broadband have allowed larger files to be pushed across the Web. RIAs take full advantage of this by allowing video, audio, RIA components, and data to be carved up into smaller sizes for network transport. RIAs do not require you to have all data and files on the client. They can be built using a component model that allows you to pull across only what you need.

Most RIAs are portable and achieve platform independence by being built with a compiled language combined with a runtime plug-in such as Flash, Curl, or Silverlight. The plug-in is the application-delivery mechanism that can run on most platforms to achieve independence.

RIAs also run in a runtime sandbox. A sandbox allows the RIA to run locally on the client's workstation in a secure environment, such as Flash. This enables an RIA to run on any platform that supports Flash—in other words, on most major platforms on the market today.

As demand for a higher degree of data visualization like charts and graphs, larger file sets, and a more immersed user experience increases, expect RIAs to not only provide these functional points, but to deliver them with a flair not yet seen on the Internet.

RIA platforms come in many different flavors. They are rapidly evolving, with more interactive tools and integrated development environments (IDEs) becoming available to developers.

With a need to provide heavy audio, video, communications, and graphics, several RIA technologies have emerged, such as the following:

- Adobe Flex/Flash

- Ajax (Asynchronous JavaScript and XML)

- OpenLaszlo

- Microsoft Silverlight

RIA Architecture Stack

Enterprise applications are built consistently with a tiered architecture that defines deliberate channels of functionality by dividing the application into tiers. As illustrated in Figure 1-2, an application is generally divided into three tiers: the client tier, the middle tier, and the data tier. Many other tiers may be added to the application stack to support various functions, including security, legacy system integration, and message brokering.

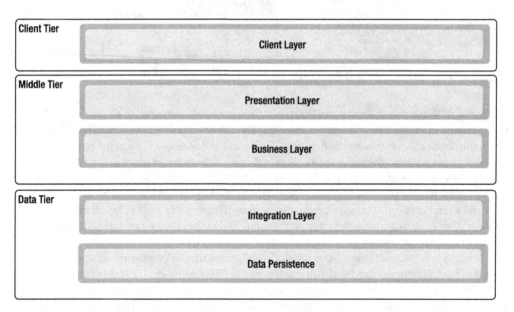

Figure 1-2. *A typical n-tier architecture*

Each tier of the architecture contains one or more layers, as follows:

- The client layer displays the user interface and application components within the user interface presented to the end user.

- The presentation layer maintains server-side session and state for the application. Session on the server is responsible for handling requests and responses between applications. State on the server is a set of user-defined variables that are persisted during a user session. The presentation layer can be in the client tier or the middle tier.

- The business layer contains the business logic for the application. This layer controls and validates business functions available to the client.

- The integration layer acts as an integration point for the middle tier. It opens up data connections through adapters and connectors to remote or local databases and data sources.

- The persistence layer controls access to databases and data sources through pooled database connections.

In a typical web application architecture, content delivery is located in the presentation layer. This layer handles the request/response transactions typical of web applications. These applications frequently need to render entire HTML pages, as each response always comprises a whole new page. This model is inefficient in many ways, most obviously because each request must refresh an entire page, thus slowing down the application's response time.

Rich clients change the game by fetching fresh content without requiring a complete page refresh. This technique replaces the request/response model with an event-driven model, as illustrated in Figure 1-3.

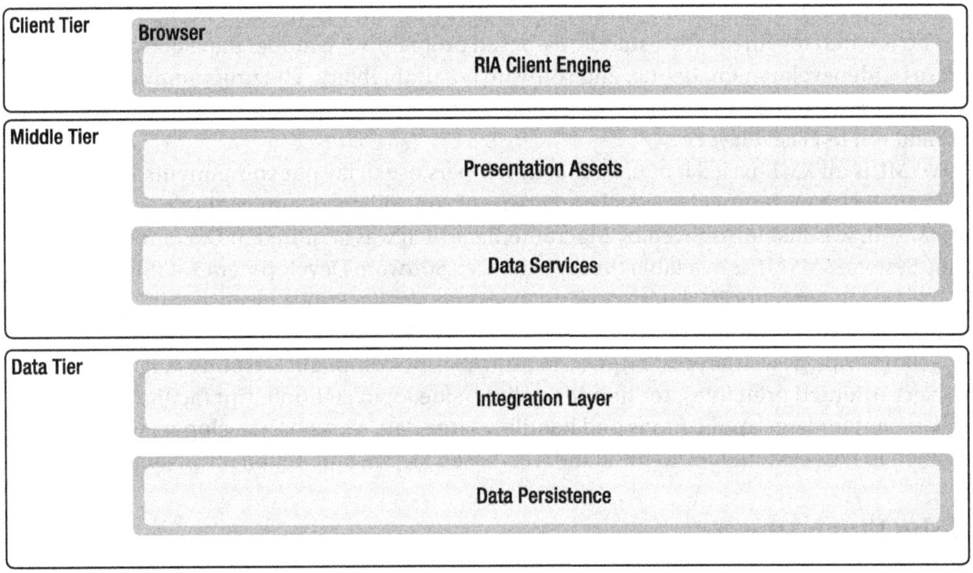

Figure 1-3. *RIA architecture*

One of the benefits of an RIA architecture is that the client browser hosts an RIA client engine like Adobe's Flash Player. This sandbox will allow the RIA to run on most platforms and most browsers. Developers are not required to write code for a specific browser or platform; they just need to code for the technology contained in the sandbox.

The middle tier of this architecture usually contains services and presentation assets such as images, XML files, and component files. The data services can be wrapped in a framework such as Spring to integrate the client with the data layer. This allows the application's components to be decoupled.

Rich clients leverage a component-driven model that allows the application to be constructed in much smaller chunks. Each component can handle its own interaction with the server through an event model. These asynchronous transactions create a lighter server load and deliver content on demand, not by page. Components can be as small as a simple question/answer poll or as large as an entire RIA.

Introducing Adobe Flex

Adobe Flex is an open source framework that runs in Adobe Flash Player to create RIAs. It combines the functionality of desktop applications with the availability of web applications. Flex leverages the best of both application types to create applications such as online e-mail applications, e-commerce applications, and business intelligence tools that provide enhanced data visualization. Flex, as a framework, extends the regular Flash application programming interface (API) to provide the benefits of Flash components integrated with Flex.

Flex has a large selection of out-of-the-box components—such as a DataGrid, Panel, and Tree—which are used to render the view of a Flex RIA. Each component can be customized down to a very granular level. Developers can change the color, border, and skin, and even extend the component to create a completely new custom component. Flex also leverages Flash transitions and animations, and supports data push and media streaming.

Flex is wired together with a standards-based programming model that supports design patterns with development, debug, and software maintainability. The programming model is made up of MXML and ActionScript. Flex applications are compiled into Flash bytecode (SWF files) and run in Flash Player.

MXML is an XML-based language that developers use to lay out components in the view of Flex applications. It provides a declarative way of controlling an application's visual appearance. MXML was first introduced by Macromedia, which was acquired in December 2005 by Adobe Systems. MXML is available through the Flex Software Development Kit (SDK), which was released in February 2008 under the open source Mozilla Public License (MPL). The MPL specification can be found at http://www.mozilla.org/MPL/MPL-1.1.html.

ActionScript, as well as JavaScript, is an ECMAScript-compliant scripting language, based on object-oriented principles, for handling client-side logic. ActionScript facilitates rapid development for large applications and handling large data sets. Java developers will find the transition to Flex easy, thanks to the standards-based MXML and ActionScript languages.

Adobe Flash Player

An introduction to Flex would not be complete without some mention of Adobe Flash Player and how it relates to Flex applications. Flash Player 9 reaches 97.7% of Internet-enabled desktops in mature markets, including the United States, Canada, United Kingdom, Germany, France, and Japan, allowing them to view Flash version 7 or higher. Figure 1-4 shows the worldwide ubiquity of Adobe Flash Player compared with other Internet technologies. You can see the official Adobe Flash Player version penetration numbers at http://www.adobe.com/products/player_census/flashplayer/version_penetration.html.

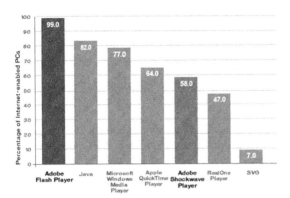

Figure 1-4. *Installations of Adobe Flash Player and other Internet player technologies (from Adobe's Flash Player Player Census page,* `http://www.adobe.com/products/player_census/flashplayer/`, *based on a Millward Brown survey conducted September 2008)*

Flash Player works on most browsers and operating systems, giving Flex applications broad cross-platform coverage. This helps to reduce the costs of new server purchases, as existing server hardware can often be used, regardless of its operating system.

Flash Player has integrated support for animations, audio/video, and graphics and drawing APIs for creating custom components. These abilities, combined with Flex, open the door to some very creative opportunities for developers.

Benefits of Adobe Flex

Flex provides the following advantages:

- Flex allows for the rapid prototyping of complex web applications.

- Flash Player eliminates the need to write browser-specific code.

- Due to the statefulness of the client, the number of server calls are reduced, compared with those required for HTML pages. This, in turn, reduces server CPU cycles and allows the client computer to power the application. The application framework eliminates the need to refresh the page every time a user gesture is processed.

- Flex has many options to run the application under, including any application server compatible with Java Platform, Enterprise Edition (Java EE, formerly J2EE), such as Tomcat, Internet Information Server (IIS), or WebLogic.

- With Flex, developers can write portlets that conform to the JSR-168 standard (see `http://jcp.org/aboutJava/communityprocess/final/jsr168/`).

Target Applications for Flex

RIAs are well suited to deliver a wide variety of application types, including interactive dashboards, business intelligence tools, self-service applications, commerce applications, and web sites. These applications share a number of characteristics that are enabled by Flex, such as the following:

- They manage process automation or work flow to augment multiple-step business processes.

- They do offline processing that allows the user to save data while disconnected from the server and automatically synchronize with the data source when the client reconnects to the server.

- They require streaming data push to the application, like a stock quote ticker.

- They aggregate media content with application logic and data.

Interactive dashboards interface with data services to bring information and analytics to decision makers. Flex creates a dynamic data visualization assembly to show data through charts, graphs, and custom components. These components can be bound to real-time data feeds for fresh data and to keep users up-to-date on the latest information.

For example, the dashboard illustrated in Figure 1-5 shows detailed sales information by using a hierarchical set of controls that drill down to the lowest level of data for an item or at the regional or store level. This dashboard is integrated, through Spring, to a data warehouse with more than 700 million rows in its main fact table. This application is used by the executive staff of a major retail company.

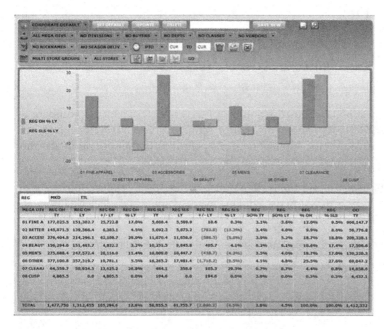

Figure 1-5. *A dashboard built by Miller & Associates*

The kinds of Flex applications that can be built as RIAs generally fall into the following categories:

Advertising and branding: Over the years, companies have developed applications using Flash to enhance their advertising and branding breadth. These applications traditionally have had a lot of content delivered through different media channels, such as phones, occasionally connected computers, and personal digital assistants (PDAs). The purpose of advertising and branding is to strengthen corporate image and to associate those images in a positive light. To help enhance those images, companies have started to utilize RIAs to deliver that message through the advertising channels, with more graphics, video, and audio.

Enterprise: Many enterprise applications handle processes that used to be labor-intensive or manual. These processes can be based on paper and are usually tied to a business work flow that drives up operating costs. These costs can be eliminated, or at least reduced, by the introduction of RIAs that streamline the processes.

Handheld devices and phones: With the advent of nanotechnology, and computer processors getting smaller and smaller and eventually dissipating less heat, we will see more and more applications pushed to the phone and smaller handheld devices. If you consider how rich the components are on the iPhone, you can see that smaller devices are starting to deliver complex applications to users. Applications are being geared toward having a web presence and a mobile presence. Mobile applications—such as e-mail, online chatting, music archives, and pictures and video—are becoming richer with features. For example, social networks in web applications are now being pushed down to mobile devices.

Public sector: Government agencies, educational institutions, and nonprofit organizations require technology to play a vital role in delivering information. As these types of organizations often have restricted information technology (IT) budgets, RIAs may seem particularly attractive to them.

Video and media: Consumers increasingly expect video and other media to be delivered to their desktops without delay. Advances in broadband have allowed video to be streamed across the Internet at high speeds, and RIAs provide a convenient way of retrieving and playing these videos for end users.

Flex Application Framework

The Flex framework is free to download from Adobe. The core Flex SDK allows developers to compile Flex from the command line. You can start with the Flex framework and begin to build applications using the editor or IDE of your choice. Unfortunately, Flex Builder, which allows you to visually build your applications and view your layouts and styling, is not free. You can build your application using Ant scripts combined with the Flex SDK and run the application to see your styling and layouts at runtime. As a professional developer, you would expect to have a series of tools that allow you to build applications quickly and help you to wire your applications together, and the Flex framework provides these tools.

BlazeDS is an open source component we will use heavily throughout this book. Flex and Adobe AIR can integrate with the BlazeDS server-side technology to communicate with back-end sources such as Spring through Java remoting and messaging. (BlazeDS was previously only available as part of Adobe LiveCycle, which was not free.)

Adobe AIR is a runtime application environment that runs on your desktop instead of inside a browser. AIR applications have access to your file system; Flex applications do not have this access. This is because they are running locally on your desktop and are in a trusted environment. A great example of an AIR application that was built for eBay can be found at http://desktop.ebay.com/.

The following three tools are included as part of Flex:

Flex Builder IDE: Flex Builder can be downloaded and installed either as a stand-alone IDE built in Eclipse or as an Eclipse plug-in. My preference is to install it as an Eclipse plug-in, which supplies the standard Eclipse components and requires applying fewer plug-ins. Installing the Flex Builder plug-in to Eclipse also allows you to leverage the Java perspective that is part of Eclipse. You will want the Java perspective to build your Spring projects.

Flex Charting: This is a set of charting and graphing components, such as bar chart, line chart, and combinations of the two. These charts enhance data visualization with visual cues that represent data and raw forms.

Adobe LiveCycle Data Services (LCDS): Formerly Flex Data Services, LCDS aids in data synchronization for Flex and Adobe AIR through remoting, messaging, data management services, and PDF document generation. All of this is not open source. For more information, see http://www.adobe.com/products/livecycle/dataservices/.

Introducing the Spring Framework

The Spring Framework is an open source framework, created by Rod Johnson to address complex design issues in enterprise application development. Spring provides an alternative solution to Enterprise JavaBeans (EJBs). Spring also provides you with wiring for your beans through its lightweight inversion of control (IoC) container.

Spring IoC and Dependency Injection

With IoC, the control of a system is inverted compared with how system control is handled with a more traditional software library. Traditional libraries expect a client to call reusable library functions, thus controlling the request and response to that client. IoC injects control from reusable components to application-specific code. Spring IoC's most important feature is dependency injection (DI). Currently, Spring has two types of DI:

Constructor injection: Dependencies are supplied through the Spring class constructor at instantiation of the class.

Setter injection: The setter methods are exposed through the Spring Framework by a dependent component. In this case, the Spring Framework uses the exposed setter methods to inject the dependency. These dependencies are defined in an external configuration file, which is loaded into web server context when the web server is started.

Spring uses DI to decouple class dependencies. The Spring Framework is responsible for instantiating a Spring bean and calling a Spring bean's setter method to inject the instantiated bean. The Spring Framework is responsible for the life cycle of a bean and handles DI through a bean's getter/setter methods.

Spring was designed to be an integration point to back-end services and able to partner with any Java EE–based server-side technology like Tomcat, without the costs and overhead of many of the leading Java EE application servers. That makes Spring an ideal solution to integrate with RIAs.

Spring Core Modules

Figure 1-6 provides a high-level look at the core modules that make up the Spring Framework.

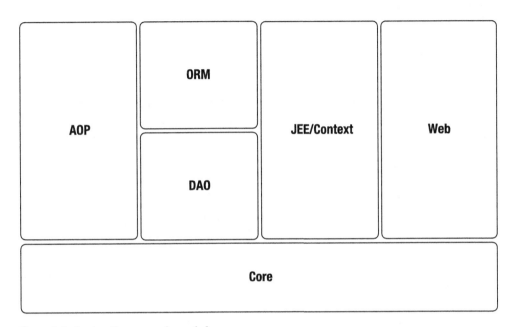

Figure 1-6. *Spring Framework modules*

The six Spring modules contribute to the framework as follows:

Core: Spring's core container provides the base functionality that governs the framework. One of the most important aspects of Spring is how IoC is realized by DI. This topic will be covered in Chapter 5.

JEE/Context: This module sits on top of the core container and extends its functionality by providing a consistent manner for controlling Spring objects. It also provides enterprise services, such as e-mail capabilities, EJBs, and adds support for internationalization (i18n) messages.

Aspect-Oriented Programming (AOP): Spring provides support for aspect-oriented programming (AOP) in this module. In Spring, *aspects* are parts of the application that cross-cut concerns by enabling modularization. For example, Spring aspects isolate logic such as logging and persistence from business logic. This can be a cleaner approach when defining common functionality, such as logging, in one component of an application. Aspects let you declaratively define the component's functionality, without needing to modify every class to which the new feature is applied.

Data Access Object (DAO): This module is a layer of abstraction for the Java Database Connectivity (JDBC) API. This layer helps to reduce the boilerplate code that is generally associated with JDBC connections, faults, result sets, processing, and so on. This module also aids in preventing problems that can result from not manually closing database connections and serves as an error message manager to help support messages from database servers.

Web: This module provides integration features geared toward building web components such as multipart file upload, IoC instantiation using servlet listeners, and web context. Spring's MVC package is probably one of the most commonly accepted approaches to designing and developing web applications today. This pattern is implemented by several Java frameworks such as Tapestry, JavaServer Faces (JSF), WebWork, and Struts, and has even been replicated in user interface frameworks such as Cairngorm and PureMVC for Flex, which is written in ActionScript.

Object-Relational Mapping (ORM): This module allows for integration of popular ORM tools such as Hibernate, TopLink, iBATIS, OBJ, and the Java Persistence API (JPA). We'll cover how to integrate Spring with ORM solutions in detail in Chapter 8.

Benefits of the Spring Framework

The following are some of the primary benefits of integrating the Spring Framework with RIAs:

- The Spring Framework allows RIA technology to bind directly to Spring beans.

- AOP modularizes cross-cutting concerns such as logging and security.

- Transaction management brings a layer of abstraction that allows you to work with nested, local, and global transactions.

- The framework allows for easier testing, since base classes are designed as JavaBeans that enable you to inject test criteria directly to the object via setter methods.

- Spring allows you to have strict layers abstracted into a series of roles, which become very evident with MVC.

- Spring is a lightweight environment that allows you to quickly build and deploy enterprise-ready applications using plain old Java objects (POJOs). This will help to increase code output in your project while using Spring.

- The data tier in Spring is a layer of abstraction that allows you to quickly change your change JDBC database access, as well as the entire ORM technology that is managing your DAO layer. This allows you to retain the code you wrote in other Spring modules when moving to a new database solution.

The Marriage of Flex and Spring

As I pointed out earlier in this chapter, there are several opportunities for integration between Flex and Spring. The data-visualization aspects of Flex and the need to quickly pull data from a lightweight service-oriented back end provide for a great opportunity to pair with the Spring

Framework. When creating a Flex object, you can bind to a remote object, which in Spring is your Java bean.

Spring makes a perfect data service source for Flex, since the integration points between the two are convenient. Through remote data binding, Flex allows you to integrate seamlessly with Spring and consume Java beans for display in the view of an RIA.

Flex can communicate with many different back-end services in several different ways. Flex is not restrained to just communicating via a remote object. It can also communicate directly using an HTTP service or a web service.

Note From my personal experiences with integrating Flex with Spring, using remote objects in this architecture has proved to be the most practical implementation for enterprise-class applications due to the binary nature of the data. Remote objects traverse the network faster than HTTP services and web services. This is not readily observed in one-to-one transaction testing of the techniques, but it is evident in large-scale applications. I will cover this topic in some of the later chapters. You'll learn how to wire applications together, some of the benefits of doing so, and how to deliver these applications with the least impact to legacy systems and the organization to which you are delivering the software solution.

One thing that Flex requires from a back-end service is a destination known in Flex as an *endpoint*. The primary communication protocol we will use in this book to call Spring services from Flex is the RemoteObject protocol. With this protocol, it is very important to understand how to provide the endpoint for Flex. You do this by creating a gateway for Flex. In Spring, you create a factory class that provides a gateway to access Spring beans. Once a factory is created and you gain access to the factory, you have full access to the objects that are served with your Spring container. The Spring factory is the most important element that integrates Flex with Spring.

Summary

This chapter explained the nature and some of the history of RIAs. It also covered Flex and the Spring Framework, followed by a discussion of how to integrate Flex with Spring and the key components needed for that integration to be successful.

This chapter also introduced Adobe Flash. As you'll see, Flex has all the advantages of Flash, as well as the ability to integrate Flash with Flex applications. Flex provides a powerful solution to build applications that manage data, video, and audio.

Spring provides a consistent way to manage Spring objects. It is based on IoC, which is realized by DI through setter and constructor injection. Spring also provides a layer of abstraction for data access through JDBC. It also integrates with ORM technologies like Hibernate, TopLink, iBATIS, OBJ, and JPA. Spring's modules include the core, AOP, DAO, ORM, web, and context containers. Those modules are the building blocks for Spring's architecture.

In the next chapter, you will start to understand how to plan projects for Flex and Spring. I will also give a practical definition of the components for the project that we will be building in this book. Last but not least, I will pass on several lessons learned from the RIA projects that I have implemented for Fortune 500 companies.

CHAPTER 2

■ ■ ■

Project Planning for Flex and Spring

In recent years, I have implemented Flex projects in many different settings. They range from business intelligence applications running against large data warehouses to simple tools that perform very specific custom business functions. From the early days with Flex 1.5 to now, I have met quite a few challenges and worked out what I consider best practices when developing Flex RIAs.

I believe in creating a consistent, modular, and repeatable architecture. The architecture must be able to support small applications as well as extremely robust enterprise applications. A key to project success is to create an architecture that new developers can rapidly understand, so that they begin to be productive on day one. I feel that the combination of Flex with Spring and Cairngorm has helped me reach the goal of a patterns-based, repeatable architecture. Cairngorm is an open source development framework that implements design patterns for building Flex user interfaces.

This chapter will serve as an introduction to the project that we will build throughout this book: the AF – Client Manager. This application will use Flex on Spring to deliver a large-scale RIA. The application will have functionality to support clients, client projects, invoices, PDF generation in Flex, and a client dashboard. You can download the source code of the entire application from this book's details page at the Apress web site (http://www.apress.com), so you can see how to build both the front end and back end.

The objective here is to define the business functionality for the application, produce the wireframes, identify the core features of the project, and relate those core features to the service layer that we will build in Spring. But first, we will look at staffing for a Flex/Spring project and also the technology required for this project. By the end of this chapter, you will have seen a solid project plan come together, giving you an idea of how to define a large-scale RIA project.

Staffing a Flex on Spring Project

After the scope of the project has been defined, it's time to determine the type of people you need for your project. It's important to ascertain the primary technology requirements to build your RIA, as discussed in the next section. By understanding the appropriate technology stack, you can better define the types of technology with which your staff should have experience.

One point to consider is that there is a smooth transition from Java development to Flex development. ActionScript is very close to JavaScript since it is based on ECMAScript. Developers will find the syntax for ActionScript familiar and will pick up on the coding aspects of Flex quickly.

The project that we will build in this book is very similar to a real-world project. It has all the components that Java and Flash developers will need to code. The combination of Flex with ActionScript 3 and MXML means that your projects can be staffed by experienced Java developers who can make the jump to building Flex applications. The developers can be divided into two groups:

Flex GUI developers: New development with Flex is primarily based on MXML. Developers with Flash experience often find it easy to start building Flex GUIs, because they generally understand ActionScript and the core Flash components and API. MXML helps developers with XML experience quickly learn how to lay out containers and components in Flex.

Flex component developers: This area relies heavily on ActionScript in general. Components can be written in MXML and in combination with ActionScript. It is important to note that ActionScript syntax is very similar to JavaScript, so programmers who have worked in JavaScript will pick up ActionScript quickly. But ActionScript also has similarities to Java, which has a much steeper learning curve than JavaScript.

Defining the Technology Stack

Every project has requirements that dictate the technologies that need to be used to get the job done. The tools I use on a daily basis are a combination of open source and commercial tools.

For the sample application, we will use as many open source projects as possible, to give you the best opportunity to build the components yourself. Some of the tools listed in this section are not open source and require you to purchase a license, but these tools are not required to compile or build any examples in this book. I've included them to give you an idea which tools are useful for building large-scale RIAs.

The technology stack for the AF – Client Manager application includes the following tools:

- MySQL is an open source relational database management system (RDBMS) that is extremely popular for building web applications.

- Adobe Flex SDK is the open source alternative to Adobe Flex Builder. The SDK allows you to compile Flex MXML and ActionScript into a SWF file. You can deploy the SWF to a web server to be accessed from there.

- Cairngorm is an open source development framework used to build patterns-based components in Flex.

- Spring is an open source framework for the Java platform that will implement services available to Flex.

- Apache Tomcat is an open source servlet container developed by Apache Software Foundation. It is a Java environment for running Java code.

- Alive PDF is an open source PDF generation library that can be integrated with Flex to create PDFs client side.

The following design tools are not required (since they are not open source, except for Eclipse), but are nice to have:

- Adobe Photoshop is a graphics editing tool that I use to create images, icons, and other graphics for RIAs. If you do not have access to Photoshop, you can download GIMP (http://www.gimp.org), which is an open source image editing tool.

- Adobe Flex Builder can be installed as a stand-alone product or integrated into Eclipse as a plug-in. I use the Eclipse plug-in version, because I use Eclipse for Java development. Using the plug-in allows you to build your projects with Ant for deployment.

- Adobe Flex Charting adds many charting types to Flex Builder, including bar, line, and bubble charts. This is a purchased add-on for Flex.

- Eclipse IDE is an open source development platform composed of tools used for building and deploying software, such as Flex Builder, Java, and Spring.

The following project management tools are also useful:

- Microsoft Project is a project management tool that allows you to create and manage project plans.

- CVS and Subversion are both source control management systems used to manage changes in your code. They also provide a way to back up your code immediately after you make changes.

Planning the AF – Client Manager Project

As we've seen in the IT industry, there is a sad trend of roughly 80% of projects failing due to going over budget, missing the implementation date, or a wide variety of other reasons. Even if the project was implemented and is in a production environment, the project can be deemed a failure if it did not meet the client's full requirements. For more information regarding IT project trends and failure rates, head over to http://www.it-cortex.com/Stat_Failure_Rate.htm. My intention here is to provide a road map to allow you to build RIAs with a solid technical design methodology that will mitigate most of the issues that cause IT projects to fail.

We must define the project's scope (sum total of all project requirements and features) in such a way that we can build the application in an iterative development cycle and keep our commitments to our clients. That way, the project will be deemed a success. If we could only put aside the corporate politics and other issues that come out of the blue, delivering a project would be that simple. Murphy's law will eventually come into play and cause some sort of trouble for the project. So we must do our best to identify the risks and find ways of mitigating them.

One of the keys to a successful project is to create strong supporting documentation. This starts with the business design documents and carries through into the technical design documents, which should be kept current throughout the life of the project. Following a proven life-cycle methodology is a good approach, which will streamline and optimize the development of the project. But whatever methodology you choose, don't get too caught up with crossing the *t*'s and dotting the *i*'s. In the end, you still have a project to deliver, and a heavy methodology can decrease productivity by adding disproportionate overhead. There's a fine balance between what is necessary for project success and self-imposed sources of inefficiency.

Now let's talk a bit about the planning stages for the project. In any project, you want to identify the key areas of project criteria that will frame the project. In building an RIA, I usually go through these four stages:

- Define a high-level list of business requirements

- Define the core features for the application

- Build the project plan

- Create the project wireframes for user interface development

The following sections discuss each of these stages for specifying the design of the AF – Client Manager project. We will define the business requirements, look at the core features of the application, better define the requirements for those features, and derive wireframes for the different view states of the application.

Defining the Business Requirements

With most IT companies, projects begin with a document that defines the business requirements. This document should express the overall goals and terms of the project, with as little reference as possible to the actual technologies used in the project. In general, the business requirements should not be directly tied to a single technology, but should be applicable in any case where the project will be built.

For example, let's say we need to build a mortgage calculator application. The business requirement for doing the calculation logic should state how the calculation will be created, not which coding language will be used. You will want to have your business requirements transferable to other languages.

The IT company has a responsibility to assess its capabilities with respect to the technologies used in the project. If the company does not have these capabilities in-house, it should either outsource them or hire staff with suitable experience. In the case of the AF – Client Manager project, the business requirements are quite simple:

> We will build an application that showcases integration between Flex and Spring, and uses best practices to link those technologies together.

Of course, a real business requirements document would be much longer than one sentence! For a real project, you would ensure that the project stakeholders have signed off on the business requirements and are ready to fund the necessary work. The goal of the business requirements document is to frame the project in such a way as to justify the necessary expenditure of capital.

Defining AF – Client Manager Core Features

The application we will build in this book will be fully functional and actually provide some sort of benefit to you. The AF – Client Manager application is very simple in what it does, but you will be able to extend it beyond what is outlined in the book.

Right from the start, it is important to subdivide each project into components so that you can delegate and separate the units of work. This lets you generate a work breakdown structure for your project. Another benefit is that you will have the opportunity to start identifying which components of the application are reusable and which components may be collected in a Flex library. In Chapter 4, I'll explain how to build a Flex library, which will allow you to transfer these components to other projects and clients in the future.

The AF – Client Manager application will be built in three main views or components: the client view, project view, and dashboard view. Here is a high-level list of the feature set we will build for the AF – Client Manager application:

- Login view

- Client manager view

- Project view

- Client/project dashboard

- File upload

- PDF generation

It is very important to define a high-level list of core features. This list will eventually drive the development of our services that will be managed by the Spring Framework.

First, we'll look at the features of the RIA from a Flex perspective. Later in the chapter, we'll define the Spring services required to feed data to Flex. To begin, I will introduce you to a term that I've started using to define assets for the project: *RIA artifacts*.

RIA Artifacts

RIA artifacts are located in a common repository that the Flex application or module can consume. This layer decouples the individual component configuration necessary to render shared resources to the browser. The following are the four categories of RIA artifacts:

Reusable components: It is very important to create your application to capitalize on areas where you can reuse components. If you're creating custom components in your Flex application, be sure to create these components in ActionScript. This may be a little more complex than creating components in MXML, but it will give you a slight performance edge. This is because the application does not need to parse the XML to determine what you are trying to accomplish at runtime.

Local images: All images are sent to a local repository so that the application can easily display the image. These are the images and icons that are used in the application, and they can be embedded in it or loaded at runtime.

Caution Be careful embedding images into you application, because the size of the image directly impacts the size of the compiled SWF. For example, if you embed a 1MB image into your application, you've just increased the size of your SWF by 1MB.

Local CSS: The style of an application can vary for each business user consuming the software. Our Cascading Style Sheet (CSS) file for the application should be a very busy file. You do not want to hard-code styles in your MXML or within your ActionScript in a Flex application. By doing so, you create the need for reworking the project if it requires rebranding or components are reappropriated for other projects in the future. Remember that you're trying to create components that can be leveraged across multiple projects and build a shared library that you or your company can exploit in the future.

Compiled modules: These modules are components that can be integrated with your Flex application that are compiled SWF files coming directly from Flash or other Flex applications. They can also be used to render common components, as well as components that have been retooled to fit a certain business need.

Now that we have talked about a few of the RIA artifacts that we want to keep track of, let's examine the core features of the application in detail.

Core Functionality

The first item to address is creating a core functionality guide from which to build our project plan. Here is the high-level guide:

- Login
- Client manager
  - Client list
  - Client details
  - Client projects
  - Client invoicing
  - Client contacts
  - Client issues
  - Client address and map
  - Client picture upload
  - Client business card upload
- Application toolbar
- Project manager
  - Project administrator
  - Project tasks/milestones
  - Project task list
  - New project
  - New/edit task

- PDF generation
- Client/project dashboard
  - Chart selection list
- File upload

This guide defines the high-level functionality that will be built in this project. The major functional points have been defined, and now we will continue with the development of the project plan.

Building the Project Plan

In RIA development, as with most project development, you might not have all of the requirements by the time you need to start executing a project plan. With RIAs, you can quickly prototype applications to help drive requirement gathering. A visual representation can help a client decide on the requirements for the application.

The first step in building a work breakdown structure is to enumerate the major aspects of our project, which we just did by defining the project guide. Now that we have a set of deliverables defined, we can produce a detailed project plan that breaks down those deliverables into a project task list. This task list will be divided into five major categories that are common to many project management methodologies:

Define: In this project phase, we define the high-level requirements, system requirements, and functionality for the application.

Design: In the design stage, we take the requirements and build our technical design for the database schema, user interface, components, and general technical functions, which could include networking, hardware, and other software considerations for the project.

Produce: This is the longest phase of the project plan. It is where we build our application and write the code. This means building out all the architecture components that are designed to support the application.

Testing: This embraces all the unit testing, system testing, and user acceptance testing in the project plan. Unit testing will run in parallel with the production of the application. It is the developer's job to test the functionality of the code to ensure it meets the stated requirements for the project. System testing generally involves a business analyst, who writes the business requirements to run regression tests against the application. Regression testing involves a set of test cases that covers all functionality for the application. User acceptance testing allows the client to get a look at the application and eventually to sign off on its functionality.

Implementation: This is the set of tasks that it takes to move your project into production. It can be as simple as setting a flag on the operating system, or as detailed as the steps it takes to set up your database from start to finish. It's important to ensure that you have captured all of the critical tasks that are required for your application to work.

In projects that I deliver, I use an iterative process to cycle through each phase of the project. Iterating through the building of project parts will help you get functionality quickly to your project sponsors and give you agility to address change requests.

Now let's take these phases of the project and build out the AF – Client Manager functions into a project plan. In this project plan, we will not apply the duration or starting day, so we are not looking at a timeline to complete this project.

The following list defines the tasks and phases for the AF – Client Manager application.

The AF – Client Manager Project Plan

```
1.  Client Manager RIA Project
2.      Design
3.          Design Database Schema
4.          Design Spring Services
5.          Design User Interface
6.      Produce
7.          Client Manager RIA
8.              Build Database Tables
9.                  Build Database Schema
10.             Screen Support Functionality
11.                 Login Process
12.                     Build Login Panel
13.                     Login Command
14.                 Client Manager View
15.                     Client List Repeater with Custom ItemRenderer
16.                     Application Toolbar
17.                     Header
18.                     Footer
19.                     Issues and Milestones Custom Component
20.                     Document Panel
21.                         File Upload
22.                     General Information Tab
23.                     Company Overview Tab
24.                     Mapping Component
26.                     Contact List Tab
27.                     Client Links Tab
28.                     Project Overview Tab
29.                     Project Information Tab
30.                     Project Issues Tab
31.                     Project Risk Tab
32.                     Financial Status Tab
33.                     Financial Invoice Tab
34.                     PDF Generation Component
35.                     RSS Subscriptions
36.                 Project Administrator View
37.                     Project Tree View Component
38.                     New/Edit Project Form
39.                     Task/Milestone list with Drag and Drop Enabled
```

40.	New/Edit Task Form
41.	Three Month Calendar Component
42.	Dashboard View
43.	Main Charting Container
44.	Project Metric List
45.	Financial Metric List
46.	Spring Services
47.	Client Service
48.	Security Service
49.	Project Service
50.	Media Service
51.	File Upload
52.	Testing
53.	Unit Testing
54.	Integrity Checks
55.	Validation Checks
56.	Systems Testing
57.	Application Regression Testing
58.	User Acceptance Testing
59.	User Signoff
60.	Implementation
61.	Database Table Builds
62.	Web Server Deployment

As you can see in the project plan, each phase is defined with sections of tasks that can be iterated through during the produce phase. For example, the client manager view section, starting with task 14, can be broken into very separate development tasks. As the header and footer are being developed by one developer, another developer can create the client list and issues and milestone components. Various parts of the system will be developed at different rates, and then integrated together as the individual components are completed. RIAs are well suited for iterative development because they are built from components.

As you see, we have quite a bit of work to do before we can implement this project. Since we have already defined our project functions and have our main business requirements set, we can move on to designing the application. The next steps are to take the defined functions and produce wireframes for the user interface.

Designing the User Interface: Producing the Wireframes

In this section, we will produce the wireframes for the application and define the functionality associated with each view state. We will review what the view state is trying to accomplish, the functions and components that make up each state, and the transitions that will occur within each view state. By *transitions*, I mean how we want to move from screen to screen and which effects we should apply. Do we want to fade from one screen and fade to the next, or do we want to use other effects, such as the wipe effect? These effects are built into the Flash engine and are leveraged in Flex.

■**Note** On projects built with Flex, I rarely use out-of-the-box components. The out-of-the-box components provided by Flex are very powerful and provide a quick means to an end with the ability to prototype applications. The downside is they generally do not fit the style you are going for with your application. You will want to create custom components to address unique needs for applications. This is where advanced skinning comes into play. *Skinning* is simply changing the appearance of components in Flex through CSS. This can be changing color, adding graphics, or even drawing custom borders in Flex components. We'll do this for the components in our application, so that you have a good understanding of what can be done outside the core components from a look-and-feel perspective.

Now that we're ready to design the application, let's get started with a login panel.

Login Panel

Figure 2-1 shows the login panel wireframe. The login features are quite simple. For this application, we will build a simple security table that will allow us to authenticate a username and password. We're not going to develop an elaborate security scheme, but I will talk about different security options in Chapter 9.

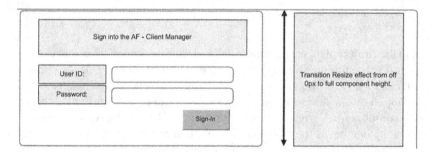

Figure 2-1. *Login panel wireframe*

Once you have successfully logged in to the application, you will be taken to the client management main screen. If you are not successfully authenticated, the application will pass back an error message to the login panel and give you another opportunity to validate your user credentials.

The login panel will have the following functions and components:

- Username and password text-input boxes

- Error message label

- Login button

When the login panel is presented, we want it to show itself at the top of the screen, starting from a zero position to its full height. This transition will give the effect that the login panel is being resized from the top of the screen. Once the resize has completed, we want to fade in the contents of the login panel so that we have a nice, clean presentation of the panel.

Client Manager Main View

Once login is successful, the application will load the default state of the application. As shown in Figure 2-2, this screen will act as the "home" state for this application. Flex applications do not have pages as HTML sites do. Pages in Flex are called either *application states* or *views*. This default view will drive the application through the menu in the header of the application. It will also list the clients you have entered in the application.

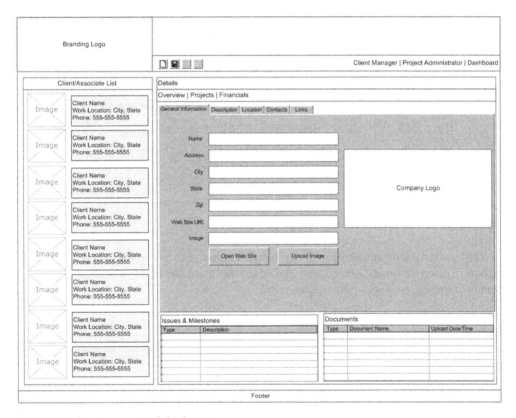

Figure 2-2. *Client manager default state*

The description tab allows you to enter a description about the client in free-form text, as shown in Figure 2-3. This could be notes to share with colleagues who might have access to this client or company information.

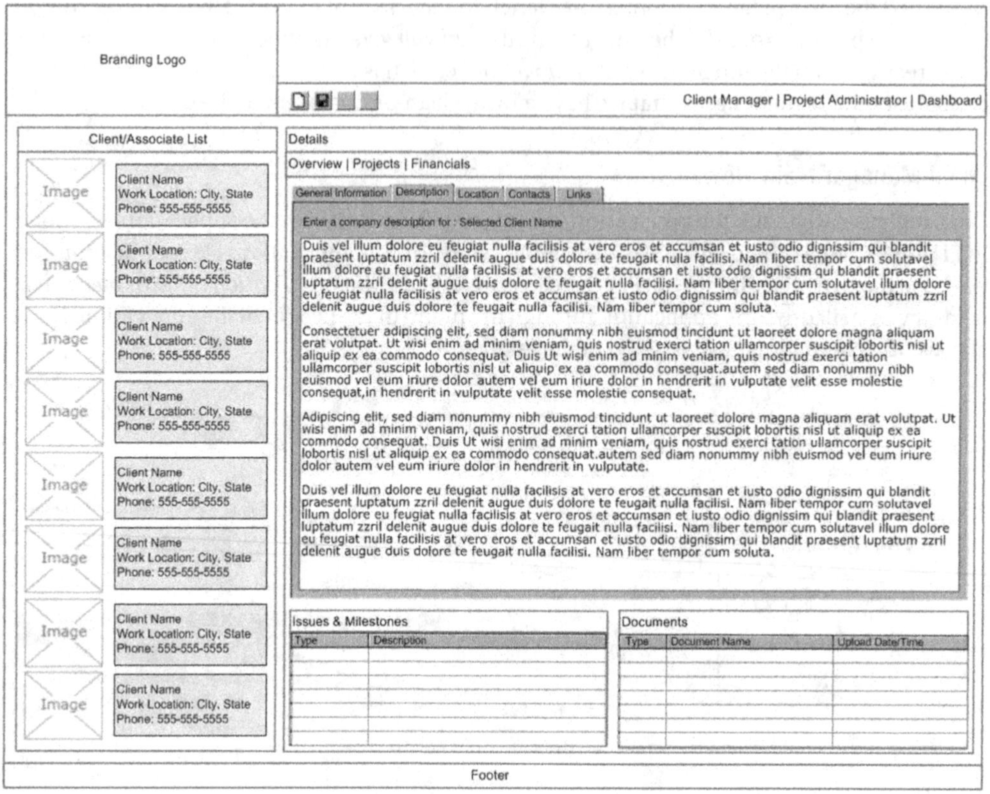

Figure 2-3. *Client manager client description*

The location will be initialized with the client's address, as shown in Figure 2-4. I will show you how to integrate Google Maps into a Flex component and display an address of choice when we initialize the component in Chapter 13.

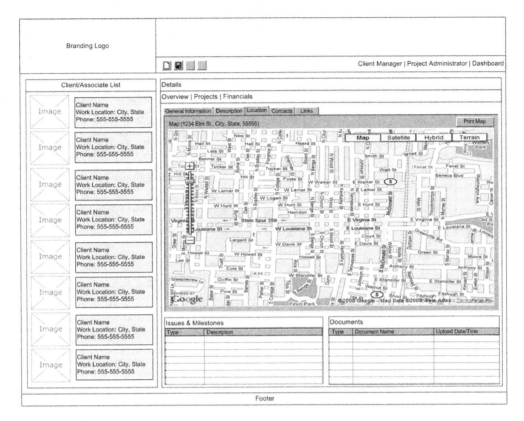

Figure 2-4. *Client manager client location*

The client manager view will be the default state for the application once you successfully authenticate your user credentials. As you can see in Figure 2-5, at the top of the wireframe, the header will contain our brand/logo, the application toolbar, and a high-level menu to the right of the header that will change the view state between the major three components of this application. This component of the application will consist of three stacked components: the header, the body, and the footer.

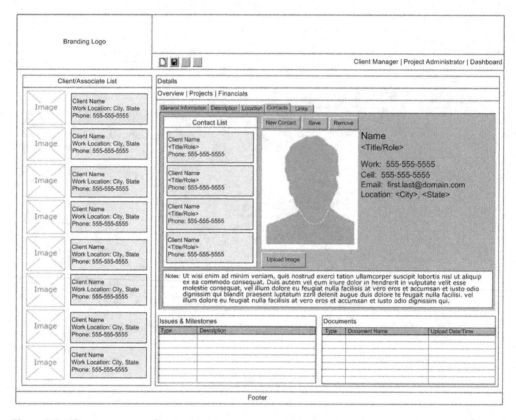

Figure 2-5. *Client manager client contacts*

On the left side will be the client list. This list will be the driver to switch between your clients or associates. We'll use the client logo, which you will be able to upload to the application, within this list, as well as the client name, city, state, and primary phone number. In Chapter 13, we'll implement this list as a `Repeater` with a custom `ItemRenderer` so that we can get the exact look and feel we want.

To the right of the client list, we will have the main details tab for the client. This will include the general information, the description, a map, and a contact list. The map will be an interface to the Google Map API. The application will be required to pass in the address of the client to display the proper location. Remember that it is very important to create components that you can reuse in other applications. This will be another example of how to create a custom component and integrate it into your application with a Flex library.

The client manager view will have the following functions and components:

- Custom client list for `Repeater` with `ItemRenderer`

- Application control bar

- Main view-switching menu

- Client details container

  - General company information component

  - Company overview component

  - Company location component

  - Company contacts component

- Client projects container

  - Project overview component

  - Project task and milestone component

  - Project information component

  - Project issues component

  - Project risks component

- Client financial container

  - Financial status component

    - Client revenue to display label

    - Post a payment component

    - Invoice status component

  - Invoice component

    - Invoice-entry component

    - Save/print as PDF component

    - Company PDF formatter component

We will use the fade effect to transition the components as you move through different components of this application.

The issues and milestones panel is a small component of the application that will give you a quick look at high-level issues and milestones tied to a project, as shown in Figure 2-6. We will color-code these issues to provide visual cues as to the severity of the issues.

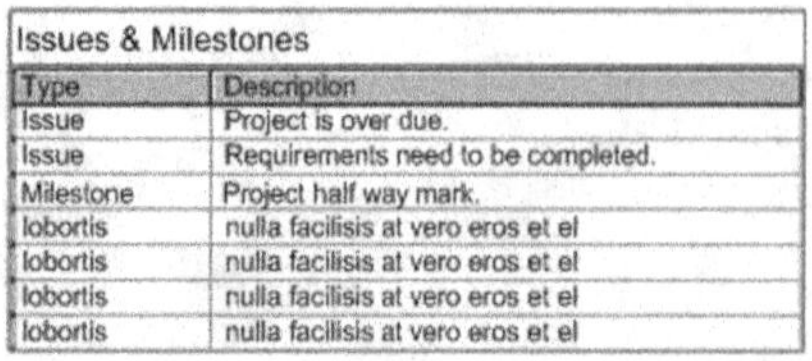

Issues & Milestones	
Type	Description
Issue	Project is over due.
Issue	Requirements need to be completed.
Milestone	Project half way mark.
lobortis	nulla facilisis at vero eros et el
lobortis	nulla facilisis at vero eros et el
lobortis	nulla facilisis at vero eros et el
lobortis	nulla facilisis at vero eros et el

Figure 2-6. *Issues and milestones panel*

The documents component, shown in Figure 2-7, will be used in a couple of places in the application. It will have the ability to upload files and tie those to projects or clients through a relationship in our database. We will carry these document relationships in our media table, which we will define shortly in our database schema.

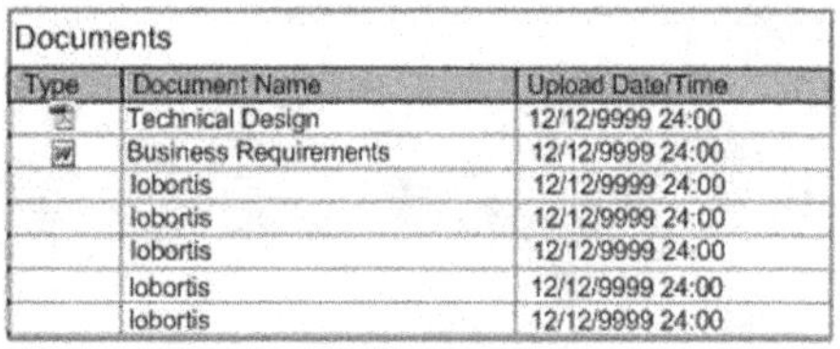

Documents		
Type	Document Name	Upload Date/Time
	Technical Design	12/12/9999 24:00
	Business Requirements	12/12/9999 24:00
	lobortis	12/12/9999 24:00
	lobortis	12/12/9999 24:00
	lobortis	12/12/9999 24:00
	lobortis	12/12/9999 24:00
	lobortis	12/12/9999 24:00

Figure 2-7. *Documents component*

We will display the type of the document, which could be PDF, Microsoft Word, Microsoft Excel, or just about any generic type we want to load in to the application. We will use a `DataGrid` to show the document type, the document name, and the time the documents were uploaded to our server.

Now that we have the main view for the client manager described, let's define the projects view.

Client Manager Projects View

The client manager projects view is a listing of projects and milestones related to the selected client, as shown in Figure 2-8. On the projects tab, you will be able to see a listing of due dates and project statuses.

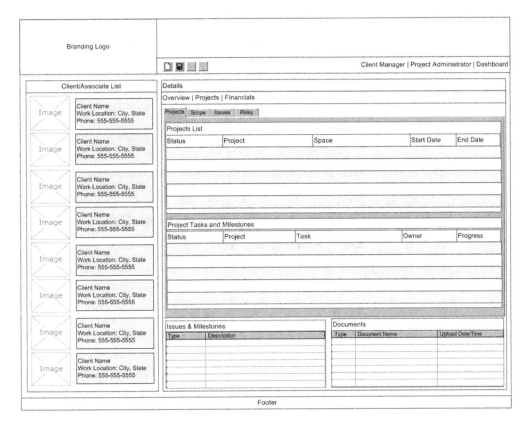

Figure 2-8. *Client manager project overview*

The description tab allows you to enter a project description and keep notes on the project in a free-form text area, as shown in Figure 2-9.

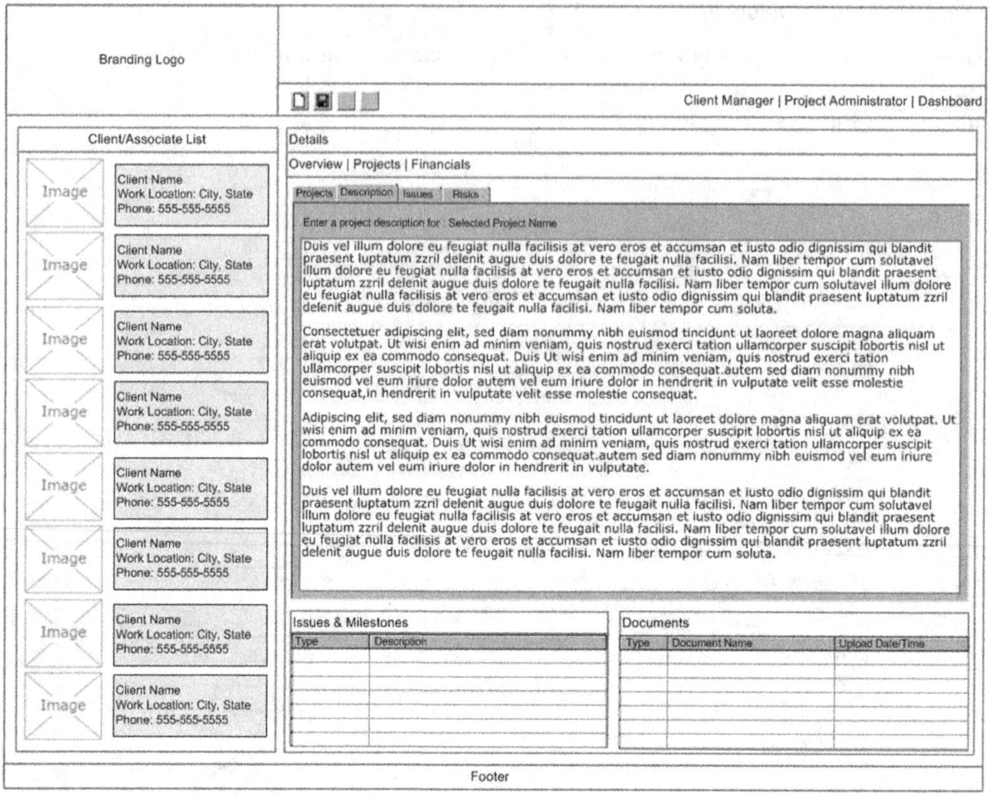

Figure 2-9. *Client manager project description*

All projects need to have issues managed closely to better serve a client or project stakeholder. The issues tab will show a list of issues for each defined project, as shown in Figure 2-10. You will be able to enter a resolution or notes for the issue selected. You will also be able to change the status of the issue.

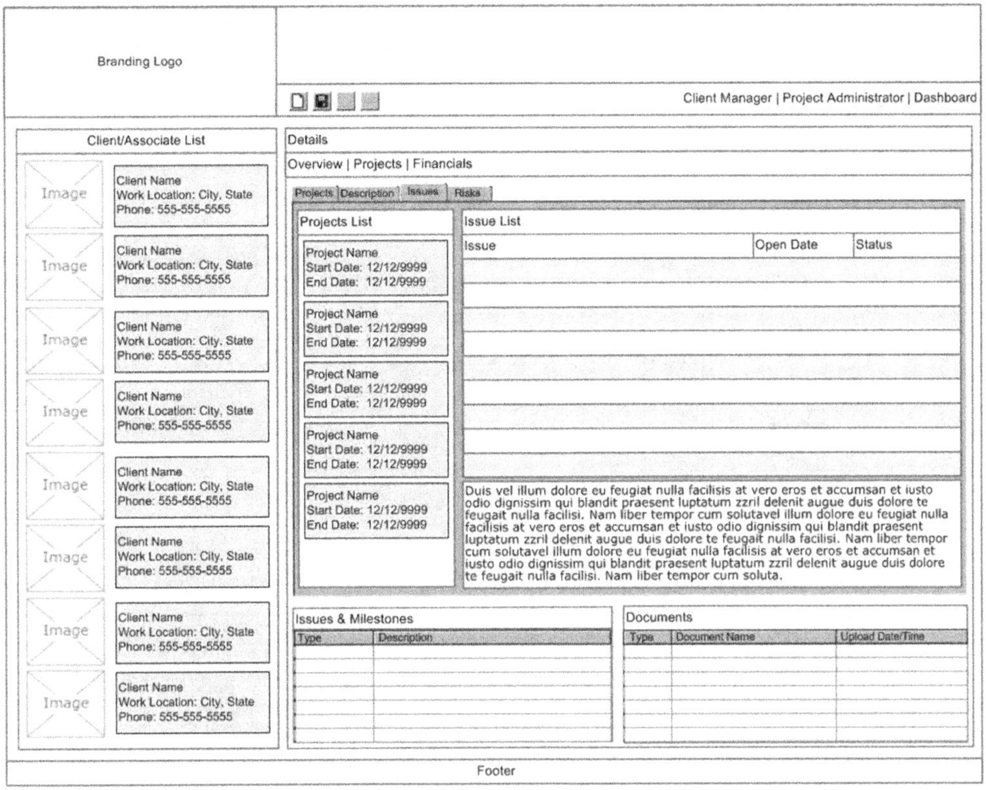

Figure 2-10. *Client manager project issues*

The projects tab is still part of the client aspect of the application. This component gives you a view into the ongoing projects and milestones that are being delivered to your clients. The main project view will show your project overview and a task and milestone overview, so that you have a quick checklist of progress for each client.

We also will include the scope and description for each project. This will allow you to keep track of the start date and end date for your projects. Along with the scope of the project, we will also have the ability to store issues for issue-tracking/resolution and project risks, as shown in Figure 2-11.

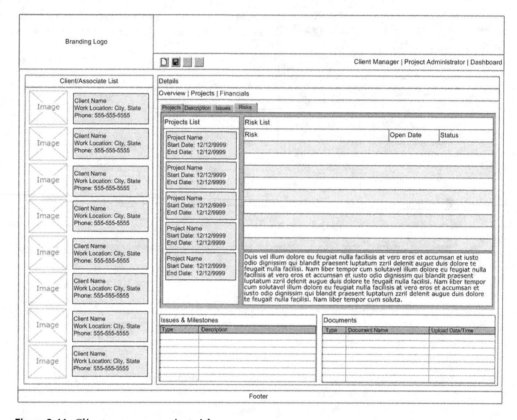

Figure 2-11. *Client manager project risks*

The last container to define for the client manager is the financial view. The financial view will provide the ability to see how your revenue is doing by client and the status of invoices submitted to those clients.

Client Manager Financial View

The financial tab will consist of two containers: one for the overall financial status of your clients, as shown in Figure 2-12, and one to invoice them, as shown in Figure 2-13. The invoice status component will use red, yellow, and green to represent the status of the payment, giving visual cues to the timeliness of payments.

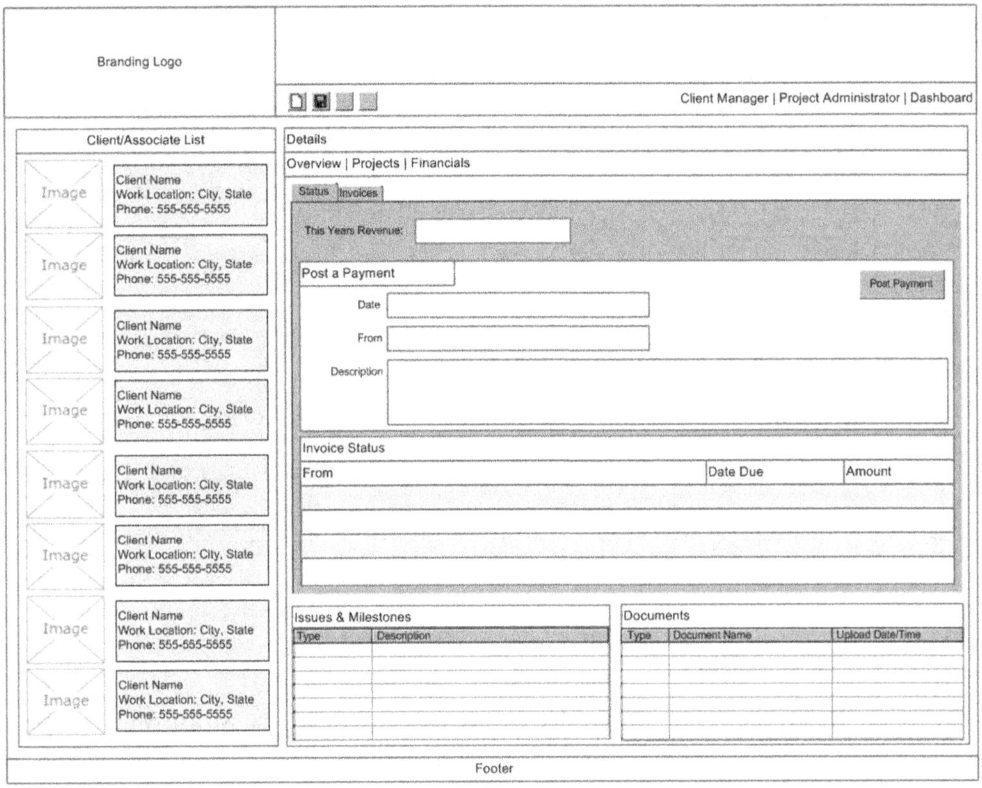

Figure 2-12. *Client manager status view*

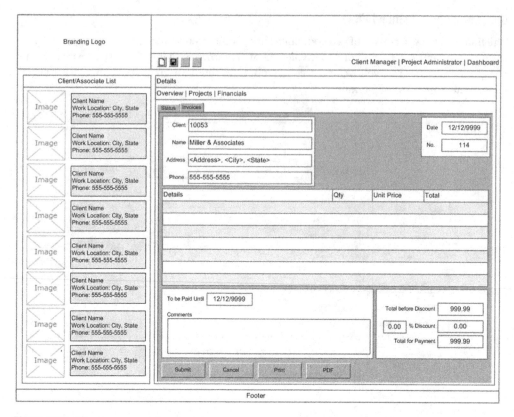

Figure 2-13. *Client manager invoice view*

Project Administrator View

The project administrator view will be driven by the same client list that we use with the client manager view. As you can see in Figure 2-14, we have four main panels that will support the addition of project tasks and milestones to a project.

The projects panel is a list of projects with the associated tasks and milestones. We will enable drag-and-drop from the task milestone list panel to the project panel to build a task list. This part of the application is not an attempt to replace tools such as Microsoft Project. It is simply a way to define critical milestones that need to be identified for the project to be successful. The advantage of this, in association with the client manager, is that you have a clear representation, by client, of the critical factors for project success.

Below the project panel is the project update/new project component. This component is very simple. It just takes the name, start date, and end date for the project.

The task/milestone panel is a listing of available tasks to add to your project. You can also add or edit a task through the new/edit task panel. This takes a task name, ID, and description of the task.

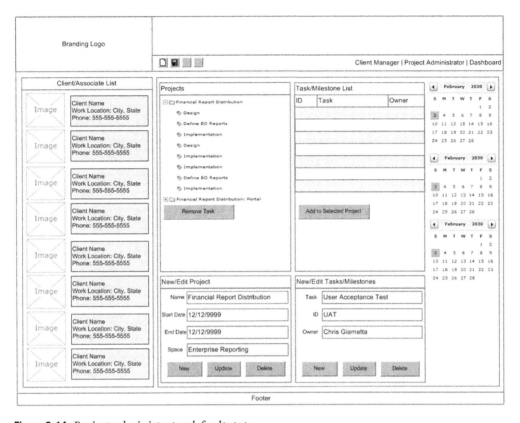

Figure 2-14. *Project administrator default state*

The project administrator view does not have a lot of moving parts, but it does play a key role in defining your projects and associating those projects with your clients. The project administrator view has the following functions and components:

- Reuse of the custom client list for `Repeater` with `ItemRenderer`

- Project tree view component

- New/edit project form

- Tasks/milestone list with drag-and-drop to the project list

- New/edit task form

- Three-month calendar view component

The only transition on this panel will be switching between the main three views of the application. We will again use the fade effect to make this happen.

Dashboard View

The dashboard is the last of the three main components of this application. As shown in Figure 2-15, it has three main parts: the charting container, the project container, and the financials container.

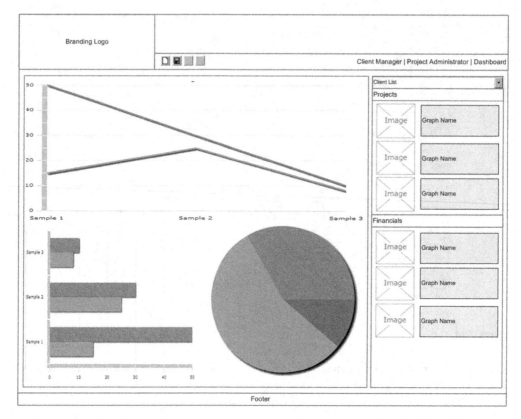

Figure 2-15. *Dashboard view*

We will have a choice of several chart types: a line chart, pie chart, and bar chart. These will be sufficient to display the information from projects and financials. Once you have chosen a chart to plot, it will display in one of the four quadrants of the charting container. The first chart will take up the top-left corner of the container. Additional charts will be placed in the remaining three quarters of the container. The view will also have the ability to dock the charts at the bottom of the charting container, if you want to have more than four charts displayed at a time. You will also be able to close a chart, as well as maximize a chart to take up the full screen.

The project container will have a list of metrics that you can run against a graph. We will start with project milestones and late milestones by client. You will also be able to map multiple projects against one another in the graphs.

In the financials container, we will show the paid invoices and late invoices by client. We will also have a revenue chart to show how clients are doing comparatively.

The dashboard view has the following functions and components:

- Main charting container

- Project metric list

- Financial metric list

Dashboards are a place in RIAs where you can really have fun with transitions and effects. If you have any artistic talent with effects, it's also a chance to show what you can do.

Wow, I said this was going to be a small project. Hey, it's only three main containers that we need to consider and build with the RIA technology, right? Since the goal is to showcase enterprise-quality applications built with Flex and Spring, you realize there's quite a bit more to do before we actually start coding this project. We are one-third through the design process, and we have built a lot of wireframes for our application. It's time to define the database schema and identify the Spring services and Spring functions that our Flex application will consume.

We will do this at a high level here, and in Chapter 11, cover in detail how to invoke the services and how to build the objects in Spring behind the services. In Chapter 11, we will also address which architecture to implement for your Flex applications by using the Cairngorm framework.

Designing the Database Schema

I have worked with many databases and data warehouses, as well as other technologies to publish data through our Flex applications. Most of the applications I build start with the database design. I use a bottom-up approach to most designs, since the data is what you are visualizing in the end. This depends greatly on the requirements and the industry in which you are working. For business applications, the bottom-up approach works great in most implementations. However, other applications, such as those for marketing products, may require a heavy investment in designing interfaces before all of the data points are defined.

The company I work for started out consulting in the data warehousing industry. We built many enterprise-scale data warehouses to support business intelligence for our clients. At one point, we realized that for a major retail client (one that we have a long-standing relationship with), we had 80% of sales data in the data warehouses, and only 20% of it was actually visible to our client. There are only so many business intelligence reports you can build through business objects and other technologies that display information in a way that is easy for the end user to consume.

This is where RIAs, and Flex in particular, really shine. We realized that we could build a custom set of tools through dashboards, business intelligence applications, and robust enterprise-quality applications, to help visualize data for our clients based on the data warehouses that we built for them.

Here's a list of the data providers that I have personally built Flex applications on top of, or have worked with our teams to develop the architecture and applications for:

- Netezza

- Oracle

- Teradata

- SAP

- MySQL

- SQL Server via .NET

- Java EE

For this application, we will keep it simple. We want the ability to quickly deploy a database that doesn't cost us an arm and a leg to have operational. The technology that we are going to use is MySQL, since it is an open source database.

Note Be sure to read the user agreement, and put in the MySQL logo and a link to the MySQL web site in your application.

Relational Database Design

Since we are keeping it simple, we'll build a simple relational database that will center on the client table. Each secondary table will associate to the client table's objectIdentifier. As you can see from Figure 2-16, the relationship between the security operator and the security access details is made through the objectIdentifier to assocObjectID.

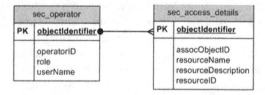

Figure 2-16. *ObjectIdentifier to assocObjectID link*

This will be the basis for the tables we will build for the entire application, with the af_client table being the parent for most relationships for a client. It will also give us a division of work for each object we build into the applications service layer. This will allow us to enforce security on changes to objects in the database by client. So with that in mind, let's take a look at the database schema, shown in Figure 2-17.

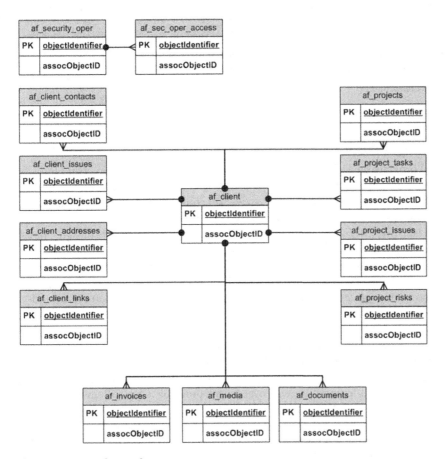

Figure 2-17. *Database schema*

Database Table Definitions

Now that we have the database schema design, we can use the tables to create domain objects in Spring and value objects in Flex. The schema will eventually serve as the object map from Flex value objects to Spring domain objects.

Value objects are not managed by Spring; they are mappings to Spring domain objects and are classes contained by Flex. In Flex, you can point your value object to a Spring domain object so it can be properly typed in Flex using the [RemoteClass] metadata tag. This tag specifies a remote class name that points to the Spring domain object. The object type must have a public constructor with no arguments. The typing of the Flex value object is done when the object is marshaled over Action Message Format (AMF) to Flex. AMF is part of BlazeDS, which is a remoting server technology provided as open source by Adobe.

■**Note** A value object in Flex has a mapping directly to the Spring domain object. It identifies the attributes based on the database tables that we have defined. These objects will be used to add, update, and delete data from our database by passing them into our Spring DAOs. These objects will also make it easy for us to display data within our Flex components.

Spring Service Design

Each Spring bean provides a necessary piece of commonly needed functionality. Our Flex application will be running in separate web contexts from our Spring service layer. We know our services will differ in business functionality, so we will compose coarser-grained service definitions to avoid having the service layer get overly cluttered.

Personally, I lean toward coarser-grained services in the architectures that I design. I have had many arguments over whether or not to break out each entity into its own service. Admittedly, this is just personal preference, and you will see this again as we define the services that will be leveraged in the AF – Client Manager application. I feel as long as the entities are part of a service's main business intent, they should be wrapped up in that service and not standalone. If an object provides a unique business function, such as the media entity for file upload, then that one entity should be its own stand-alone service.

Spring provides the service layer by allowing you to define core business services that separate interface from implementation. All services and DAOs are provided through DI. There is transparent support for transaction management, exposing services through remote interfaces and security. Spring exposes beans for remote access over several protocols, such as Remote Method Invocation (RMI), Internet Inter-ORB Protocol (IIOP), Xfire, HttpInvoker, Burlap, and AMF (which we will use for our application). Figure 2-18 shows a diagram depicting the Spring service layer in relation to domain objects and the DAO layer.

I know this book is about wiring Spring and Flex together, but we need to consider one thing about building our service layer. User-interface technologies come and go faster than server-side technologies. We want to build our Spring service layer in such a way that it is not bound or tied directly to the user-interface technology we decide to use. The only piece that will have a direct reflection in a Flex application will be the Spring factory that we build. Building your service layer in an agnostic way toward Flex will allow you to port that layer and extend it to other user-interface technologies in the future. This also allows you to hook this layer into older technology with which your client or your enterprise may want to interface.

Our services in general are being built to deliver as much functionality as possible in a scalable, robust manner. The design of the services requires a serious evaluation to determine the best granularity of the services in the defined architecture. We want to make sure that our service layer is scalable, robust, and conforms to standards.

The architecture of how our services are delivered will be discussed in detail in Chapter 12. We will define the architecture so that will be building a centralized location for our services, called AF–Central Data Services.

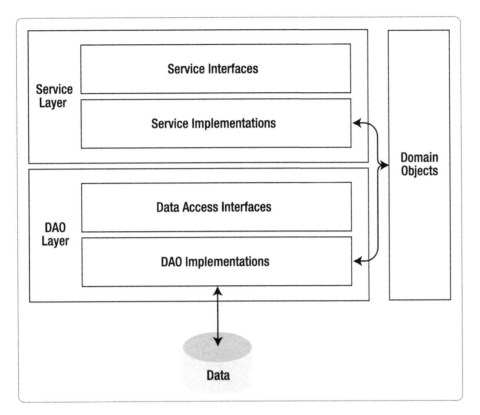

Figure 2-18. *Spring service layer with DAO access*

Summary

In this chapter, you were introduced to the AF – Client Manager project. We explored the features and functions of the application that we will build in the remainder of this book. We planned the features of the application and what they do. We employed a step-by-step process to design the application from the user interface down to the database schema.

We began with a discussion of the roles Java developers will fulfill working on a RIA project, and how transition to Flex development is smoothed due to the similarities between Java and Flex syntax and development environments. We then discussed defining business requirements.

The project plan was laid out as a task list that defines every feature of the application. Within the project planning stages, the wireframes and database schema were built. The Spring service layer architecture was defined to support the design.

At this point, you should have a good understanding of the scope of the AF – Client Manager project that we will build and a general understanding of what it takes to plan an RIA project.

CHAPTER 3

■■■

The Tools for the Job

After all the planning in Chapter 2, we are now ready for the actual project startup and configuration. We are not quite to the point where we will start coding the project. This chapter will tell you what you need to get your development environment ready for the produce phase of the project. I am going to explain the procedures I go through before I write any code.

We will go over the tools that integrate into the Eclipse IDE to support the development of Flex projects. You will also learn about building Flex projects via command-line scripts using Ant. Finally, we will set up three projects in our Eclipse IDE. The first project will be our Flex project. It will demonstrate how to define the Flex project's folder structure using an MVC pattern. The second project will be a Flex Library project, which will contain any custom classes that we build for the application. The Flex library will eventually be compiled and integrated into the main Flex project. Finally, we will create our Spring project. We will also define the architecture and folder structure for that project, so that you get a good understanding of where the Spring beans reside.

Flex and Spring Tool Set

Most developers understand the need for a robust tool set to enhance the development of any project. With all RIA projects, we don't want to deal with a cumbersome set of tools due to the number of touch points associated with these projects. We want to streamline the development process as much as possible, so we can get down to the business of building an RIA. For me, this is the opportunity to build a dynamic user interface by extending the out-of-the-box components in Flex, as well as creating a robust service implementation with Spring.

We will use the following development tools for the AF – Client Manager application we'll build in this book (introduced in the previous chapter):

- Apache Ant

- Eclipse

- Version control system (Subversion or CVS)

- Spring IDE (if you don't want to use the Eclipse Java perspective)

- Adobe Flex Builder

- Flex SDK

As you can see, we're going to keep it simple. I do not like to clutter up my development environment with plug-ins or tools that I rarely use. I like to keep things as efficient as possible and not lose time dealing with processes that bog me down.

I use Flex Builder on a daily basis to create Flex applications for my clients. I realize that Flex Builder is a commercial tool that is not free. You are not required to get Flex Builder, since you can build Flex applications using Ant. However, you can download Flex Builder from http://www.adobe.com/downloads/ for a trial or if you have a license key.

Building Flex SDK Applications with Ant

Unless you are building a very simple application, compiling and deploying the application needs to be automated. Creating a build script for large-scale applications can be a mini project within the main project when you need to compile hundreds or thousands of Flex or Spring source files. And after you compile the application, you need to deploy the compiled binaries to a runtime environment. Java developers usually use a build tool like Ant or Maven to take care of the heavy lifting of building and deploying their applications.

For my own work, I use Flex Builder combined with Ant to build and deploy my projects. Here, I will explain how to use Ant combined with the Flex SDK, since the Flex SDK is open source. The Flex SDK includes the Flex framework and Flex compiler. It enables you to program Flex applications using any IDE available to you.

Installing the Flex SDK and Ant

You can download the Flex SDK from http://www.adobe.com/products/flex/flexdownloads/index.html. Then unzip the contents of the downloaded file to your workstation. The SDK contains the Flex libraries, binaries for compiling applications, tools, documentation, and samples needed for you to use in building applications. I usually locate it with my other Adobe products in the Adobe folder (C:\Program Files\Adobe\flex_sdk_3).

You also need to install Ant on your workstation. Download Ant from http://ant.apache.org. You can install Ant by taking the contents of the zip archive and moving them to the directory of your choice on your workstation, such as C:\ant. Once you have done that, you need to add the Ant bin directory to your operating system's environment variables, as follows:

```
Path=C:\apache-ant-1.7.1\bin
```

Next, open a command-line terminal and enter ant. If you have Ant installed correctly with the path set, you should see something like this:

```
C:\ant
Buildfile: build.xml does not exist!
Build failed
```

This is a good failure! You have installed Ant successfully and are ready to build your Flex applications.

You also need access to the Flex compiler mxmlc. Add the following operating system environment variable to the path:

```
C:\Program Files\Adobe\flex_sdk_3\bin
```

Now check that you have access to the Flex compiler. In a command-line terminal, enter mxmlc. You should get the following results:

```
C:\mxmlc
Adobe Flex Compiler (mxmlc)
Version 3.1.0 build 2710
Copyright (c) 2004-2007 Adobe Systems, Inc. All rights reserved.

mxmlc [options] [defaultVar]
Use 'mxmlc -help' for more information.
```

With that done, you are almost ready to build a Flex application using Ant. But, of course, you need to create a Flex application first.

Creating a Sample Flex Application

To demonstrate how to build an application with Ant, we'll use a simple application with a button that pops up a message when clicked. Listing 3-1 shows this test application.

Listing 3-1. *FlexAntTest.mxml Application to Be Built with Ant*

```xml
<?xml version="1.0" encoding="utf-8"?>
<mx:Application
    xmlns:mx="http://www.adobe.com/2006/mxml"
    layout="absolute">
    <mx:Script>
        <![CDATA[
            import mx.controls.Alert;
        ]]>
    </mx:Script>

    <mx:Button label="Do It!" click="Alert.show('Ant Test!')" />

</mx:Application>
```

We will cover Flex MXML and ActionScript in much more detail in Chapter 4. For now, we're just using a basic application that doesn't do much other than handle a button click.

Building any application requires steps for the compilation of the code as well as the deployment of the application. Even with an application as simple as the one in Listing 3-1, several steps are involved:

1. Allow the Flex SDK's mxmlc to compile the FlexAntTest.mxml file.

2. Create an HTML wrapper for the Flex application from a template that comes with the Flex SDK.

3. Clean the deployment directory on your web server.

4. Copy the newly built files to the clean directory on your web server.

These four steps are fairly detailed to just build and move one Flex file to a web server. This process can get very complex when you include Spring source and large-scale Flex applications. That is why it is important to let a build process perform the heavy lifting, so you don't have a maintenance nightmare.

Creating a Build Script

We are ready to create a build script that Ant will use to build the sample Flex application. Listing 3-2 shows a basic Ant build script that uses Flex Ant tasks.

Listing 3-2. *Basic Ant Script Using Flex Ant Tasks for Flex SDK (build.xml)*

```xml
<?xml version="1.0" encoding="utf-8"?>
<project name="FlexAntTest" basedir=".">
    <taskdef resource="flexTasks.tasks" classpath=
        "${basedir}/flexTasks/lib/flexTasks.jar"/>
    <property name="FLEX_HOME" value="C:\Program Files\Adobe\flex_sdk_3"/>
    <property name="APP_ROOT" value="src"/>
    <property name="OUTPUT_DIR" value="bin" />
    <property name="APP_NAME" value="FlexAntTest" />

    <target name="init">
        <delete dir="${OUTPUT_DIR}" />
        <mkdir dir="${OUTPUT_DIR}" />
    </target>
    <target name="wrapper">
        <html-wrapper
            title="Flex Ant Test"
            file="index.html"
            height="300"
            width="400"
            bgcolor="red"
            application="app"
            swf="${APP_NAME}"
            version-major="9"
            version-minor="0"
            version-revision="0"
            history="true"
            template="express-installation"
            output="${OUTPUT_DIR}"/>
    </target>
```

```
    <target name="main" depends="init,wrapper">
        <mxmlc file="${APP_ROOT}/${APP_NAME}.mxml"
            output="${OUTPUT_DIR}/${APP_NAME}.swf"
            keep-generated-actionscript="true">
        <load-config
            filename="${FLEX_HOME}/frameworks/flex-config.xml"/>
            <source-path path-element="${FLEX_HOME}/frameworks"/>
        </mxmlc>
    </target>
</project>
```

The script in Listing 3-2 takes a few arguments. `FLEX_HOME` needs to be set to your root install directory for the Flex SDK you installed (`C:\Program Files\Adobe\flex_sdk_3\bin`). `APP_ROOT` is the location of the Flex application you wish to compile. You define the application name in the `APP_NAME` property and the compiled output in `OUTPUT_DIR`.

The first task in this script is to clean the output directory. This is done in the `init` task. That will delete all contents in the output directory and make a new directory if it is not already created.

The second task is to create the Flex HTML wrapper and associated files. If the wrapper files are created properly, you will see an `index.html` file that wraps the compiled `FlexAntTest.swf`. The HTML file is what you will use to run the application from a web server. You do not want to call `FlexAntTest.swf` in a URL; you should always call `index.html` to run your application.

The main task is the task responsible for compiling your Flex application and deploying it to the output directory. You can set the output directory to a web server location of your choice. The `flex-config.xml` file contains compiler settings that tell Flex's `mxmlc` compiler how to compile Flex code.

You can get much more advanced than we did in this simple Ant demonstration; for example, by adding the ability to execute unit testing, creating ASDocs (similar to Javadocs, but for ActionScript), and generating a WAR file for deployment. It is up to you and your organization to decide the best practices for deploying your Flex applications.

Eclipse IDE

Eclipse is an open source developer environment written mostly in Java that you can use to build Spring and Flex applications. It is composed of a workbench that controls the following items:

- *Perspectives*, which are groups of views and code editors tailored to a programming language; for example, there is Java perspective.

- *Views*, which are visual components used to navigate areas of a perspective. Most notable and used is the main navigation view for your source code, such as the package explorer in the Java perspective.

- *Editors*, which support code highlighting and code completion, and allow you to modify and save your work.

Eclipse allows you to add plug-ins to support your code development needs. Through this plug-in system, Eclipse can be extended to use other programming languages such as Java and Flex. It also can use plug-ins for version control systems and other tools you need to develop applications or deal with software environment issues.

I am using Eclipse Classic 3.4.1, which you can download from http://www.eclipse.org/downloads/. For installation instructions for Eclipse, see this book's appendix. You also need to have Java installed on your workstation to support Eclipse. We will be using Java 1.5 for the examples in this book.

For our development throughout this book, you may want to download the following plug-ins for Eclipse:

Adobe Flex Builder: Flex Builder is the development IDE used to build and deploy Flex applications. It comes in two forms: an Eclipse plug-in and a stand-alone environment called Flex Builder, which is built on the Eclipse framework.

Spring IDE: The Spring IDE is a visual tool to manage files used by the Spring Framework. You can get more information regarding how to install this Eclipse plug-in from http://springide.org/project/wiki/SpringideInstall.

Subclipse: If you use Subversion (SVN), you will want to install Subclipse. Subclipse is an Eclipse plug-in that adds support to manage your files with Subversion in Eclipse. Otherwise, you can open the CVS perspective that is installed with Eclipse (Window ➤ Open Perspective ➤ Other ➤ CVS Repository Exploring).

Version Control System

A version control system is a system designed to store all changes to files by multiple developers. Source code control is extremely important for large-scale RIA projects. It ensures that developers do not lose their work and allows them to quickly share their work with other developers on the project.

Version control systems typically have a central repository to house the files. Users get the files from the repository (check out), modify them, and then put them back into the repository (check in).

Different version control systems coordinate changes by multiple people in various ways. The traditional method is to "lock" a file when someone checks it out, preventing other users from checking that file out or in until the user working with the file checks it back in. A concurrent versioning system does not incur these locks when someone is editing a file. In concurrent systems, when multiple versions of the files are checked in and all the changes are merged, the user is responsible for correcting the file to its proper state.

Note When using a version control system, you want to make sure that you don't overwrite other developers' changes, by merging your code with theirs if they checked in the file before you. This is where it is important to have communication among team development members and to bear in mind that you are working in a collaborative work environment to build the project.

A very popular version control system is Subversion. However, for our examples, we will use CVS, which is a freely available open source, concurrent revision control system. We are using CVS because it has a built-in client packaged with Eclipse. You are not required to install and set up a source control server to execute the examples throughout this book. It is, however, in your best interest to make sure to always back up your code as you make changes. (I have had a few very bad days when I lost work due to not backing up my changes in CVS.)

Spring IDE

The Spring IDE might not be for everyone. It is a plug-in for Eclipse to build Spring applications with support for Spring 2.x, Spring Web Flow, AOP, and JavaConfig. Spring IDE 2.x is compatible with Eclipse 3.3.

If you wish to use the Spring IDE in Eclipse, you will need to use the Eclipse update manager to install and download the plug-in from `http://springide.org/updatesite/`. This can be done in Eclipse by choosing Help ➤ Software Updates ➤ Find and Install. You will be prompted to search for updates on currently installed features and to search for new features to install. Select "Search for new features to install," and you will see the Install dialog box. After selecting a mirror site from which to download the Spring IDE, as shown in Figure 3-1, you will see a list of features for the Spring IDE and their dependencies, as shown in Figure 3-2.

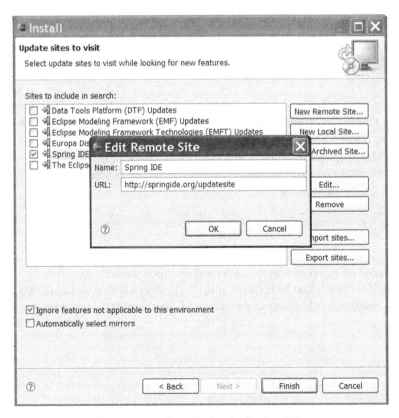

Figure 3-1. *Creating a new update site for the Spring IDE*

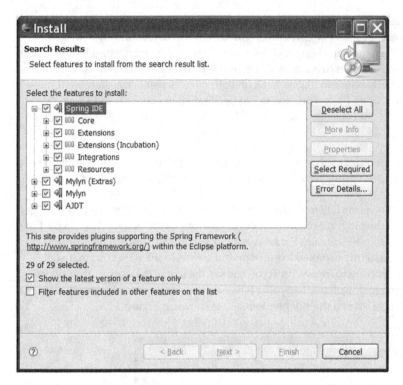

Figure 3-2. *Selecting the Spring IDE features and dependencies*

■**Note** For Spring IDE 2.x, Eclipse 3.2.x is required for installation. You do not need to check the Dependencies feature if you are running Eclipse 3.3 or later. That feature is intended for Eclipse 3.2 only. Optionally, you can install Mylyn and AspectJ Development Tools (AJDT), with which the Spring IDE integrates. Mylyn is a task-focused interface that simplifies workspace management for developers by tracking tasks you are delivering. AJDT supports Spring 2.x AOP development.

Flex Builder

Flex Builder is a commercial product from Adobe built on the Eclipse platform. As you know, Flex development can be done in any text editor, but using Flex Builder will help you learn Flex quicker by providing code editing, debugging, and a rich set of components to lay out your applications

The Flex Builder design view makes it easy for you to assemble and preview your application interfaces. It also provides a set of tools to enable skinning of your application. You can set properties on each component in your application that tie into your CSS. There are also options to import professionally done graphics and skins from Flash, Photoshop, or other supported graphical design tools.

There are two ways to install Flex Builder: as a stand-alone application or as an Eclipse plug-in. Either way will give you the same tool set to build a Flex application. There are no hits to performance or functionality for the compiled SWF. That said, we also want to build our Spring services in Eclipse. This forces us to use the Eclipse plug-in version of the Flex Builder. As I've mentioned in the previous chapter, this is the version I prefer, since it provides the other benefits that come with the base version of Eclipse. The main benefit is that the Java perspective is ready to use for your Eclipse project with Spring applied. It also has CVS and Ant views that you can easily plug in. If you prefer a different IDE for your Java development, you can use the stand-alone Flex Builder instead of the plug-in.

Setting Up Your Project Directory Structure

The directory structure we will use for the sample AF – Client Manager application is a semi-standard structure employed in many Flex web development projects. The first thing we need to do to set up the structure is to define a namespace for the project. This will allow us to organize our code in a series of folders so that our files can eventually be checked into CVS and shared among the team. A standard structure also helps with starting up new projects quicker and moving code between projects.

Creating a Flex Project

The first task is to create our new Flex project. To do so in Eclipse, select File ➤ New ➤ Flex Project. If you do not see the option to create a new Flex project, you may need to select Other from the menu to find the Flex project option.

You will be presented with a simple wizard to guide you through the process. Type in af_ClientManager for the project name, as shown in Figure 3-3, and then click the Finish button. For now, we will just accept the wizard's defaults for this project. Later, we will customize our directory structure for the project.

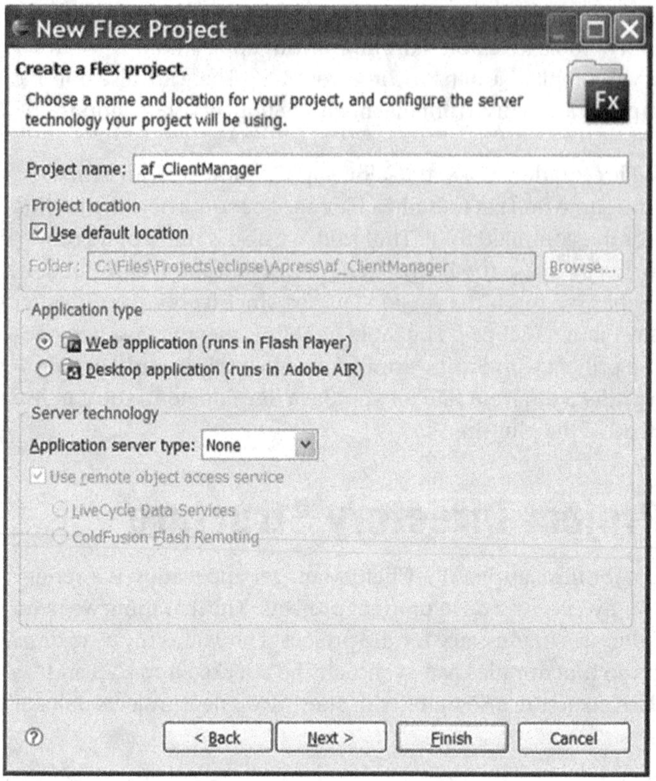

Figure 3-3. *Using the Flex Project wizard*

For this project, there is one library that is important to download and install. This is the Cairngorm library, which we will use to set up our Flex application framework for data persistence and messaging. Cairngorm is a developer framework you can use to build a patterned-based architecture for your Flex applications. It is based on the MVC pattern to help organize your project. You can download the latest version of the regular Cairngorm framework from Adobe Labs at http://opensource.adobe.com/wiki/display/cairngorm/Downloads. I will discuss Cairngorm in much more detail in Chapter 7.

Once you have downloaded the framework, extract Cairngorm.swc into your project libs directory. To make sure that the library is applied to your project, open the project properties (by right-clicking the project and selecting Properties or by choosing Project ➤ Properties), and then open the Library path tab under the Flex Build Path. Check that you have a Cairngorm.swc link to your project. Your Properties dialog box should look something like the one shown in Figure 3-4.

Now that we've created our project and have the Cairngorm library linked into the project, we can create our project folder structure.

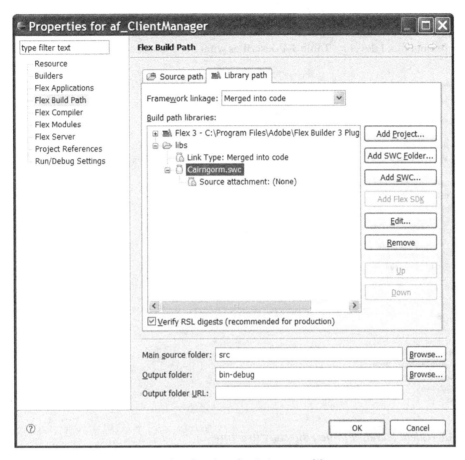

Figure 3-4. *Flex project properties showing the Cairngorm library*

Creating the Flex Project Directory Structure

Just as programming styles are different from developer to developer, so are folder structures from architecture to architecture. Development firms have different ideas about how you should name your folders and what the primary function of each folder should be. For my company, I have defined a folder structure that enhances the architecture and does an excellent job of organizing the code that we write. Without this sort of organization, we would run the risk at creating a project that becomes a tangled ball of yarn and has no long-term maintainability or reusability.

Reusability is one of the goals we are shooting for with those components and Flex. I do not like to waste time reinventing the wheel with every new project that comes along. It's also important to create a sense of branding for your company through the components that you build over time when developing a series of projects. From a pure business perspective, developing a series of tangible assets is something that can boost your company's financial performance.

With all that said, let's get down to the folder structure that we will be working with on our project. Figure 3-5 shows the layout of AF – Client Manager, which is very similar to the layout of any new project that I develop. Table 3-1 describes what each folder contains.

Figure 3-5. *AF – Client Manager project directory structure*

Table 3-1. *Flex Project Directories*

Directory	Purpose
html-template	Holds the HTML wrapper and Flash Player install files that are deployed with your application. The HTML wrapper works as the index.html in your web server location. If you modify any of the files in this directory, they will be moved to the bin-debug and bin-release folders.
bin-debug	Where Flex places all of the resources when performing a local Flex build for debugging purposes. This is a default folder that Flex Builder will create.
bin-release	When you are ready to release the source code to the web server, you export the release build to this directory by selecting Project ➤ Export Release Build in Eclipse.
libs	Holds the SWC files for externally built Flash and Flex components such as Cairngorm and Flash preloaders.
src	Web root of the Flex project and associated components. Contains the main MXML and ActionScript source code, as well as any CSS files needed for the project. Specific configuration files such as the crossdomain.xml and .flexProperties files are also held here.

Table 3-1. *Flex Project Directories*

Directory	Purpose
assets	Holds the icons, images, and CSS files used throughout the application, as well as the sample XML data files.
com	The root level of the package namespace. It is the first folder you will find in the root folder src.
business	Holds all delegates that are responsible for sending requests to the HTTP services and listening for the response.
command	Cairngorm structure that holds the commands that use the delegates to communicate with the HTTP service calls. Commands consist of execute and result functions for sending and retrieving data from the HTTP service call.
control	Cairngorm controllers that catch the events raised from the front-end system and call the proper commands.
model	Holds the singleton instance for the model of the application. There can be submodels extended from the main model. This layer will hold the data objects for the components.
services	Contains the service definitions and endpoints for the application.
view	Contains all of the viewable representations of the model information, including dialog boxes, components, views, etc.
vo	Holds model-related data stored in individual and collection-based value objects.

Setting Up the Flex Library Project

I've touched on the importance of creating a common set of components and building your own library to house those components. Now the rubber hits the road. We will create that component library to reuse throughout our projects. This is the ultimate way to share your components across applications and also create a set of standard components for your organization to leverage.

To create a new Flex Library project in Eclipse, select File ➤ New ➤ Flex Library Project. The project name usually will just be your company name followed by _lib. As you can see in Figure 3-6, I have used af_lib. The af refers to my AppFoundation project, which is a series of RIA applications and tools that I have built over the years.

Figure 3-6. *Flex Library project directory structure*

The directory structure for your library consists of a namespace (com/af/components) and a binary directory (bin) where your SWC file will be compiled. The compiled SWC file is very similar to the Cairngorm.swc file that we linked to our main Flex project. Once you have your SWC compiled—af_lib.swc, in this case—you could take this file and drop it directly into your main application's lib folder, and it will be applied to your project automatically. What is really nice is that once your library is linked into the project, you will have code completion for your library components.

The com/af/components namespace will be used to reference our components throughout our Flex applications and will also serve to organize components within their functional space. For example, if you were to extend the Flex DateChooser component, you would create a folder under the components called dateChooser. You would likely name the component CustomDateChooser so any developer who wants to use that component knows that it was extended at some point. In fact, this is exactly what we will do in the next chapter to demonstrate creating a custom component.

Setting Up the Spring Project

Getting started with the Spring project requires creating a new Java project within the Eclipse IDE. To do so, select File ➤ New ➤ Java Project. Using the wizard, give your project a name and accept the default configurations, as shown in Figure 3-7.

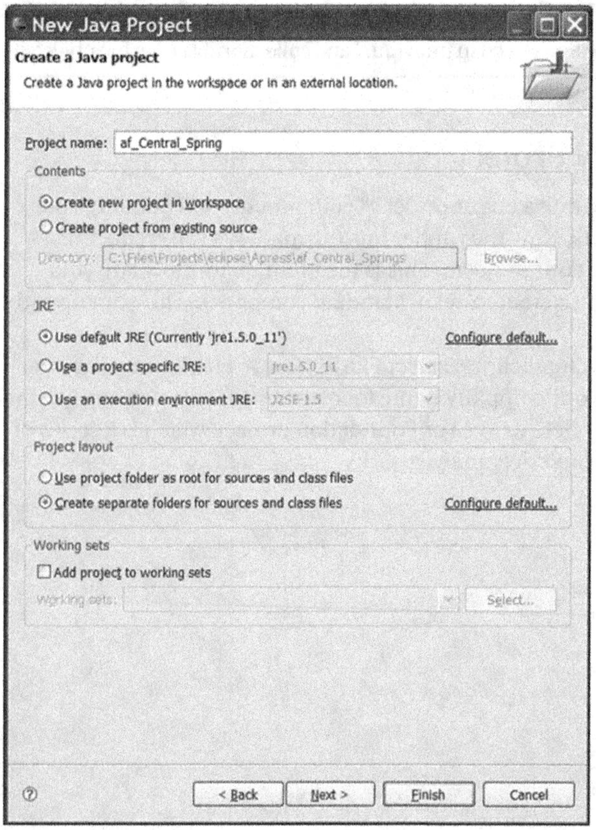

Figure 3-7. *Using the Java Project wizard*

Now that you have created the new project, you will want to go ahead and download the Spring libraries for the project. Download the Spring Framework from http://www. springframework.org/download. Copy the single Spring JAR file into your lib directory of the Spring project. This will link the library to your project so you can extend it and use the different functionality of those components.

As you can you can see in Figure 3-8, we have a different set of directory structures to support the architecture. However, notice that the Flex project and the Spring project have a lot in common. This is a key point that shows developers how easy it is to move from Java to Flex.

Figure 3-8. *Spring project directory structure*

Table 3-2 describes the directories in the Spring project directory structure. These directories are created by hand, based on the package structure com/af/...

Table 3-2. *Spring Directories*

Directory	Purpose
bin	Contains the compiled .class files for the Spring project
build	Holds the WAR file generated by an Ant build
src/com	Holds all the Java source files
tests/com	Contains all unit testing Java source associated with the src/com files
factories	Holds the Spring factory files that will act as the gateway for Flex
servlet	Contains any Java servlets used in the application, such as file upload servlets

Table 3-2. *Spring Directories (Continued)*

Directory	Purpose
core	Contains all the Spring interfaces, beans, and components
dao	Holds the DAOs (interface-driven Spring beans), including the code for ORM access
domain	Holds the domain objects we will use to pass typed object data back and forth from Flex, such as a customer object with attributes like name, age, sex, and phone number
services	Holds interface-driven Spring beans that are accessible from Flex, as well as the implementation of the services, and injects the DAOs for data persistence

Sharing the Project with CVS

As discussed earlier, we're using CVS as the revision control system to build a project. This is not required, but is highly recommended.

To access the CVS perspective in Eclipse, select Window ➤ Open Perspective ➤ Other. Then select CVS Repository Exploring, as shown in Figure 3-9.

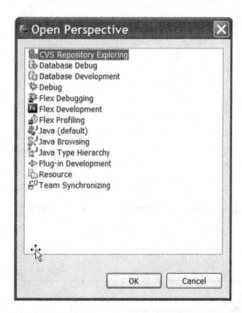

Figure 3-9. *CVS perspective selection in Eclipse*

You'll see that Eclipse has taken you to the CVS Repository Exploring perspective. You can switch perspectives quickly with the pick list in the top-right corner of the Eclipse IDE.

Connecting to a CVS repository is simple. In the CVS repositories view, select Add CVS Repository, and you will be prompted to enter the specifics of your CVS repository, as shown in Figure 3-10.

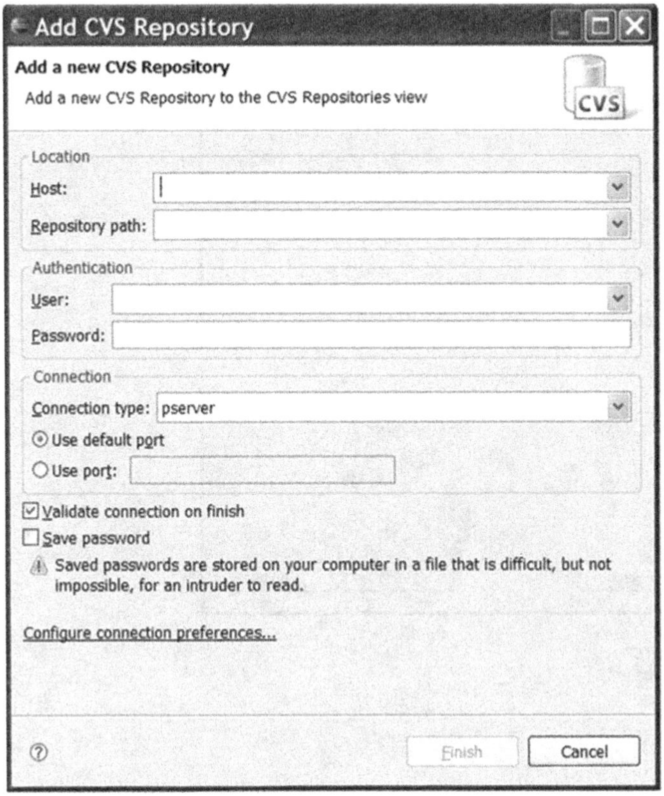

Figure 3-10. *Adding a new CVS repository*

Success! You should have a live connection to your CVS repository and now can share your project, so that your team has access to the project template that you have just created.

To share your project, right-click the project name and select Team ➤ Share Project. Then select the CVS repository that you just added, and accept the defaults provided by this wizard. You will see a dialog box that allows you to review and commit resources to the repository, as shown in Figure 3-11. Once you're sure of what you want to commit to the repository, click Finish. The wizard will create a new project on the CVS server, and submit all of the directory structure and source code that is in your project.

Once the commit process is complete, you will notice a change to your project structure. The text "[Server Name or IP]" will now appear next to your root project name.

⊟ 📷 >af_ClientManager[Server Name or IP]

Now that you have the Flex project committed to CVS, repeat this same process for your Spring project and your Flex Library project to share them through CVS.

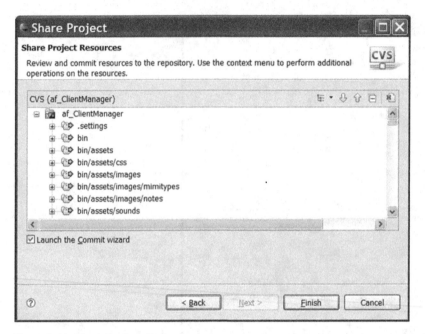

Figure 3-11. *Share Project dialog box*

Summary

This chapter covered how to build Flex applications using Ant. This will allow you to deliver Flex applications without requiring costly purchases. Not only can you build the application, but you can also use Ant to run unit tests and deploy your application to the destination of your choice. Ant also works well in Eclipse, which is the IDE we are using to build and deploy our sample application.

We also covered the benefits of using a version control system to share and maintain your code. Two good choices for version control systems if you use Eclipse are CVS and Subversion. Both products offer Eclipse integration through plug-ins. Visual cues allow you to see when you have modified code and need to commit your changes.

Next, we talked about the Eclipse IDE, which allows you to edit code and add tools needed to do your job. We covered the Spring IDE and the benefits it brings, such as Spring 2.x, Spring Web Flow, AOP, and JavaConfig. It is up to you to decide if you need this plug-in.

Finally, we set up the project directory structure for our sample application. We created the main two Flex project types we will use, along with the Spring project.

Now we are ready to discuss the architecture we will deploy for Flex and Spring in detail. The next chapter introduces Flex and explains how it can be used in RIA projects.

■ ■ ■

## CHAPTER 4

Introduction to Flex Applications

At this point, you should understand how to create a new project in Flex and the basic folder structure for your project. This chapter introduces Flex applications. It will serve to set the tone for understanding RIAs, as well as getting started with Flex. We'll cover the major components of Flex and the areas that you need to have a clear understanding of before we start building this book's sample project.

Introducing MXML and ActionScript

In general, a Flex application is laid out with an MXML (Flex's extensible markup language similar to HTML) file, coupled with ActionScript to support the application logic. Let's start with a quick overview of MXML and ActionScript.

MXML

MXML is used to define the user interface layouts and controls of an application. MXML allows you to structure your application components with a parent-child relationship that lays out the application in many different ways.

User Interface Containers and Components

User interface components in Flex are those that you use to build your different views. You can use many different components, such as `<mx:DataGrid>`, `<mx:TextBox>`, `<mx:TabNavigator>`, `<mx:Listbox>`, and so on. These components are flexible in that you can skin them, extend them into custom components, and change their size and shape.

Containers, on the other hand, are used to wrap these components to derive your visual layout. Containers have the same flexibility as components and have the option of being visible or not, based on the requirements of your application. They act as the framework to shift and maneuver components through transitions and effects. Examples of containers are `mx:HBox`, `mx:VBox`, `mx:Panel`, and `mx:HDividedBox`.

In developing a Flex application, the first MXML file to consider is the main application component, as shown in Listing 4-1.

Listing 4-1. *Flex Application Container*

```
<?xml version="1.0" encoding="utf-8"?>
<mx:Application
    xmlns:mx="http://www.adobe.com/2006/mxml"
    layout="absolute">

    <mx:HBox>
        <mx:Button />
        <mx:Button />
    </mx:HBox>
</mx:Application>
```

The code in Listing 4-1 does nothing more than define the application and the child components located in the application. As you can see, the <mx:HBox> container lays out two buttons horizontally across the application. So far, this is just a skeleton application that has minimal usefulness, other than to show you how to create a basic Flex application. But it is a first step toward demonstrating how to build real working applications from reusable components.

To better understand what I mean by creating reusable components in Flex, let's move the buttons from the main Flex application container to their own MXML component and reference the new component from the main application. To do this, we create a component called ButtonComponent.mxml and access it from our main application, as shown in Listings 4-2 and 4-3.

Listing 4-2. *ButtonComponent Component (ButtonComponent.mxml)*

```
<?xml version="1.0" encoding="utf-8"?>
<mx:Canvas
    xmlns:mx="http://www.adobe.com/2006/mxml" >

    <mx:Button />

</mx:Canvas>
```

Listing 4-3. *Revised Main Application Container*

```
<?xml version="1.0"?>
<mx:Application
    xmlns:mx="http://www.adobe.com/2006/mxml"
    xmlns:local="*">

    <local:ButtonComponent />

</mx:Application>
```

Once you have created your ButtonComponent in your application, go ahead and start typing the component's name: <ButtonC.... If you are using Flex Builder, you should see a menu pop up, offering you code completion for that MXML component. Since the component we built is local to the root application, we do not require a namespace to find a component.

MXML Tags

In Flex, ActionScript classes correspond to MXML tags. When you create a Flex application, the application interrogates the MXML tags to generate the appropriate ActionScript classes. These tags help to shape and structure the different Flex components that are used within an application. The structure may define the height and width of a component or container, as well as all attributes that the specified ActionScript class has defined. Listing 4-4 shows an example of using MXML tags.

Listing 4-4. *Flex MXML Tag Example*

```
<?xml version="1.0"?>
<mx:Application
      xmlns:mx="http://www.adobe.com/2006/mxml"
      xmlns:local="*">

      <mx:Panel id="mainPnl"
            title="MXML Tags"
            height="200" width="200"
            paddingLeft="10"
            paddingRight="10"
            paddingBottom="10"
            paddingTop="10"
            horizontalAlign="center">

            <mx:RadioButton id="rb" label="On" />
            <mx:Button id="submitBtn" label="Do It" />
      </mx:Panel>
</mx:Application>
```

MXML Namespaces

Namespaces in MXML are used to locate components and containers for you to use in your applications. They act as an alias to the location of the core components that come with Flex Builder, or a series of custom components you have defined yourself.

The default namespace in Flex is xmlns:mx="http://www.adobe.com/2006/mxml". You will notice the alias mx is the namespace object to access all components in the mx object, thus:

```
<mx:Button id="btnNamespace" />
<mx:VBox id="vbxNamespace" />
```

To define a custom namespace, we need to create a new folder. Let's call the folder views. In the views folder, create a new MXML component called NamespaceTest.mxml. We fill out the NamespaceTest.mxml component as shown in Listing 4-5, and add it to a new Flex application as shown in Listing 4-6.

Listing 4-5. *NamespaceTest.mxml Component*

```
<?xml version="1.0" encoding="utf-8"?>
<mx:Canvas xmlns:mx="http://www.adobe.com/2006/mxml"
      width="400" height="300">

      <mx:Panel title="Namespace Example"
            paddingLeft="10"
            paddingRight="10"
            paddingBottom="10"
            paddingTop="10"
            horizontalAlign="center">

            mx:Button label="Do It"/>

      </mx:Panel>
</mx:Canvas>
```

Listing 4-6. *Main Application for the NamespaceTest.mxml Component*

```
<?xml version="1.0"?>
<mx:Application
      xmlns:mx="http://www.adobe.com/2006/mxml"
      xmlns:view="view.*"
      horizontalAlign="center"
      verticalAlign="middle">

      <view:NamespaceTest width="100%" height="100%" />

</mx:Application>
```

If you are using Flex Builder, you should notice that the new namespace is in the code completion menu when you start typing `<Namespa....`

Selecting your new component will add the `view` namespace to the `<mx:Application>` beginning MXML tag automatically. You now have access to any component you put in the `view` folder through the namespace alias. This is a key point, as you will be using namespaces consistently as you progress to larger applications.

ActionScript

ActionScript is used in Flex applications to prescribe custom behavior for the application. This behavior can involve a wide range of functionality, such as triggering events, displaying dialog boxes, and creating custom classes. ActionScript has advantages over MXML for this purpose, as it is a procedural language and syntactically similar to JavaScript.

If you want to create dynamic components or process creative effects and transitions in your application, you will require ActionScript to build those components. ActionScript has a full complement of variable types (`String`, `Array`, `int`, and so on), and allows you to build methods to execute from MXML and ActionScript. Moreover, if you have a button that you want to grow in size on mouse-over, you can use MXML to support that effect. But if you want a user gesture to generate an action on your view, you will need to create ActionScript methods to support those user gestures.

The `<mx:Script>` tag in MXML is one way to define a location for ActionScript in a component. The methods in this tag are accessible and scoped to the component in which they are created. Each variable and method can be public, private, or protected. This allows you to communicate between components if necessary.

■**Caution** Tightly coupling components can cause maintenance issues and works against reuse of components. It is not a good practice to allow component-to-component communication using `Application.` `application` or `this.parentApplication`. The goal of an RIA is to create a loosely coupled architecture, and using those two references can create cross-component dependencies that you will most likely need to correct in the future.

The only place you want public methods and variables will be in ActionScript classes that are created to support common business functions such as models, submodels, and value objects.

Handling Data in Flex

In your Flex applications, you can use data binding to supply data to objects throughout your applications. Data validation is important for applications that take data as input. And for data coming into your components, you will probably want to set standard formatting.

Data Binding

Data binding is the process of linking Flex objects to data objects. One benefit of data binding is that when data is updated to the data provider, the data propagates to the view component objects that are bound to that data provider.

As you become more advanced in your Flex architecture, you will see the true benefits of binding to data objects in your applications model. This will be one of the core principles I will cover when discussing the Cairngorm framework in Chapter 10.

Currently, Flex offers several ways to bind data between objects. You can use one of the following approaches:

- Curly braces ({})

- The `<mx:Binding>` tag in MXML

- ActionScript expressions

- ActionScript bindings

Let's look at each of these approaches.

Using Curly Braces {}

Data binding requires a source object, a destination object, and a triggering event that causes the data to be copied from the source to the destination. This triggering event can range from data being pushed from another component, to a change in the state of a component (if the data binding is tied to a component tag like an `<mx:HSlider>` value tag), to the initialization of a component.

In our example, we will define an `Array` that will be loaded to an `ArrayCollection` in the initialize tag of the application shown in Listing 4-7.

Listing 4-7. *Data Binding Using Curly Braces Syntax*

```
<?xml version="1.0"?>
<mx:Application xmlns:mx="http://www.adobe.com/2006/mxml"
      horizontalAlign="center" verticalAlign="middle"
      initialize="initComp();">

      <mx:Script>
      <![CDATA[
            import mx.collections.*
            private var STATES_ARRAY:Array=
            [{label:"AR", data:"Arkansas"},
            {label:"OH", data:"Ohio"},
            {label:"TX", data:"Texas"}];

            // Declare an ArrayCollection variable for states.
            // Make it Bindable so it can be bound to a container ({statesAC})
            [Bindable] public var statesAC:ArrayCollection;

            // Initialize statesAC ArrayCollection variable from the Array.
            private function initComp():void
            {
                  statesAC = new ArrayCollection(STATES_ARRAY);
            }
      ]]>
      </mx:Script>

      <mx:Panel title="Using the Curly Braces for Data Binding"
            paddingLeft="10" paddingRight="10" paddingBottom="10" paddingTop="10"
            horizontalAlign="center">

            <mx:ComboBox dataProvider="{statesAC}"/>
      </mx:Panel>
</mx:Application>
```

Once initialization is complete, you will notice that the `<mx:ComboBox>` is loaded with the states array, as shown in Figure 4-1. The initialize tag on the application acted as the trigger to load the data from the statesAC (source) to the ComboBox.dataProvider (destination). Notice how the statesAC ArrayCollecation is bound to the `<mx:ComboBox>` through the curly braces {statesAC}.

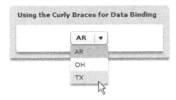

Figure 4-1. *Result of running the curly braces example*

Using the <mx:Binding> Tag in MXML

The <mx:Binding> tag can be used as an alternative to the curly braces syntax. This requires the
same source and destination objects as the curly braces syntax, and is essentially the same
as that technique, but is located in the tag properties. The main difference is that you use the
<mx:Binding> tag to completely separate your view. In the MVC architecture, the <mx:Binding>
tag is your controller, which separates the view from the model. Another benefit is that you can
source multiple <mx:Binding> tags from the same destination. Listing 4-8 shows an example of
using this syntax.

Listing 4-8. *Data Binding Using the <mx:Binding> Tag in MXML Syntax*

```
<?xml version="1.0" encoding="utf-8"?>
<mx:Application xmlns:mx="http://www.adobe.com/2006/mxml" layout="absolute"
    horizontalAlign="center" verticalAlign="middle">

        <!-- Model: for contacts -->
        <mx:Model id="contacts">
            <contact>
                <name>
                        <first>{"John"}</first>
                        <last>{"Doe"}</last>
                </name>
            </contact>
        </mx:Model>

    <!-- View: User Interface components and containers -->
    <mx:Panel title="Use the mx:Binding tag in MXML"
            paddingLeft="10" paddingRight="10" paddingBottom="10" paddingTop="10"
            horizontalAlign="center">

        <mx:Form>
          <mx:FormItem label="First Name" >
                <mx:TextInput id="firstName" />
          </mx:FormItem>

          <mx:FormItem label="Last Name">
                <mx:TextInput id="lastName" />
          </mx:FormItem>
        </mx:Form>
    </mx:Panel>
```

```
<!-- Controller: Used to bind data from the Model to the View -->
<mx:Binding
        source="contacts.name.first"
        destination="firstName.text"
/>

<mx:Binding
        source="contacts.name.last"
        destination="lastName.text"
/>
</mx:Application>
```

Figure 4-2 shows the runtime application view of this example.

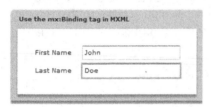

Figure 4-2. *Result of running the Binding tag example*

Using ActionScript Expressions for Data Binding

Another way to bind data is through ActionScript expressions. You can bind expressions using curly braces directly in ActionScript to return a value when a user gesture is executed.

In the example in Listing 4-9, the user types her first name and last name in the <mx:TextInput> boxes, which have their text property bound through the ActionScript embedded in the <mx:Model> tag. The first name and last name will show up as output in the two labels that are bound to the <mx:Model> attributes.

Listing 4-9. *Data Binding Through ActionScript Expressions*

```
<?xml version="1.0" encoding="utf-8"?>
<mx:Application xmlns:mx="http://www.adobe.com/2006/mxml" layout="absolute"
     horizontalAlign="center" verticalAlign="middle">

    <!-- Model: for contacts -->
    <mx:Model id="contacts">
        <contact>
            <name>
                <first>{firstNameInput.text}</first>
                <last>{lastNameInput.text}</last>
            </name>
        </contact>
    </mx:Model>
```

```
    <!-- View: User Interface components and containers -->
    <mx:Panel title="Binding ActionScript Expressions"
            paddingLeft="10" paddingRight="10" paddingBottom="10" paddingTop="10"
            horizontalAlign="center">
        <mx:Form>
            <mx:FormItem label="First Name" >
                <mx:TextInput id="firstNameInput"/>
            </mx:FormItem>

            <mx:FormItem label="Last Name">
                <mx:TextInput id="lastNameInput"/>
            <mx:FormItem>

            <mx:FormItem label="First Name" >
                <mx:Label id="firstName"
                        text="{contacts.name.first}"
                        fontSize="15" fontWeight="bold" />
            </mx:FormItem>

            <mx:FormItem label="Last Name">
                <mx:Label id="lastName"
                        text="{contacts.name.last}"
                        fontSize="15" fontWeight="bold" />
            </mx:FormItem>
        </mx:Form>
    </mx:Panel>
</mx:Application>
```

Figure 4-3 shows the runtime application view for the example in Listing 4-9.

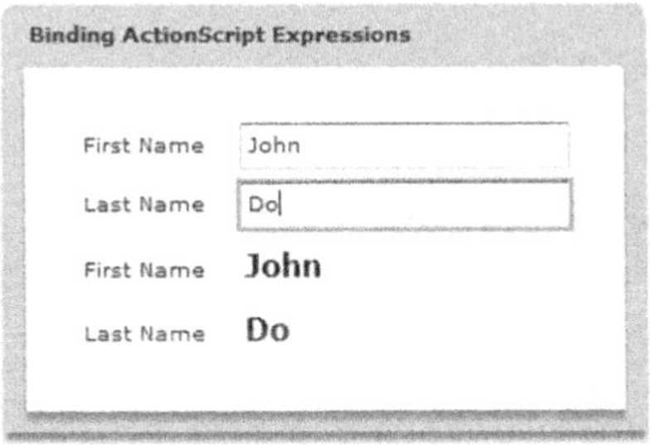

Figure 4-3. *Result of running the ActionScript expressions binding example*

Using ActionScript Bindings for Data Binding

The most prevalent way to bind data is by using the curly braces syntax, as discussed earlier. For my projects, using ActionScript bindings is probably the least common approach, since every application I build now is based on an MVC architecture pattern.

The example in Listing 4-10 uses the mx.binding.utils.BindingUtils class. This class must be imported to your script and gives you access to the bindProperty() method, which lets you define a destination/property and source/object. The destination is the model you plan to host the data, and the property declares where you will host the actual data. The source is the location from which you will obtain the data element. It is usually a property from an MXML tag—TextInput.text, in this example.

Listing 4-10. *Data Binding Through the ActionScript BindingUtils Class*

```
<?xml version="1.0" encoding="utf-8"?>
<mx:Application xmlns:mx="http://www.adobe.com/2006/mxml" layout="absolute"
      horizontalAlign="center" verticalAlign="middle"
      initialize="initComp();">

    <!-- Model: for contacts -->
    <mx:Model id="contacts">
         <contact>
             <name>
                   <first/>
                   <last/>
             </name>
         </contact>
    </mx:Model>

    <mx:Script>
         <![CDATA[
         import mx.binding.utils.BindingUtils;

         private function initComp():void
         {
             // Updates the model
             BindingUtils.bindProperty(contacts, "name.first",
                   firstNameInput, "text");
             BindingUtils.bindProperty(contacts, "name.last",
                   lastNameInput, "text");

             // Reads from the model to update the status text
             BindingUtils.bindProperty(firstName, "text",
                   contacts, "name.first");
             BindingUtils.bindProperty(lastName, "text", contacts,
                   "name.last");
         }
         ]]>
    </mx:Script>

    <!-- View: User Interface components and containers -->
    <mx:Panel title="BindingUtils Class in ActionScript"
         paddingLeft="10" paddingRight="10" paddingBottom="10" paddingTop="10"
         horizontalAlign="center">
         <mx:Form>
```

```
        <mx:FormItem label="First Name" >
            <mx:TextInput id="firstNameInput"/>
        </mx:FormItem>

        <mx:FormItem label="Last Name">
            <mx:TextInput id="lastNameInput"/>
        </mx:FormItem>

        <mx:FormItem label="First Name" >
            <mx:Label id="firstName" text="{contacts.name.first}"
                fontSize="15" fontWeight="bold" />
        </mx:FormItem>

        <mx:FormItem label="Last Name">
            <mx:Label id="lastName" text="{contacts.name.last}"
                fontSize="15" fontWeight="bold" />
        </mx:FormItem>
    </mx:Form>
    </mx:Panel>
</mx:Application>
```

Figure 4-4 shows the result of running the example in Listing 4-10.

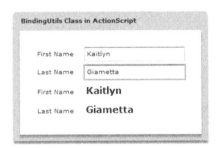

Figure 4-4. *Result of running the ActionScript BindingUtils class example*

Validating Data

Data validators in Flex are important to understand when building applications that take data as input. Form-driven applications or those with a business work flow usually require validation of data types such as e-mail addresses, ZIP codes, numeric types, alpha types, dates, and so on.

Flex offers validators to cover most of the common scenarios. You also have the option of creating custom validators if needed. Here, we will take a look at three common ways to use validators:

- Triggering validation through ActionScript

- Triggering validation through data bindings

- Triggering validation through events

Triggering Validation Through ActionScript

To trigger validation programmatically, you use the Validator class in Flex. The Validator class and its subclasses have a method called validate(), which allows you to invoke a specific validator directly.

The Validator.listener property is set to listen for changes to the object assigned to the listener. The listener is required to apply changes to the source object being validated.

In the example shown in Listing 4-11, the validator is defined in the doValidation() method, which is invoked from the <mx:Button> click event. The doValidation() method sets a listener on the <mx:TextInput> object. Once the button is clicked, the data validator validates the data in the source object the listener is listening to.

Listing 4-11. *Data Validation Through ActionScript*

```
<?xml version="1.0"?>
<mx:Application xmlns:mx="http://www.adobe.com/2006/mxml">

    <mx:Script>
        <![CDATA[
        import mx.validators.DateValidator;

        private var validator:DateValidator = new DateValidator();

        private function doValidation():void
        {
            validator.allowedFormatChars = "/-";
            validator.listener=myDate;
            validator.validate(myDate.text);
        }
        ]]>
    </mx:Script>

    <mx:Panel title="Validation through ActionScript"
        paddingLeft="10" paddingRight="10" paddingBottom="10" paddingTop="10"
        horizontalAlign="center">

        <mx:Label text="Enter a date to be validated (mm/dd/yyyy):"/>
        <mx:TextInput id="myDate"/>
        <mx:Button label="Do It" click="doValidation();"/>
    </mx:Panel>
</mx:Application>
```

Figure 4-5 shows the results of running the example in Listing 4-11.

Figure 4-5. *Result of running the data validation through ActionScript example*

Triggering Validation Through Data Bindings

You can use a validator with data bindings to validate either the source or destination of the binding. In this scenario, you use the default event `valueCommit` on your selected control to trigger the validation. With bound data, Flex updates the data destination every time the source changes, which triggers validation on the control. This has the effect of validating every character that is typed into a component in your application. Listing 4-12 shows an example of triggering validation through data bindings.

Listing 4-12. *Data Validation Through Data Bindings*

```
<?xml version="1.0"?>
<mx:Application xmlns:mx="http://www.adobe.com/2006/mxml">

    <!-- Define a data model for storing the date. -->
    <mx:Model id="userData">
        <userInfo>
            <email>{emailInput.text}</email>
            <phone>{phoneInput.text}</phone>
        </userInfo>
    </mx:Model>

    <!-- Define the EmailValidator and PhoneNumberValidator. -->
    <mx:EmailValidator
        source="{emailInput}"
        property="text"/>

    <mx:PhoneNumberValidator
        source="{phoneInput}"
        property="text" />

    <mx:Panel title="Validation through Data Bindings"
        paddingLeft="10" paddingRight="10" paddingBottom="10" paddingTop="10"
        horizontalAlign="center">

        <mx:Label text="Enter an email address:"/>
        <mx:TextInput id="emailInput"/>
        <mx:TextInput id="phoneInput"/>
    </mx:Panel>
</mx:Application>
```

Figure 4-6 shows the result of running the example in Listing 4-12.

Figure 4-6. *Result of running the data validation with data bindings example*

Triggering Validation Through Events

You can trigger validation through events by setting the `trigger` and `triggerEvent` properties on the validator to the event you want to fire the validation. The `trigger` property specifies the component or object that will fire the event that will cause validation to occur. The `triggerEvent` is the event that triggers the validation. Flex dispatches events when certain user gestures are made. In the example in Listing 4-13, the click event for the `<mx:Button>` will trigger the valida-tion of the `<mx:TextInput>` object.

Listing 4-13. *Data Validation Through Events*

```
<?xml version="1.0"?>
<mx:Application xmlns:mx="http://www.adobe.com/2006/mxml">

        <!-- US currency validator -->
        <mx:CurrencyValidator
                source="{currencyUS}"
                property="text"
                alignSymbol="left"
                trigger="{validateButton}"
                triggerEvent="click"/>

        <mx:Panel title="Validation through Events"
                paddingLeft="10" paddingRight="10" paddingBottom="10" paddingTop="10"
                horizontalAlign="center">

                <mx:Label text="Enter a US-formatted number:"/>
                <mx:TextInput id="currencyUS"/>
                <mx:Button label="Do It" id="validateButton"/>
        </mx:Panel>
</mx:Application>
```

Figure 4-7 shows the result of running the example in Listing 4-13.

Figure 4-7. *Result of running the data validation through events example*

Formatting Data

Data formatters in Flex allow you to set standard data output configurations on raw data coming into your components. Common formatters in Flex are CurrencyFormatter, DateFormatter, NumberFormatter, PhoneFormatter, and ZipCodeFormatter.

These formatters convert raw data into a string before the data is rendered in a control. The formatters are all subclasses of the mx.formatters.Formatter class, which has a format() method to which you can pass in a String to be formatted.

Listing 4-14 uses an <mx:DateFormatter> defined in MXML to format a selected date from an <mx:DateField> control. When you change the date, the <mx:DateFormatter> is triggered for the bound text field in the TestArea.text tag. This is bound using curly braces.

Listing 4-14. *Data Formatting Using MXML Formatters*

```
<?xml version="1.0"?>
<mx:Application xmlns:mx="http://www.adobe.com/2006/mxml">

    <!-- Define a date formatter and its properties -->
    <mx:DateFormatter id="dateFrm"
        formatString="MM/DD/YY"  />

    <mx:Panel title="Date Formatter"
        paddingLeft="10" paddingRight="10" paddingBottom="10" paddingTop="10"
        horizontalAlign="center">

        <mx:DateField id="dteField"/>
        <mx:TextArea text="{dateFrm.format(dteField.text)}" />
    </mx:Panel>
</mx:Application>
```

Figure 4-8 shows the result of running the example in Listing 4-14.

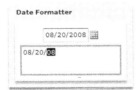

Figure 4-8. *Result of running the date formatter*

Creating Custom Components with ActionScript

ActionScript certainly has advantages over MXML when it comes to creating custom components. ActionScript allows you to get down to the lower levels of the Flex component API to extend and enhance out-of-the-box components. You can also create brand-new components, whether these share part of the core Flex components or are wholly original.

ActionScript is compiled, whereas MXML is interpreted at runtime. This makes Action-Script a better choice for writing custom components, although many of these are a blend of ActionScript and MXML, just like your application files. Pure ActionScript components generally take more time to develop, since you must code every interaction, but they lend themselves to reuse throughout your application and in future ones. This is why we create custom ActionScript components!

One component in Flex that is difficult to give custom skinning to is the `<mx:DateChooser>`. For our AF – Client Manager application, we will create a custom `<mx:DateChooser>` component that allows us to configure the dates and skin the component dynamically. This will require creating a base class for the new component, adding the method we want to override, and then adding the new functionality to the component.

Creating the Base ActionScript Class

The first task is to create a base class for our new component. The class is made up of a package. You will want to include your company or project as part of the package name in a domain name structure, which will look as follows for the Flex namespace:

```
xmlns:component="com.af.components.datechooser.*"
```

Using the company/project as part of the domain name structure helps to keep similar components from multiple vendors separate. You will reference this component in ActionScript with the `import` statement and in MXML through the namespace alias.

Listing 4-15 shows the base ActionScript class for our custom date chooser, and Listing 4-16 shows the main application file.

Listing 4-15. *Basic ActionScript Class CustomDateChooser (CustomDateChooser.as)*

```
package com.af.components.datechooser
{
     import mx.controls.DateChooser;

     public class CustomDateChooser extends DateChooser
     {
          public function CustomDateChooser()
          {
          }
     }
}
```

Listing 4-16. *Main Application File for CustomDateChooser*

```
<?xml version="1.0"?>
<mx:Application xmlns:mx="http://www.adobe.com/2006/mxml"
      xmlns:custom="com.af.components.datechooser.*">

      <custom:CustomDateChooser />

</mx:Application>
```

Let's take a look at the newly created component <custom:CustomDateChooser>. We created this new custom component and put it in the datechooser folder in our package.

When creating a component in Flex, you need to understand that all components modify the behavior of existing components. In this case, we want to extend the core <mx:DateChooser> component in Flex. By extending the <mx:DateChooser> class, <custom:CustomDateChooser> inherits all attributes of the <mx:DateChooser> class. This is very important for later, since we will override some of those attributes to change the behavior of this class.

One last item to note here is the constructor for the class: CustomDateChooser(). This is where we will put style overrides and data providers, if needed.

In the main application, notice the namespace alias custom. The alias gives you access to the component as an MXML tag (<custom:CustomDateChooser/>). Running this application will produce an <mx:DateChooser> extended through the new custom class.

Overriding Component Functions

The next step is to determine if we need or want to extend current base class functionality. You can override base class methods in the extended ActionScript class. To override a method, add the method to your custom class with the same method name prefixing the method with the override keyword. The following code overrides the updateDisplayList() in the <mx:DateChooser> base class:

```
package com.af.components.datechooser
{
      import mx.controls.DateChooser;

      public class CustomDateChooser extends DateChooser
      {
            public function CustomDateChooser()
            {
            }

            override protected function
                  updateDisplayList(unscaledWidth:Number,
                                    unscaledHeight:Number):void
            {
                  super.updateDisplayList(unscaledWidth,
                                          unscaledHeight);
            }
      }
}
```

Within the updateDisplayList, notice the super.updateDisplayList() method. The call to super.updateDisplayList() causes Flex to invoke the superclass's updateDisplayList() method. This allows you to get the superclass's functionality, as well as override some or all of it in your custom updateDisplayList() method. Whether you are required to call the super() method depends on your functional needs. You do need to call the super() method before your code to add your specific functionality. To completely replace the base method, do not call the super() method.

Now that we have built the new class and added the method we want to override, we need to add the new functionality to the component.

Adding Functionality to the Component

Establishing your component's requirements before you start to build it is very important. Creating your own component is one of the more complex aspects of Flex programming. Expertise in building custom components is a big asset to an individual developer or a team.

The goal of our sample component is to support specific business requirements that are not supported with an out-of-the-box Flex component. The requirements are as follows:

- Add the ability to create a gradient background to the DateChooser. For this, we need to remove the header, body, and border backgrounds.

- Add the ability to hide the month forward button, month back button, and the year display. We will use this component in the AF – Client Manager application in a such way that we do not want the user to change the month.

- Reformat the month and year display to appear as *MMMM YY* (as in January 99).

The following sections detail how to take this set of simple tasks and create a complex, custom reusable component.

Allowing a Gradient Background

The first requirement is to allow the component to have a gradient background that can be manipulated via CSS. The first thing we need to do with our new CustomDateChooser class is remove the header, body, and border backgrounds. To make this happen, we need to override the graphics in the base class so they do not load. Then we can fit in a gradient background. We need to use the mx_internal namespace so we have access to protected variables in the base class. Once this is done, we can assign the base class graphics to locally declared graphics variables. We can then use the clear() methods on the graphics object to clear the graphic from the component. Usually, these graphics are drawn at runtime to display certain aspects of a component.

The following code accomplishes our objectives:

```
override protected function updateDisplayList(unscaledWidth:Number,
    unscaledHeight:Number):void
{
    super.updateDisplayList(unscaledWidth, unscaledHeight);

    // Remove the header
    var calHG:Graphics = calHeader.graphics;
    calHG.clear();
```

```
    // Remove the body
    var calBody:Graphics = background.graphics;
    calBody.clear();

    // Remove the border
    var calBorder:Graphics = border.graphics;
    calBorder.clear();
}
```

Hiding the Month Buttons and Year Display

If you take a look at the DateChooser class in Flex, you will notice two mx_internal variables: fwdMonthButton:Button and backMonthButton:Button. These variables are actually buttons that are used at the top of the DateChooser component to cycle through months. For this new component, we want the ability to stop cycling through months.

To make these two variables available to MXML to set a visible state, we need to add a couple more lines of code to our class. We need to create two private Boolean variables to capture the state we need the buttons to be in—visible or not visible—as follows:

```
private var _fwdMonthButtonVisible:Boolean = true;
private var _backMonthButtonVisible:Boolean = true;
```

The default is true, so the core functionality is there at the beginning with the option to hide the buttons.

Now that we have the variables defined, we need a way to set them in MXML. Adding setters and getters to an ActionScript class will allow you to see the variables as a component attribute in the MXML tag. You will be able to see this using the code-completion function in Flex Builder. In this case, we only need setters for the Boolean values, as follows:

```
public function set fwdMonthButtonVisible(value:Boolean):void
{
    if (value == _fwdMonthButtonVisible)
        return;

    _fwdMonthButtonVisible = value;
}
public function set backMonthButtonVisible(value:Boolean):void
{
    if (value == _backMonthButtonVisible)
        return;

    _backMonthButtonVisible = value;
}
```

With the setters in place, we only need to add the Boolean check to the UpdateDisplayList() method. Make sure that the base class variable checks against our newly created variables that are set at the MXML tag level.

```
override protected function updateDisplayList(unscaledWidth:Number,
        unscaledHeight:Number):void
{
        super.updateDisplayList(unscaledWidth, unscaledHeight);

        // Remove the header
        var calHG:Graphics = calHeader.graphics;
        calHG.clear();

        // Remove the body
        var calBody:Graphics = background.graphics;
        calBody.clear();

        // Remove the border
        var calBorder:Graphics = border.graphics;
        calBorder.clear();

        // Validate button visibility
        fwdMonthButton.visible = _fwdMonthButtonVisible;
        backMonthButton.visible = _backMonthButtonVisible;
}
```

Reformatting the Month and Year Display

To format the date display to show the *MMMM YY* format, we will not use a DateFormatter, since the month and year are IUITextField types, which are not date formats. We will treat them as String values.

The only piece of the display date we need to format is the year. We just want the last two characters of the year String, so we will use the String classes subStr() method to do the job. Here is the code to format the yearDisplay variable that belongs to the DateChooser base class:

```
override protected function updateDisplayList(unscaledWidth:Number,
        unscaledHeight:Number):void
{
        super.updateDisplayList(unscaledWidth, unscaledHeight);

        // Format and move the year
        yearDisplay.text = String(monthDisplay.text) + " " +
        String(yearDisplay.text).substr(2,2);
        yearDisplay.width = this.width;
        yearDisplay.move(0, monthDisplay.y);

        displayDate = yearDisplay.text;
}
```

The subStr() method takes a start index and length to pull from the String. We are starting in position 2, which is the third character for the year, since the index is zero-based. We set the length at 2 to get the last two characters of the year and apply a concatenated string of the DateChooser monthDisplay.text and yearDisplay.text, and override its yearDisplay.text.

Next, we want to give the yearDisplay the width of the scoped CustomDateChooser so we have enough room to display the new String. We also want to move the yearDisplay along the y axis of the component to be sure it is properly centered. The last item of interest is setting the yearDisplay.text to a local Bindable variable called displayDate. This is set so we can easily access the display date from other components that may need to track this information.

Creating a Skinnable Gradient Background

Now we have a class that has stripped all of the graphics from its component and displays only the two buttons, year, and calendar. Next, we want to add a way to apply a gradient background through a CSS file.

Remember that we removed the border and background from this component since it was not directly styled. Now we need to add an <mx:VBox> that we can style with a new class we will configure shortly. As shown in Listing 4-17, we set the width and height of the <mx:VBox> to match that of the CustomDateChooser.

Listing 4-17. *CustomDateChooser Class Ready to Be Styled (CustomDateChooser.as)*

```
package com.af.components.datechooser
{
    import flash.display.Graphics;

    import mx.containers.VBox;
    import mx.controls.DateChooser;
    import mx.core.mx_internal;

    use namespace mx_internal;

    public class CustomDateChooser extends DateChooser
    {
        [Bindable] public var displayDate:String;
        private var _yearDisplayVisible:Boolean = true;
        private var _fwdMonthButtonVisible:Boolean = true;
        private var _backMonthButtonVisible:Boolean = true;
        public var highlightDaysArray:Array = new Array();
        private var gradientContainer:VBox = new VBox();

        public function CustomDateChooser():void
        {
            this.addChild(gradientContainer);
        }

        override protected function
            updateDisplayList(unscaledWidth:Number,
                              unscaledHeight:Number):void
        {
            var borderColor:Number = getStyle("borderColor");
            var borderThickness:Number = getStyle("borderThickness");
            var headerHeight:Number = getStyle("headerHeight");
```

```
        super.updateDisplayList(unscaledWidth, unscaledHeight);

        // Remove the header
        var calHG:Graphics = calHeader.graphics;
        calHG.clear();

        // Remove the body
        var calBody:Graphics = background.graphics;
        calBody.clear();

        //Remove the border
        var calBorder:Graphics = border.graphics;
        calBorder.clear();

        // Hide some of the date chooser controls
        fwdMonthButton.visible = _fwdMonthButtonVisible;
        backMonthButton.visible = _backMonthButtonVisible;
        monthDisplay.visible = false;

        // Format and move the year
        yearDisplay.text = String(monthDisplay.text) + " " +
        String(yearDisplay.text).substr(2,2);
        yearDisplay.width = this.width;
        yearDisplay.move(0, monthDisplay.y);

        displayDate = yearDisplay.text;

        yearDisplay.visible = _yearDisplayVisible;

        gradientContainer.height = this.height;
        gradientContainer.width = this.width;
    }
    public function set fwdMonthButtonVisible(value:Boolean):void
    {
        if (value == _fwdMonthButtonVisible)
            return;

        _fwdMonthButtonVisible = value;
    }
    public function set backMonthButtonVisible(value:Boolean):void
    {
        if (value == _backMonthButtonVisible)
            return;
```

```
            _backMonthButtonVisible = value;
        }
        public function set yearDisplayVisible(value:Boolean):void
        {
            if (value == _yearDisplayVisible)
                return;

            _yearDisplayVisible = value;
        }
    }
}
```

Figure 4-9 shows our custom component at this point. In the next section, we will take a look at adding styles with CSS, and then apply styles to our CustomDateChooser component.

Figure 4-9. *CustomDateChooser runtime view without a gradient background*

Adding Styles with CSS

CSS, not to be confused with application skinning, is used to add styles to your application components. You use CSS to change the look and feel of the application through fonts, colors, and layout properties throughout the application. These elements can be added at a global level or to individual components. They can even be added to an entire component set like Button, or you can have individual styles that can be read in by different Button instances through the setStyle property.

CSS styles are compiled into the Flex SWF file, rather than parsed at runtime by your web browser. In Flex, you have several options for applying styles to your applications:

- Code inline style declarations in a component.

- Use the <mx:Style> tag in a component.

- Use the setStyle() method to set styles on a component.

- Use the top-level MXML tag names in your CSS to apply global styles to a component.

Using Inline Style Declarations on MXML Tags

Inline CSS refers to using CSS elements within your MXML tags. You can set the same properties on the component as in a CSS file. This is best for setting layout constraints on your components, and setting font and color styles. As your application grows, you will come to regret setting detailed styling at the component level; this is generally a bad practice. Overall, doing it wrong will create a mess in your application.

In practice, the only time I use inline styling is when setting padding and basic layout configurations in a component/application, because generally, layouts will not change much (compared to font sizes and other font parameters). Here is an example of how I might add layout properties to a component:

```
<mx:Panel
      id="mainPanel"
      title="Custom component example"
      paddingLeft="10"
      paddingRight="10"
      paddingBottom="10"
      paddingTop="10"
      horizontalAlign="center"
      verticalAlign="middle"
/>
```

This styling is contained in the component in which the `<mx:Panel>` will be presented.

Caution Keep in mind the difference between global and component styles. Global styles should be in CSS files. Individual layout styles can be in the component itself, or your CSS can get out of control.

Using the <mx:Style> Tag

Using the `<mx:Style>` tag in MXML will apply styles locally. The syntax of the contents of the `<mx:Style>` tag is the same as an external CSS file. These definitions apply to the local component and all the children of the component. If you put these in the root application file, you can apply styles to your entire application.

A potential issue with this technique is that if you put `<mx:Style>` tags all over your application, you run the risk of creating a monster to correct when you maintain the code. The key is to keep all style declarations in one location.

You write your component and custom styles between the `<mx:Style>` start tag and `</mx:Style>` end tag, like this:

```
<mx:Style>
      Application
      {
            fontFamily: Verdana;
            fontSize: 14;
            color: #CCCCCC;
      }
```

```
        .customStyle
    {
            color: #FFFFFF;
    }
</mx:Style>
```

Ideally, you do not want a bunch of <mx:Style> declarations in application components. One use would be in a custom component, but even with those, you might want to set a style in an external CSS file.

The best location for your styles is in an external CSS file. In your application, you can take the previous example and move it to an external CSS file intact, except for the <mx:Style> tags. You simply use the <mx:Style> tag's source property to reference the new CSS file, like this:

```
<mx:Style source="assets/css/style.css"/>
```

The contents of this file in this case would be as follows:

```
Application
{
        fontFamily: Verdana;
        fontSize: 14;
        color: #CCCCCC;
}
.customStyle
{
        color: #FFFFFF;
}
```

Using the setStyle() Method

The setStyle() method is accessible in every component in Flex. It allows you to override the default style for the component by creating a CSS element that the component uses. This is the method we will use for our CustomDateChooser component.

First, let's apply a global background color to every <mx:VBox> used in the application. We need to create the CSS entry for the tag, as follows:

```
VBox
{
        backgroundColor: #000000;
}
```

Note You may be wondering why I used the syntax backgroundColor instead of background-color. In Flex, you can use the property name, and Flex will translate that to the appropriate style name. Either way will work.

Since we used <mx:VBox> as the CSS tag name, it is applied to every <mx:VBox> in our Flex application. This is good in some cases for creating consistent styles for items like Button components. However, in most applications, you probably would not want every <mx:VBox> to have a black background. Let's give it a new color and use a custom CSS tag name, as follows:

```
.customVBoxBGColor
{
        backgroundColor: #CCCCCC;
}
```

The dot preceding the name types it as a custom tag that we can leverage in our application. Here is the Flex code using the styleName property on the <mx:VBox> to apply the new light-gray color:

```
<?xml version="1.0"?>
<mx:Application xmlns:mx="http://www.adobe.com/2006/mxml"
     xmlns:custom="com.af.components.datechooser.*">

     <mx:Style source="assets/css/style.css"/>

     <mx:VBox styleName="customVBoxBGColor" width="212" height="193" />

</mx:Application>
```

Be sure to add the style reference to your <mx:Application>. This always goes in the root of your application.

Currently, our CustomDateChooser component has no background graphics. We will apply a gradient background through CSS, to provide maximum flexibility for the look and feel of our custom component.

We added an <mx:VBox> to the component so it has a container that we can easily style. We could do this directly through CSS, but our custom component will have rounded corners, and there is a little issue with most containers in Flex when you apply a background color: 90-degree border edges stick out on each corner when you round the corners of the component. To work around this, we will write another custom class that will redraw the border of the component and apply a gradient to the <mx:VBox> in our CustomDateChooser, as shown in Listing 4-18.

Listing 4-18. *RoundedGradientBorder Class (RoundedGradientBorder.as)*

```
package com.af.components.graphics
{
        import flash.display.*;
        import flash.geom.*;
        import flash.utils.*;

        import mx.core.EdgeMetrics;
        import mx.skins.halo.HaloBorder;
        import mx.utils.ColorUtil;
        import mx.utils.GraphicsUtil;
```

```
public class RoundedGradientBorder extends HaloBorder
{
    private var topCornerRadius:Number;            // top corner radius
    private var bottomCornerRadius:Number; // bottom corner radius
    private var fillColors:Array; // fill colors (two)
    private var setup:Boolean;

    private function setupStyles():void
    {
        fillColors = getStyle("fillColors") as Array;
        if (!fillColors) fillColors = [0xFFFFFF, 0xFFFFFF];

        topCornerRadius = getStyle("cornerRadius") as Number;
        if (!topCornerRadius) topCornerRadius = 0;

        bottomCornerRadius = getStyle("bottomCornerRadius") as Number;
        if (!bottomCornerRadius) bottomCornerRadius = topCornerRadius;
    }

    override protected function
        updateDisplayList(unscaledWidth:Number,
                          unscaledHeight:Number):void
    {
        super.updateDisplayList(unscaledWidth, unscaledHeight);

        setupStyles();

        var _graphics:Graphics = this.graphics;
        var _border:EdgeMetrics = borderMetrics;
        var _width:Number = unscaledWidth - _border.left - _border.right;
        var _height:Number = unscaledHeight - _border.top -
            _border.bottom;

        // Create a Matrix gradient fill
        var matrix:Matrix = new Matrix();
        matrix.createGradientBox(_width,_height,1.57,0,0);
        graphics.beginGradientFill("linear", fillColors,
            [1,1], [0, 255], matrix, SpreadMethod.PAD);
        var tr:Number = Math.max(topCornerRadius-2, 0);
        var br:Number = Math.max(bottomCornerRadius-2, 0);

        // Draw a complex rounded rectangle
        _graphics.drawRoundRectComplex(_border.left,_
            border.top, _width, _height, tr, tr, br, br);
        _graphics.endFill();
    }
}
```

This class digs into some of the drawing capabilities in Flex. As you can see, we are extending the HaloBorder class and overriding the updateDisplayList() method, much as we did with the same method in our CustomDateChooser class. The essence of this class is that we are looking for CSS styles that will be used in drawing the new border. We take the topCornerRadius and bottomCornerRadius to use when we draw the complex rounded rectangle. The other parameter we take is the fillColors array. This allows us to create that gradient look we want.

We also need to make a change to the CustomDateChooser class. The style for the <mx:VBox> needs to be set to show our new gradient border. In the constructor of the class, add the following code:

```
public function CustomDateChooser():void
{
    gradientContainer.setStyle("styleName", "CustomDateChooser");
    this.addChild(gradientContainer);
}
```

The setStyle() method is accessible from the component in ActionScript. It takes in a style property and a new value to look up. This value is located in your CSS file. For this component, we need to create a CustomDateChooser CSS entry, as shown in Listing 4-19.

Listing 4-19. *CustomDateChooser CSS Declaration*

```
CustomDateChooser
{
    borderStyle: solid;
    borderThickness: 2;
    borderColor: #72BAE6;
    borderSkin:
     ClassReference("com.af.components.graphics.RoundedGradientBorder");
    fillColors: #FFFFFF, #C6E3F6;
    fillAlphas: 1, 1;
    dropShadowEnabled: true;
    topCornerRadius: 12;
    bottomCornerRadius: 12;
    cornerRadius: 12;
    headerHeight: 30;
}
```

Now that we have the code in place, let's take a look at the results. Figure 4-10 shows the styled custom component.

As you can see, we now have a nice, gradient-filled background, which starts with white at the top and transitions into a light blue. The border's corners are rounded smoothly, with a slight drop shadow on the component.

What we've done might seem like a lot of work up front, but now we can reap the rewards of creating a custom component. Another huge benefit is that you can apply the RoundedGradientBorder class to any container to create a nice gradient background.

Figure 4-10. *CustomDateChooser runtime view with gradient background*

Skinning

Skinning is different from pure CSS in that it actually changes visual elements of a component. You can use CSS to apply skins to components, as they are both intertwined. Skinning can be graphical and programmatic.

Application skins can come from external Flash SWF files or from other asset libraries linked to your Flex project. Skinning is a bit more complex than basic CSS styling, as it requires assets not directly created in Flex.

The easiest way to skin a Flex application is through image assets. Using the Embed metadata tag allows you to set images to components that accept images.

■**Note** Embedding images will increase the size of your compiled SWF by the size of the image.

To demonstrate skinning, we will change the button skins for the next and previous month buttons in our CustomDateChooser component. I created a couple of new assets in Adobe Photoshop to be our new buttons, in PNG format. Add the following in the CSS file:

```
DateChooser
{
    prevMonthSkin: Embed("assets/images/icon_BtnLeft.png");
    nextMonthSkin: Embed("assets/images/icon_BtnRight.png");
}
```

By embedding the new images in DateChooser, we effectively globally change the month skins for every DateChooser we use in our application, as shown in Figure 4-11. prevMonthSkin and nextMonthSkin are properties on the <mx:DateChooser> tag. As noted, the assets you embed in your CSS can also come from a SWF file created from Flash.

Figure 4-11. *CustomDateChooser runtime view with buttons reskinned*

Using Flex Libraries

In Flex, you can build custom component libraries that you can use across multiple projects and share with other developers. Flex library projects are an integral part of creating reusable components. Using them is a good way to reduce the amount of work you need to do in the future as you grow your code repositories. A library generates a SWC file, instead of a SWF file like a regular Flex project.

You can use the libraries in a few different ways in your projects:

Integrated with the Flex application: You can drop a SWC library into the Flex project's libs directory to get access to the components. Once you drop the SWC into the directory, Flex will pick up on the change and integrate the library into your project. Then you will have access to the components in the library SWC. This approach compiles the library SWC into the Flex project's SWF, thus increasing the size of your SWF. This is the most convenient and common way to use library components.

Externalized library: Externalizing the library from the Flex project will keep the SWC from being compiled into the SWF. Use this approach if you need to cut down on your SWF size. The components of the SWC are loaded into memory when needed at runtime.

Runtime shared library (RSL): RSLs are similar to dynamically linked libraries (DLLs) in Windows and are available only in Flex projects. You will want to investigate this solution if you have multiple applications that need to share components of a Flex library. Again, these components are loaded only when needed and are loaded into memory once. They are cached and shared across all applications that need to use that component.

To complete our custom component example, we will move `CustomDateChooser` and `RoundedGradientBorder` to a Flex library. The first thing we need to do here is create a new Flex library project to hold our custom ActionScript components. In Eclipse, select File ➤ New ➤ Flex Library Project. Give it a project name, as shown in Figure 4-12, and then click the Finish button. (You don't need the AIR libraries unless you are building an AIR application, which we are not doing in this example.)

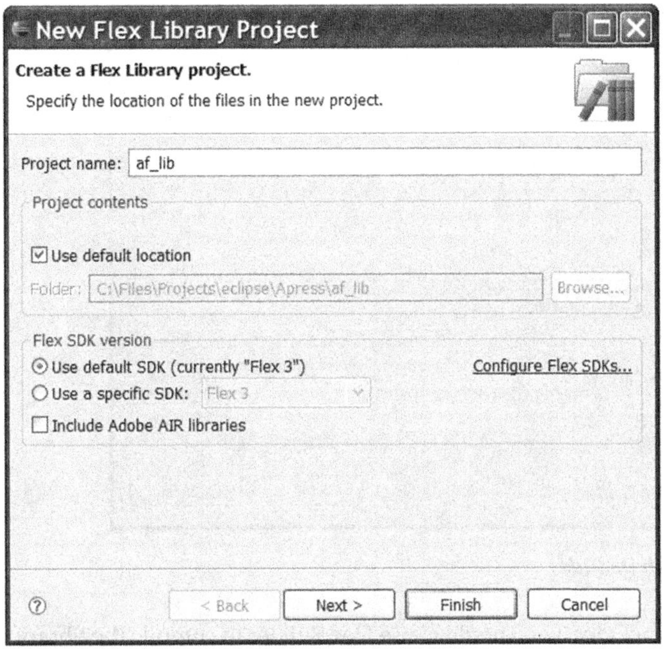

Figure 4-12. *Creating a new Flex Library project in Eclipse*

We already created the package structure for our two custom classes in the Flex project of `com/af/components`. Take the `com` directory from the Flex project and move it to the Flex Library project. Then select the elements you want compiled into the SWC. Open the project properties by right-clicking the project and selecting Properties, or by selecting Project ➤ Properties. Open the Classes tab under the Flex Library Build Path, and check the top-level check box on `com`, as shown in Figure 4-13.

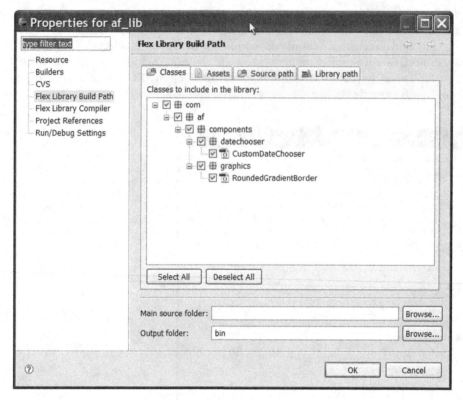

Figure 4-13. *Flex library build path includes*

By selecting the build path includes, you should cause Flex Builder to compile the library SWC for you. You will find the SWC in the bin directory of the Flex Library project. Take this SWC and drop it into the Flex project libs directory to integrate the components with the Flex project. You now have access to the components through the SWC library and can use them like this:

```
<?xml version="1.0"?>
<mx:Application xmlns:mx="http://www.adobe.com/2006/mxml"
     xmlns:af="com.af.components.datechooser.*">

    <mx:Style source="assets/css/style.css"/>

    <mx:Panel id="mainPanel" title="Gradient Filled Example"
         paddingLeft="10" paddingRight="10" paddingBottom="10" paddingTop="10"
         horizontalAlign="center">

        <af:CustomDateChooser />

    </mx:Panel>
</mx:Application>
```

When I added the `CustomDateChooser` to the application, Flex Builder's code completion found the class and added a new namespace alias to the application tag.

Note I have stressed the importance of reusable components in this chapter. That principle is a core element to building a strong set of code that provides immense value to your developers and organization.

Summary

This chapter provided a 30,000-foot view of Flex and some of the core elements of the technology that you need to understand to successfully build the AF – Client Manager project, or any other large-scale Flex project. I suggest referring to other books that cover the Flex programming language in more detail, such as *Flex Solutions: Essential Techniques for Flex 2 and 3 Developers* by Marco Casario (friends of ED, 2007).

This chapter started with an introduction to the roles of MXML and ActionScript in Flex. You learned about MXML tags, namespaces, and user interface containers and controls. Then we took a look at data binding, validation, and formatting. Next, we covered creating custom components. ActionScript is similar to coding Java and will be what you use to create many of your custom components.

This chapter also covered the use of CSS to skin and style your Flex applications. Styles are changes to elements of a component. Skinning refers to the use of external assets, like a button skin created in Flash, to change the appearance of a component or part of a component.

The topics covered in this chapter could well have whole books devoted to them. The important thing to realize is that there are many granular levels that can be addressed with Flex, and there is always something new to learn. The deeper you go, the more dynamic your applications will be.

■ ■ ■

## CHAPTER 5

Introduction to Spring

All Java applications, whether they are basic programs or complex enterprise applications, are composed of a set of objects, which are the building blocks and/or services that fulfill data requests. In this chapter, we will discuss how the Spring Framework combines the building blocks (classes and objects) for an application into a whole entity through its components.

Chapter 1 briefly introduced the Spring Framework and its modules. This chapter will serve as an overview of important aspects of Spring that will be built upon in upcoming chapters. Since Spring is so broad, I will not cover every aspect of it in this book. However, you will get the ammunition you need to build fully functional services for your Flex applications to consume.

The Spring Framework is hosted by SpringSource (`http://www.springsource.org`) and can be downloaded from `http://www.springsource/org/download`. Spring addresses Java/Java EE development by organizing your middle-tier objects and takes care of the plumbing that is usually left up for you to create. Spring can also work in any architecture layer while running in any runtime environment.

Upon finishing the chapter, you will have a solid understanding of how to properly wire your Spring beans, implement a Spring MVC solution with Flex, create bean factories, and test your Spring application code.

Spring Bean Wiring

In Chapter 1, you learned that Spring uses inversion of control (IoC) and dependency injection (DI) to provide wiring for beans. Here, we'll take a closer look at these features.

Inversion of Control (IoC)

The IoC container, also called the *core container*, wires Spring beans together. It is also responsible for the configuration and creation of objects in Spring.

In most cases, when an object needs references to data, it does a lookup or retrieval from an external data repository. IoC allows the component to not require information regarding the location of the data source, thus cleaning up the process of data retrieval through inverting the direction of the retrieval.

The core container manages its POJOs by passing a reference to those resources. The component does not need to know how or where to get its data; it only needs to have the ability to handle the data passed into it. This removes the requirement for you to write code to handle those lookups, and simplifies your coding and testing.

IoC helps to create layers of abstraction through your Spring applications. Spring's core container provides a central location for accessing objects, called the *application context*. The application context can be configured as Java 5 annotations or as an XML file that contains the signatures of each bean that is created in a Spring application.

IoC has been referred to as the Hollywood Principle—"don't call us; we'll call you." That is the main difference between a class library and framework: you call a class library, but a framework calls you.

Dependency Injection (DI)

The Spring Framework uses DI to realize the goals of IoC. A Spring bean or POJO declares attributes with getter and setter methods or constructors, which allow dependencies to be provided to them, instead of looking up their dependencies for those attributes. DI is realized when the Spring Framework creates its context. It uses an XML file or annotations to determine which objects need to be instantiated and injected—that is, which objects to create and which getter and setter methods need to be called. In the XML file or annotations, you'll have entries describing every bean definition used in the Spring context.

When an object references another object by defining it as a bean, its description in the XML file or annotations has a reference to the used object. When the Spring context is initialized, Spring finds this entry description, instantiates the object, and calls the setter method on the object to set its attributes. This allows a programmer to change the bean that is referenced as an attribute, without recompiling the container object by changing the entry in the XML file (as long as the dependent object implements the same interface or method calls).

IoC is responsible for resolving dependencies between beans. As noted in Chapter 1, Spring's core container offers two types of DI to inject resources and objects; setter injection and constructor injection.

Setter Injection

Setter injection uses setter methods to inject resources and objects. As an example, Listing 5-1 shows a class that takes in an attribute for age. Setter injection is used to inject the age into the bean's setAge() method by the Spring context, as defined in the XML configuration file or by annotations. As you can see in Listing 5-2, the configuration file, the age of 21 is set on the class SetterInjectionBean. This will occur when the bean is loaded into context at the startup of the web server on which this bean resides.

Listing 5-1. *Setter Injection Example*

```
package com.af.flexonspring.chapter5;

public class SetterInjectionBean
{
      private int age;

      public int getAge()
      {
            return this.age;
      }
```

```
        public void setAge(int age)
        {
                this.age = age;
        }
}
```

Listing 5-2. *Spring Configuration File for the Setter Injection Example*

```xml
<?xml version="1.0" encoding="UTF-8" ?>
<beans xmlns="http://www.springframework.org/schema/beans"
      xmlns:xsi="http://www.w3.org/2001/XMLSchema-instance"
      xsi:schemaLocation="http://www.springframework.org/schema/beans
      http://www.springframework.org/schema/beans/spring-beans-2.5.xsd">

      <bean id="guestListService"
            class="com.af.flexonspring.chapter5.SetterInjectionBean">
            <property name="age" value="21"/>
      </bean>
</beans>
```

Constructor Injection

Constructor injection calls a constructor within a class to inject resources and objects, rather than using setters to inject dependencies. It is common to create a default constructor for code compatibility. Listing 5-3 shows a constructor injection example. It obtains the same results as the example in Listing 5-1. The only difference is in the Spring configuration file, shown in Listing 5-4, where the <constructor-arg> tag is used to inject 21 as the age in the bean.

Listing 5-3. *Constructor Injection Example*

```java
package com.af.flexonspring.chapter5;

public class ConstructorInjectionBean
{
      private int age;

public ConstructorInjectionBean() {};

      public ConstructorInjectionBean(int age)
      {
            this.age = age;
      }
      public int getAge()
      {
            return this.age;
      }
}
```

Listing 5-4. *Spring Configuration File for the Constructor Injection Example*

```xml
<?xml version="1.0" encoding="UTF-8" ?>
<beans xmlns="http://www.springframework.org/schema/beans"
       xmlns:xsi="http://www.w3.org/2001/XMLSchema-instance"
       xsi:schemaLocation="http://www.springframework.org/schema/beans
       http://www.springframework.org/schema/beans/spring-beans-2.5.xsd">

    <bean id="guestListService"
          class="com.af.flexonspring.chapter5.ConstructorInjectionBean">
        <constructor-arg value="21"/>
    </bean>
</beans>
```

Spring MVC

MVC is a popular design pattern for Java-based frameworks such as JSF, Struts, WebWork, and Tapestry. Many RIA applications are built using the MVC pattern.

■**Note** MVC was conceived by Trygve Reenskaug at Xerox PARC in 1979 while working with Smalltalk. It originated in desktop applications and now is in many web applications.

Spring MVC is a framework that aids in integrating web MVC architectures. It is used for managing application state, validation, and work flow. The Spring MVC integration with the Servlet API has made it easier to handle web requests. The Spring Web MVC layer is designed to provide support for many view technologies, such as JavaServer Pages (JSP), Java Swing, and Adobe Flex.

A benefit to using Spring MVC with other Spring applications is that you can inject other Spring beans into the Spring MVC controllers.

Note that when integrating Flex with Spring—the main subject of this book—calling servlets is not generally the first choice for integrating Flex and Spring, and it is not the approach we will take for this book's main sample application (AF – Client Manager). As you'll learn in the next chapter, you are better off making Remoting calls directly to the Spring service via Flex's AMF gateway.

However, it is still worthwhile to understand how Spring MVC works with Flex. Here, we'll look at the key interfaces and components that make up Spring MVC, and then go over an example.

Spring MVC Components

With Spring MVC, the model, controller, and view work as follows:

Model: The model contains a collection of objects that are required by the view. It can contain business rules and data needed to render for the view, which is populated by the controller.

Controller: The controller implements the controller interface. It can subclass a helper class or be annotated using @Controller. Controllers are required to package view objects with the model data that is sent to the services. The controller is nothing more than a Spring bean.

View: The view is the layout and container to which the model data is returned. The view could be a JSP for traditional web applications that could render a home page. However, we are not using JSPs for our view. We are using Adobe Flex. Flex can integrate with Spring MVC by calling JSPs through its HTTPService protocol. This protocol simply calls an endpoint URL. The HTTPService implements a request/response model, even though the response in Flex is called the *result*.

Next, we will build a simple Flex application that uses an HTTPService call to render our view in Flex.

Building a Sample Spring MVC Application with Flex As the View

As an example, we will push data to a Flex application to show how to connect to the Spring MVC framework. This application will simply return rushing stats for an American football player entered into a Flex application. As I mentioned earlier, I am not going to discuss in detail the integration architecture between Flex and Spring MVC, since the Flex RemoteObject protocol is a better choice for Flex and Spring integration (covered in Chapter 6).

Building the sample Flex and Spring MVC application involves the following steps:

1. Configure the web server.

2. Build the Player model.

3. Create the Player controller.

4. Set up the service.

5. Build a Flex application to call the Player service.

Configuring the Web Server

This example will require us to run the Spring application on a web server. The servlet container of choice here will be Tomcat.

We need to configure two files for our Spring MVC application: web.xml and springMVC-servlet.xml. These two files are required to acquire the Spring beans and activate the context for the web server.

The web.xml file, shown in Listing 5-5, sets up the servlet mapping, servlet, and application context that will be loaded into the servlet context when the web server is started.

Listing 5-5. *The web.xml Configuration File for the Spring MVC Example*

```
<?xml version="1.0" encoding="UTF-8"?>
<web-app>
    <display-name>springMVC</display-name>
```

```
        <!-- APPLICATION CONTEXT -->
        <context-param>
                <param-name>contextConfigLocation</param-name>
                <param-value>
                        /WEB-INF/springMVC-servlet.xml
                </param-value>
        </context-param>

        <!-- SERVLET -->
        <servlet>
                <servlet-name>springMVC</servlet-name>
                <servlet-class>
                        org.springframework.web.servlet.DispatcherServlet
                </servlet-class>
                <load-on-startup>0</load-on-startup>
        </servlet>

        <!-- SERVLET MAPPING -->
        <servlet-mapping>
                <servlet-name>springMVC</servlet-name>
                <url-pattern>*.htm</url-pattern>
        </servlet-mapping>
</web-app>
```

The springMVC-servlet.xml file is shown in Listing 5-6. This file initializes the MVC framework and gives access to the controllers, as well as defines beans we will call from the Flex application.

Listing 5-6. *The springMVC-servlet.xml Configuration File for the Spring MVC Example*

```
<?xml version="1.0" encoding="UTF-8"?>
<!DOCTYPE beans PUBLIC "-//SPRING//DTD BEAN//EN"
        "http://www.springframework.org/dtd/spring-beans.dtd">
<beans>
        <!-- SPRING SERVICES -->
        <bean id="playerService"
                class="com.af.springMVC.services.PlayerServiceImpl">
        </bean>

        <!-- CONTROLLER FOR EXPOSING THE SERVICE -->
        <bean id="playerController"
                class="com.af.springMVC.controller.PlayerController">
                <property name="sessionForm">
                        <value>true</value>
                </property>
                <property name="commandName">
                        <value>player</value>
                </property>
```

```xml
            <property name="commandClass">
                  <value>com.af.springMVC.model.Player</value>
            </property>
            <property name="playerService">
                  <ref bean="playerService" />
            </property>
            <property name="formView">
                  <value>player</value>
            </property>
            <property name="successView">
                  <value>playerStats.htm</value>
            </property>
</bean>

<!-- CONTROLLER FOR HANDLING FLEX FORM INPUT -->
<bean id="playerStatsController"
      class="com.af.springMVC.controller.PlayerStatsController">
</bean>

<!-- URL MAPPING -->
<bean id="urlMapping"
      class="org.springframework.web.servlet.handler.SimpleUrlHandlerMapping">
      <property name="urlMap">
            <map>
                  <entry key="/playerStats.htm">
                        <ref bean="playerStatsController" />
                  </entry>
            </map>
      </property>
</bean>

<!-- VIEW RESOLVER -->
<bean id="viewResolver"
      class="org.springframework.web.servlet.view. ➥
        InternalResourceViewResolver">
      <property name="viewClass">
            <value>org.springframework.web.servlet.view.JstlView</value>
      </property>
      <property name="prefix">
            <value>/WEB-INF/jsp/</value>
      </property>
      <property name="suffix">
            <value>.jsp</value>
      </property>
</bean>
```

```
                    <!-- MESSAGE SOURCE  -->
                    <bean id="messageSource"
                          class="org.springframework.context.support.ResourceBundleMessageSource">
                          <property name="basename">
                                  <value>messages</value>
                          </property>
                    </bean>
          </beans>
```

Building the Player Model

The model is responsible for holding the data that is presented to the view. The model in the Spring MVC framework is implemented with beans. As shown in Listing 5-7, the `Player` bean has only two attributes: the player's first name and last name. This bean implements the setters and getters for the player's attributes. This example will provide a simple string for any name you enter in the Flex application. We are not hooking into a live data source, and there is no real business logic for this example.

Listing 5-7. *The Player Bean*

```java
package com.af.springMVC.model;

import java.io.Serializable;

public class Player implements Serializable
{
      static final long serialVersionUID = 2L;

      private String firstName;
      private String lastName;

      public String getFirstName()
      {
          return firstName;
      }

      public void setFirstName(String firstName)
      {
          this.firstName = firstName;
      }

      public String getLastName()
      {
          return lastName;
      }
```

```
        public void setLastName(String lastName)
        {
                this.lastName = lastName;
        }
}
```

Creating the Player Controller

The PlayerController class, shown in Listing 5-8, is required to implement the ModelAndView that encapsulates the model and view data to be displayed in Flex. In this case, the data is the results from asking the Player bean for player information. The PlayerController also creates a PlayerService that is injected by Spring. The PlayerStatsController, shown in Listing 5-9, is responsible for taking input parameters from the Flex application and applying them to the results sent back to Flex.

You will need the following JAR files to build the Spring MVC project:

- spring.jar

- commons-logging.jar

- jstl.jar

- spring-web.jar

- spring-webMVC.jar

Listing 5-8. *PlayerController.java for the Spring MVC Application*

```
package com.af.springMVC.controller;

import javax.servlet.ServletException;
import javax.servlet.http.HttpServletRequest;
import javax.servlet.http.HttpServletResponse;

import org.springframework.validation.BindException;
import org.springframework.web.servlet.ModelAndView;
import org.springframework.web.servlet.mvc.SimpleFormController;
import org.springframework.web.servlet.view.RedirectView;

import com.af.springMVC.services.PlayerService;

public class PlayerController extends SimpleFormController
{
        private PlayerService playerService;
```

```java
        public ModelAndView onSubmit(HttpServletRequest request,
            HttpServletResponse response, Object command, BindException errors)
            throws ServletException
        {
            return new ModelAndView(new RedirectView(getSuccessView()));
        }

        public PlayerService getPlayerService()
        {
            return playerService;
        }

        public void setPlayerService(PlayerService playerService)
        {
            this.playerService = playerService;
        }
}
```

Listing 5-9. *PlayerStatsController.java for the Spring MVC Application*

```java
package com.af.springMVC.controller;

import javax.servlet.http.HttpServletRequest;
import javax.servlet.http.HttpServletResponse;

import org.apache.commons.logging.Log;
import org.apache.commons.logging.LogFactory;
import org.springframework.web.servlet.ModelAndView;
import org.springframework.web.servlet.mvc.Controller;

import com.af.springMVC.model.Player;
import com.af.springMVC.services.PlayerServiceImpl;

public class PlayerStatsController implements Controller
{
        private static final Log log = LogFactory.getLog(PlayerStatsController.class);
        private PlayerServiceImpl playerService = new PlayerServiceImpl();

        public ModelAndView handleRequest(HttpServletRequest request,
            HttpServletResponse response) throws Exception {

            Player player = new Player();
            player.setFirstName(request.getParameter("firstName"));
            player.setLastName(request.getParameter("lastName"));
```

```
        String playerStats = playerService.getPlayerInfo(player);
        String xml = "<root><message>"+playerStats+"</message></root>";

        return new ModelAndView("success", "xml", xml);
    }
}
```

Setting Up the Service

The service in this example is extremely trivial. The PlayerService does nothing more than return a String. It does not retrieve data from a DAO implementation. The service is made available through the controller configuration. Listings 5-10 and 5-11 show the PlayerServiceImpl.java and PlayerService.java classes.

Listing 5-10. *PlayerServiceImpl.java*

```
package com.af.springMVC.services;

import java.io.Serializable;
import org.apache.commons.logging.Log;
import org.apache.commons.logging.LogFactory;

import com.af.springMVC.model.Player;

public class PlayerServiceImpl implements Serializable, PlayerService
{
    private String stats;

    public String getPlayerInfo(Player player)
    {
        return player.getFirstName() + " " + player.getLastName() + " " +
          this.stats;
    }

    public String getStats()
    {
        return stats;
    }

    public void setStats(String stats)
    {
        this.stats = stats;
    }
}
```

Listing 5-11. *PlayerService.java*

```java
package com.af.springMVC.services;

import com.af.springMVC.model.Player;

public interface PlayerService
{
     public String getPlayerInfo(Player player);
}
```

Building a Flex Application to Call the PlayerService

The last piece of this puzzle is to build a Flex application to front the Spring MVC back-end services. The Flex application, shown in Listing 5-12, uses the HTTPService protocol to call the player service.

Listing 5-12. *Flex Application to Support the View of the Player Data*

```xml
<?xml version="1.0" encoding="utf-8"?>
<mx:Application xmlns:mx="http://www.adobe.com/2006/mxml"
     layout="vertical" backgroundColor="white">

     <mx:HTTPService id="getStatsService"
          url="http://localhost:8080/SpringMVC/playerStats.htm"
          resultFormat="e4x" method="POST"
          result="getStatsResult(event)" fault="faultHandler(event)"/>

     <mx:Script>
          <![CDATA[
          import mx.rpc.events.FaultEvent;
          import mx.controls.Alert;
          import mx.rpc.events.ResultEvent;

          public function getStats() : void
          {
               var params:Object = new Object();

               params.firstName = firstName.text;
               params.lastName = lastName.text;

               getStatsService.send(params);
          }
          public function getStatsResult(event:ResultEvent):void
          {
               Alert.show("Result = " + event.result);
          }
```

```
            public function faultHandler(event:FaultEvent):void
            {
                    Alert.show("Fault = " + event.fault);
            }
            ]]>
     </mx:Script>

    <mx:Panel id="mainPanel"
        title="Flex SpringMVC Example"
        paddingLeft="10" paddingRight="10"
        paddingBottom="10" paddingTop="10"
        horizontalAlign="center">

            <mx:Form>

                    <mx:FormItem label="First Name: ">
                            <mx:TextInput id="firstName"/>
                    </mx:FormItem>

                    <mx:FormItem label="Last Name: ">
                            <mx:TextInput id="lastName"/>
                    </mx:FormItem>

                    <mx:Button id="getStatsBtn" label="Get Stats"
                        click="getStats();" />

            </mx:Form>
        </mx:Panel>
</mx:Application>
```

You will need to compile the application files in Eclipse. Once that is done, copy the WEB-INF folder and contents to the Tomcat server web apps directory you set up for the application. In this case, it will be <tomcat-install-directory>/<context-root>/WEB-INF.

This application is a simple view that allows the user to input a first and last name. As you can see, when the user clicks the getStatsBtn, a call to the getStatsService is executed. The parameters from the first and last names are entered into the param object. That object is then sent in the post to the Spring MVC servlet.

The HTTPService protocol in Flex handles a couple items of interest. It allows the developer to set a result method to handle the ResultEvent from the server. The ResultEvent contains the data returned from the server. In this application, we are displaying the result XML in an Alert control, as shown in Figure 5-1.

Chris Giametta [104 Rushing Yards] [33
Receiving Yards] [1 Ru TD]

Figure 5-1. *Result from running the Flex application*

Spring Factories

As collections of objects are important to Java, Spring provides the bean factory container to help
with multiple beans. Let's take a closer look at the bean factory, and then use one in an example.

Bean Factories

BeanFactory is the container in Spring that instantiates, configures, and manages multiple
beans and is at the center of the Spring container. In order to start a bean factory, you need two
things: POJOs and metadata. The metadata can be reflected as XML or annotations. The metadata is passed into bean definitions during application startup.

The beans generally work with one another through dependences. These dependencies
are based on configuration data that BeanFactory uses. Figure 5-2 illustrates what a typical
bean factory will contain.

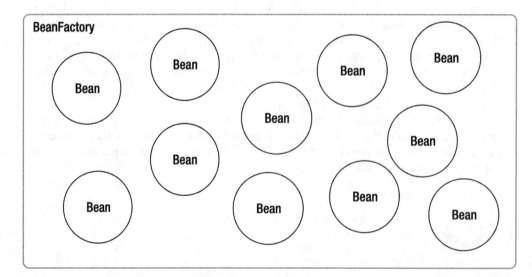

Figure 5-2. *Typical bean factory*

The configuration XML file for the bean factory simply congregates all beans in a configurable location, which is read into the web context when the application is started. Listing 5-13 shows a basic bean configuration file.

Listing 5-13. *Basic Bean Configuration File*

```
<beans>
        <bean></bean>
        <bean></bean>
        <bean></bean>
        <bean></bean>
        <bean></bean>
</beans>
```

The nice thing about this approach is that you can configure your beans without compiling the source code, as long as you are not adding a new bean or changing bean attributes. In most cases, you will be required to complete a new source build to push your code to a web server.

The beans are basically single instances of a bean ID or name and can be simple POJOs. Having a single place to locate your services makes life easier when adding new services and hooking Flex applications into those services.

Building a Sample Spring Service

To demonstrate the use of bean factories, we will create a simple Spring service that gets a guest list. This list is nothing more than a list of names that is injected to the implementation of the service. I don't want a Hello World application in this book, so I will take one step beyond a typical Hello World example.

Setting Up the Spring Project

For the sample application to compile correctly, you need to have access to two JAR files:

- `spring.jar`

- `commons-logging.jar`

Be sure to add the libraries to your project in Eclipse by right-clicking the project name and selecting Properties. The JARs should be in the root `/libs` directory and then added to the properties of the project. Figure 5-3 shows the Properties window in Eclipse.

With the project ready, building the sample application will involve the following steps:

1. Build a simple bean.

2. Build a service to access the bean.

3. Initialize the bean in the `applicationContext.xml` file.

4. Create a Spring application.

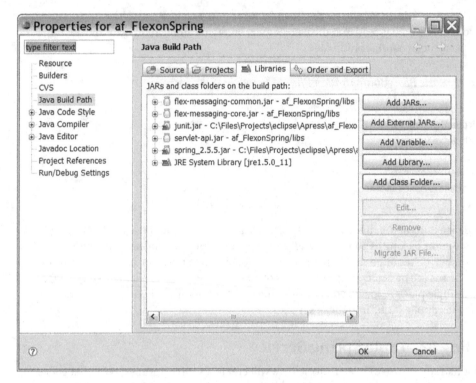

Figure 5-3. *Properties for the Spring project in Eclipse*

Building a Simple Bean

The first item of interest is to build a bean for our service. This bean is part of the IoC container. Beans defined in the IoC container are nothing more than a pool of components you have access to by referencing the service with which they are associated.

The GuestListService is a simple POJO with a method to print the guest list to the system console. This bean does not have a constructor, as no arguments need to be passed to the bean at instantiation. Listing 5-14 shows the GuestListServiceImpl class.

Listing 5-14. *Bean Implementation (GuestListServiceImpl.java)*

```
package com.af.flexonspring.chapter5.beanfactory;

import java.lang.reflect.Array;
import java.util.List;

public class GuestListServiceImpl implements GuestListService
{
    private List<Object> guestList;
```

```java
    /**
     * Prints the guestList to the console
     */
    public void printGuestList()
    {
        for(Object g : guestList)
        {
            System.out.println(g);
        }
    }
    /**
     * Gets the guestList
     */
    public List<Object> getGuestList()
    {
        return guestList;
    }
    /**
     * Sets the guestList
     */
    public void setGuestList(List<Object> guestList)
    {
        this.guestList = guestList;
    }
}
```

Building a Service to Access the Bean

Now that we have a basic bean implementation, we need to create the service that will extend and use the GuestListService. This is a bare-bones example, with no real data source or ORM component. Its purpose is simply to illustrate the basic wiring in the Spring Framework. We also want to build our application back end in a service-oriented architecture to allow for as much reuse as possible. Flex may not always be the front-end technology we want to hook into our back-end services.

Listing 5-15 shows our GuestListService service.

Listing 5-15. *GuestListService Service (GuestListService.java)*

```java
package com.af.flexonspring.chapter5.beanfactory;

public interface GuestListService
{
    void printGuestList();
}
```

GuestListService is a fine-grained service with only one method to implement.

I have had many arguments with fellow architects regarding the best practice for building services. The argument is almost always tied to the granularity of the business components located in the service. In large-scale enterprise systems, having a single service for every business function can become overwhelming if you have a service tied to each entity. For example, having a GuestListService that implements createGuestList(), retrieveGuestList(), updateGuestList(), and deleteGuestList() would be preferable. Most services we create will have the standard create, retrieve, update, and delete (CRUD) methods and custom methods needed to resolve that unit of business functionality.

On the other side of that coin is the bad practice of congregating all service methods into one service. This is not modular and creates a maintenance mess. Not only that, it does not properly define the units of business functionality to a degree of granularity that logically represents what the service is meant to do.

That said, I feel there is a fine line when creating services. They should always represent how the units of business functionality have been divided among the various business units. Most services I build contain the CRUD aspects of multiple business units (of course, only the ones that logically fit together). When you architect your services, it is up to you to determine what approach fits your organization best and what level of service granularity makes the most sense.

Initializing the Bean in applicationContext.xml

The application context XML file is used to define which beans you have access to in your application. In our example, we are defining a bean with an id of guestListService and giving it a type of GuestListServiceImpl. We have created a property, guestList, which will inject a list of four guests to our bean. When the application initializes the application's context, those data values will be injected. Listing 5-16 shows the applicationContext.xml file for our example.

Listing 5-16. *The applicationContext.xml Bean Configuration File for GuestListService*

```xml
<?xml version="1.0" encoding="UTF-8" ?>
<beans xmlns="http://www.springframework.org/schema/beans"
      xmlns:xsi="http://www.w3.org/2001/XMLSchema-instance"
      xsi:schemaLocation="http://www.springframework.org/schema/beans
          http://www.springframework.org/schema/beans/spring-beans-2.5.xsd">


    <bean id="guestService"
          class="com.af.flexonspring.chapter5.beanfactory.GuestListServiceImpl">
        <property name="guestList">
            <list>
                <value>Guest One</value>
                <value>Guest Two</value>
                <value>Guest Three</value>
                <value>Guest Four</value>
            </list>
        </property>
    </bean>
</beans>
```

Creating a Spring Application

Spring can be used to enhance almost any Java or Java EE application. Spring is built in Java and runs in the JVM. Spring's core container maintains the beans so you can retrieve them from the main application's context. The basic implementation of the IoC container is BeanFactory.

However, we want to avoid using BeanFactory directly. Instead we want to use the application context for our applications. ApplicationContext is a subclass of BeanFactory. It inherits all functionality from BeanFactory and adds much more. You would want to use BeanFactory directly only if you require a low-memory footprint for your application. In other situations, use the ApplicationContext interface to load your beans.

The GuestListMain class, shown in Listing 5-17, is a standard Java application with a main() method.

Listing 5-17. *GuestListMain.java Using ApplicationContext*

```
package com.af.flexonspring.chapter5.beanfactory;

import org.springframework.context.ApplicationContext;
import org.springframework.context.support.ClassPathXmlApplicationContext;

public class GuestListMain
{
    public static void main(String[] args) throws Exception
    {
        ApplicationContext context =
            new ClassPathXmlApplicationContext("applicationContext.xml");

        GuestListService guestListService =
            (GuestListService) context.getBean("guestListService");

        guestListService.printGuestList();
    }
}
```

The first line of the main() method creates the ApplicationContext and reads in the applicationContext.xml file. The next line sets up the GuestListService so we have access to the methods in the service. Once the application context is initialized and we have a hook to the service, we simply call the printGuestList() method located in GetServiceBean. The output is nothing more than a listing of guest names. Here is the output from the console in Eclipse when I ran the Spring application:

```
Sep 5, 2008 10:52:49 PM org.springframework.core.CollectionFactory <clinit>
Sep 5, 2008 10:52:49 PM
org.springframework.beans.factory.xml. ➡
XmlBeanDefinitionReader loadBeanDefinitions
INFO: Loading XML bean definitions from class path resource [ApplicationContext.xml]
Sep 5, 2008 10:52:49 PM org.springframework.context.support. ➡
```

```
AbstractRefreshableApplicationContext refreshBeanFactory
INFO: Bean factory for application context [org.springframework.context.support. ➥
ClassPathXmlApplicationContext;hashCode=27130879]:
org.springframework.beans.factory.support.DefaultListableBeanFactory defining beans
[guestListService]; root of BeanFactory hierarchy
Sep 5, 2008 10:52:49 PM org.springframework.context.support. ➥
AbstractApplicationContext refresh
INFO: 1 beans defined in application context [org.springframework. ➥
context.support.ClassPathXmlApplicationContext;hashCode=27130879]
Sep 5, 2008 10:52:49 PM org.springframework.context.support. ➥
AbstractApplicationContext initMessageSource
INFO: Unable to locate MessageSource with name 'messageSource': using default
[org.springframework.context.support. ➥
DelegatingMessageSource@79a2e7]
Sep 5, 2008 10:52:49 PM org.springframework.context.support. ➥
AbstractApplicationContext initApplicationEventMulticaster
INFO: Unable to locate ApplicationEventMulticaster with name
'applicationEventMulticaster': using default
[org.springframework.context.event. ➥
SimpleApplicationEventMulticaster@120bf2c]
Sep 5, 2008 10:52:49 PM org.springframework.beans.factory.support. ➥
DefaultListableBeanFactory preInstantiateSingletons
INFO: Pre-instantiating singletons in factory [org.springframework.beans.factory. ➥
support.DefaultListableBeanFactory defining beans [guestListService]; ➥
root of BeanFactory hierarchy]

Guest One
Guest Two
Guest Three
Guest Four
```

As I mentioned, if you need a small memory footprint, you could use BeanFactory directly, as shown in Listing 5-18.

Listing 5-18. *GuestListMainBF.java Using BeanFactory*

```
package com.af.flexonspring.chapter5.beanfactory;

import org.springframework.beans.factory.BeanFactory;
import org.springframework.beans.factory.xml.XmlBeanFactory;
import org.springframework.core.io.FileSystemResource;
```

```
public class GuestListMainBF
{
    public static void main(String[] args) throws Exception
    {
        BeanFactory factory =
            new XmlBeanFactory(new FileSystemResource("applicationContext.xml"));

        GuestListService guestListService =
            (GuestListService) factory.getBean("guestListService");
        guestListService.printGuestList();
    }
}
```

Testing with Spring

A thorough review of testing would require more than a section in a book. However, I do want to cover enough information to show basic test setup and execution within a Spring application. First, let's look briefly at testing types, and then demonstrate testing our sample service using JUnit within our service's application context.

Unit Testing and Test-Driven Development

Unit testing is something that should be required for every enterprise project for ensuring quality and enabling testing to support changes in application code. It is inevitable that every application will eventually undergo changes to address requirements, defects, or enhancements.

Unit testing is the process of testing each individual unit of code in isolation, to ensure that it is functioning properly. A unit test is generally the lowest level of testing that can occur within an application. In object-oriented programming, a smallest unit would be a method belonging to a particular class. The goal is to isolate each method within its own test, making it independent of all other tests.

Unit testing offers useful benefits to developers, including managing change, simplifying integration, separating code into components, and even documenting your code.

To gain the full benefits of unit testing, a developer must be disciplined enough to create unit tests at the beginning of the software development process. *Test-driven development* (TDD) is a development process in which developers create their unit test for each class before writing it. This helps developers to think about exactly what they want their classes to do, and helps to avoid issues even before writing any classes.

Before you begin writing tests, you should have a clear understanding of the technical requirements, functional requirements, and nonfunctional requirements for your class. For example, suppose you have an application that returns a string that defines your credit report rating. Here are the requirements that you might need to test for:

- If your credit score is less than 620, then return `'poor'`.

- If your credit score is greater than 620 and less than 680, then return `'fair'`.

- If your credit score is greater than 720, then return `'excellent'`.

These requirements could be implemented with a single method that would determine, based on your credit score, where you fall within the definitions of those number ranges. This would require you to write three test cases to check for these three scenarios.

The next step is to create your class and any code that is part of the class based on your requirements. Implementation of this class is complete when all the tests have passed. You will basically be implementing small pieces of code while testing each segment of code as you write the class. This can eventually get you to a point where you have the cleanest code possible for the functionality you are attempting to implement.

The third step is to run the automated test. This part of the process is very red and green, as in passing and failing the individual test cases. Either the test passed or the test failed, and you're not finished until all test cases pass. If your tests are failing, you should go back and refactor your code until you're able to get all tests to pass.

Integration and Systems Testing

The other side of the coin is integration testing, which is a process of testing multiple models combined into a testing group. Integration testing is the phase of the project that is prior to systems testing. Systems testing occurs when the project is ready to integrate all aspects of the application together and move them to a model office environment so that the application can be run as a whole.

Integration testing is an important part of the project delivery process and should be performed incrementally throughout the development life cycle. It brings together major project components that require collaboration. Integration testing will be performed to determine if the components are working together based on system requirements.

A good example of a functional unit that should be integration-tested is a component that needs to access the database. Since testing the database requires multiple components and multiple layers of the application—such as JDBC, SQL statements, and services to execute the data retrieval—it makes sense to perform an integration test on those components.

Testing GuestListService

Now we are ready to test our `GuestListService`. Two testing packages are currently popular on the Java platform:

- JUnit (`http:/junit.org/`) is a testing framework that is used to write and run automated tests within your Java applications.

- TestNG (`http://testng.org/doc/`) is a framework that evolved from JUnit and has added many more powerful features, such as Java Development Kit (JDK) 5 annotations, data-driven testing, parameter support, and test groups.

Here, we will cover testing the `GuestListService` service using JUnit within our service's application context. We'll write our test case and then run the automated test.

As you've seen, GuestListService is a very simple service. Since the service does nothing more than return a list of guests and has no business logic associated with that, our test is extremely simplistic. It has only one requirement: retrieve a guest list and display the guest list.

To test the GuestListService, download the following JAR files:

- Spring-test_2.5.jar (http://www.mvnrepository.com/artifact/org.springframework/spring-test/2.5)

- JUnit-4.5.jar (http://junit.org/)

The Spring test libraries are part of the Spring Framework with dependencies project. You can build the Spring test JAR from the project if you desire. I pulled the zip archive from the Maven Repository site and converted it to a JAR file. Simple put, you can change the .zip to .jar to use the library.

Our testing will start with the implementation of the service. Listing 5-19 shows the GuestListServiceTest source code and the results from running the test in Eclipse.

Listing 5-19. *GuestListServiceTest JUnit Test*

```
package com.af.springtests;

import org.springframework.context.ApplicationContext;
import org.springframework.context.ApplicationContextAware;
import org.springframework.test.context.ContextConfiguration;
import org.springframework.test.context.junit4.SpringJUnit4ClassRunner;

import com.af.flexonspring.chapter5.beanfactory.services.GuestListService;

import org.junit.Before;
import org.junit.Test;
import org.junit.runner.RunWith;

@RunWith(SpringJUnit4ClassRunner.class)
@ContextConfiguration(locations = "applicationContext.xml")
public class GuestListTests implements ApplicationContextAware
{
    private GuestListService guestListService;

    private ApplicationContext applicationContext;

    public void setApplicationContext(ApplicationContext applicationContext)
    {
        this.applicationContext = applicationContext;
    }
```

```
        @Before
        public void init()
        {
                guestListService =
                    (GuestListService) applicationContext.getBean("guestListService");
        }

        @Test
        public void testPrintGuestList()
        {
                guestListService.printGuestList();
        }
}
```

This test case is annotated using the Spring test library from the Spring Framework with dependencies project. The Spring test library works in conjunction with JUnit and allows you to annotate your test classes. Notice that the test class implements ApplicationContextAware. The implementation of ApplicationContextAware requires you to specify the Spring test runner used to run you test. In this case, the test runner is SpringJUnit4ClassRunner.class, which is defined with the @RunWith annotation.

In the GuestListTests class, we use @ContextConfiguration to locate the applicationContext. xml file. We then create an init() method and annotate it with @Before to initialize the application context. In this case, ApplicationContext and GuestListService are initialized to be used within the test. The context is initialized when we get the handle on the application context from our startup context for the application. The application context has been set using the setApplicationContext setter for the test class. If you were performing database tests with inserts, you would use the @After annotation to clean up your inserts at the end of the test cycle.

To tag a method to execute during the unit test, use the @Test annotation before the method name. Once you have tagged test methods, you can use the initialized application context to get a service to test. For our test, this is done by using the applicationContext. getBean("guestListService") method to access the bean loaded in the context we want to test in the init() method. Once we have a handle on the bean, we can call the printGuestList() method, which will retrieve the list and print it to the console. In Eclipse, you will notice a JUnit console with the results of the test that has been run, as shown in Figure 5-4.

In this case, we are just running tests against one method. This is about as simple as it gets when it comes to testing a Spring service. Your real applications will be much larger, so you'll have a much longer list of tests to run. Those tests can be automated and evaluated whenever you make changes within your code through Ant scripts. It is a good practice to build your test cases upfront. This helps things to run more smoothly when a change occurs, and improves the quality of your code right from the start of the production phase.

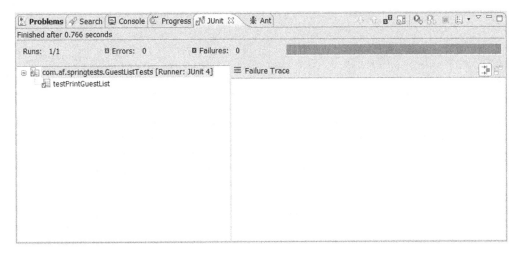

Figure 5-4. *JUnit test results in Eclipse*

Summary

This chapter covered several basic building blocks of Spring that will be indispensable as we move forward. As I said at the beginning of the chapter, I cannot go into every aspect of Spring in this book. What I hope I've done here is set the stage for building the enterprise application example that will materialize over the coming chapters.

You learned the IoC container wires Spring beans together and is responsible for the configuration and creation of objects in Spring. To realize the goals of the IoC, DI is used. Spring's core container offers two types of DI to inject resources and objects: setter injection and constructor injection.

Spring also provides an MVC application framework to deliver objects and resources to different view technologies. You learned that the MVC design pattern is used across many RIA solutions as well as with Spring.

Next, we looked at bean factories. Spring provides the bean factory container to instantiate, configure, and manage multiple beans. You learned that the bean factory is the basic type of Spring's IoC container implementation, and the more advanced solution is called application context. Application context is an extension of the bean factory.

Testing application code should always be part of a developer's day-to-day processes when delivering high-quality code. We looked at unit and integration testing in projects. Unit testing is performed by the developer on their individual components. Integration testing can require multiple developers, since it is the testing of components that collaborate with each other. For test-driven development, developers create test cases that are implemented with a testing package like JUnit or TestNG.

In the next chapter, you will see how to perform integration for Spring and Flex, and discover some integration best practices.

CHAPTER 6

■ ■ ■

Flex and Spring Integration Architecture

Flex is quickly becoming one of the standard options for building interactive RIAs. For several years, Spring has been among the more popular Java frameworks used to deliver content to different view technologies.

This chapter will cover integrating Flex with Spring. We will dive into the best practices for delivering a solid Flex/Spring architecture and how to simplify the architecture where possible. As I have stated earlier, I believe in creating a consistent, modular, and repeatable architecture. The architecture we define here will support small applications as well as robust enterprise applications. The emphasis will be on architecting the Spring and Flex communication layers.

To build the examples in this chapter, you can use the Ant scripts in the appendix of this book, or you can download the source code from this book's details page at the Apress web site (http://www.Apress.com). If you have Flex Builder, you can use it to build all of the examples.

Transport Architecture

Many applications are implemented with a three-tier architecture, as illustrated in Figure 6-1. Data is stored in the database. The web server runs Java services that access the database and retrieve the information. The Java classes are responsible for the business logic that receives a call from the client tier, assembles the information from the database, and returns the result. The client tier utilizes browser technology that runs a Flash application to provide an interface to the user and calls the Java services for required information. The client workstations call the Tomcat server, which calls the database to gather data and executes the Spring services that contain the application's business logic. The framework of choice here is Flex on Spring.

To access the database, several ORM solutions are available, including iBATIS and Hibernate. The ORM framework also uses DI. It provides a method of issuing SQL queries and transforming the returned rows into objects to be used by mapped Spring beans. We will discuss iBATIS and Hibernate in detail in Chapter 8.

In this architecture, the compiled Flex and Spring code resides on the Tomcat server. The client workstations download the Flex SWF and associated files, which contain the hooks into the Spring services.

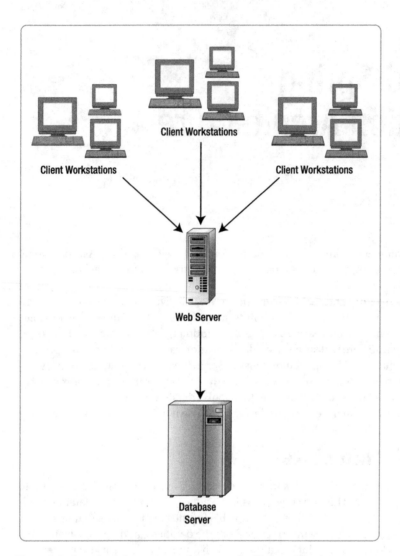

Figure 6-1. *Standard three-tier architecture for Flex and Spring*

The Three Flex Communication Protocols

Flex offers asynchronous communication through Remote Procedure Call (RPC) and real-time communication options. The main Flex communication protocols are HTTPService, WebService, and RemoteObject.

Before we jump in and discuss these three protocols, let's clear up which back-end servers Flex can use. Just to give you some examples, Table 6-1 shows several server-side technology options and how I have integrated Flex with them. This table does not cover all options for Flex, as it can send and receive SOAP calls and use web services to communicate with a wide variety of server-side solutions.

Table 6-1. *Some Flex Integration Options for Server-Side Technologies*

Server Technology	Integration Technology	Flex Protocol
Java EE	GraniteDS	RemoteObject
Java EE	LiveCycle DS, BlazeDS	RemoteObject
.NET	WebORB .NET	RemoteObject
PHP	WebORB PHP	RemoteObject
SAP	BSPs	HTTPService
Spring MVC	JSPs	HTTPService
Spring	Spring BlazeDS Integration	RemoteObject
Spring	AMF via `SpringFactory`	RemoteObject

HTTPService Protocol

Flex's HTTPService protocol serves as a mechanism for Flex clients to communicate with back-end XML-based services using XML over HTTP(S). These back-end services are non-SOAP entities, sometimes referred to as representational state transfer (REST) services. Figure 6-2 illustrates the HTTPService request/response model.

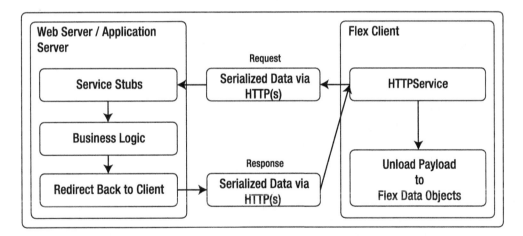

Figure 6-2. *HTTPService request/response model*

The HTTPService contains a URL attribute that is the actual URL of the web service or data file you wish to call. The data is transferred in plain text over an HTTP channel that can handle XML files, JSP pages, ASP pages, SAP BSP pages, or a PHP script.

Most HTTPService communication is done using the HTTP GET and POST methods. The GET method is used for getting data from the server. You can send parameters that are appended to the query string and passed to the URL. The POST method sends data to the server. In a POST method, the transfer parameters are hidden, since they are appended to the request object, rather than being copied into the URL.

HTTPService is good for situations where you need to get data to your Flex client quickly. However, these services can be cumbersome if you are required to handle the XML in your Flex application. Third-party libraries like JavaScript Object Notation (JSON) can help with the data exchange between Flex and the server-side technology with which you are integrating.

Listings 6-1 and 6-2 show a Flex HTTPService example. In this example, the Flex application calls an RSS service to return the blog entries on my AppFoundation.com blog. The results are returned in XML format and converted to an object by setting the HTTPService resultFormat attribute to object. The example then uses the result method onComplete(ResultEvent) to push the returned items into a local ArrayCollection. The ArrayCollection is bound to an <mx:repeater>, which traverses each item and generates a custom item renderer for each item.

Listing 6-1. *HTTPService Example to Read an RSS Blog Feed (RSSReader.mxml)*

```
<?xml version="1.0" encoding="utf-8"?>
<mx:Application xmlns:mx="http://www.adobe.com/2006/mxml"
    xmlns:local="*"
    width="100%" height="100%"
    verticalGap="0"
    creationComplete="httpRSS.send()">

    <mx:HTTPService id="httpRSS"
        url="{AF_RSS_FEED_URL}" resultFormat="object"
        result="onComplete(event)" fault="onFault(event)"
        showBusyCursor="true"/>

    <mx:Script>
        <![CDATA[
            import mx.rpc.events.FaultEvent;
            import mx.rpc.events.ResultEvent;
            import mx.controls.Alert;
            import mx.formatters.DateFormatter;
            import flash.net.navigateToURL;
            import mx.collections.ArrayCollection;

            public var AF_RSS_FEED_URL:String =
                "http://www.appfoundation.com/blogs/giametta/feed?format=xml";
            public var AF_COMPANY_BLOG:String =
                "http://www.appfoundation.com/blogs/giametta/";
            public var AF_HOME_PAGE:String =
                "http://www.appfoundation.com";

            [Bindable]
            private var externalData:ArrayCollection;
```

```
            private function onComplete(event:ResultEvent):void
            {
                var tmp:Object = event.result.rss.channel.item;
                var items:Array = new Array();
                for( var i:String in tmp ) {
                    items.push(tmp[i]);
                }
                externalData = new ArrayCollection(items);
            }
            private function onFault(event:FaultEvent):void
            {
                Alert.show(event.fault.faultString, 'Error');
            }
            private function processURL(url:String):void
            {
                var request:URLRequest = new URLRequest(url);
                navigateToURL(request);
            }
            private function rollOutHandler(event:Event):void
            {
                moreNews.setStyle("color", 0x28568F);
            }
            private function rollOverHandler(event:Event):void
            {
                moreNews.setStyle("color", 0x5B88BA);
            }
        ]]>
    </mx:Script>

    <mx:Panel title="HTTPService Example"
        paddingLeft="10" paddingRight="10" paddingBottom="10" paddingTop="10"
        horizontalAlign="center" width="416" height="377">
        <mx:HBox width="100%"
                horizontalAlign="left" verticalAlign="middle"
                paddingLeft="5" paddingRight="10">
            <mx:Image source="assets/images/icon_RSS.png" height="16" width="16"
                useHandCursor="true" buttonMode="true" mouseChildren="false"
                click="{processURL(AF_RSS_FEED_URL)}" toolTip="RSS Source"/>
            <mx:Label text="Latest AF News" styleName="frontPageHeaderText"/>
            <mx:Spacer width="100%"/>
            <mx:Label id="moreNews" text="More News >>"
                    rollOut="rollOutHandler(event)"
                    rollOver="rollOverHandler(event)"
                    styleName="hyperLinkText" click="{processURL(AF_COMPANY_BLOG)}"
                    useHandCursor="true" buttonMode="true" mouseChildren="false"/>
        </mx:HBox>
```

```
            <mx:Spacer height="5" />
            <mx:HRule height="10" width="100%"/>
            <mx:VBox width="100%" height="100%" verticalGap="0"
                paddingLeft="5" paddingRight="10">
              <mx:Repeater width="100%"
                    id="rp" count="6"
                  dataProvider="{ externalData }" >
                  <local:RSSEntryRenderer blogItem="{rp.currentItem}"
                        verticalGap="0" />
              </mx:Repeater>
            </mx:VBox>
            <mx:Label text="www.appfoundation.com"
                rollOut="rollOutHandler(event)" rollOver="rollOverHandler(event)"
                styleName="hyperLinkText" click="{processURL(AF_HOME_PAGE)}"
                useHandCursor="true" buttonMode="true" mouseChildren="false"/>
      </mx:Panel>
 </mx:Application>
```

Listing 6-2. *HTTPService Example to Display Blog Entries (RSSEntryRenderer.mxml)*

```
<?xml version="1.0"?>
<mx:VBox xmlns:mx="http://www.adobe.com/2006/mxml"
    width="100%"
    verticalScrollPolicy="off" horizontalScrollPolicy="off"
    verticalGap="0"
    creationCompleteEffect="{moveItem}">


    <mx:Script>
        <![CDATA[
            import mx.formatters.DateFormatter;
            import flash.events.Event;

            [Bindable]
            public var blogItem:Object = new Object();

            private function formatDate(date:String):String
            {
                var df:DateFormatter = new DateFormatter();
                df.formatString = "DD MMM YY";
                return df.format(date);
            }
```

```
        private function processURL(url:String):void
        {
                var request:URLRequest = new URLRequest(url);
                navigateToURL(request);
        }
        public function rollOutHandler():void
        {
            container.setStyle("fillcolors", 0xFFFFFF);
        }
        public function rollOverHandler():void
        {
                container.setStyle("fillcolors", [0xF2F2F2, 0x000000]);
        }
    ]]>
</mx:Script>
<mx:HBox id="container" width="100%" horizontalAlign="left"
        creationCompleteEffect="Fade"
        click="processURL(blogItem.link)" verticalGap="0"
         rollOver="{rollOverHandler()}" rollOut="{rollOutHandler()}">
        <mx:Label width="25%" text="{formatDate(blogItem.pubDate)}"
                color="0x999999"/>
        <mx:TextArea paddingLeft="10" paddingRight="10" editable="false"
                selectable="false"
            width="100%" borderStyle="none" backgroundAlpha="0"
            useHandCursor="true" buttonMode="true" mouseChildren="false"
            htmlText="{blogItem.title}" ></mx:TextArea>
</mx:HBox>
<mx:HRule width="100%" />
<mx:Move id="moveItem" target="container" xFrom="500" xTo="0"/>
</mx:VBox>
```

This is actually a pretty cool little component you can use on your web pages. It runs in its own little world, with its HTTPService gathering data from my blog. You can easily replace my link with your blog's link. The component is fairly interactive, allowing users to click and jump to the blog entries or view the entire RSS from the blog. I also added an effect in the item renderer. Be sure you bind the effect using curly braces binding (discussed in Chapter 4), so the effect will happen on the creationComplete of the component.

Figure 6-3 shows the output from running the HTTPService example.

HTTPService Example

📶 Latest AF News		More News >>
14 Aug 08	Flex/Flash Developer	
09 Jul 07	Internet Explorer: Setting Focus on Flex Apps / Flash Player	
12 Jun 07	Tomcat 5 Tip: Multiple Flex 2 Projects	
11 May 07	Eclipse Tip: Flex and Java Project Performance	
09 May 07	Flex, Spring, iBATIS, Cairngorm: Bringing It All Together	

www.appfoundation.com

Figure 6-3. *HTTPService runtime results*

WebService Protocol

As you saw in the previous section, HTTPServices are non-SOAP messages over HTTP. WebServices, on the other hand, are SOAP messages over HTTP. Figure 6-4 illustrates the WebService request/response model.

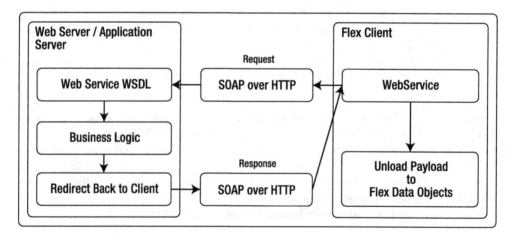

Figure 6-4. *WebService request/response model*

The <mx:WebService> MXML tag is used to declare a web service in Flex. The Web Services Description Language (WSDL) attribute is the URL location for the web service you wish to consume. WSDL is a messaging format that describes messages that a web service comprehends. Once you define the web service and give it an ID, you can use the webServiceID.send() to invoke the web service. Parameters that are appended to the send() method can be defined either in ActionScript or as part of the `<mx:request>` tag in MXML. They can also be input to the send() method directly, like this:

```
webServiceID.send(textInput.text, textInput2.text).
```

Two other important attributes for a web service are the fault and result handlers. These will reference ActionScript methods to handle errors and data results from the web service you call. The Flex application is able to process the data for the result handler when the web service has completed its execution. The fault handler is called when you get an error from the web service invocation.

Listings 6-3 and 6-4 show a Flex WebService example that pulls weather information from public web services and renders it in a browser window. It requires the GetWeatherByZipCode web service, which is publicly available from http://www.webservicex.net.

Listing 6-3. *WebService Example to Get Weather Information from www.webservicex.net (WeatherService.mxml)*

```
<?xml version="1.0" encoding="utf-8"?>
<mx:Application xmlns:mx="http://www.adobe.com/2006/mxml"
     xmlns="*">

     <mx:WebService id="weatherService"
          wsdl="http://www.webservicex.net/WeatherForecast.asmx?WSDL"
          useProxy="false" showBusyCursor="true"
          fault="Alert.show(event.fault.faultString), 'Error'"
           result="onResult(event)" >
          <mx:operation name="GetWeatherByZipCode" resultFormat="e4x" >
               <mx:request>
                    <ZipCode>{zipcode.text}</ZipCode>
               </mx:request>
          </mx:operation>
     </mx:WebService>

     <mx:Script>
          <![CDATA[
               import mx.messaging.SubscriptionInfo;
               import mx.controls.dataGridClasses.DataGridColumn;
               import mx.rpc.events.ResultEvent;
               import mx.managers.CursorManager;
               import mx.controls.Alert;

               default xml namespace = "http://www.webservicex.net";

               [Bindable] private var xmlResult:XML;
               [Bindable] private var weatherData:XMLList;
               [Bindable] private var location:String;
```

```
private function getLocalWeather():void
{
        weatherService.GetWeatherByZipCode.send();
}
private function onResult(event:ResultEvent):void
{
        xmlResult = XML(event.result);

        var xmlResultNode:XML =
            xmlResult.GetWeatherByZipCodeResult[0];
        var xmlDetailsNode:XML = xmlResultNode.Details[0];

        location = xmlResultNode.PlaceName.text() + ", "
                        + xmlResultNode.StateCode.text();

        weatherData = xmlDetailsNode.WeatherData;
}
private function setRendererObject(obj:Object):Object
{
        var xmlItem:XML = XML(obj);
        var rObj:Object = new Object();
        var day:String = xmlItem.Day.text().toString();

        day = day.substr(0,day.indexOf(","));
        rObj.Day = day;
        rObj.WeatherImage = xmlItem.WeatherImage.text();
        rObj.MaxTemperatureF = xmlItem.MaxTemperatureF.text();
        rObj.MinTemperatureF = xmlItem.MinTemperatureF.text();
        // The last node of this Web Service returns empty
        // weather data
        // This is just to account for the image being blank
        // in the item renderer
        if(rObj.WeatherImage.toString() == "")
        {
           rObj.WeatherImage = "assets/images/icon_DefaultImage.png";
        }
        return rObj;
    }
    ]]>
</mx:Script>

<mx:Panel id="myPanel" width="521" height="245" title="WebService Example"
    paddingTop="10" paddingBottom="10" paddingLeft="10" paddingRight="10"
    horizontalScrollPolicy="off" verticalScrollPolicy="off">
```

```
        <mx:HBox>
              <mx:Label width="100%" text="Please enter a zip code:"/>
              <mx:TextInput id="zipcode" text="75025"/>
              <mx:Button label="Get Weather" click="getLocalWeather()"/>
        </mx:HBox>

        <mx:Text id="txtLocation" htmlText="{location}"
              styleName="locationFont"/>

        <mx:HBox>
              <mx:Repeater id="rp" dataProvider="{weatherData}">
                    <WeatherRenderer
                          weatherItem="{setRendererObject(rp.currentItem)}"
                          verticalGap="0" />
              </mx:Repeater>
        </mx:HBox>
    </mx:Panel>
</mx:Application>
```

Listing 6-4. *WebService Example to Display Weather Information (WeatherRenderer.mxml)*

```
<?xml version="1.0"?>
<mx:VBox xmlns:mx="http://www.adobe.com/2006/mxml"
    width="100%"
    verticalScrollPolicy="off" horizontalScrollPolicy="off"
    verticalGap="0"
    creationCompleteEffect="{zoom}">

    <mx:Script>
          <![CDATA[
                import mx.controls.Alert;
                import mx.formatters.DateFormatter;
                import flash.events.Event;

                [Bindable]
                public var weatherItem:Object;
          ]]>
    </mx:Script>

    <mx:VBox id="container" horizontalAlign="center" verticalGap="0"
          verticalAlign="middle" styleName="WeatherPanel" >
          <mx:Label text="{weatherItem.Day}" />
          <mx:VBox verticalGap="0" horizontalAlign="center">
                <mx:Image id="img" source="{weatherItem.WeatherImage}"/>
```

```
            <mx:HBox width="100%">
                    <mx:Label text="Low" fontWeight="bold" />
                    <mx:Label text="High" fontWeight="bold"/>
            </mx:HBox>
            <mx:HBox width="100%">
                    <mx:Label text="{weatherItem.MinTemperatureF}"
                            styleName="temperatureFont"/>
                    <mx:Label text="{weatherItem.MaxTemperatureF}"
                            styleName="temperatureFont"/>
            </mx:HBox>
        </mx:VBox>
    </mx:VBox>
    <mx:Zoom id="zoom" />
</mx:VBox>
```

In the `<mx:WebService>` tag, notice that the WSDL attribute points to the web service the example is calling: `http://www.webservicex.net/WeatherForecast.asmx?WSDL`. This web service requires a ZIP code, which is taken from the `<mx:TextInput>` box. The ZIP code is passed into the WebService protocol through the `<mx:operation>` tag's request parameters. To get results formatted in ECMAScript for XML (E4X), you need to define a namespace for the web service, which is set as `xml namespace = "http://www.webservicex.net";` by default. WebService is invoked when you click the Get Weather button, as shown in Figure 6-5.

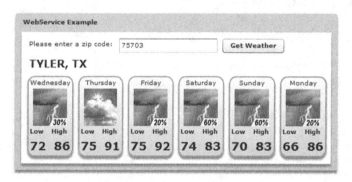

Figure 6-5. *WebService example runtime results*

Also note the result and fault attributes on the `<mx:WebService>` tag. They work in the same way as the result and fault attributes for HTTPService. The results are sent the result method. If an error occurs on the service, the fault method will be called. WebService can be invoked through ActionScript as well.

RemoteObject Protocol

The RemoteObject protocol is the fastest communication method for data services that Flex offers. The class gives you access to back-end classes through AMF encoding. This binary protocol uses Java classes directly to provide data to Flex. AMF is not a transport protocol. The RemoteObject component uses HTTP to transport binary ActionScript over the communication channel. Figure 6-6 shows the RemoteObject architecture.

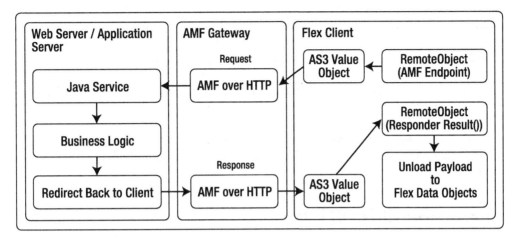

Figure 6-6. *RemoteObject request/response model*

Besides being substantially faster than any other means of communication in Flex, another benefit of using RemoteObject is that you can send and receive strongly typed objects to and from the server. Serialization and deserialization take place on the server side with Remoting, which is enabled through the AMF gateway (also known as a Remoting gateway). You can send simple and complex objects to the server, as well as custom objects that you need in your Flex application. These value objects in Flex can be mapped to the server-side object by adding a RemoteClass metadata tag to your value object class, like this:

```
[RemoteClass(alias="com.af.domain.SomeJavaObject")]
```

■**Note** You can use RemoteObjects in Flex without binding to Java objects. When Flex objects are bound to Java objects, they are transformed into the Java objects they represent through the RemoteClass metadata tag. If a Flex object is not bound to a corresponding Java object, it is transformed into a hashmap.

Setting up RemoteObject communications is a little more involved than setting up HTTPService or WebService communications. As you have seen, HTTPService and WebService can be executed directly in the Flex application, without requiring any Flex server-side components to be created or configured. RemoteObject requires a Flex server-side component to access the Java service, such as BlazeDS, LiveCycle Data Services (DS), or ColdFusion. In our examples, we will use BlazeDS, an open source Flex server, to facilitate communication with our Java/Spring services via AMF.

As you have seen, three protocols can act as the transport layer between Flex and its server counterparts. When communicating with Spring, the RemoteObject protocol used with the AMF gateway has shown itself to be much more efficient, because its payload is in binary format. This results in smaller packet sizes. RemoteObject is faster through the pipe than WebService and HTTPService, since they use XML as their payload format.

Furthermore, handling XML in Flex can become a performance issue if you have a requirement to parse it on the Flex side. Working with XML in Flex is slightly more difficult when building enterprise applications that have many custom components. Working with pure objects, on the other hand, is a much smoother transition for developers and has applied "common sense" when binding objects to the Flex controls, since the attributes of the objects are exposed to the developer. With XML, Flex does not control the object as it does with value objects defined in Flex.

I believe that RemoteObject should be used in enterprise applications every time it is an option. RemoteObject is a good fit for working with push techniques, where data is pushed from one application to another in real time.

In the remainder of this chapter, we will work through an example that demonstrates how to use Flex RPC RemoteObject. But first, let's take a look at how Flex fits into the enterprise architecture.

Flex in the Enterprise

As illustrated in Figure 6-7, Flex fits nicely within existing enterprise architectures. We need to add a layer for Flex data integration to grant us access to business logic located in the services layer. Services do not need to be built directly for Flex to consume them. Flex, through its many communication protocols, can adapt to the existing environment and call those available services that may not be built directly for Flex. That makes a solid case for using Flex for new project development and for application modernization projects that extend legacy systems. The Flex data integration layer is required only for Flex projects that will use RPC services, the Flex Message Service, and Flex Data Management Services.

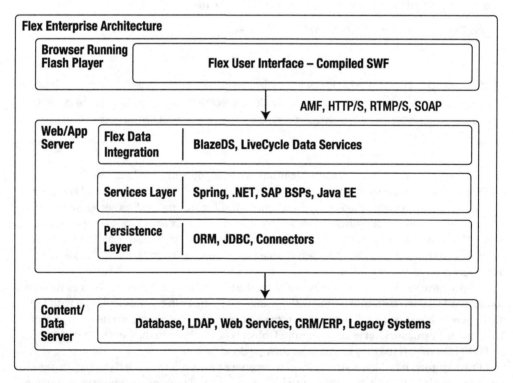

Figure 6-7. *How Flex fits in the enterprise architecture*

I have discussed Flex's RPC services in regard to RemoteObject, and will continue to expand on that subject in the following sections. The Flex Message Service supports applications such as peer-to-peer applications that need real-time data feeds to integrate with messaging technologies, such as the Java Message Service (JMS). Calls made through a messaging service are queued in case of a network failure. This provides the foundation to build offline applications that have a reliable means to get their data. The Flex Message Service supports collaboration, data push, and publish/subscribe techniques.

Flex Data Management Services make it easier to synchronize data between the Flex client and data services. These services allow you to implement data synchronization, paging, and occasionally connected clients (OCCs). All of these techniques can be implemented with high scalability and without any performance hits to the client, while ensuring that data integrity is secured. Flex Data Management Services can allow client synchronization by propagating data from one client to the other when a user makes an update.

Using Flex RPC RemoteObject

To demonstrate using RemoteObject, we will build a simple Spring application, reusing the GuestListService we created in Chapter 5. We will work through two examples, each demonstrating a different solution for integrating Flex and Spring:

- Using the SpringFactory class with BlazeDS

- Using the Spring BlazeDS Integration project

Our first steps for both solutions are to configure the web server and install BlazeDS.

Configuring the Web Server

We will use Tomcat to administer our web server responsibilities. See this book's appendix for instructions on installing Tomcat on your server.

For this example, we will need to create two folders in <tomcat-install-directory>\webapps. One will be created when we install BlazeDS, and the other will contain the Flex application.

I usually have many Flex projects deployed on my Tomcat server at any given time—five to ten projects will be running. I used to get memory errors when I run three of these larger Flex applications. Now I use a couple of Java options that have helped with server memory allocation with Flex applications:

-Xms and -Xmx: I usually start with a lower -Xms (minimum heap size) number so the heap can build up to the -Xmx (maximum heap size) if needed. This way, I do not partition a portion of memory that may not be used. I use the following setting on development and production servers:

```
-Xms 256m -Xmx 1024m
```

MaxPermSize: Class and method objects on the Java Virtual Machine (JVM) are held as reflective data by the permanent size generation. MaxPermSize is an addition to the -Xmx value. I have set the following MaxPermSize in development and production:

```
-XX:MaxPermSize=128m
```

You can set these parameters in Tomcat using the Java VM tab of the Configure Tomcat application. Be sure you have enough physical memory on the web server for which you are allocating memory.

■**Caution** Later versions of Tomcat may have the `-Xms`, `-Xmx`, and `MaxPermSize` parameters located in specific fields in the configuration for Tomcat. Adding these lines to versions later than Tomcat 5.*x* could cause your server to not start.

Installing BlazeDS

BlazeDS extends the Flex framework. It provides an integration point for Flex by managing data transfer and integrating with existing applications and infrastructure. It is implemented as a Java web application and will run inside web containers of popular Java application servers such as Tomcat, JBoss, Adobe JRun, IBM WebSphere, and BEA WebLogic.

■**Note** If you want a subscription to enterprise BlazeDS support, you will need to purchase that with Live-Cycle Data Services.

To understand how applications communicate with a BlazeDS server, we need to look at how BlazeDS is built. BlazeDS is a message-based architecture that uses channels to communicate to and from the client. The channels are grouped into channel sets. For example, there is an AMF channel and an HTTP channel that handle AMF encoding and the HTTP protocol, respectively.

The BlazeDS server supports the Flex RPC components such as Producer, Consumer, RemoteObject, HTTPService, and WebService. If you look at the Flex RPC components supplied with the Flex SDK or in Flex Builder, you will see access to create RemoteObject, Producer, and Consumer components. However, you cannot send messages or get messages directly with those components without having a Flex server installed. BlazeDS is the Flex server technology we will use to give Flex access to our Spring services.

Let's take a look at the steps to set up access to Spring services on a BlazeDS server.

Installing the BlazeDS Server

The first thing we need to do is install BlazeDS on the Tomcat server. BlazeDS offers a turnkey installation. The turnkey installation contains both Tomcat and a deployed BlazeDS WAR. If you are like me, you already have several applications running on your Tomcat server. The second option is to get just the BlazeDS binary distribution. This is simply a zip file with the BlazeDS WAR.

Follow these steps to install BlazeDS on Tomcat:

1. Download and install JDK 1.5 or higher and make sure you have your `JAVA_HOME` variable pointed to the JDK install location.

2. Download the BlazeDS server install files—either `blazeds_turnkey_<version>.zip` or `blazeds_bin_<version>.zip`.

3. Move the `blazeds.war` file to `<tomcat-install-directory>`/webapps.

4. Start Tomcat. This will deploy a fresh BlazeDS server, ready to be configured for a Flex project.

5. Enter the following URL into your browser:

   `http://localhost:8080/blazeds/messagebroker/amf`

6. If you get a blank screen, you have installed BlazeDS correctly, and the AMF gateway is available to send requests over.

Implementing the Service

In our Spring application for this example, we need to change a couple of architecture components. We must move the `ApplicationContext` instantiation from the Java `Main()` method to loading it from a context parameter in the Tomcat application's `web.xml` file. Starting Tomcat will load the `ApplicationContext` into the web application's context and set up the proper channels to access the beans defined.

We also need an implementation of the Spring bean. In this case, we will create an implementation class called `GuestListServiceImpl`, which implements the `GuestListService`. This is the class that makes its methods available for consumption when the Tomcat server is started. Listings 6-5, 6-6, and 6-7 show the three Spring components that make up this service. These are located in the `com.af.flexonspring.chapter6` package.

To compile this project, you will need the following JAR files:

- `servlet-api.jar`

- `spring.jar`

- `flex-messaging-common.jar`

- `flex-messaging-core.jar`

- `commons-logging.jar`

Listing 6-5. *GuestListService.java*

```
package com.af.flexonspring.chapter6.services;

import java.util.List;

import com.af.flexonspring.chapter6.domain.Guest;

public interface GuestListService
{
     public List<Guest>  getGuestList();
}
```

Listing 6-6. *GuestListServiceImpl.java*

```java
package com.af.flexonspring.chapter6.services;

import java.util.ArrayList;
import java.util.List;
import java.io.Serializable;

import com.af.flexonspring.chapter6.domain.Guest;

public class GuestListServiceImpl implements Serializable, GuestListService
{
      public List<Guest>  getGuestList()
      {
            List<Guest> guestList = new ArrayList<Guest>();

            guestList.add(new Guest("Guest One"));
            guestList.add(new Guest("Guest Two"));
            guestList.add(new Guest("Guest Three"));
            guestList.add(new Guest("Guest Four"));
            return guestList;
      }
}
```

Listing 6-7. *Guest.java*

```java
package com.af.flexonspring.chapter6.domain;

import java.io.Serializable;

public class Guest implements Serializable
{
      private String guestName;

      public Guest(String guestName)
      {
            this.guestName = guestName;
      }

      public String getGuestName()
      {
            return guestName;
      }

      public void setGuestName(String guestName)
      {
            this.guestName = guestName;
      }
}
```

In this application, Flex makes an RPC call to the BlazeDS server to consume the guestListService we created in Spring. To run this code, create a new Flex application, as shown in Listing 6-8, and use Ant or Flex Builder to build it. For instructions on building the application using Ant, see the appendix of this book.

Listing 6-8. *Flex RemoteObjects Application*

```
<?xml version="1.0" encoding="utf-8"?>
<mx:Application xmlns:mx="http://www.adobe.com/2006/mxml">

    <mx:RemoteObject id="ro"
            destination="guestListService"
            endpoint="http://localhost:8080/blazeds/messagebroker/amf"
            result="resultHandler(event)"
            fault="faultHandler(event)"/>

    <mx:Script>
        <![CDATA[
                import mx.collections.ArrayCollection;
                import mx.rpc.events.ResultEvent;
                import mx.rpc.events.FaultEvent;
                import mx.utils.ObjectUtil;
                import mx.controls.Alert;
                import mx.utils.StringUtil;

                [Bindable]
                private var guestListDP:ArrayCollection = new ArrayCollection();

                private function resultHandler(event:ResultEvent):void
                {
                        guestListDP = ArrayCollection(event.result);
                }
                private function faultHandler(event:FaultEvent):void
                {
                        Alert.show( ObjectUtil.toString(event.fault) );
                }
        ]]>
    </mx:Script>

    <mx:Panel title="RemoteObject Example"
            paddingLeft="10" paddingRight="10" paddingBottom="10" paddingTop="10"
            horizontalAlign="center" width="416" height="377">
```

```
            <mx:Button label="Get Guest List" click="ro.getGuestList()"/>
            <mx:DataGrid id="dg" dataProvider="{guestListDP}"
                    width="260" height="180">
                <mx:columns>
                        <mx:DataGridColumn headerText="Guest Name"
                                dataField="guestName"   />
                </mx:columns>
            </mx:DataGrid>
        </mx:Panel>
</mx:Application>
```

The application executes the `<mx:RemoteObject>` call on the click of the Get Guest List button. The results of the call are a list of Guest objects returned from the Spring service. Notice the list is bound to the `<mx:DataGrid>` through the guestListDP, which is cast to a Flex ArrayCollection.

Integrating Flex and Spring with SpringFactory

The SpringFactory class was built to bridge the gap between Flex's AMG gateway and access to Spring beans via RemoteObject calls. In this first example of using the RemoteObject protocol, we will employ SpringFactory as our solution, so you will have a complete understanding of setting up your web server to host Flex and Spring.

Installing Spring on BlazeDS

Now that there is a BlazeDS server installed, we need to make the Spring Framework available to our BlazeDS server. Follow these steps to install the Spring.jar file and set up the context listener:

1. Download the Spring Framework from http://springframework.org.download. The version I am using is Spring Framework 2.5.x. Go ahead and download the version with dependencies.

2. Once you have the zip file, locate the Spring.jar file and move it to your *<tomcat-install-directory>*/webapps/blazeds/lib folder.

3. Set up a context-param and listener for the Spring Framework. Open *<tomcat-install-directory>*/webapps/blazeds/WEB-INF/web.xml and add the following context-param and listener at the bottom of the file, before the </web-app> tag:

```
<context-param>
        <param-name>contextConfigLocation</param-name>
        <param-value>/WEB-INF/applicationContext.xml</param-value>
</context-param>

<listener>
        <listener-class>
            org.springframework.web.context.ContextLoaderListener
        </listener-class>
</listener>
```

Note If you plan to create a project that deploys BlazeDS with Spring in Eclipse, you will want to edit the web.xml file in your project, instead of the Tomcat installation directory on your server.

We now have access to the Spring Framework from our BlazeDS web applications, and the ApplicationContext for the registered Spring beans will be available to the BlazeDS web application context. We are ready to register the Spring beans.

Registering Spring Beans

Now that you have installed BlazeDS, we need an example for integrating Flex RemoteObject RPC calls to Spring. We need to define a service and register the Spring beans on the Tomcat server running BlazeDS. For now, we can use the GuestListService that we built in Chapter 5. It will be more than sufficient to demonstrate exactly how to integrate Flex with Spring.

As you know, Flex clients can communicate with many different server technologies, including Java objects. Spring beans are Java objects, so shouldn't we be able to communicate directly with Spring beans from Flex? The short answer is yes, with a little help.

As explained in Chapter 1, Spring is built on the concept of DI through the Spring IoC container. The idea behind Spring is to let the container inject dependencies into the objects that will be running on our BlazeDS server. We want the BlazeDS server to allow the Spring container to take care of instantiating the Spring beans. By default, when a Flex client makes an RPC call to a BlazeDS server, the BlazeDS server attempts to instantiate the Java objects. The key to make this work for Spring is to create a factory to enable the usage of components to BlazeDS. We do not want BlazeDS to instantiate Spring beans directly, because that would not properly implement DI and therefore would not work for our architecture.

Spring beans require the ApplicationContext to be accessible from Flex applications. The ApplicationContext file will define the beans that will be available for Flex and will allow Flex to inject data values into those beans via the services that are exposed.

Here are the steps to create applicationContext.xml:

1. Create a new file named applicationContext.xml in <*tomcat-install-directory*>/webapps/blazed/WEB-INF.

2. Register the GuestListService bean in the applicationContext.xml file as follows:

```
<?xml version="1.0" encoding="UTF-8" ?>
<!DOCTYPE beans PUBLIC "-//SPRING//DTD BEAN//EN"
      "http://www.springframework.org/dtd/spring-beans.dtd">
<beans>
      <bean id="guestService"
            class="com.af.flexonspring.chapter6.services.GuestListServiceImpl"/>
</beans>
```

If you look at GuestListServiceImpl in Listing 6-6 (shown earlier in this chapter), you will notice that I have coded the return data directly into a generic List of Guest domain objects. I will demonstrate how to map beans through properties when we build the AF – Client Manager application in the upcoming chapters, as it will be a much more complex example of a real-world application. For now, we need to cover the basics of setting up a Spring service.

Creating and Registering SpringFactory

The other objects in the architecture for this example make up the business logic and data containers for the application, as well as configuration. These objects include Spring beans, Flex user interface components, and objects to configure context for the Tomcat server, as well as a few specialized objects to handle the underpinnings of the transport architecture.

One specialized object that warrants description here is the SpringFactory object. Any class that is within the application's classpath on the Tomcat server can be called by a client of Tomcat. The context of the object is within the Tomcat JVM.

In order for the Spring beans to have been properly initialized by Spring, they must be instantiated within a Spring context, or the Spring Framework must be instantiated by reading the configuration and properly instantiating all the beans. This can be done from within the Tomcat context by a Tomcat object instantiating the Spring context and then calling the Spring objects. It can also be done with entries within the Tomcat configuration files to instantiate the Spring context so that it is available to any classes within the Tomcat context. The previously described methods make the application dependent on Tomcat, either through configuration or an object within the Tomcat context.

The Flex client in this case uses RemoteObject calls to get data from the middle tier, Tomcat. These objects are created from within the Flex context on the server. In order for the classes to have the proper Spring context, the BlazeDS server must be configured to instantiate the Spring context. The SpringFactory class properly instantiates this context and forwards the call to the classes. *The SpringFactory class is the most important component of this solution and is critical to successfully integrating Flex with Spring.*

The SpringFactory class, shown in Listing 6-9, was created by Jeff Vroom of Adobe Systems.

Listing 6-9. *SpringFactory Java Class (by Jeff Vroom of Adobe Systems)*

```
package com.af.common.factories;

import org.springframework.context.ApplicationContext;
import org.springframework.web.context.support.WebApplicationContextUtils;
import org.springframework.beans.BeansException;
import org.springframework.beans.factory.NoSuchBeanDefinitionException;

import flex.messaging.FactoryInstance;
import flex.messaging.FlexFactory;
import flex.messaging.config.ConfigMap;
import flex.messaging.services.ServiceException;

/**
 * This interface is implemented by factory components which provide
 * instances to the flex messaging framework.
 *
 * @author Jeff Vroom
 */
public class SpringFactory implements FlexFactory
{
    private static final String SOURCE = "source";
```

```java
/**
 * This method can be used to initialize the factory itself.
 * It is called with configuration parameters from the
 * factory tag which defines the id of the factory.
 */
public void initialize(String id, ConfigMap configMap) {}

/**
 * This method is called when we initialize the definition of an instance
 * which will be looked up by this factory.  It should validate that
 * the properties supplied are valid to define an instance.
 * Any valid properties used for this configuration must be accessed to
 * avoid warnings about unused configuration elements.  If your factory
 * is only used for application scoped components, this method can simply
 * return a factory instance which delegates the creation of the component
 * to the FactoryInstance's lookup method.
 */
public FactoryInstance createFactoryInstance(String id, ConfigMap properties)
{
    SpringFactoryInstance instance =
        new SpringFactoryInstance(this, id, properties);
    instance.setSource(properties.getPropertyAsString(SOURCE,
        instance.getId()));
    return instance;
} // end method createFactoryInstance()

/**
 * Returns the instance specified by the source
 * and properties arguments.  For the factory, this may mean
 * constructing a new instance, optionally registering it in some other
 * name space such as the session or JNDI, and then returning it
 * or it may mean creating a new instance and returning it.
 * This method is called for each request to operate on the
 * given item by the system so it should be relatively efficient.
 * <p>
 * If your factory does not support the scope property, it
 * report an error if scope is supplied in the properties
 * for this instance.
 */
public Object lookup(FactoryInstance inst)
{
    SpringFactoryInstance factoryInstance = (SpringFactoryInstance) inst;
    return factoryInstance.lookup();
}
```

```
static class SpringFactoryInstance extends FactoryInstance
{
    SpringFactoryInstance(SpringFactory factory, String id,
        ConfigMap properties)
    {
        super(factory, id, properties);
    }


    public String toString()
    {
        return "SpringFactory instance for id =
            " + getId() + " source=" + getSource() + " scope=" + getScope();
    }

    public Object lookup()
    {
        ApplicationContext appContext =
          WebApplicationContextUtils.getWebApplicationContext(
          flex.messaging.FlexContext.getServletConfig().getServletContext());
        String beanName = getSource();

        try
        {
            return appContext.getBean(beanName);
        }
        catch (NoSuchBeanDefinitionException nexc)
        {
            ServiceException e = new ServiceException();
            String msg = "Spring service named '" +
                    beanName + "' does not exist.";
            e.setMessage(msg);
            e.setRootCause(nexc);
            e.setDetails(msg);
            e.setCode("Server.Processing");
            throw e;
        }
        catch (BeansException bexc)
        {
            ServiceException e = new ServiceException();
            String msg = "Unable to create Spring service named '" +
                    beanName + "' ";
            e.setMessage(msg);
            e.setRootCause(bexc);
            e.setDetails(msg);
            e.setCode("Server.Processing");
            throw e;
```

```
        }
      }
    }
  }
}
```

This factory will allow you to use Spring services as RemoteObject RPC calls from Flex. This is the bridge between BlazeDS and Spring. There is only one configuration item we need to implement to set up the SpringFactory class.

Follow these steps to download and configure SpringFactory:

1. Download SpringFactory from Adobe Exchange at http://www.adobe.com/cfusion/ exchange/. You will likely need to perform a search of the Adobe Exchange for "Spring and Flex" to find the source for the SpringFactory class (shown in Listing 6-9). This class is also available with the downloadable source code for this book.

2. Move the SpringFactory.java to the package com.af.common.factories, or a location you prefer, in your Spring project to compile it. You will notice you require a few Flex Data Services JAR files to compile SpringFactory: Flex-messaging-core.jar, Flex-messaging-common.jar, and Spring.jar. These JAR files are found in <tomcat-install-directory>/webapps/blazeds/lib. You will also want to copy those two JAR files into your Spring project in Eclipse.

3. Build the Spring project and move the SpringFactory class to the <tomcat-install-directory>/webapps/blazeds/WEB-INF/classes directory. In the classes directory, you should see com/af/common/factories/SpringFactory.class and SpringFactory$SpringFactoryInstance.class. The SpringFactory$SpringFactoryInstance.class file is created when you run the Tomcat server. You will need to have the servlet-api.jar file referenced in your classpath to build the SpringFactory.

4. The last item is to register the SpringFactory class for BlazeDS to consume. Edit the services-config.xml file located in the <tomcat-install-directory>/webapps/ blazeds/WEB-INF/flex directory. Add the following lines in services-config.xml to register the SpringFactory class:

```
<factories>
    <factory id="spring"
            class="com.af.common.factories.SpringFactory"/>
</factories>
```

With that done, we are ready to configure our Flex Remoting services so we have a destination from which Flex can access the Spring beans.

Configuring Flex Remoting Configuration and Project Files

The last configuration item for using Flex RPC RemoteObject calls to Spring services is to locate and apply the target for the Flex application to hit. You will want to enter a destination for every Spring bean or service that should be exposed to Flex for consumption. Here are the steps to set up the Flex Remoting destination:

1. Locate the `remoting-config.xml` file in `<tomcat-install-directory>`/webapps/blazeds/WEB-INF/flex.

2. Add the following entry to set the `guestListService` destination in `remoting-config.xml`:

```
<destination id="guestListService">
    <properties>
        <factory>spring</factory>
        <source>guestListService</source>
    </properties>
</destination>
```

3. Copy all compiled Spring code to the `<tomcat-install-directory>`/webapps/blazeds/WEB-INF/classes directory.

4. Start the Tomcat server.

What follows is the `<mx:RemoteObject>` definition in MXML that accesses the `guestListService`:

```
<mx:RemoteObject id="ro"
        destination="guestListService"
        endpoint="http://localhost:8080/blazeds/messagebroker/amf"
        result="resultHandler(event)"
        fault="faultHandler(event)"/>
```

Notice the `destination` name is the same as the `destination id` located in the `remoting-config.mxml` file. Flex uses the RemoteObject destination to look up objects on the BlazeDS server. The endpoint for our `<mx:RemoteObject>` points to the AMF gateway running within the BlazeDS web context on Tomcat.

We have completed the entire setup for the Flex BlazeDS server and Spring configuration to access our beans and services. Now, let's go ahead and implement a RemoteObject example that consumes the `GuestListService` available via our Spring application.

Running the Application

To run the application after you build it with Ant, you can deploy it to your BlazeDS server by moving the appropriate files to the server.

After you compile the Flex application (Listing 6-8), copy the following files to the `<tomcat-install-directory>`/webapps/blazeds folder:

- `GuestList.swf`

- `GuestList.html`

- `playerProductInstall.swf`

- `AC_OETags.js`

These files will run the Flex application based on the `GuestList.html` wrapper file. The `playerProductInstall.swf` file is used as part of the Flash version detection process when the application is run on a computer. If the version is not supported by the Flex application, it will prompt the user to download and install the latest version of Flash. Upon completion of the download and install, the Flex application can be run. The AC_OETags.js file is the JavaScript file that detects which version of Flash you have installed on your computer when the application is run.

After compiling the Spring project, either through Eclipse or Ant, copy or use the Ant script to move the com/af/flexonspring/chapter6/* files to the <tomcat-install-directory>/webapps/blazeds/WEB-INF/classes folder.

Earlier in the chapter, you set up your BlazeDS server and created or updated many configuration files. These files include web.xml and applicationContext.xml, registering the SpringFactory, and setting the remoting-config.xml destinations. You may want to run through the configuration of these entities once more to ensure everything is correctly formatted and typed.

After you've located the files as instructed, start your Tomcat server and type the following URL to access the application in a web browser, if you are running Tomcat on the defined 8080 port:

```
http://localhost:8080/blazeds/GuestList.html
```

You should see the results shown in Figure 6-8.

Figure 6-8. *RemoteObject runtime results*

Integrating Flex and Spring with Spring BlazeDS Integration

In December 2008, SpringSource released the first milestone for the Spring BlazeDS Integration (SBI) project. The SBI suite is designed as a best practice solution for integrating Flex and Spring. Its main goal is to simplify communication between Flex and Spring by providing Remoting and messaging capabilities in combination with BlazeDS, while keeping the project open source.

The current release is the foundation of the project. It includes wiring Spring beans for Flex RemoteObject, HTTPService, and WebService calls. The project will include support for integrating Spring Security with BlazeDS, integration with BlazeDS message services, and building a Spring 3.0 RESTful architecture that uses AMFView.

I believe this solution will become the mainstay for Flex and Spring integration. It does not get rid of all configuration items required for using `SpringFactory`, but it does clean up quite a bit of the locations for configurable items. It also provides a familiar process for wiring your beans and removes the need for a transport component such as `SpringFactory`, since it provides a set of libraries that handles communication.

Since we have already set up a BlazeDS server, there are only a few steps to complete to start using the SBI solution.

To use SBI, you need to be sure you have the following requirements covered to run the server:

- Java 5 or above

- Spring 2.5 with dependencies or above

- Adobe BlazeDS 3.2 or above

- Spring MVC dependency JARs from the Spring 2.5 with dependencies download:

    - `spring-web.jar`

    - `spring-beans.jar`

    - `spring-context.jar`

    - `spring-context-support.jar`

    - `spring-core.jar`

    - `spring-tx.jar`

    - `spring-webmvc.jar`

Installing SBI

You should already have installed the BlazeDS server. If not, go ahead and do so now, following the directions provided earlier in the "Installing BlazeDS" section. After you have BlazeDS installed, you will need to download Spring, Spring MVC, and the SBI libraries, as follows:

1. Download the Spring Framework from `http://www.springsource.org/download`. The version I am using is Spring Framework 2.5.*x*. Be sure to download the version with dependencies.

2. Once you have the zip file, locate the `Spring.jar` file with the dependency JARs in the preceding list, and move them to your *<tomcat-install-directory>*`/webapps/blazeds/lib` folder.

3. Download the SBI project from `http://www.springsource.org/download`. Open the zip file and move the `org.springframework.flex-1.`*x* JAR file to your *<tomcat-install-directory>*`/webapps/blazeds/lib` folder.

You now have access to the SBI framework from BlazeDS, which will wire Spring beans to Flex Remoting calls. In this example, we are using RemoteObject to call the server from Flex. The next steps will cover setting up the configuration files required to support server-side calls from Flex.

Setting Up the BlazeDS MessageBroker

The `MessageBroker` is a the SBI component responsible for handling HTTP messages from the Flex client. The `MessageBroker` is managed by Spring instead of BlazeDS. Messages are routed to the Spring-managed `MessageBroker` via the Spring `DispatcherServlet`. Listing 6-10 shows the `web.xml` file.

Listing 6-10. *The web.xml File for SBI*

```xml
<?xml version="1.0" encoding="UTF-8"?>

<!DOCTYPE web-app PUBLIC "-//Sun Microsystems, Inc.//DTD Web
Application 2.3//EN" "http://java.sun.com/dtd/web-app_2_3.dtd">

<web-app>
    <display-name>Spring BlazeDS Integration Samples</display-name>
    <description>Spring BlazeDS Integration Sample Application</description>

    <!-- Http Flex Session attribute and binding listener support -->
    <listener>
        <listener-class>flex.messaging.HttpFlexSession</listener-class>
    </listener>

    <!-- The front controller of this Spring Web application,
    responsible for handling all application requests -->
    <servlet>
        <servlet-name>Spring MVC Dispatcher Servlet</servlet-name>
        <servlet-class>
            org.springframework.web.servlet.DispatcherServlet
        </servlet-class>
        <init-param>
            <param-name>contextConfigLocation</param-name>
            <param-value>/WEB-INF/applicationContext.xml</param-value>
        </init-param>
        <load-on-startup>1</load-on-startup>
    </servlet>

    <!-- Map all *.spring requests to the DispatcherServlet for handling -->
    <servlet-mapping>
        <servlet-name>Spring MVC Dispatcher Servlet</servlet-name>
        <url-pattern>/spring/*</url-pattern>
    </servlet-mapping>

    <welcome-file-list>
        <welcome-file>index.htm</welcome-file>
    </welcome-file-list>
</web-app>
```

The DispatcherServlet is configured to bootstrap Spring's WebApplicationContext. There are two things to notice in the definition. First, the <servlet-class> has changed to allow Spring to manage the MessageBroker itself:

```
From:
<servlet-class>
    flex.messaging.MessageBrokerServlet
</servlet-class>

To:
<servlet-class>
    org.springframework.web.servlet.DispatcherServlet
</servlet-class>
```

The other item of interest in the web.xml file is the mapping of the DispatcherServlet to Flex requests. You will want to add a channel in the <tomcat-install-directory>/webapps/blazeds/WEB-INF/flex/services-config.xml to support the mapping definition, such as the following:

```
<channel-definition id="my-amf" class="mx.messaging.channels.AMFChannel">
    <endpoint url=
        "http://{server.name}:{server.port}/{context.root} ➥
        /spring/messagebroker/amf"
        class="flex.messaging.endpoints.AMFEndpoint"/>
    <properties>
        <polling-enabled>false</polling-enabled>
    </properties>
</channel-definition>
```

The first steps set up a channel with a servlet mapping to the channel using the HandlerMapping located in <tomcat-install-directory>/webapps/blazeds/WEB-INF/applicationContext.xml. The HandlerMapping is responsible for mapping all paths to the Spring-managed MessageBroker. I have set the path to /*, which will map any URL that comes across the channel to the Spring-managed MessageBroker. You can define more specific paths for allowing requests to be processed if you need to secure your server at the URL level. The requests that are mapped to the MessageBroker from the MessageBrokerHandlerAdapter are located in Spring's WebApplicationContext. The following two beans need to be entered in the applicationContext.xml file for this application:

```
<bean class="org.springframework.web.servlet.handler.SimpleUrlHandlerMapping">
    <property name="mappings">
        <value>
            /*=mySpringManagedMessageBroker
        </value>
    </property>
</bean>

<bean class="org.springframework.flex.messaging.servlet. ➥
    MessageBrokerHandlerAdapter"/>
```

One more bean needs to be defined in the application context. The `MessageBrokerFactoryBean` bootstraps and exposes the Spring-managed `MessageBroker` so you can wire your beans or services. The following entry in the `applicationContext.xml` file is required:

```
<bean id="springManagedMessageBroker"
    class="org.springframework.flex.messaging.MessageBrokerFactoryBean" />
```

After we look at the Remoting configuration, I'll show you the full listing of the `applicationContext.xml` file (Listing 6-11).

Flex Remoting Directly to Exposed Spring Beans

Spring manages the `MessageBroker` to allow beans to be wired for direct Remoting calls by Flex. This allows you to remove much of the configuration that was located in the `remoting-config.xml` file. You can use the `applicationContext.xml` file to wire your beans for Remoting through the `MessageBroker`, which will serialize and deserialize objects between Java and the Flex AMF data types.

You do not need to configure any Remoting destinations in the `remoting-config.xml` file with SBI. This reduces a good part of the BlazeDS configuration, since you are no longer required to keep this file up-to-date. In future releases of SBI, the requirement to have the `remoting-config.xml` file will be removed.

All you need in your `<tomcat-install-directory>`/webapps/blazeds/WEB-INF/flex/ `remoting-config.xml` are the following configuration items, which are in the native BlazeDS installation:

```
<?xml version="1.0" encoding="UTF-8"?>
<service id="remoting-service"
    class="flex.messaging.services.RemotingService">

    <adapters>
        <adapter-definition id="java-object"
        class="flex.messaging.services.remoting.adapters.JavaAdapter"
        default="true"/>
    </adapters>

    <default-channels>
        <channel ref="my-amf"/>
    </default-channels>

</service>
```

Now you are ready to wire your beans in the application context. This will be very familiar to Spring developers, and it simplifies the process of exposing Spring beans for Flex Remoting.

For this example, we will use the `guestListService` defined earlier in Listings 6-5, 6-6, and 6-7. There are no changes required to the Spring source code to support using SBI. You define your beans in the same way:

```
<bean id="guestService"
    class="com.af.flexonspring.chapter6.services.GuestListServiceImpl"/>
```

The FlexRemotingServiceExporter is a new entry in the application context. It is required by SBI to export Spring-managed services for Flex Remoting. The GuestListService is registered to the MessageBroker through the springManagedMessageBroker reference to the MessageBrokerFactoryBean:

```
<bean id="guestService"
    class="org.springframework.flex.messaging.remoting. ➥
    FlexRemotingServiceExporter">
      <property name="messageBroker" ref="springManagedMessageBroker"/>
      <property name="service" ref="guestListService"/>
</bean>
```

As you can see, we have cut down on the configuration effort with a much cleaner process than using SpringFactory. Over time, as SBI evolves, it will offer a much tighter integration solution for Flex and Spring.

Listing 6-11 shows a complete listing of the application context XML file for this example, which contains all of the configuration items we have discussed.

Listing 6-11. *The applicationContext.xml File for SBI*

```
<?xml version="1.0" encoding="UTF-8"?>
<beans xmlns="http://www.springframework.org/schema/beans"
    xmlns:xsi="http://www.w3.org/2001/XMLSchema-instance"

xsi:schemaLocation="
        http://www.springframework.org/schema/beans
        http://www.springframework.org/schema/beans/spring-beans-2.5.xsd">

    <!-- Maps request paths at /* to the BlazeDS MessageBroker -->
    <bean class="org.springframework.web.servlet.handler.SimpleUrlHandlerMapping">
        <property name="mappings">
            <value>
                /*=springManagedMessageBroker
            </value>
        </property>
    </bean>

    <!-- Dispatches requests mapped to a MessageBroker -->
    <bean class="org.springframework.flex.messaging.servlet. ➥
    MessageBrokerHandlerAdapter"/>

    <!-- Bootstraps and exposes the BlazeDS MessageBroker -->
    <bean id="springManagedMessageBroker"
    class="org.springframework.flex.messaging.MessageBrokerFactoryBean" />
```

```
<!-- Expose the guestListService bean for BlazeDS remoting -->
<bean id="guestService"
class="org.springframework.flex.messaging.remoting.FlexRemotingServiceExporter">
    <property name="messageBroker" ref="springManagedMessageBroker"/>
    <property name="service" ref="guestListService"/>
</bean>

<bean id="guestListService"
        class="com.af.flexonspring.chapter6.services.GuestListServiceImpl"/>
```

```
</beans>
```

Running the Application

To run this application, you need to make a minor change to the Flex source code in Listing 6-8. Modify the destination to match the guestService bean in the applicationContext.xml file and match the endpoint tag to the channel defined in services-config.xml.

Here's the entry in applicationContext.xml:

```
<bean id="guestService"
    class="org.springframework.flex.messaging.remoting.FlexRemotingServiceExporter">
    <property name="messageBroker" ref="springManagedMessageBroker"/>
    <property name="service" ref="guestListService"/>
</bean>
```

And here's the entry in services-config.xml:

```
<channel-definition id="my-amf" class="mx.messaging.channels.AMFChannel">
    <endpoint url="http://{server.name}:{server.port}/{context.root} ➥
    /spring/messagebroker/amf"
    class="flex.messaging.endpoints.AMFEndpoint"/>
    <properties>
        <polling-enabled>false</polling-enabled>
    </properties>
</channel-definition>
```

Finally, here is the Flex source code (Listing 6-8) that needs changes:

```
<mx:RemoteObject id="ro"
        destination="guestService"
        endpoint="http://localhost:8080/blazeds/spring/ ➥
          messagebroker/amf"
        result="resultHandler(event)"
        fault="faultHandler(event)"/>
```

I've highlighted the changes to show you where they match up in the configuration files.

After you make the changes to the Flex source code, you can run the application to get the same results as in the SpringFactory example, shown earlier in Figure 6-8, by going to the following URL:

```
http://localhost:8080/blazeds/GuestList.html
```

Summary

We covered quite a bit of ground in this chapter, including how to retrieve data for Flex using the WebService, HTTPService, and RemoteObject protocols. The preferred approach is to use RemoteObject in conjunction with Spring.

You've seen that Spring is very versatile in allowing Flex to communicate with it. You learned how the SpringFactory class and the SBI solution from SpringSource and Adobe play key roles in integrating Flex with Spring. BlazeDS provides factory support and allows you to create Spring beans to be consumed by the Flex RemoteObject protocol.

You also learned what it takes to configure a BlazeDS server with Flex and Spring on Tomcat. Of course, Tomcat isn't the only web/application server on which you can run Flex and Spring. The technology can run on several popular Java application servers, such as JBoss, Adobe JRun, IBM WebSphere, and BEA WebLogic.

In the next chapter, you will learn about architecting the view for your Flex applications by using the Cairngorm and PureMVC frameworks.

CHAPTER 7

■■■

Architecting the View:
Cairngorm and PureMVC

In previous chapters, you have seen that Flex can be built out of the box to obtain data from external data sources. This works fine with small Flex applications that have only one or few view states. However, when it comes to building enterprise-scale applications in Flex, the basics just won't cut it. To avoid a "big ball of yarn" (many point-to-point connections between Flex components) infrastructure, you need to define a standard and consistent architecture for your Flex applications.

Several Flex application development frameworks offer solutions to Flex development through design patterns. These include Cairngorm, PureMVC, MVCS, and Mate. The purpose of a development framework or architecture is to create a consistent development process that is repeatable, maintainable, and developer-friendly. When determining which architecture to use for your Flex user interface, you need to consider what best fits your organization and developers' skills, as each solution is different and generally based on different design patterns, or slight modifications of those patterns.

In this chapter, we will take a look at PureMVC and Cairngorm. We will build an application to manage contacts in both frameworks. I will leave it up to you to decide which architecture best fits your development interest.

For the sample AF – Client Manager application, we will apply Cairngorm as the application framework (in Chapter 13). This is because Cairngorm is hosted and built by Adobe. It is being evolved to fit enterprise developers' needs. There is also a general view that PureMVC has a more involved learning curve than Cairngorm. I'll let you be the judge of that.

Keep in mind that I recommend using these architectures for medium-scale to large-scale applications only. I feel there is a diminished return on your time investment if you are building a small Flex component and using a heavy framework to implement the underpinnings for that component.

Using PureMVC

PureMVC, created by Cliff Hall, is an ActionScript-based framework that Flex leverages to handle data transport from Flex view components to external services like Spring services. PureMVC is based on the MVC metapattern, in which the model, view, and controller are implemented as singletons. It is a solid solution for projects with multiple developers.

PureMVC Components

The PureMVC framework is designed to represent the application in three tiers to separate coding responsibilities into those tiers. The facade is also a singleton that is created to provide a single interface for communication throughout the application. Figure 7-1 illustrates the core objects in PureMVC and their relationships.

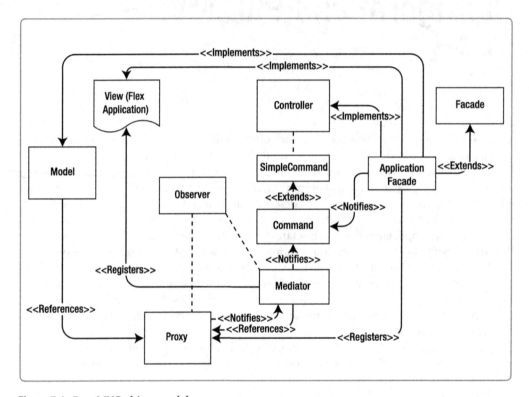

Figure 7-1. *PureMVC object model*

The PureMVC programming model is made up of the following components:

Value object: The PureMVC value object is nothing more than a mapping to your Spring beans. This value object is used to help match incoming domain objects from Spring; in the case of this book's examples, to use in the Flex views.

Events: PureMVC uses the core flash.event class to dispatch events throughout the framework.

Facade: The facade is responsible for holding the model, view, and controller in the memory cache. It also initializes each of those three main singletons in the PureMVC framework, as well as provides the point of access to their public methods.

Controller: The controller is responsible for maintaining and registering the commands in the application.

Command: Commands are a way in which view components can interface with the model. A command can interface with proxies, mediators, and other commands. Commands are generally used to initiate application startup and shutdown, as well as to implement business logic for the application.

Model: The model provides a layer to access and change application data through creating proxies.

Proxy: Proxies represent a layer of abstraction that exposes business functions to the application by fronting data objects. They are a means to engage with remote services such as Spring services to retrieve data. They contain the data result and fault handlers that are implemented through the `IResponder` class.

Mediator: The mediator classes in PureMVC act as a connector between view components and the view's data. Mediators facilitate state changes and data updates for the related views. In other words, mediators front views in PureMVC.

Observer: The commands, proxies, and mediators communicate with each other through notifications, which are mapped names to observer lists. The observers are notified when a notification is sent from the view. Notifications are not Flex events, even though they implement `flash.event`. They are used for communication between objects only in the PureMVC framework.

PureMVC Framework Implementation for Flex

The PureMVC framework does a very good job of creating decoupled layers to use for building application components. As mentioned, PureMVC is built on the three main singletons of model, view, and controller. You cannot directly manipulate these entities. Instead, you develop proxy classes to access the model, mediator classes to update and change state on the view, and commands to direct traffic via the controller.

The framework does not limit how you can access data through Flex. You have the common options of using the RemoteObject, WebService, and HTTPService protocols to call external Spring services, as explained in Chapter 6.

The framework is built on notifications broadcast through the model, view, and controller. The model will broadcast notifications only to the other layers; it does not listen for notifications. The view, on the other hand, will broadcast and listen for notifications. The controller will also broadcast notifications and will listen by invoking commands.

Here are the steps for building a PureMVC application:

1. Ensure the (Java) service is defined in the delegate.

2. Create the delegate class to implement the Spring service method stubs.

3. Create a data proxy for handling results and faults when attempting to access Spring services.

4. Create mediators to present and update the view.

5. Create commands in the controller to give view components a conduit to model data, and create the `ApplicationStartupCommand` to initialize the application.

6. Set up a concrete facade to handle communication between the model, view, and controller.

7. Add events to the view to invoke service calls.

To show how to leverage PureMVC for the transport layer in a Flex application, we will walk through a sample application. We will build a contact management view component that will engage the PureMVC framework to handle application communication.

Setting Up a PureMVC Flex Project

Begin by downloading the PureMVC framework with the ActionScript 3 port from http://www.puremvc.org. You will want to get the PureMVC Standard for AS3. Version 2.0.4 was used to create the example in this chapter.

Once you have downloaded the PureMVC framework, locate PureMVC_AS3_2_0_4.swc in the zip file. Create a project named PureMVC_flex and copy the SWC to your Flex project's libs directory. Open the project's properties and ensure the SWC is loaded and referenced in the project. The Library path tab under the Flex Build Path should look like Figure 7-2.

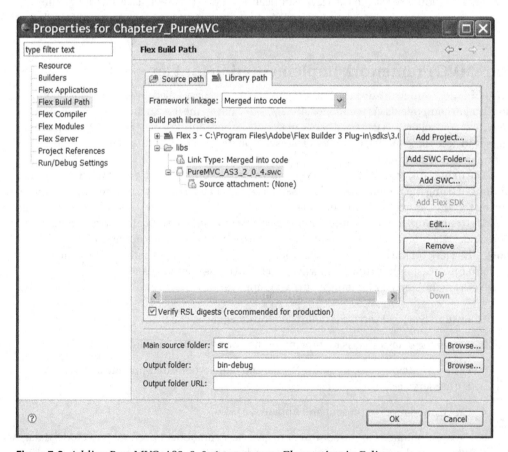

Figure 7-2. *Adding PureMVC_AS3_2_0_4.swc to your Flex project in Eclipse*

For the sample application, we will implement four methods in a proxy: `AddContact()`, `DeleteContact()`, `GetContacts()`, and `UpdateContact()`. The mediator will interact with the proxy class, `ContactProxy`, on behalf of the view to get data by invoking the Spring services. Each of the methods is accessed through a notification that is processed in the mediator class for contacts. The `ApplicationFacade` is responsible for directing traffic through custom notification constants that are defined there.

Creating an HTTPService

The service definitions in PureMVC go in the delegate. Each delegate will have a service entry that describes the handle the service will be called within Flex, as shown in Listing 7-1.

Listing 7-1. *HTTPService Destination in the Delegate*

```
private var responder : IResponder;
private var contactService : HTTPService;

public function ContactDelegate( responder : IResponder )
{
     this.contactService = new HTTPService();
     this.contactService.url="assets/xml/Contacts.xml";

     this.responder = responder;
}
```

In this example, we are creating an HTTPService to open and read the contents of the `Contacts.xml` file, shown in Listing 7-2. The data results are sent to the `ContactProxy` via the `IResponder` we have defined in the service call.

Listing 7-2. *The Contacts.xml File*

```
<?xml version="1.0" encoding="utf-8"?>
<contacts>
     <contact>
          <contact_id>1</contact_id>
          <name>Chris Giametta</name>
          <email>chris.giametta@myemail.com</email>
     </contact>
     <contact>
          <contact_id>2</contact_id>
          <name>Cole Giametta</name>
          <email>cole.giametta@myemail.com</email>
     </contact>
     <contact>
          <contact_id>3</contact_id>
          <name>Kaitlyn Giametta</name>
          <email>kaitlyn.giametta@myemail.com</email>
     </contact>
```

```
        <contact>
                <contact_id>4</contact_id>
                <name>Kristi Giametta</name>
                <email>kristi.giametta@myemail.com</email>
        </contact>
</contacts>
```

Creating the Delegate Class

The ContactDelegate will store a reference to the data service we are going to call. The getContactsService invokes the HTTPService and notifies the responder when the service has completed its call. Once the call is complete, the response is handled by the proxy and set by the result argument located in the proxy that is referenced. In this case, it is the ContactProxy. If a fault occurs in the service call, the ContactProxy will be notified of the fault, and the error message will be passed to it. Listing 7-3 shows the delegate that invokes the HTTPService to get contacts.

Listing 7-3. *Delegate That Invokes an HTTPService to Get Contacts (ContactDelegate.as)*

```
package com.af.cep.model.business
{
        import mx.rpc.AsyncToken;
        import mx.rpc.IResponder;
        import mx.rpc.http.HTTPService;

        public class ContactDelegate
        {
                private var responder : IResponder;
                private var contactService : HTTPService;

                public function ContactDelegate( responder : IResponder )
                {
                        this.contactService = new HTTPService();
                        this.contactService.url="assets/xml/Contacts.xml";

                        this.responder = responder;
                }
                public function getContactsService() : void
                {
                        var token:AsyncToken = contactService.send();

                        token.addResponder( responder );
                }
        }
}
```

Creating Data Proxies for Result and Fault Handling

The proxy for the contact application implements IResponder to handle responses from data services, which requires us to add result and fault methods. The result method is called when the delegate responds to a call from the service. The fault method is called if the delegate receives an error from the service.

We also need to create methods to invoke the delegate service stubs. The delegate is created to get data and is passed a reference to the proxy that can handle data results. We can also send notifications from proxies. For example, in the result of the getContacts() call, we populate the contact list in the ContactProxy with the service XML result. The proxy is a good place to transform data between the server and application. It also can represent any form of data, such as application constants. We then send a notification through the ApplicationFacade to let it know that we have loaded the contacts successfully. Listing 7-4 shows the ContactProxy.

Listing 7-4. *Proxy Responsible for Interacting with the Delegate to Handle Contact Events (ContactProxy.as)*

```
package com.af.cep.model
{
     import com.af.cep.*;
     import com.af.cep.model.business.ContactDelegate;
     import com.af.cep.model.vo.ContactVO;

     import mx.collections.ArrayCollection;
     import mx.rpc.IResponder;

     import org.puremvc.as3.interfaces.*;
     import org.puremvc.as3.patterns.proxy.Proxy;

     public class ContactProxy extends Proxy implements IProxy, IResponder
     {
          public static const NAME:String = "ContactProxy";

          public function ContactProxy ( data:Object = null )
          {
               super ( NAME, data );
          }
          public function getContacts():void
          {
               var delegate : ContactDelegate = new ContactDelegate( this );
               delegate.getContactsService();
          }
          public function result( rpcEvent : Object ) : void
          {
               data = rpcEvent.result.contacts.contact as ArrayCollection;
               sendNotification( ApplicationFacade.LOAD_CONTACTS_SUCCESS );
          }
```

```
public function fault( rpcEvent : Object ) : void
{
    data = new ArrayCollection();
    errorStatus = "Could Not Load Contact List!";
    sendNotification( ApplicationFacade.LOAD_CONTACTS_FAILED );
}
public function addContact():void
{
    if( contact != null )
    {
        contactListDP.addItem( contact );
    }
}
public function updateContact():void
{
    var dpIndex : int = -1;

    if( contact != null )
    {
        for ( var i:int = 0; i < contactListDP.length; i++ )
        {
            if ( contactListDP[i].contact_id ==
                contact.contact_id )
            {
                dpIndex = i;
            }
        }
        contactListDP.setItemAt( contact, dpIndex );
    }
}
public function deleteContact():void
{
    if( contact != null )
    {
        for ( var i:int=0; i < contactListDP.length; i++ )
        {
            if ( contact.contact_id ==
                contactListDP[i].contact_id )
            {
                contactListDP.removeItemAt(i);
            }
        }
    }
}
```

```
        public function get contactListDP():ArrayCollection
        {
                return data as ArrayCollection;
        }

        public var contact:ContactVO = new ContactVO();
        public var errorStatus:String;
    }
}
```

The proxy class uses the ContactVO, shown in Listing 7-5, as a data reference to hold contact data and passes the object into event calls.

Listing 7-5. *The Contact Value Object (ContactVO.as)*

```
package com.af.cep.model.vo
{
    public class ContactVO
    {
        public var contact_id:int;
        public var name:String;
        public var email:String;

        public function ContactVO(){}
    }
}
```

Updating and Presenting the View with Mediators

The ApplicationMediator, shown in Listing 7-6, is a proxy for the main Flex application view. A mediator can be built for each view component in the Flex application (and should be, in my opinion). It is up to the developer to determine the granularity of mediators to views. In this case, we have only one component outside the main application, the ContactPanel.mxml. In the ApplicationMediator, we create and register a mediator for each view component that will support the view component by listening for events dispatched from the view, sending notifications for the view based on the events that are dispatched, and maintaining the state of the view directly through public methods and public properties on the view.

Listing 7-6. *Mediators That Process Application and View Interests (ApplicationMediator.as)*

```
package com.af.cep.view
{
    import com.af.cep.ApplicationFacade;
    import com.af.cep.model.*;
    import com.af.cep.model.vo.ContactVO;
    import com.af.cep.view.viewcomponents.*;
```

```
import org.puremvc.as3.interfaces.*;
import org.puremvc.as3.patterns.mediator.Mediator;

public class ApplicationMediator extends Mediator implements IMediator
{
    public static const NAME:String = "ApplicationMediator";

    public function ApplicationMediator(viewComponent:Object)
    {
        super(NAME, viewComponent);

        facade.registerMediator(new ContactsMediator( app.contactPanel));

        contactProxy = ContactProxy(facade.retrieveProxy(
            ContactProxy.NAME));
    }
    override public function listNotificationInterests():Array
    {
        return [ApplicationFacade.GET_CONTACTS];
    }
    override public function handleNotification(
        notification:INotification):void
    {
        switch (notification.getName())
        {
            case ApplicationFacade.GET_CONTACTS:
                contactProxy.contact = null;
                break;
        }
    }
    protected function get app():PureMVCExample
    {
        return viewComponent as PureMVCExample;
    }

    private var contactProxy:ContactProxy;
  }
}
```

The ContactsMediator, shown in Listing 7-7, is responsible for interacting with ContactPanel. In the constructor for the class, notice that it requires a viewComponent, which is the ContactPanel, so it can reference the ContactPanel's properties. We also list all notifications this mediator is interested in, as well as handle those notifications. Lastly, we add functions to process retrieval of contacts, adding contacts, deleting contacts, and updating contacts.

Listing 7-7. *The Contacts Mediator (ContactsMediator.as)*

```
package com.af.cep.view
{
     import com.af.cep.ApplicationFacade;
     import com.af.cep.model.ContactProxy;
     import com.af.cep.model.vo.ContactVO;
     import com.af.cep.view.viewcomponents.ContactPanel;

     import flash.events.Event;

     import org.puremvc.as3.interfaces.*;
     import org.puremvc.as3.patterns.mediator.Mediator;

     public class ContactsMediator extends Mediator implements IMediator
     {
          public static const NAME:String = "ContactsMediator";

          public function ContactsMediator(viewComponent:Object)
          {
               super(NAME, viewComponent);

               contactProxy =
                    ContactProxy(facade.retrieveProxy(ContactProxy.NAME));

               contactPanel.addEventListener(
                    ContactPanel.GET_CONTACTS, getContacts);
               contactPanel.addEventListener(
                    ContactPanel.ADD_CONTACT, addContact);
               contactPanel.addEventListener(
                    ContactPanel.UPDATE_CONTACT, updateContact);
               contactPanel.addEventListener(
                    ContactPanel.DELETE_CONTACT, deleteContact);
               contactPanel.addEventListener(
                    ContactPanel.SELECTED_CONTACT, setSelectedContact);
          }
          override public function listNotificationInterests():Array
          {
               return [ApplicationFacade.LOAD_CONTACTS_SUCCESS,
                    ApplicationFacade.LOAD_CONTACTS_FAILED];
          }
          override public function handleNotification(
               notification:INotification):void
          {
               var selectedItem:Object = new Object();
```

```
            switch (notification.getName())
            {
                  case ApplicationFacade.LOAD_CONTACTS_SUCCESS:
                       contactPanel.dgContact.dataProvider =
                              contactProxy.contactListDP;
                       break;
                  case ApplicationFacade.LOAD_CONTACTS_FAILED:
                       break;
            }
      }

      public function clearFormItems():void
      {
            contactPanel.clearFormItems();
      }

      protected function get contactPanel():ContactPanel
      {
            return viewComponent as ContactPanel;
      }
      private function getContacts(event:Event = null):void
      {
            sendNotification(ApplicationFacade.GET_CONTACTS);
      }
      private function addContact(event:Event = null):void
      {
            sendNotification(ApplicationFacade.ADD_CONTACT,
              {name:contactPanel.fullName.text,
               email:contactPanel.emailAddress.text});
            contactPanel.clearFormItems();
      }
      private function setSelectedContactevent:Event = null ):void
      {
            sendNotification(ApplicationFacade.SELECTED_CONTACT,
                 contactPanel.dgContact.selectedItem);
      }
      private function deleteContact( event:Event = null ):void
      {
            sendNotification(ApplicationFacade.DELETE_CONTACT);
            contactPanel.clearFormItems();
      }
      private function updateContact(event:Event = null):void
      {
            sendNotification( ApplicationFacade.UPDATE_CONTACT,
              {name:contactPanel.fullName.text,
               email:contactPanel.emailAddress.text});
      }
```

```
            private var contactProxy:ContactProxy;
    }
}
```

Creating Commands for View Access to Model Data

For our example, we will create commands as follows:

- Initialize the application: `ApplicationStartupCommand`

- Register the `ContactProxy` and initiate the first data call: `ModelInitCommand` and `ViewInitCommand`

- Execute basic create, read, update, and delete (CRUD) functions for the application: `AddContactCommand`, `DeleteContactCommand`, `UpdateContactCommand`, and `SelectContactCommand`

The `ApplicationStartupCommand` is shown in Listing 7-8. Notice that it extends `MacroCommand`, which allows you to sequentially execute multiple subcommands. In this case, the overridden function `initializeMacroCommand()` will add two subcommands: `ModelInitCommand` and `ViewInitCommand`. By sequentially creating these subcommands, we can control how the application is initialized and ensure the view is completely finished rendering before we attempt to push data to it.

Listing 7-8. *ApplicationStartupCommand That Initializes the View and Model (ApplicationStartupCommand.as)*

```
package com.af.cep.controller
{
    import org.puremvc.as3.patterns.command.*;
    import org.puremvc.as3.interfaces.*;

    public class ApplicationStartupCommand extends MacroCommand
    {
        override protected function initializeMacroCommand() :void
        {
            addSubCommand( ModelInitCommand );
            addSubCommand( ViewInitCommand );
        }
    }
}
```

The `ModelInitCommand`, shown in Listing 7-9, is responsible for registering the `ContactProxy` with the model, which is accessible through the `ApplicationFacade`. All commands are implemented by overriding the public `execute()` function.

Listing 7-9. *ModelInitCommand.as*

```
package com.af.cep.controller
{
    import org.puremvc.as3.interfaces.*;
    import org.puremvc.as3.patterns.command.*;
    import org.puremvc.as3.patterns.observer.*;

    import com.af.cep.*;
    import com.af.cep.model.*;

    public class ModelInitCommand extends SimpleCommand
    {
        override public function execute( note:INotification ) :void
        {
            facade.registerProxy(new ContactProxy());
        }
    }
}
```

In Listing 7-10, you can see that the ViewInitCommand implements the execute() function. A STARTUP notification with a reference to the associated view component is sent by the main application from the sendNotification() method in the ApplicationFacade at application startup. This reference to the view component is used to register the ApplicationMediator using the reference on the notification's body. The ApplicationMediator will then register all mediators that need to be created. The last item of interest in the ViewInitCommand is the notification that is sent via the ApplicationFacade to get all contacts.

Listing 7-10. *ViewInitCommand.as*

```
package com.af.cep.controller
{
    import com.af.cep.*;
    import com.af.cep.model.*;
    import com.af.cep.view.ApplicationMediator;

    import org.puremvc.as3.interfaces.*;
    import org.puremvc.as3.patterns.command.*;
    import org.puremvc.as3.patterns.observer.*;

    public class ViewInitCommand extends SimpleCommand
    {
        override public function execute( notification:INotification ) :void
        {
            facade.registerMediator( new ApplicationMediator(
                notification.getBody() ) );
```

```
                    var contactProxy:ContactProxy = facade.retrieveProxy(
                        ContactProxy.NAME ) as ContactProxy;
                    contactProxy.getContacts();

                    sendNotification( ApplicationFacade.GET_CONTACTS );
                }
            }
    }
```

The AddContactCommand, DeleteContactCommand, UpdateContactCommand, and
SelectContactCommand commands, shown in Listings 7-11 through 7-14, are used to execute
basic CRUD functions for the application. The commands are registered in the ApplicationFacade
using the PureMVC registerCommand() method.

Listing 7-11. *AddContactCommand.as*

```
package com.af.cep.controller
{
        import com.af.cep.ApplicationFacade;
        import com.af.cep.model.ContactProxy;
        import com.af.cep.model.vo.ContactVO;
        import com.af.cep.view.ContactsMediator;

        import org.puremvc.as3.interfaces.INotification;
        import org.puremvc.as3.patterns.command.SimpleCommand;

        public class AddContactCommand2 extends SimpleCommand
        {
            override public function execute(notification:INotification):void
            {
                var noteBody:Object = notification.getBody();
                var contactProxy:ContactProxy =
                    ContactProxy(facade.retrieveProxy(ContactProxy.NAME));

                contactProxy.contact = new ContactVO();
                contactProxy.contact.contact_id =
                        contactProxy.contactListDP.length+1;
                contactProxy.contact.name = noteBody.name;
                contactProxy.contact.email = noteBody.email;
                contactProxy.addContact();
            }
        }
}
```

Listing 7-12. *DeleteContactCommand.as*

```
package com.af.cep.controller
{
    import com.af.cep.model.ContactProxy;

    import org.puremvc.as3.interfaces.INotification;
    import org.puremvc.as3.patterns.command.SimpleCommand;

    public class DeleteContactCommand extends SimpleCommand
    {
        override public function execute(notification:INotification):void
        {
            var contactProxy:ContactProxy =
                ContactProxy(facade.retrieveProxy(ContactProxy.NAME));

            contactProxy.deleteContact();
        }
    }
}
```

Listing 7-13. *UpdateContactCommand.as*

```
package com.af.cep.controller
{
    import com.af.cep.model.ContactProxy;
    import com.af.cep.view.ContactsMediator;

    import org.puremvc.as3.interfaces.INotification;
    import org.puremvc.as3.patterns.command.SimpleCommand;

    public class UpdateContactCommand extends SimpleCommand
    {
        override public function execute(notification:INotification):void
        {
            var noteBody:Object = notification.getBody();
            var contactProxy:ContactProxy =
                ContactProxy(facade.retrieveProxy(ContactProxy.NAME));
            var contactsMediator:ContactsMediator =
                ContactsMediator(facade.retrieveMediator(
                    ContactsMediator.NAME));
            contactProxy.contact.name = noteBody.name;
            contactProxy.contact.email = noteBody.email;
            contactProxy.updateContact();

            contactsMediator.clearFormItems();
        }
    }
}
```

Listing 7-14. *SelectContactCommand.as*

```
package com.af.cep.controller
{
      import com.af.cep.model.ContactProxy;
      import com.af.cep.model.vo.ContactVO;

      import org.puremvc.as3.interfaces.INotification;
      import org.puremvc.as3.patterns.command.SimpleCommand;

      public class SelectContactCommand extends SimpleCommand
      {
            override public function execute(notification:INotification):void
            {
                  var noteBody:Object = notification.getBody();
                  var contactProxy:ContactProxy =
                        ContactProxy(facade.retrieveProxy(ContactProxy.NAME));
                  contactProxy.contact = new ContactVO();
                  contactProxy.contact.contact_id = noteBody.contact_id;
                  contactProxy.contact.name = noteBody.name;
                  contactProxy.contact.email = noteBody.email;
            }
      }
}
```

Building the ApplicationFacade for Model, View, and Controller Communication

The ApplicationFacade, shown in Listing 7-15, is a single point of contact for mediators, proxies, and commands to interact with each other while being abstracted from the model, view, and controller. It needs to be created only one time for the entire application. This concrete Facade is a subclass used to define notification constants that will be leveraged throughout the model, view, and controller, as well as creating mappings with commands to notifications.

Listing 7-15. *ApplicationFacade That Implements the Model, View, and Controller (ApplicationFacade.as)*

```
package com.af.cep
{
      import com.af.cep.controller.*;
      import com.af.cep.model.*;
      import com.af.cep.view.*;

      import org.puremvc.as3.interfaces.*;
      import org.puremvc.as3.patterns.facade.*;
      import org.puremvc.as3.patterns.proxy.*;
```

```
public class ApplicationFacade extends Facade
{
    public static const STARTUP:String = "startup";
    public static const SHUTDOWN:String = "shutdown";

    public static const LOAD_CONTACTS_SUCCESS:String =
        "loadContactsSuccess";
    public static const LOAD_CONTACTS_FAILED:String =
        "loadContactsFailed";

    public static const GET_CONTACTS:String = "getContacts";
    public static const ADD_CONTACT:String = "addContact";
    public static const UPDATE_CONTACT:String = "updateContact";
    public static const DELETE_CONTACT:String = "deleteContact";
    public static const SELECTED_CONTACT:String = "selectedContact";

    public static function getInstance() : ApplicationFacade
    {
        if (instance == null) instance = new ApplicationFacade();
            return instance as ApplicationFacade;
    }
    override protected function initializeController() : void
    {
        super.initializeController();
        registerCommand(STARTUP, ApplicationStartupCommand );
        registerCommand(SELECTED_CONTACT, SelectContactCommand);
        registerCommand(ADD_CONTACT, AddContactCommand);
        registerCommand(UPDATE_CONTACT, UpdateContactCommand);
        registerCommand(DELETE_CONTACT, DeleteContactCommand);
    }
    public function startup(app:PureMVCExample):void
    {
        sendNotification(STARTUP, app);
    }
}
}
```

Adding Events to the View

As you have seen in the ViewInitCommand (Listing 7-10), we created a ContactProxy to call the getContacts() service. This was handled at the startup of the application. The result was the population of the dgContact DataGrid in the ContactPanel with a list of contacts.

To add, delete, and update contacts, we need to dispatch events upon the click user gestures for those actions. Listing 7-16 shows the ContactPanel code with the click events, as well as the entire layout for this application.

Listing 7-16. *MXML View for the ContactPanel in PureMVC (PureMVCExample.mxml)*

```
<?xml version="1.0" encoding="utf-8"?>
<mx:Canvas xmlns:mx="http://www.adobe.com/2006/mxml">

    <mx:Script>
        <![CDATA[
        import mx.validators.ValidationResult;
        import mx.controls.Alert;
        import mx.collections.ArrayCollection;

        import flash.net.*;
        import com.af.cep.*;

        public static const GET_CONTACTS:String = "getContacts";
        public static const ADD_CONTACT:String = "addContact";
        public static const UPDATE_CONTACT:String = "updateContact";
        public static const DELETE_CONTACT:String = "deleteContact";
        public static const SELECTED_CONTACT:String = "selectedContact";

        [Bindable]
        public var contacts : ArrayCollection;

        public function getContacts():void
        {
            dispatchEvent(new Event(GET_CONTACTS));
        }

        public function selectContact():void
        {
            if(dgContact.selectedItem != null)
            {
                fullName.text = dgContact.selectedItem.name;
                emailAddress.text = dgContact.selectedItem.email;
                dispatchEvent(new Event(SELECTED_CONTACT));
            }
        }

        public function addContact() : void
        {
            dispatchEvent(new Event(ADD_CONTACT));
        }
```

```
        public function deleteContact():void
        {
            if(dgContact.selectedItem != null)
            {
                dispatchEvent(new Event(DELETE_CONTACT));
             }
        }


        public function updateContact():void
        {
            if(dgContact.selectedItem != null)
            {
                dispatchEvent(new Event(UPDATE_CONTACT));
            }
        }


        public function clearFormItems():void
        {
            fullName.text = "";
            emailAddress.text = "";
        }


        public function navigateToAF(event:MouseEvent):void
        {
            var u:URLRequest = new URLRequest("http://www.appfoundation.com");
            navigateToURL(u,"_blank");
        }
        ]]>
</mx:Script>


<mx:Panel styleName="CustomPanelBlueGrey">
    <mx:Panel height="100%" styleName="CustomPanelBlueGreen">
        <mx:VBox height="100%">
            <mx:ApplicationControlBar x="2" y="2"
                paddingTop="0" paddingLeft="3" horizontalGap="0"
                width="100%" height="22"
                styleName="ApplicationControlBarBlack"
                cornerRadius="4">
                <mx:Image
                 source="assets/images/icon_halfArrowYellow.png"/>
                <mx:Label text="MY CONTACTS"
                    fontWeight="bold" color="white" fontSize="13" />
```

```
</mx:ApplicationControlBar>
<mx:HBox height="100%" styleName="greyFill">
    <mx:VBox>
        <mx:Form id="addcontactForm" width="100%">
            <mx:HBox width="100%"
                    horizontalAlign="left">
                    <mx:Text text="Maintain Contacts:"
                        fontSize="12"/>
            </mx:HBox>

            <mx:FormItem label="Name: " width="100%">
                <mx:TextInput id="fullName"
                    width="100%" color="black"/>
            </mx:FormItem>

            <mx:FormItem label="Email: " width="100%">
                <mx:TextInput id="emailAddress"
                    width="100%" color="black"/>
            </mx:FormItem>

            <mx:HBox width="100%"
                    horizontalAlign="right">
                    <mx:Button label="Add Contact"
                        click="addContact()" />
                    <mx:Button label="Update Contact"
                        click="updateContact()" />
                    <mx:Button label="Delete Contact"
                        click="deleteContact()" />
            </mx:HBox>
        </mx:Form>
    </mx:VBox>

    <mx:VRule height="100%" strokeColor="#DDDDDD"/>

    <mx:VBox paddingTop="15" paddingLeft="15"
            paddingRight="15" paddingBottom="15">
        <mx:Text text="Contact List:" fontSize="12"/>

        <mx:DataGrid id="dgContact"
                height="243" styleName="greyFill"
                change="selectContact()"
                click="selectContact()">
```

```
                              <mx:columns>
                                   <mx:DataGridColumn
                                       headerText="Name"
                                       dataField="name"/>
                                   <mx:DataGridColumn
                                       headerText="Email"
                                       dataField="email"/>
                              </mx:columns>
                         </mx:DataGrid>
                    </mx:VBox>
               </mx:HBox>
          </mx:VBox>
     </mx:Panel>
     <mx:HBox width="100%" >
          <mx:Image source="assets/images/icon_appFoundationSmall.png"
                    click="navigateToAF(event)"
                    alpha=".75" rollOverEffect="alphaFadeIn"
                    rollOutEffect="alphaFadeOut"
                    useHandCursor="true" buttonMode="true" mouseChildren="false"
                    toolTip="AppFoundation.com"/>
     </mx:HBox>
</mx:Panel>


<mx:Fade id="alphaFadeOut" duration="350" alphaFrom="1.0" alphaTo="0.75"/>
<mx:Fade id="alphaFadeIn"   duration="350" alphaFrom="0.75" alphaTo="1.0"/>
</mx:Canvas>
```

Listing 7-17 shows the main application source code, to give you a complete picture of the application. The main application instantiates an instance for the `ApplicationFacade` to be used as a single instance throughout the application.

Listing 7-17. *PureMVCExample.mxml Application*

```
<?xml version="1.0" encoding="utf-8"?>
<mx:Application
     xmlns:mx="http://www.adobe.com/2006/mxml"
     xmlns:viewcomponents="com.af.cep.view.viewcomponents.*"
     xmlns:mvc="com.af.cep.*"
     pageTitle="PureMVC Sample Project"
     horizontalAlign="center" verticalAlign="middle"
     creationComplete="facade.startup(this)">

     <mx:Script>
          <![CDATA[
          import com.af.cep.*;
```

```
        private var facade:ApplicationFacade = ApplicationFacade.getInstance();

    ]]>
  </mx:Script>

  <viewcomponents:ContactPanel id="contactPanel" />

</mx:Application>
```

Figure 7-3 shows the results of running the application. This completes the PureMVC example. We'll now turn our attention to Cairngorm, and demonstrate the use of that framework by re-creating the same contacts management application.

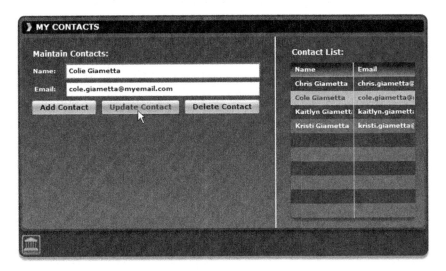

Figure 7-3. *Runtime results of the PureMVC and Cairngorm example applications*

Using Cairngorm

Cairngorm is an architectural framework that is essentially a collection of design patterns, including the MVC, front controller, and command patterns. It was originally developed by iteration::two, which was acquired by Macromedia in 2005. Macromedia is now part of Adobe, and Cairngorm is a piece of the Adobe Engagement Platform. Cairngorm is used as an event model to make and receive calls from the server. Cairngorm shines when you have more than one developer working on the same code base. This is the primary reason I have chosen Cairngorm as the de facto standard for Flex development for my company. Cairngorm has helped to tame the chaos associated with developing large-scale RIAs.

Cairngorm Components

Figure 7-4 illustrates the objects in the Cairngorm framework and their relationships.

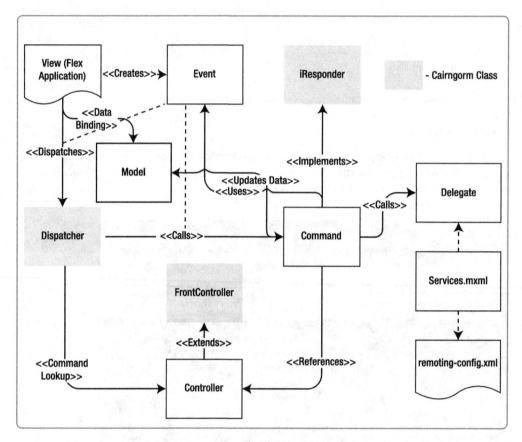

Figure 7-4. *Cairngorm object model*

The Cairngorm programming model is made of the following components:

Value object: The Cairngorm value object acts as a marker interface to help improve readability of code. The value object is nothing more than a mapping to your Spring beans. This object is used to help transform incoming object lists to map to Flex view objects, such as an <mx:Datagrid> dataProvider attribute.

Event: The event contains the type of object that will be processed when the event is dispatched. The event type is set by the initialization of the event. The controller listens for specific event types based on the event definition, and is tied to a corresponding command to execute when the event is triggered.

Front controller. The FrontController class binds events, triggered by user actions, to specified commands. That marriage of these two components allows Flex to detect user gestures and return data to the model.

Command: The command is responsible for initiating internal or external calls through the business delegate and is bound by the controller to an event. A command can interact within the application and doesn't require the IResponder interface to be set.

Business delegate: The delegate sets the responder that handles data returned as the result of a service call. In general, I try to match my delegates to my Spring service method implementations.

Service locator. The service locator is where you specify your RemoteObject, WebService, or HTTPService definitions.

Model locator. The model locator is used to instantiate the application's model and/or submodels. The model locator grants access to Flex data objects in which the command store results. The views for the application access these data objects through data binding to the model.

That should give you a high-level view of the framework components. Let's now take a closer look at the model in Cairngorm.

A model in a Cairngorm application is a global ActionScript singleton object that contains attributes ready for data binding. Components in views (MXML files) are bound to the attributes in these models.

Each individual view could contain a handle (a pointer or a variable) on the data used by components in that view. This would tightly couple the view to the specific data and the call to the server. It would also bind that data to that specific view. If another view needed the same data, it would either need to have a handle on the view or to get the data for itself.

To reduce the coupling between the view and data, a model is introduced to abstract the layers. The model holds the data used in the application. Different models contain different groups of data. To retrieve the correct model, a singleton class named ModelLocator is used. When a command processes the results of a call to the server, it puts the data returned in the proper model. Using a model to hold data, a view to format/display data, and a command to control the data in this way creates an MVC pattern within the Flex application.

Since the data for the Flex application is contained within models found by the model locator, multiple views can reference the same data. Views can also change how the data is formatted, without needing to modify the data or how it is retrieved from the server. Figure 7-5 illustrates the relationship between the model, view, and controller in Cairngorm.

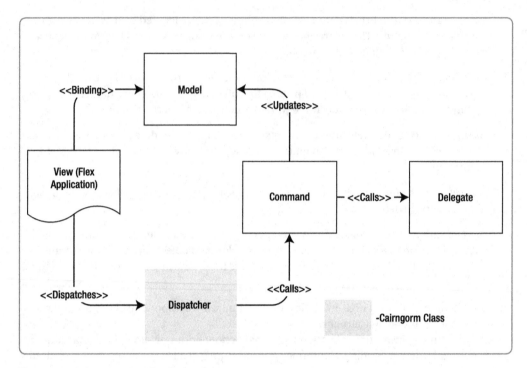

Figure 7-5. *Cairngorm MVC relationship*

Cairngorm Framework Implementation for Flex

The Cairngorm framework is an event pattern framework that allows for a consistent method of calling and handling faults and the return of data from the server. The method utilized for calling the server from Flex can be RemoteObject, WebService, or HTTPService calls (as discussed in Chapter 6). In most of the applications I have built, I have created RemoteObjects to work with Cairngorm service locators. RemoteObjects send binary data to the server, and that data is processed by the AMF gateway and serialized into value objects that Spring services use.

Once Cairngorm objects have been created to make a call, a view that needs data from the server just needs to code a few of steps to retrieve that data. The view creates an event specific to the type of call it wants to make. When it creates the event, it passes any parameters/variables required to the new event object. Finally, the view uses a Cairngorm object to dispatch the event, as in the following example of getting a list of contacts from the Spring service:

```
var event : GetContactsEvent = new GetContactsEvent();
CairngormEventDispatcher.getInstance().dispatchEvent( event );
```

The key to ensuring that the call to the server works properly is creating and setting up the call within the Cairngorm framework. There are seven basics steps to do so:

1. Ensure the (Java) service is defined in `WEB-INF\flex\remoting-config.xml`.

2. Ensure the service is defined in `Services.mxml`.

3. Create the delegate class to implement the Spring service method stubs.

4. Add the event/command association to the controller, and add the `addCommand()` method call that binds the event constant to the command object. You can add the event constant to the controller or to the event itself. It is up to you to determine what you like in this regard. Adding the event constant to the control will create a circular reference from the controller, to command, to event. Having all of the event constants in the controller does keep all event tags in one place, to ensure you do not duplicate event names or command-to-event mappings. I put the event constant in the event, which is what you will find in the Adobe examples as well.

5. Create the event classes.

6. Create the command classes.

7. Add the call to the view.

To demonstrate these steps, we will build the same Flex application we built using PureMVC: an application that manages a contact list and implements the CRUD aspects of a contact service.

Setting Up a Cairngorm Flex Project

Before you get started building the sample application, you need to download the Cairngorm library for our project. You will find the download files here:

`http://opensource.adobe.com/wiki/display/cairngorm/Downloads`

For the examples in the book, we will use Cairngorm 2.2.1. I suggest downloading the documents and source.

■**Note** You do not need Cairngorm Enterprise 2.2.1, unless you plan to use it in conjunction with LiveCycle Data Services. Download only the base Cairngorm installation.

Next, you need to get the Cairngorm library into your Flex project. Unzip the Cairngorm zip file and move the `Cairngorm.swc` file to your project's `libs` directory. If you're using Flex Builder, it should pick up the SWC when it is dropped into the `libs` directory. If not, open the project properties in Eclipse and add the library through the Library path tab under the Flex Build Path, as shown in Figure 7-6. After that is done, you are ready to start building a project with Cairngorm.

For our sample application, we will implement four events to manipulate data for the application: `AddContactEvent`, `DeleteContactEvent`, `GetContactsEvent`, and `UpdateContactEvent`. Each event has a corresponding command that is linked to the event via the controller. The delegate will hold the method invocations to the Spring service. For this example, we will not have persistence to an actual database. That will come in Chapter 8.

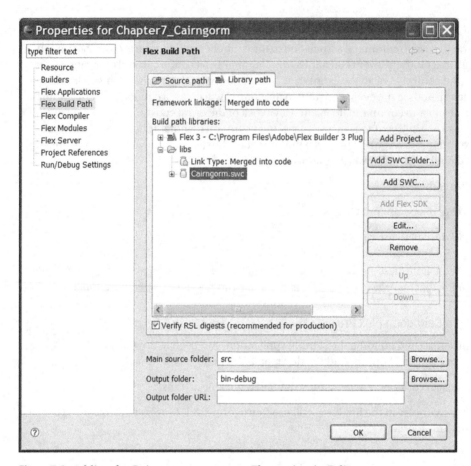

Figure 7-6. *Adding the Cairngorm.swc to your Flex project in Eclipse*

Configuring remoting-config.xml

The `remoting-config.xml` file contains references to the Spring services. Each service has an entry in the `remoting-config.xml` file that describes the handle the service will be called within Flex and the name of the service on the server. The file can be found in your BlazeDS server, located in `<tomcat-install-directory>`/webapps/blazeds/flex. Listing 7-18 shows the entry.

Listing 7-18. *RemoteObject Destination Entry in remoting-config.xml*

```
<destination id="contactService">
    <properties>
        <factory>spring</factory>
        <source>contactService</source>
    </properties>
</destination>
```

Configuring Services in Flex

The service must be defined in the Services.mxml file in the com/af/cep/services directory in the Flex project. This entry tells the Cairngorm framework which services will be used in the framework. It defines an id tag on the `<mx:RemoteObject>` that Cairngorm will use to reference a service and the destination defined in the remote-services.xml file that it references. Typically, the same name is used for both. Listing 7-19 shows the entry.

Listing 7-19. *Services Configuration for the ServiceLocator in Services.mxml*

```
<?xml version="1.0" encoding="utf-8"?>
<cairngorm:ServiceLocator
     xmlns:mx="http://www.adobe.com/2006/mxml"
     xmlns:cairngorm="com.adobe.cairngorm.business.*">

     <mx:RemoteObject
         id="contactService"
         destination="contactService"
         showBusyCursor="true">
     </mx:RemoteObject>

</cairngorm:ServiceLocator>
```

Creating the Models and Value Objects

To support the application data, you need to create a model for binding and value objects to create custom data types for the application to use. In the case of the contact example, we need a value object to hold contact attributes, with a model to hold contact data for the Flex application. Listings 7-20 and 7-21 show the code to support the application data in the form of a main model with one submodel for adding contacts. Listing 7-22 defines a contact value object that will be used throughout the application.

Listing 7-20. *Cairngorm Model Locator (ModelLocator.as)*

```
package com.af.cep.model
{
     import com.adobe.cairngorm.model.ModelLocator;
     import mx.collections.ArrayCollection;
     import mx.controls.DataGrid;
     import com.af.cep.vo.ContactVO;

     [Bindable]
     public class ModelLocator implements com.adobe.cairngorm.model.ModelLocator
     {
          private static var modelLocator : com.af.cep.model.ModelLocator;
```

```
                    public static function getInstance() : com.af.cep.model.ModelLocator
                    {
                        if ( modelLocator == null )
                            modelLocator = new com.af.cep.model.ModelLocator();

                        return modelLocator;
                    }

                    public function ModelLocator()
                    {
                        if ( com.af.cep.model.ModelLocator.modelLocator != null )
                        throw new Error( "Only one ModelLocator instance " +
                            "should be instantiated" );
                    }

                    public var addcontact : AddContact = new AddContact();
                    public var contacts : ArrayCollection = new ArrayCollection();
                    public var contactDG : DataGrid = new DataGrid;
                    public var contact : ContactVO = new ContactVO;
                }
        }
```

Listing 7-21. *Cairngorm Submodel (AddContact.as)*

```
package com.af.cep.model
{
        import com.af.cep.vo.ContactVO;

        public class AddContact
        {
            [Bindable]
            public var contactVO : ContactVO;
            [Bindable]
            public var isPending : Boolean;
            [Bindable]
            public var statusMessage : String;
        }
}
```

Listing 7-22. *Cairngorm Contact Value Object (ContactVO.as)*

```
package com.af.cep.vo
{
        import com.adobe.cairngorm.vo.ValueObject;

        [Bindable]
        [RemoteClass(alias="com.af.vms.domain.Contact")]
```

```
    [Bindable]
    public class ContactVO
    {
        public var contacts: Array;

        public var objectIdentifier: Number;
        public var name: String;
        public var email:String;
    }
}
```

Creating the Contact Delegate Class

We need a delegate class for each service. This class defines how Cairngorm makes the call to the service, with the specific method name and parameters. Within the delegate class, a method needs to be defined for each method call that will be made to the Spring service. This method calls the specific Spring service method with the parameters the method requires. Listing 7-23 shows an example of the contact delegate with each method defined to invoke the Spring service associated with it.

Listing 7-23. *Cairngorm Delegate Class to Invoke Back-End Services*

```
package com.af.cep.model.business
{
    import mx.rpc.IResponder;
    import mx.rpc.events.FaultEvent;
    import com.adobe.cairngorm.business.Responder;
    import com.adobe.cairngorm.business.ServiceLocator;
    import com.af.cep.vo.ContactVO;
    import mx.rpc.AsyncToken;
    import mx.rpc.events.ResultEvent;

    public class ContactDelegate
    {
        private var responder : IResponder;
        private var service : Object;

        public function ContactDelegate( responder : IResponder )
        {
            this.service = ServiceLocator.getInstance().getService(
                "contactService" );
            this.responder = responder;
        }
        public function addContact( contactVO : ContactVO ): void
        {
            var call:AsyncToken = service.insertContact(contactVO);
             call.addResponder( responder );
        }
```

```
        public function updateContact( contactVO : ContactVO ): void
        {
            var call:AsyncToken = service.updateContact(contactVO);
             call.addResponder( responder );
        }
        public function deleteContact( contactVO : ContactVO ): void
        {
            var call:AsyncToken = service.deleteContact(
                 contactVO.objectIdentifier);
            call.addResponder( responder );
        }
        public function getContacts(): void
        {
            var call:AsyncToken = service.getContacts();
             call.addResponder( responder );
        }
    }
}
```

Adding Events and Commands to the Controller

The event and the command that the event uses to issue the call to the server must be associ-ated with each other. This is done within the Event class itself.

First, we need to define a constant in the event for the Cairngorm framework to use. The value of the string constant is arbitrary, but it must be unique to the application. Here is an example of the constant entry:

```
public static const EVENT_GET_CONTACTS:String = "get_contacts";
```

The controller has the code that adds all available commands to the Cairngorm framework. The addCommand() method call adds the command to the system, associating it with an event constant. This makes the command object accessible to the controller object. The following is an example of that call:

```
addCommand(GetContactsEvent.EVENT_GET_CONTACTS, GetContactsCommand);
```

Listing 7-24 shows the complete view of the controller class for the contact application example.

Listing 7-24. *Cairngorm Controller Event-to-Command Mappings and Constants*

```
package com.af.cep.control
{
    import com.adobe.cairngorm.control.FrontController;
    import com.af.cep.commands.*;
    import com.af.cep.commands.events.AddContactEvent;
    import com.af.cep.commands.events.DeleteContactEvent;
    import com.af.cep.commands.events.GetContactsEvent;
    import com.af.cep.commands.events.UpdateContactEvent;
```

```
public class ContactController extends FrontController
{
     public function ContactController()
     {
     addCommand( AddContactEvent.EVENT_ADD_CONTACT, AddContactCommand );
     addCommand( GetContactsEvent.EVENT_GET_CONTACTS, GetContactsCommand );
     addCommand( UpdateContactEvent.EVENT_UPDATE_CONTACT,
          UpdateContactCommand );
     addCommand( DeleteContactEvent.EVENT_DELETE_CONTACT,
          DeleteContactCommand );
     }
}
}
```

Creating the Cairngorm Events

Next, we must create event classes for each service call the application needs to make. In this case, four events that represent basic CRUD calls will be created. The events will contain parameters that need to be populated with data required by server-side methods. This class associates itself with the event constant, telling Cairngorm which type of event object this is, so that Cairngorm can call the associated command object. The event object also contains any parameters required for the command to execute a service call. If the service call does not require any parameters, then the event object does not contain any. Listings 7-25 through 7-28 show examples of the events we need for the application.

Listing 7-25. *Cairngorm Event for Adding a Contact (AddContactEvent.as)*

```
package com.af.cep.commands.events
{
     import com.adobe.cairngorm.control.CairngormEvent;
     import com.af.cep.vo.ContactVO;
     import com.af.cep.control.ContactController;

     public class AddContactEvent extends CairngormEvent
     {
          public static const EVENT_ADD_CONTACT : String = "addContact";
          public var contactVO : ContactVO;

          public function AddContactEvent( contactVO : ContactVO )
          {
               super( ContactController.EVENT_ADD_CONTACT );
               this.contactVO = contactVO;
          }
     }
}
```

Listing 7-26. *Cairngorm Event for Deleting a Contact (DeleteContactEvent.as)*

```
package com.af.cep.commands.events
{
    import com.adobe.cairngorm.control.CairngormEvent;
    import com.af.cep.vo.ContactVO;
    import com.af.cep.control.ContactController;

    public class DeleteContactEvent extends CairngormEvent
    {
        public static const EVENT_DELETE_CONTACT : String = "deleteContact";
        public var contactVO : ContactVO;

        public function DeleteContactEvent( contactVO : ContactVO )
        {
            super( EVENT_DELETE_CONTACT );
            this.contactVO = contactVO;
        }
    }
}
```

Listing 7-27. *Cairngorm Event for Getting a Contact (GetContactsEvent.as)*

```
package com.af.cep.commands.events
{
    import com.adobe.cairngorm.control.CairngormEvent;
    import com.af.cep.vo.ContactVO;
    import com.af.cep.control.ContactController;

    public class GetContactsEvent extends CairngormEvent
    {
        public static const EVENT_GET_CONTACTS : String = "getContacts";
        public function GetContactsEvent()
        {
            super(EVENT_GET_CONTACTS );
        }
    }
}
```

Listing 7-28. *Cairngorm Event for Updating a Contact (UpdateContactEvent.as)*

```
package com.af.cep.commands.events
{
    import com.adobe.cairngorm.control.CairngormEvent;
    import com.af.cep.vo.ContactVO;
    import com.af.cep.control.ContactController;
```

```
public class UpdateContactEvent extends CairngormEvent
{
        public static const EVENT_UPDATE_CONTACT : String = "updateContact";
        public var contactVO : ContactVO;

        public function UpdateContactEvent( contactVO : ContactVO )
        {
                super( EVENT_UPDATE_CONTACT );
                this.contactVO = contactVO;
        }
}
}
```

Creating the Cairngorm Commands

The command class is an object that Cairngorm uses to process user gestures in the Flex application. It is most commonly used to invoke server-side methods through a business delegate. It is also used to manipulate the application state and data through the implementation of business logic in this layer of Cairngorm. A command contains three methods:

- execute(): Calls the delegate to make the service call

- result(): Defines how to handle the results that come back from the server

- fault(): Defines what to do if an error occurs

Examples of these three methods for the four events we have defined are shown in Listings 7-29 through 7-32.

Listing 7-29. *Cairngorm Command for Adding a Contact (AddContactCommand.as)*

```
package com.af.cep.commands
{
    import mx.rpc.events.ResultEvent;
    import mx.rpc.IResponder;

    import com.adobe.cairngorm.business.Responder;
    import com.adobe.cairngorm.commands.Command;
    import com.adobe.cairngorm.control.CairngormEvent;

    import com.af.cep.model.business.ContactDelegate;
    import com.af.cep.commands.events.AddContactEvent;
    import com.af.cep.model.ModelLocator;
    import com.af.cep.vo.ContactVO;

    public class AddContactCommand implements Command, IResponder
    {
        private var model : ModelLocator = ModelLocator.getInstance();
```

```
public function execute( event : CairngormEvent ) : void
{
    model.addcontact.isPending = true;

    var delegate : ContactDelegate = new ContactDelegate( this );
    var addcontactEvent : AddContactEvent = AddContactEvent( event );
    delegate.addContact( addcontactEvent.contactVO );
}

public function result( data:Object ) : void
{
    var event:ResultEvent = data as ResultEvent;

    model.addcontact.isPending = false;
    model.contacts.addItem(model.addcontact.contactVO);
}
public function fault( info:Object ) : void
{
    model.addcontact.statusMessage = "Could not send contact " +
        "information to the server.";
    model.addcontact.isPending = false;
}
    }
}
```

Listing 7-30. *Cairngorm Command for Deleting a Contact (DeleteContactCommand.as)*

```
package com.af.cep.commands
{
    import mx.rpc.events.ResultEvent;
    import mx.rpc.IResponder;
    import mx.collections.ArrayCollection;

    import com.adobe.cairngorm.business.Responder;
    import com.adobe.cairngorm.commands.Command;
    import com.adobe.cairngorm.control.CairngormEvent;

    import com.af.cep.model.business.ContactDelegate;
    import com.af.cep.commands.events.DeleteContactEvent;
    import com.af.cep.model.ModelLocator;
    import com.af.cep.vo.ContactVO;

    public class DeleteContactCommand implements Command, IResponder
    {
        private var model : ModelLocator = ModelLocator.getInstance();
```

```
        public function execute( event : CairngormEvent ) : void
        {
            model.addcontact.isPending = true;

            var delegate : ContactDelegate = new ContactDelegate( this );
            var deleteContactEvent : DeleteContactEvent =
                DeleteContactEvent( event );
            delegate.deleteContact( deleteContactEvent.contactVO );
        }
        public function result( data:Object ) : void
        {
            var event:ResultEvent = data as ResultEvent;
            model.addcontact.isPending = false;
             (model.contactDG.dataProvider as
                ArrayCollection).removeItemAt(model.contactDG.selectedIndex);
        }
        public function fault( info:Object ) : void
        {
            model.addcontact.statusMessage = "Could not send contact " +
                "information to the server.";
            model.addcontact.isPending = false;
        }
    }
}
```

Listing 7-31. *Cairngorm Commands for Getting a Contact (GetContactsCommand.as)*

```
package com.af.cep.commands
{
    import mx.rpc.events.ResultEvent;
    import mx.rpc.IResponder;
    import mx.collections.ArrayCollection;

    import com.adobe.cairngorm.business.Responder;
    import com.adobe.cairngorm.commands.Command;
    import com.adobe.cairngorm.control.CairngormEvent;

    import com.af.cep.model.business.ContactDelegate;
    import com.af.cep.commands.events.GetContactsEvent;
    import com.af.cep.model.ModelLocator;
    import com.af.cep.vo.ContactVO;

    public class GetContactsCommand implements Command, IResponder
    {
        private var model : ModelLocator = ModelLocator.getInstance();
```

```
        public function execute( event : CairngormEvent ) : void
        {
            model.addcontact.isPending = true;
            var delegate : ContactDelegate = new ContactDelegate( this );
            var getContactsEvent : GetContactsEvent =
                    GetContactsEvent( event );
            delegate.getContacts();
        }
        public function result( data:Object ) : void
        {
            var event:ResultEvent = data as ResultEvent;
            model.addcontact.isPending = false;
            model.contacts = ArrayCollection(event.result);
        }
        public function fault( info:Object ) : void
        {
            model.addcontact.statusMessage = "Could not send contact " +
                    "information to the server.";
            model.addcontact.isPending = false;
        }
    }
}
```

Listing 7-32. *Cairngorm Command for Updating a Contact (UpdateContactCommand.as)*

```
package com.af.cep.commands
{
    import mx.rpc.events.ResultEvent;
    import mx.rpc.IResponder;
    import mx.collections.ArrayCollection;

    import com.adobe.cairngorm.business.Responder;
    import com.adobe.cairngorm.commands.Command;
    import com.adobe.cairngorm.control.CairngormEvent;

    import com.af.cep.model.business.ContactDelegate;
    import com.af.cep.commands.events.UpdateContactEvent;
    import com.af.cep.model.ModelLocator;
    import com.af.cep.vo.ContactVO;

    public class UpdateContactCommand implements Command, IResponder
    {
        private var model : ModelLocator = ModelLocator.getInstance();
```

```
        public function execute( event : CairngormEvent ) : void
        {
            model.addcontact.isPending = true;
            var delegate : ContactDelegate = new ContactDelegate( this );
            var updateContactEvent : UpdateContactEvent =
                UpdateContactEvent( event );
            delegate.updateContact( updateContactEvent.contactVO );
        }
        public function result( data:Object ) : void
        {
            var event:ResultEvent = data as ResultEvent;
            model.addcontact.isPending = false;
              (model.contactDG.dataProvider as ArrayCollection).setItemAt(
                    model.contact, model.contactDG.selectedIndex);
        }
        public function fault( info:Object ) : void
        {
            model.addcontact.statusMessage = "Could not send contact " +
                "information to the server.";
            model.addcontact.isPending = false;
        }
    }
}
```

Adding the Calls to the View

The final step is to add the actual call to the Flex view that dispatches these events. To better decouple the view, we will break out the view components from the main application container. The main application container, located at the root of your Flex project, should contain only the main application setup parameters and components. This application is small and has only a few containers to display the data. Listing 7-33 shows the source code for the Flex application, and Listing 7-34 shows the associated ContactPanel.mxml file.

Listing 7-33. *Main Cairngorm Application (CairngormExample.mxml)*

```
<?xml version="1.0" encoding="utf-8"?>
<mx:Application
    xmlns:mx="http://www.adobe.com/2006/mxml"
    xmlns:services="com.af.cep.services.*"
    xmlns:control="com.af.cep.control.*"
    xmlns:view="com.af.cep.view.*"
    pageTitle="Cairngorm Sample Project"
    horizontalAlign="center" verticalAlign="middle">
```

```
<!-- ======================================================================= -->
    <!-- the ServiceLocator where we specify the remote services -->
    <services:Services id="addcontactServices"/>

    <!-- the FrontController, containing Commands specific to this application -->
    <control:ContactController id="controller"/>
<!-- ======================================================================= -->


    <view:ContactPanel id="addcontactPanel" />

</mx:Application>
```

Listing 7-34. *The ContactPanel in Cairngorm (ContactPanel.mxml)*

```
<?xml version="1.0" encoding="utf-8"?>
<mx:Canvas
    xmlns:mx="http://www.adobe.com/2006/mxml"
    xmlns:view="com.appfoundation.cep.view.*"
    initialize="initComp()">

    <mx:Script>
        <![CDATA[
                import mx.validators.ValidationResult;
                import mx.collections.ArrayCollection;

                import flash.net.*;

                import com.adobe.cairngorm.control.CairngormEventDispatcher;

                import com.af.cep.commands.events.*;
                import com.af.cep.model.AddContact;
                import com.af.cep.vo.ContactVO;
                import com.af.cep.model.ModelLocator;

                [Bindable]
                public var model : ModelLocator = ModelLocator.getInstance();

                [Bindable]
                public var addcontact : AddContact;

                [Bindable]
                public var contacts : ArrayCollection;
```

```
private function initComp():void
{
     // Get a list of contacts from the Spring services.
     var event : GetContactsEvent = new GetContactsEvent();
     CairngormEventDispatcher.getInstance().dispatchEvent(
          event );
}
public function selectContact():void
{
     if(dgContact.selectedItem != null)
     {
          fullName.text = dgContact.selectedItem.name;
          emailAddress.text = dgContact.selectedItem.email;
     }
}
public function addContact() : void
{
     // Bind to the addcontact model
     addcontact = model.addcontact;
     var contactVO : ContactVO = new ContactVO();
     contactVO.name = fullName.text;
     contactVO.email = emailAddress.text;

     // Bind the new contact to the contactVO model object
     model.addcontact.contactVO = contactVO;

     var event : AddContactEvent = new AddContactEvent(
          contactVO );
     CairngormEventDispatcher.getInstance().dispatchEvent(
          event );

     clearFormItems();
}
public function deleteContact():void
{
     if(dgContact.selectedItem != null)
     {
          var contactVO : ContactVO = new ContactVO();
          contactVO = ContactVO(dgContact.selectedItem);

          var event : DeleteContactEvent =
               new DeleteContactEvent( contactVO );
          CairngormEventDispatcher.getInstance().dispatchEvent(
               event );

          clearFormItems();
     }
}
```

```
            public function updateContact():void
            {
                    if(dgContact.selectedItem != null)
                    {
                            // bind to the addcontact model
                            addcontact = model.addcontact;
                            var contactVO : ContactVO = new ContactVO();
                            contactVO.name = fullName.text;
                            contactVO.email = emailAddress.text;
                            contactVO.objectIdentifier =
                                    dgContact.selectedItem.objectIdentifier;

                            var event : UpdateContactEvent =
                                    new UpdateContactEvent( contactVO );
                            CairngormEventDispatcher.getInstance().dispatchEvent(
                                    event );

                            model.contact = contactVO;
                            clearFormItems();
                    }
            }
            public function clearFormItems():void
            {
                    fullName.text = "";
                    emailAddress.text = "";
            }
            public function navigateToAF(event:MouseEvent):void
            {
                    var u:URLRequest =
                            new URLRequest("http://www.appfoundation.com");
                    navigateToURL(u,"_blank");
            }
        ]]>
    </mx:Script>

    <mx:Binding source="model.contacts" destination="dgContact.dataProvider" />

    <mx:Panel styleName="CustomPanelBlueGrey">
        <mx:Panel height="100%" styleName="CustomPanelBlueGreen">
            <mx:VBox height="100%">
                    <mx:ApplicationControlBar x="2" y="2" paddingTop="0"
                            paddingLeft="3" horizontalGap="0"
                            width="100%" height="22"
                            styleName="ApplicationControlBarBlack"
                            cornerRadius="4">
```

```
    <mx:Image
        source="assets/images/icon_halfArrowYellow.png"/>
    <mx:Label text="MY CONTACTS" fontWeight="bold"
            color="white" fontSize="13" />
</mx:ApplicationControlBar>
<mx:HBox height="100%" styleName="greyFill">
    <mx:VBox>
        <mx:Form id="addcontactForm" width="100%">
            <mx:HBox width="100%"
                    horizontalAlign="left">
                    <mx:Text text="Maintain Contacts:"
                            fontSize="12"/>
            </mx:HBox>

            <mx:FormItem label="Name: " width="100%">
                    <mx:TextInput id="fullName"
                            width="100%" color="black"/>
            </mx:FormItem>

            <mx:FormItem label="Email: " width="100%">
                    <mx:TextInput id="emailAddress"
                            width="100%" color="black"/>
            </mx:FormItem>

            <mx:HBox width="100%"
                    horizontalAlign="right">
                    <mx:Button label="Add Contact"
                     enabled="{ !addcontact.isPending }"
                     click="addContact()" />
                    <mx:Button label="Update Contact"
                     enabled="{ !addcontact.isPending }"
                     click="updateContact()" />
                    <mx:Button label="Delete Contact"
                     enabled="{ !addcontact.isPending }"
                     click="deleteContact()" />
            </mx:HBox>
        </mx:Form>
    </mx:VBox>

    <mx:VRule height="100%" strokeColor="#DDDDDD"/>

    <mx:VBox paddingTop="15" paddingLeft="15"
        paddingRight="15" paddingBottom="15">
        <mx:Text text="Contact List:" fontSize="12"/>
```

```
                                <mx:DataGrid id="dgContact" height="243"
                                        styleName="greyFill"
                                        change="selectContact()"
                                        click="selectContact()">
                                    <mx:columns>
                                            <mx:DataGridColumn
                                                    headerText="Name"
                                                    dataField="name"/>
                                            <mx:DataGridColumn
                                                    headerText="Email"
                                                    dataField="email"/>
                                    </mx:columns>
                                </mx:DataGrid>
                            </mx:VBox>
                        </mx:HBox>
                    </mx:VBox>
            </mx:Panel>
            <mx:HBox width="100%" >
                    <mx:Image source="assets/images/icon_appFoundationSmall.png"
                            click="navigateToAF(event)"
                            alpha=".75" rollOverEffect="alphaFadeIn"
                            rollOutEffect="alphaFadeOut"
                            toolTip="AppFoundation.com"/>
            </mx:HBox>
        </mx:Panel>

        <mx:Fade id="alphaFadeOut" duration="350" alphaFrom="1.0" alphaTo="0.75"/>
        <mx:Fade id="alphaFadeIn"  duration="350" alphaFrom="0.75" alphaTo="1.0"/>
</mx:Canvas>
```

The Cairngorm application has exactly the same look and feel as the PureMVC example we created earlier in this chapter (see Figure 7-3).

Summary

In this chapter, we looked at the top two frameworks used to build Flex applications. Both Cairngorm and PureMVC add value when developing applications with multiple developers. These frameworks organize the project well and help with maintaining the project when it is completed. Of course, you do not need to have a development framework to build Flex applications. However, I strongly suggest that you consider using one on medium- to large-scale applications. If you are creating applications with only one view and very little code, for example, using a development framework may be overkill. Still, you might want to consider a solution that creates a consistent environment in which to work.

Both the PureMVC and Cairngorm frameworks are solid for enterprise development of Flex applications. The reasons for using one over the other are insignificant, as both are very viable solutions for getting the job done well. The following are some of the differences between these two frameworks:

- In PureMVC, you do not do data binding between the model and views. as you do in Cairngorm. You can bind data from mediators to views, which would create tight coupling between the two layers. PureMVC requires mediators to directly manipulate the view, whereas Cairngorm holds the data elements on the model, which is globally accessed.

- Cairngorm has a service locator to separate your RemoteObject, WebService, and HTTPService definitions, which are then used in the delegate. PureMVC has you define them in the delegate or multiple delegates. Technically, you could create a singleton in PureMVC to act as a service locator if you were inclined to do so.

- With PureMVC, views require mediators to push data updates to the view. Cairngorm has the view binding to a model.

The one big weakness in Cairngorm is where PureMVC shines. Cairngorm has no built-in observer or notification system. When data is returned to a Cairngorm command, it has no way to invoke state changes on the view. PureMVC's notifications do exactly that. They invoke changes to the state of the view by notifying the view component's proxy that changes need to occur. To address this weakness in Cairngorm, you can create an observer for your application or use Flash events.

In the next chapter, we will take a detailed look at data persistence for Flex and Spring applications, including using ORM technologies within the Spring application.

CHAPTER 8

■ ■ ■

Data Persistence

We have covered how to transport data to and from Flex views with Spring beans through the RemoteObject, WebService, and HTTPService protocols. We also looked at how Flex developer frameworks such as Cairngorm and PureMVC aid in the movement of data. Now we need to integrate Spring with a data source using JDBC and ORM tools in the Spring DAO layer.

In this chapter, you will learn how to persist data in databases. This chapter will serve as an introduction to popular database connectivity frameworks integrated with the Spring Framework. It will also introduce database transaction management with Spring transactions.

The purpose of using JDBC or an ORM component is to provide APIs through which you can execute SQL statements against a database. Both JDBC and ORM components in Spring allow you to call the basic CRUD functions to create, read, update, and delete data from relational databases.

After completing this chapter, you will be able to use a DAO framework in Spring to access data and expose that data to Flex applications.

Spring Database Transaction Management

The Spring Framework provides a layer of abstraction for transaction management to allow you to consistently program across different transaction APIs, such as JDBC, Hibernate, JPA, and Java Data Objects (JDO). Spring provides support for both programmatic and declarative transaction management, as does EJB. However, EJB requires coupling with a Java Transaction API (JTA) that handles callbacks. Spring, on the other hand, does not require a JTA implementation (although it's possible to use one). It provides a callback mechanism that abstracts away the transaction management of the actual implementation from your code.

I'm not going to go into a trite monologue of how transactions relate to some real-world action. Simply put, transaction management in Spring presents a transaction as an action that is either successful or fails, and is fully rolled back as if it never happened. Transactions play a pivotal role in Spring, ensuring that data integrity is maintained and never left in a corrupted state. Without them, there is a chance that business logic cannot be properly executed due to data being out of sync with the logic.

Before we jump into some transaction examples in Spring, we need to look at the four transaction descriptions that make up ACID:

Atomic: Transactions are a combination of actions that make up a transaction. Atomicity ensures that either all parts of a transaction are successful or it is fully rolled back. If there is a failure, the database acts like the entire transaction never occurred.

Consistent: The state of the system will always stay the same, regardless of whether the transaction was successful or failed, and the data should never be corrupted from a failed transaction. If the transaction violates the database's consistency rules, then it should be rolled back.

Isolated: The effects of one transaction should be isolated from other transactions so that data that is modified by one transaction does not cause data to be returned in a state of flux to another transaction. Since transactions can occur concurrently, concurrent reads and writes to the same data should not be allowed.

Durable: The state of the data will be permanent once the transaction has completed. This involves storing the data in some form of persistent storage and ensuring that the data cannot be modified if there is a system outage.

Spring Transaction Managers

Spring provides transaction managers that delegate work to platform-specific transaction implementations through either JTA or the transaction manager's framework; Spring does not manage transactions directly. Spring provides transaction managers for J2EE Connector Architecture (JCA), JDBC, JMS, Hibernate, JDO, JPA, TopLink, and others.

Spring's transaction managers are tailored to the specific persistence solution you decide to use. To use transactions in Spring, you will need to define a transaction manager bean in your application context.

JDBC and iBATIS Transactions

The most basic transaction manager is the DataSourceTransactionManager, which provides support for JDBC and iBATIS transactions. iBATIS is a persistence framework that allows you to map SQL to Java objects. You will want to wire the manager into your application using the following <bean> tag in your applicationContext.xml file:

```
<bean id="transactionManager"
      class="org.springframework.jdbc.datasource.DataSourceTransactionManager">
      <property name="dataSource"><ref local="dataSource"/></property>
</bean>
```

The property dataSource references a local bean in your applicationContext.xml named dataSource. The dataSource bean can be either an org.springframework.jdbc.dataSource or org.apache.commons.dbcp.BasicDataSource, depending on your preference. Listing 8-1 shows an example of using org.apache.commons.dbcp.BasicDataSource, and Listing 8-2 (later in the chapter) uses org.springframework.jdbc.dataSource, for a JDBC data source.

Listing 8-1. *JDBC DriverManagerDataSource Bean*

```
<bean id="dataSource" class="org.apache.commons.jdbc.DriverManagerDataSource">
    <property name="driverClassName">
        <value>${jdbc.driverClassName}</value>
    </property>
    <property name="url">
        <value>${jdbc.url}</value>
    </property>
    <property name="username">
        <value>${jdbc.username}</value>
    </property>
    <property name="password">
        <value>${jdbc.password}</value>
    </property>
</bean>
```

In the `org.springframework.jdbc.dataSource` package, you can define either a `DriverManagerDataSource` or `SingleConnectionDataSource`. The `DriverManagerDataSource` will return a new connection every time a user requests a connection. The `SingleConnectionDataSource` returns the same connection every time a connection is requested. Neither of these data sources allows connection pooling. As you can see, these two options are good solutions for small applications, but you should consider other options when delivering large applications.

Hibernate Transactions

If you have selected Hibernate as your ORM solution, you will need to use the `HibernateTransactionManager`. How you reference this transaction manager depends on which version of Hibernate you are using. For Hibernate 2, you need to declare its bean with the following XML:

```
<bean id="transactionManager"
    class="org.springframework.orm.hibernate.HibernateTransactionManager">
    <property name="sessionFactory"><ref local="sessionFactory"/></property>
</bean>
```

If you are using Hibernate 3, you will need to declare a different version of the `HibernateTransactionManager`. Note the different package names in the Hibernate 2 and Hibernate 3 bean definitions.

```
<bean id="transactionManager"
    class="org.springframework.orm.hibernate3.HibernateTransactionManager">
    <property name="sessionFactory"><ref local="sessionFactory"/></property>
</bean>
```

The sessionFactory property is wired to the Hibernate SessionFactory in the same applicationContext.xml file. The HibernateTransactionManager will delegate transaction management to a Hibernate Transaction object, which will call the commit() method with a successful transaction or the rollback() method when a transaction fails.

Programmatic Transactions

If you need finely grained controls on your transactions, you will want to employ programmatic transaction management instead of declarative transactions, since declarative transactions are declared at the method level. The advantage of using Spring's transaction management is you do not require JTA or other frameworks to manage transactions.

As you will see in this chapter, Spring offers several different templates to use for data persistence. For transactions, a transaction template can be used in conjunction with a transaction manager. Transaction templates help control the transaction management for a transaction. Programmatic transactions use a transaction template that encapsulates the code block that you want to be transactional. This creates a callback class that implements the TransactionCallback interface.

Spring's JDBC framework helps clean up your JDBC code by handling database resource management and exception handling with its JdbcTemplate class. The JdbcTemplate class does not provide transaction management itself. That is handled by the TransactionTemplate, which is a helper class that handles transaction life cycle. Exceptions are defined on the TransactionTemplate's execute method. The PlatformTransactionManager interface is passed an implementation of a DataSourceTransactionManager into the setTransactionManager method, which wraps the SimpleJdbcInsert class for use in the EcommerceDaoImpl DAO. In the SimpleJdbcInsert class, the SimpleJdbcTemplate handles the insert transaction in the DAO.

The following demonstrates how to make a method transactional from the EcommerceDaoImpl class. This example is not a full implementation in Spring.

```
private PlatformTransactionManager transactionManager;
private SimpleJdbcInsert insertProduct;

public class EcommerceDaoTTImpl extends SimpleJdbcTemplate
    implements EcommerceJdbcDao
{
public void setTransactionManager(PlatformTransactionManager transactionManager)
{
     this.transactionManager = transactionManager;
}

public void insertProduct(final Product product)
{
     TransactionTemplate transactionTemplate =
         new TransactionTemplate(transactionManager);
```

```
transactionTemplate.execute(new TransactionCallbackWithoutResult()
{
    protected void doInTransactionWithoutResult(TransactionStatus status)
    {
        Number newId = insertProduct.executeAndReturnKey(
            new BeanPropertySqlParameterSource(product));
            product.setProductID(newId.intValue());
    }
});
}
}
```

The insertProduct() method resides in a DAO class. To make this database call transactional, we wrap the executeAndReturnkey method of the SimpleJdbcInsert call in the TransactionTemplate. Since we had no result to be returned from the query, we implemented the TransactionCallbackWithoutResult interface. If you are expecting to return data from the database call, use TransactionCallback instead.

There are two ways a rollback will occur: by calling the setRollbackOnly() method on the TransactionalStatus object or by throwing an exception from the call. Otherwise, the data will be committed when the transaction completes.

Declaring Transactions

Spring's support for declarative transaction management is applied through the Spring AOP framework. It provides three ways to support declarative transactions. The first is to declare transactions by proxying beans using Spring AOP. This has always been supported by Spring. The other two ways were introduced with Spring 2.0, which allows annotation-driven and XML-declared transactions.

To create a transaction using a proxy template, you need to use the TransactionProxyFactoryBean. This creates lengthy Spring configuration files that are difficult to maintain. Therefore, we'll avoid that approach, and look at XML-declared and annotation-driven transactions.

XML-Declared Transactions

With Spring 2.0, some new configuration elements were added to support declaring transactions. The new elements are in the tx namespace and can be added to the XSD schema in your applicationContext.xml configuration file. I have highlighted the new elements in Listing 8-2.

Spring 2.0 also shipped with an AspectJ aspects library, which can be used to make most objects transactional. AspectJ allows you to annotate objects that use aspects to address modularization of concerns across many objects.

Note You also need to include the aop namespace in the XSD schema. Spring's AOP configuration elements are required for declaring transaction configuration elements.

Listing 8-2. *Declaring a Transaction with XML in applicationContext.xml*

```xml
<?xml version="1.0" encoding="UTF-8"?>
<beans xmlns="http://www.springframework.org/schema/beans"
       xmlns:xsi="http://www.w3.org/2001/XMLSchema-instance"
       xmlns:aop="http://www.springframework.org/schema/aop"
       xmlns:tx="http://www.springframework.org/schema/tx"
       xsi:schemaLocation="
            http://www.springframework.org/schema/beans
            http://www.springframework.org/schema/beans/spring-beans-2.5.xsd
            http://www.springframework.org/schema/tx
            http://www.springframework.org/schema/tx/spring-tx-2.5.xsd
            http://www.springframework.org/schema/aop
            http://www.springframework.org/schema/aop/spring-aop-2.5.xsd">

    <tx:advice id="txAdvice" transaction-manager="txManager">
        <tx:attributes>
            <tx:method name="insert*" propagation="REQUIRED"/>
            <tx:method name="*" propagation="SUPPORTS"/>
        </tx:attributes>
    </tx:advice>

    <aop:config>
        <aop:advisor
            pointcut="execution(* com.af.services.ProductsService.*(..))"
            advice-ref="txAdvice"/>
    </aop:config>

    <bean id="propertyConfigurer" class="org.springframework.beans.factory. ➥
        config.PropertyPlaceholderConfigurer">
    <property
name="location"><value>classpath:../application.properties</value></property>
    </bean>
    <bean id="dataSource" class="org.apache.commons.dbcp.BasicDataSource"
            destroy-method="close">
        <property name="driverClassName">
            <value>
                    ${jdbc.driverClassName}
            </value>
        </property>
        <property name="url"><value>${jdbc.url}</value></property>
        <property name="username"><value>${jdbc.username}</value></property>
        <property name="password"><value>${jdbc.password}</value></property>
    </bean>
```

```
        <bean id="txManager" class="org.springframework.jdbc.datasource. ➡
            DataSourceTransactionManager">
                <property name="dataSource" ref="dataSource"/>
        </bean>

        <!--Transactional service bean -->
        <bean id="productsService" class="com.af.services.ProductsService"/>

</beans>
```

One of the elements provided by the tx namespace is <tx:advice>. This element advises Spring on how to implement transactions for methods defined in it. Attributes are defined in <tx:advice> using the <tx:attributes> element. This element contains <tx:method> tags that set the transaction properties for that method that requires transaction management. In Listing 8-2, you can see that any method that starts with insert requires a transaction to run. Anything else falls into the second method definition that uses a wildcard. Those methods do not require a transaction, but will support a transaction if one exists.

The use of <tx:advice> alone does not define a complete transaction; it defines only an AOP advice to set method properties to use within a transaction. AOP reduces cross-cutting concern code by reducing the need to repeat the code throughout your Spring application.

To complete the transaction, we need to define which beans must be advised. To complete the loop, we need to define an advisor with the <aop:config> element. The <aop:advisor> sets a pointcut to advise all methods within a specific bean—in this case, the ProductsService bean. The pointcut entry, pointcut="execution(* com.af.services.ProductsService.*(..))", specifies that advice should be applied on any method in the ProductsService bean when a method is executed with any return type and any set of input parameters. Pointcuts are used to control when an advice is executed by joining points of interest in Spring code.

As you can see, declaring transactions in the application context through XML makes transactions easier to work with. However, using annotation-driven transactions will clean up your applicationContext.xml definitions further, and they work within a Java 5 environment.

Annotation-Driven Transactions

Annotation-driven transactions require less configuration than XML-declared transactions. Instead of the <tx:advice> element, you use the <tx:annotation-driven> element. Just add one line to your applicationContext.xml file (compare that to all of the lines of XML necessary to support <tx:advice>). Here it is:

```
<tx:annotation-driven transaction-manager="txManager"/>
```

That's it. You only need to add the element and associate it with a specific transaction manager that supports the ORM solution you choose for database persistence, as in this example:

```
<bean id="txManager"
        class="org.springframework.orm.hibernate3.HibernateTransactionManager">
        <property name="sessionFactory"><ref local="sessionFactory"/></property>
</bean>
```

Figure 8-1 illustrates the Spring bean wiring for annotation-driven transactions.

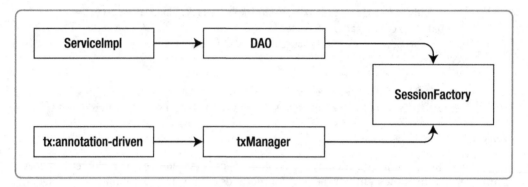

Figure 8-1. *Spring bean wiring with annotations*

You can see a complete example of using annotations in Listing 8-20, later in this chapter. This allows you to define transaction properties on the methods within your Spring beans. It cleans up your configuration quite a bit and allows you to concentrate where you would rather be working in your Spring code.

Annotations allow you to define metadata within your code instead of configuration files. The <tx:annotation-driven> element directs Spring to look for the annotation @Transactional within all Spring beans loaded in context and advise the method with the defined advice. The advice transaction parameters are set on the @Transactional annotation. Listing 8-3 shows an example of a class that has been made transactional with annotations.

Listing 8-3. *Making ProductsServiceImpl Transactional with Annotations*

```
package com.af.core.services;

import com.af.core.dao.ProductsDao;
import com.af.core.domain.Product;

import java.io.Serializable;

import org.springframework.transaction.annotation.Propagation;
import org.springframework.transaction.annotation.Transactional;

@Transactional(propagation=Propagation.SUPPORTS, readOnly=true)
public class ProductsServiceImpl implements Serializable, ProductsService
{
    @Transactional(propagation=Propagation.REQUIRED, readOnly=true)
    public void insertProduct(Product product)
    {
        ecommerceHibernateDao.insertProduct(product);
    }
}
```

In Listing 8-3, the class is made transactional by defining a @Transactional annotation above the class definition. Within the class, the insertProduct() method was annotated as transactional with a propagation status of REQUIRED so it requires a transaction. Any other methods added to this class will support transactions due the propagation setting of SUPPORTS at the class level. You have the option to set the propagation setting to what is required for your methods.

Annotations can also be added at the interface level to require that all implementations of a service be transactional. Listing 8-4 shows the interface for ProductsService made transactional. If you annotate at the interface or class level, all methods will be made transactional with the parameters you set.

Listing 8-4. *Annotating the ProductsService at the Interface Level*

```
package com.af.core.services;

import com.af.core.domain.Product;

import org.springframework.transaction.annotation.Propagation;
import org.springframework.transaction.annotation.Transactional;

@Transactional(propagation=Propagation.SUPPORTS, readOnly=true)
public interface ProductsService
{
    @Transactional(propagation=Propagation.REQUIRED, readOnly=false)
    void insertProduct(Product product);
}
```

We will use transactions in the upcoming examples in this chapter, which demonstrate how to use ORM frameworks to persist data.

Setting Up for Data Persistence

Spring has several options for ORM solutions, which are listed in Table 8-1. In this chapter, we will look at using JDBC, iBATIS, and Hibernate. The implementations of the various ORM solutions are very similar. Once you understand how to use one ORM solution, you will find it easy to move to another ORM solution.

Table 8-1. *Spring ORM Solutions*

ORM Package	Open Source	Download URL
Hibernate	Yes	http://www.hibernate.org/6.html
iBATIS	Yes	http://ibatis.apache.org/javadownloads.cgi
Java Data Objects (JDO)	Yes, with commercial version available	http://db.apache.org/jdo/downloads.html
EJB3 Persistence (JPA)	Yes, with commercial version available	http://java.sun.com/javaee/technologies/persistence.jsp
Oracle TopLink	No, commercial	http://www.oracle.com/technology/products/ias/toplink/jpa/download.html

To demonstrate how to persist data with Spring, we need an application that will require us to execute the CRUD operations. Suppose we are developing an e-commerce site that will display products that can be purchased online. One of the first design steps will be to create the table structure for the relational database. First, we need to create a table to hold the products.

I have chosen to use MySQL Community Server (http://dev.mysql.com/downloads) as my database. MySQL Community Server is an open source relational database. See Chapter 11 for more information about MySQL.

Caution If you are upgrading your MySQL database, I strongly suggest that you back up all of your data before installing a new version of your database. This applies to any database solution you choose.

To create the product table in MySQL, execute the SQL statement shown in Listing 8-5. The ProductID will be set as the primary key for the table. (Note that this is used in this example only.)

Listing 8-5. *Create Table SQL for the Product Table in MySQL*

```
CREATE TABLE `apress`.`product` (
      `ProductID`                 INTEGER NOT NULL AUTO_INCREMENT,
      `SKU`                       VARCHAR(45),
      `ProductName`               VARCHAR(120),
      `ProductDescription`        VARCHAR(200),
      `supplierID`                VARCHAR(45),
      `categoryID`                VARCHAR(45),
      `UnitPrice`                 VARCHAR(45),
      `UnitQuantity`              INTEGER,
      `MSRP`                      VARCHAR(45),
      `availableSize`             VARCHAR(45),
      `availableColors`           VARCHAR(45),
      `size`                      VARCHAR(45),
      `color`                     VARCHAR(45),
      `Image`                     VARCHAR(45),
   PRIMARY KEY(`ProductID`)
)
ENGINE = InnoDB;
```

Once that is complete, you can go ahead and create a class to support the table. The domain object in Spring will be named the same as the table, Product, as shown in Listing 8-6.

Listing 8-6. *The Product Domain Object*

```
package com.af.core.domain;

public class Product implements java.io.Serializable
{
```

```
    private int productID;
    private String SKU;
    private String productName;
    private String productDescription;
    private int supplierID;
    private int categoryID;
    private int unitQuantity;
    private float unitPrice;
    private float MSRP;
    private String availableSize;
    private String availableColors;
    private String size;
    private String color;
    private String image;
  // Constructors, Getters and Setters
}
```

This domain object will be used with JDBC, iBATIS, and Hibernate. We will share this object between the three different data-access techniques to show how domain objects can be shared throughout a Spring application when the data access objects change. One of the benefits of Springs DAO layer is that you can switch ORM and JDBC solutions without rewriting much code in your application—that is, if you implement the DAO pattern correctly in Spring.

One of the mistakes developers make is combining presentation and business logic in the data access layer. You want to keep the data access logic separated and contained in DAOs. In building the e-commerce site to display products, we will be interchanging three persistence solutions, and you will see how to keep the DAOs separate from the other layers to ensure you have a smooth transition when changing your ORM or JDBC solution.

For the e-commerce application, we need to create a DAO to support insert, update, delete, and retrieve operations, each of which is carried out by a DAO method, as shown in Listing 8-7. These four methods should be defined in the DAO interface to allow for different implementation technologies such as Hibernate and iBATIS. As we progress through the different data access solutions, these interfaces and classes will evolve to fit the solution.

Listing 8-7. *The EcommerceDao Interface*

```
package com.af.core.dao;

import com.af.core.domain.Product;
import java.util.List;

public interface EcommerceDao
{
     public List<Product> getProducts();
     public int deleteProduct(Product product);
     public int insertProduct(Product product);
     public int updateProduct(Product product);
}
```

To gain access to the data layer, we need to create a service layer bean to inject data into and call the data access layer. To do so, we need to create an interface that is implemented by the e-commerce service. This code will reside in the service layer and not change when you migrate to a different ORM solution. By keeping code in the proper application layers, you eliminate the need for rework by building components in Spring that serve a separate purpose than the data access layer.

Listings 8-8 and 8-9 show the EcommerceService and EcommerceServiceImpl that will be wired into the ApplicationContext for this application.

Listing 8-8. *EcommerceService*

```
package com.af.core.services;

import com.af.core.domain.Product;
import java.util.List;

public interface EcommerceService
{
        public abstract List<Product> getProducts() throws Exception;

        public abstract int insertProduct(Product product) throws Exception;

        public abstract int deleteProduct(Product product) throws Exception;

        public abstract int updateProduct(Product product) throws Exception;
}
```

Listing 8-9. *EcommerceServiceImpl*

```
package com.af.core.services;

import com.af.core.dao.EcommerceDao;
import com.af.core.domain.Product;

import java.util.List;
import java.io.Serializable;

public class EcommerceServiceImpl implements Serializable, EcommerceService
{
        // Injected by Spring
        EcommerceDao ecommerceDao;

        public EcommerceDao getEcommerceDao()
        {
                return ecommerceDao;
        }
```

```
    public void setEcommerceDao(EcommerceDao ecommerceDao)
    {
            this.ecommerceDao = ecommerceDao;
    }


    // Products
    public List<Product> getProducts() throws Exception
    {
            return ecommerceDao.getProducts();
    }

    public int insertProduct(Product product) throws Exception
    {
            return ((Integer)ecommerceDao.insertProduct(product));
    }

    public int deleteProduct(Product product) throws Exception
    {
            return ((Integer)ecommerceDao.deleteProduct(product));
    }

    public int updateProduct(Product product) throws Exception
    {
            return ((Integer)ecommerceDao.updateProduct(product));
    }
}
```

Again, this bean will not change if there are any changes to this application's ORM solutions. The only upgrade we will need for these beans is to make them transactional.

The properties in Table 8-2 are held in the application.properties file, which is read into context during the initialization of the application when your web server starts. You can see the application.properties file in Listing 8-10.

Table 8-2. *JDBC Properties for Database Connectivity*

Property	Value
driverClassName	com.mysql.jdbc.Driver
url	jdbc.mysql://localhost:3306/apress
username	af
password	afpass

Listing 8-10. *The application.properties File*

```
# JDBC Connection information
jdbc.driverClassName=com.mysql.jdbc.Driver
jdbc.url=jdbc:mysql://localhost/apress
jdbc.username=af
jdbc.password=afpass
```

As you can see, application.properties is loaded into context for your Spring application. Those properties are then used as a BasicDataSource bean or directly in the configuration of an ORM solution in ApplicationContext. The following is an example of a propertyConfigurer bean that uses the property values from application.properties. The propertyConfigurer bean is located in the applicationContext.xml file.

```
<!-- START Load application properties -->
    <bean id="propertyConfigurer"
          class="org.springframework.beans.factory.config. ➥
             PropertyPlaceholderConfigurer">
          <property name="location">
                <value>WEB-INF/application.properties</value>
          </property>
    </bean>
<!-- END Load application properties -->
```

Note You will need to include commons-collections.jar in your project library to use the data source implementations in the Apache Commons Database Connection Pool (DBCP). You can download the JAR file from http://commons.apache.org/collections.

This application is running on a BlazeDS server and requires the following JAR files, along with the JARs installed with your BlazeDS server:

- commons-codec-1.3.jar

- commons-collections.jar

- commons-dbcp-1.2.2.jar

- commons-httpclient-3.0.1.jar

- commons-logging.jar

- commons-pool-1.4.jar

- concurrent.jar

- mysql-connector-java-5.1.7.jar

- spring.jar

Those are the basic building blocks for our application. It is ready to access data from the MySQL database. The first data persistence solution we will explore uses JDBC.

Using JDBC

As you've learned, the Spring Framework offers integration with many persistence technologies such as Hibernate, iBATIS, and JPA, to name a few. Despite this, developers are still writing database solutions with JDBC. JDBC is written on top of SQL, which allows you to work at lower levels with your data. JDBC also lets you take advantage of a database's proprietary features, where other ORM solutions might allow limited access or even refuse to allow access to those features.

Using JDBC Directly

There are some issues that come with using JDBC directly. With the power to work at a more granular level to finely tune your persistence layer, you will notice that you require more steps to deliver the payload than with an ORM solution. You are required to code more of the interaction pieces, which results in more lines of code that can be bypassed by using an ORM solution. For example, to insert a row into your database using traditional JDBC, you need to execute a few steps:

1. Open a database connection.

2. Create a prepared statement.

3. Bind incoming parameters from an object type.

4. Execute the prepared statement.

5. Handle exceptions.

6. Clean up your database connection and statement resources.

The code shown in Listing 8-11 implements these six steps to insert a row into the `product` table.

Listing 8-11. *Using Traditional JDBC to Insert a Row into the Product Table*

```
private static final String PRODUCT_INSERT =
    "INSERT INTO product(SKU, productName, productDescription, supplierID)" +
    "VALUES(?,?,?,?)";

public void insertProduct(Product product)
{
    Connection con = null;
    PreparedStatement stmt = null;
    try
    {
```

```
            con = dataSource.getConnection();
            stmt = con.preparedStatement(PRODUCE_INSERT);

            stmt.setString(1, product.getSKU());
            stmt.setString(2, product.getProductName());
            stmt.setString(3, product.getProductDescription());
            stmt.setInt(4, product.getSupplierID());

            stmt.execute();
        } catch (SQLException e)
        {
            // Handle exception
        } finally
        {
            If(stmt != null) {stmt.close(); }
            If(con!= null) { con.close(); }
        }
    }
}
```

Notice how much code was written to execute an insertion into the database. That is a good amount of code required to manage database interactivity. This is where Spring can help with its JDBC templates. Spring's JDBC framework will clean up your JDBC code, adding a layer of abstraction to boilerplate functions that interact with databases. It also handles resource management and fault handling for you. This leaves you free to write code only to move data in and out of databases.

Using Spring JDBC Templates

Spring offers three JDBC templates for working with data access technologies such as JDBC, JDO, and Hibernate:

JdbcTemplate: This is the most primitive of Spring's JDBC templates. It is the central class in Spring's JDBC core package. It abstracts away the creation and release of resources for JDBC and executes SQL queries.

NamedParameterJdbcTemplate: This template adds support for coding JDBC statements using named parameters instead of statements using classic placeholders (?). This class wraps the JdbcTemplate to do much of the work.

SimpleJdbcTemplate: This is an upgrade to the JdbcTemplate. It takes advantages of Java 5 features, such as generics and variable parameter lists, to further simplify the use of JDBC. Note that SimpleJdbcTemplate requires Java 5 or above.

These templates give a layer af abstraction and implement methods for providing the data source and configuration parameters associated with the data access solutions.

For our e-commerce application example, we'll use the SimpleJdbcTemplate. The bean configuration required to use SimpleJdbcTemplate in Spring starts with defining the bean in the applicationContext.xml file, as shown in Listing 8-12. We will reuse the ecommerceDao and ecommerceService beans with each of the three data persistence solutions.

Listing 8-12. *The Bean Definitions in applicationContext.xml for the JDBC Implementation*

```
<?xml version="1.0" encoding="UTF-8" ?>
<!DOCTYPE beans
        PUBLIC "-//SPRING//DTD BEAN//EN"
        "http://www.springframework.org/dtd/spring-beans.dtd">
<beans>
<!-- START JDBC DAO config -->
    <bean id="ecommerceDao" class="com.af.core.dao.jdbc.EcommerceJdbcDaoImpl">
            <property name="dataSource" ref="dataSource" />
    </bean>
<!-- END JDBC DAO config -->
<!-- START Service config -->
    <bean id="ecommerceService" class="com.af.core.services.EcommerceServiceImpl">
            <property name="ecommerceDao"><ref bean="ecommerceDao"/></property>
    </bean>
<!-- ENDService config -->
</beans>
```

We have already written the service layer and the interface for the ecommerceDao bean, as you can see earlier in Listings 8-7, 8-8, and 8-9. Since that is done, all you need to do is write the code for the EcommerceDao implementation. This is the component that will change when you migrate to a new ORM solution. It is an interchangeable part of the Spring DAO architecture. For this bean, we will define four functions: getProducts(), deleteProduct(), insertProduct(), and updateProduct(), as shown in Listing 8-13. These will serve as the base CRUD operations to execute for the Product domain object.

Listing 8-13. *The EcommerceDaoImpl with JDBC Support*

```
package com.af.core.dao.jdbc;

import java.util.List;
import javax.sql.DataSource;

import org.springframework.jdbc.core.namedparam.BeanPropertySqlParameterSource;
import org.springframework.jdbc.core.simple.ParameterizedBeanPropertyRowMapper;
import org.springframework.jdbc.core.simple.SimpleJdbcTemplate;
import org.springframework.dao.DataAccessException;

import com.af.core.dao.EcommerceDao;
import com.af.core.domain.Product;

public class EcommerceDaoImpl implements EcommerceDao
{
    private SimpleJdbcTemplate simpleJdbcTemplate;
```

```
        public void setDataSource(DataSource dataSource)
        {
            this.simpleJdbcTemplate = new SimpleJdbcTemplate(dataSource);
        }
        public List<Product> getProducts()
        {
            List<Products> productList = simpleJdbcTemplate.query(
                "SELECT * FROM product",
                ParameterizedBeanPropertyRowMapper.newInstance(Products.class));
            return productList;
        }
        public void deleteProduct(Product product) throws DataAccessException
        {
            simpleJdbcTemplate.update("DELETE FROM product WHERE productID =
                :productID");
        }
        public void insertProduct(Product product)
        {
            simpleJdbcTemplate.update(
                "INSERT into product VALUES('', " +
                ":SKU," +
                " :productName, " +
                " :productDescription, " +
                " :supplierID, " +
                " :categoryID, " +
                " :unitQuantity, " +
                " :unitPrice, " +
                " :MSRP, " +
                " :availableSize, " +
                " :availableColors, " +
                " :size, " +
                " :color, " +
                " :image ",
                new BeanPropertySqlParameterSource(product));
        }
        public void updateProduct(Product product)
        {
            simpleJdbcTemplate.update(
                "UPDATE product SET  supplierID        = :supplierID, " +
                "                    productName       = :productName, " +
                "                    productDescription = :productDescription, " +
                "                    SKU               = :SKU, " +
                "                    categoryID        = :categoryID, " +
                "                    unitQuantity      = :unitQuantity, " +
                "                    unitPrice         = :unitPrice, " +
                "                    MSRP              = :MSRP, " +
                "                    availableSize     = :availableSize, " +
```

```
        "              availableColors    = :availableColors, " +
        "              size               = :size, " +
        "              color              = :color, " +
        "              image              = :image " +
        "WHERE productID = :productID",
    new BeanPropertySqlParameterSource(product));
    }
}
```

As you can see in Listing 8-13, we have implemented a clean structure of CRUD operations for the Product domain object.

Notice that there is no exception catching at this level. That is because the JdbcTemplate catches those exceptions at a lower level than we need to code. A SQLException is handled internally by JdbcTemplate and will be translated to a more generic JDBC exception like BatchUpdateException, DataTruncation, SQLException, or SQLWarning, and then rethrown for the application to catch.

In the updateProduct() method, notice the use of named parameters from the Product domain object to give each parameter in the SQL an explicit name to map to. The order of the bound parameters is not important, since each parameter is bound by name to the associated table field name.

JDBC is the most basic solution for working with a relational database. As you have seen, Spring offers options to abstract away the boilerplate code associated with classic JDBC through JdbcTemplate options. Even though Spring manages most of the tedium of working with JDBC, it can still become a maintenance issue as applications grow large. To help better manage persistence needs in Spring, you may want to consider switching from JDBC to a more robust persistence solution like iBATIS or Hibernate.

Using iBATIS

The iBATIS framework works on a dependency injection model. However, iBATIS's primary responsibilities are to issue queries to a database, receive the results of the query, and transform the rows returned into objects. iBATIS does this by using an XML configuration file that contains what iBATIS calls *SQL maps* (however, the file can contain references to multiple files, each with SQL maps). The SQL maps define how a query should be transformed into an object.

The SQL map file has an entry called a ResultSet, which defines an object used and which columns of a result set are matched to attributes in the object. The SQL map file also contains entries that define the SQL and which ResultSet should be used for the results returned. A query can also have an entry for an object passed in whose attributes are used in the query. The iBATIS XML allows for powerful dynamic building of the SQL through variable substitution and conditional statements.

Domain objects contain data that will be passed back to the client by Spring service calls. Each service has an interface used for reference to it, and Spring injects the implementation of that interface, as defined in the Spring configuration file. Services can utilize other services.

DAOs are responsible for getting the data from the database. Each DAO has an interface and an implementation class for the same reasons as the services. They are beans that implement or extend iBATIS framework objects. They have methods defined in them for CRUD or utility operations on the database. The implementation DAOs are defined in the Spring configuration file for injection into the Spring beans that use them. These DAOs get the data from the database by making calls on the iBATIS framework and passing in which statement defined in the SQL map file(s) to use. Domain objects represent rows from the database. They simply contain attributes and getters/setters for those attributes.

A Case for iBATIS

iBATIS is not a fully functional ORM solution. It is a cross between ORM and pure JDBC.

iBATIS is basically an object-to-relational database binding framework. The SQL maps bind Spring domain objects directly to database table fields. The SQL used to query a database is held in SQL map files, which are XML files. Therefore, I use iBATIS when I need to manage large, complicated SQL statements by hand.

Let's say you are building a Flex application that is chartered to integrate with a large data warehouse. I have built many business intelligence tools in Flex that query data warehouses with more than 700 million rows in the main fact table. The data warehouses are tuned for those types of interactions. However, you must be sure to have full access and control over the SQL for performance considerations. Database administrators generally have a specific SQL structure they will want you to deliver to query their databases. As a data warehouse grows, you may need to quickly tweak (going through proper change control channels of course) your SQL to adapt to those changes.

This is where iBATIS has value. The SQL is stored outside the compiled code, and you can update it quickly to adapt to changes. Having the ability to quickly adapt to changes in the data sets allows you to keep the Flex and Spring applications from being bogged down with performance issues.

Using iBATIS for Data Persistence

To use iBATIS, you will first need to download a version that works with Java 5 and Spring 2.5 or above. You can download iBATIS from the iBATIS for Java Downloads site (http://ibatis.apache.org/javadownloads.cgi).

To gain access to iBATIS, you will need to add a bean definition in your applicationContext.xml file for iBATIS's SqlMapClientTemplate, as shown in Listing 8-14, as well as a dataSource object, DAO bean, and service bean. The SqlMapClientTemplate references the SqlMapClient, which implements the SqlMapClientFactoryBean. The SqlMapClient accesses the dataSource bean and sets the location of the SQL map XML files used to hold the SQL that iBATIS executes.

Listing 8-14. *The iBATIS SqlMapClientTemplate Definition in applicationContext.xml*

```
<beans>
     <!-- START Load application properties -->
     <bean id="propertyConfigurer"
          class="org.springframework.beans.factory.config. ➥
             PropertyPlaceholderConfigurer">
          <property name="location">
                <value>classpath:../application.properties</value>
          </property>
     </bean>
     <!-- END Load application properties -->
```

```xml
<!-- START DB connection info -->
<bean id="dataSource" class="org.apache.commons.dbcp.BasicDataSource"
    destroy-method="close">
    <property name="driverClassName">
        <value>${jdbc.driverClassName}</value>
    </property>
    <property name="url"><value>${jdbc.url}</value></property>
    <property name="username"><value>${jdbc.username}</value></property>
    <property name="password"><value>${jdbc.password}</value></property>
</bean>

<bean id="transactionManager"
    class="org.springframework.jdbc.datasource ➡
    .DataSourceTransactionManager">
    <property name="dataSource"><ref local="dataSource"/></property>
</bean>
<!-- END DB connection info -->

<!-- START iBATIS config -->
<bean id="sqlMapClientTemplate"
    class="org.springframework.orm.ibatis.SqlMapClientTemplate">
    <property name="sqlMapClient" ref="sqlMapClient" />
</bean>

<bean id="sqlMapClient"
    class="org.springframework.orm.ibatis.SqlMapClientFactoryBean">
    <property name="dataSource" ref="dataSource" />
    <!-- this needs to point to where the sql-map-config.xml file is -->
    <property name="configLocation"
        value="classpath:../sql-map-config.xml" />
</bean>
<!-- END iBATIS config -->

<!-- START DAO config -->
<bean id="ecommerceDao" class="com.af.core.dao.ibatis.EcommerceDaoImpl">
    <property name="sqlMapClientTemplate" ref="sqlMapClientTemplate" />
</bean>
<!-- END DAO config -->

<!-- START Service config -->
<bean id="ecommerceService" class="com.af.core.services.EcommerceServiceImpl">
    <property name="ecommerceDao"><ref bean="ecommerceDao"/></property>
</bean>
<!-- ENDService config -->
</beans>
```

All JDBC and JNDI information is configured in the Spring applicationContext.xml configuration file.

Configuring the SQL Map for Product

The sql-map-config.xml file contains the path of XML files that contain iBATIS SQL maps. You need to create separate SQL maps for each DAO bean. Listing 8-15 sets the location for the Product bean. The resource is Product.xml, which will hold the SQL to query the database and the mappings back to the Product domain object. The SQL maps can be put in the directory of your choice on your web server. In this example, the SQL map is located in <tomcat-install-directory>/webapps/SpringDataPersistence/WEB-INF/sqlmaps.

Listing 8-15. *The iBATIS SQL Map Configuration (sql-map-config.xml)*

```
<?xml version="1.0" encoding="UTF-8" ?>
<!DOCTYPE sqlMapConfig PUBLIC "-//ibatis.apache.org//DTD SQL Map Config 2.0//EN"
    "http://ibatis.apache.org/dtd/sql-map-config-2.dtd">

<sqlMapConfig>
    <sqlMap resource="../sqlmaps/Product.xml" />
</sqlMapConfig>
```

The XML files found in the sqlmaps directory contain the mappings of database tables to domain objects and SQL queries. Listing 8-16 shows the details of the Product CRUD operations using iBATIS.

Listing 8-16. *The iBATIS SQL Map for Product (Product.xml)*

```
<?xml version="1.0" encoding="UTF-8" ?>
<!DOCTYPE sqlMap
    PUBLIC "-//ibatis.apache.org//DTD SQL Map 2.0//EN"
    "http://ibatis.apache.org/dtd/sql-map-2.dtd">

<sqlMap namespace="Product">

    <typeAlias alias="product" type="com.af.core.domain.Product"/>

    <resultMap id="productsResult" class="product">
        <result property="productID"          column="ProductID"/>
        <result property="SKU"                column="SKU" />
        <result property="productName"        column="ProductName" />
        <result property="productDescription" column="ProductDescription" />
        <result property="supplierID"         column="SupplierID" />
        <result property="categoryID"         column="CategoryID" />
        <result property="unitQuantity"       column="UnitQuantity" />
        <result property="unitPrice"          column="UnitPrice" />
        <result property="MSRP"               column="MSRP" />
        <result property="availableSize"      column="AvailableSize" />
        <result property="availableColors"    column="AvailableColors" />
```

```xml
            <result property="size"                   column="Size" />
            <result property="color"                  column="Color" />
            <result property="image"                  column="Image" />
    </resultMap>

    <sql id="product_table" >
        product
    </sql>

    <select id="getProducts" resultMap="productsResult" parameterClass="product">
        SELECT * FROM <include refid="product_table"/>
    </select>

<insert id="insertProduct" parameterClass="product">
      INSERT into <include refid="product_table"/>(
        SKU,
        ProductName,
        ProductDescription,
        SupplierID,
        CategoryID,
        UnitQuantity,
        UnitPrice,
        MSRP,
        AvailableSize,
        AvailableColors,
        Size,
        Color,
        Image)
                        values( #SKU#,
                                #productName#,
                                #productDescription#,
                                #supplierID#,
                                #categoryID#,
                                #unitQuantity#,
                                #unitPrice#,
                                #MSRP#,
                                #availableSize#,
                                #availableColors#,
                                #size#,
                                #color#,
                                #image#)
      <selectKey resultClass="int">
          SELECT distinct last_insert_id() FROM <include refid="product_table"/>
      </selectKey>
    </insert>
```

```
        <update id="updateProduct" parameterClass="product">
            UPDATE <include refid="product_table"/>
                    set SKU                    = #SKU#,
                          ProductName          = #productName#,
                          ProductDescription   = #productDescription#,
                          SupplierID           = #supplierID#,
                          CategoryID           = #categoryID#,
                          UnitQuantity         = #unitQuantity#,
                          UnitPrice            = #unitPrice#,
                          MSRP                 = #MSRP#,
                          AvailableSize        = #availableSize#,
                          AvailableColors      = #availableColors#,
                          Size                 = #size#,
                          Color                = #color#,
                          Image                = #image#
        WHERE ProductID = #productID#
    </update>

    <delete id="deleteProduct" parameterClass="product">
        DELETE from <include refid="product_table"/> WHERE ProductID = #productID#
    </delete>
</sqlMap>
```

Now we have defined four queries to work with your database. As you can see, the SQL can be quickly modified without requiring a compile if changes are needed.

In the Product SQL map (Listing 8-16), we have defined an alias to the Product domain object. This alias is used in the resultMap to give iBATIS a reference to the domain object.

The resultMap is a mapping of domain object attributes to database table fields. In this case, the Product domain object is mapped to the product database table. We are allowing iBATIS to determine the attribute types. You can specify both the Java attribute types and database field types, if needed.

Another alias used in Listing 8-16 is wrapped in the <sql> tag. I suggest setting an alias for your database tables used in SQL maps at the top of the file. That alias is used in every query for the table name. This helps eliminate the need to maintain every query in your SQL maps if a table name changes. This way, you are required to change the table name in only one location.

You should also notice the four tags for insert, select, update, and delete. These are the four basic CRUD operations you create in the SQL map. You need to give an id in these tags so the DAO can locate the query. The parameterClass dictates which type of object will be used in the query. This can range from Product to int or an alias, for example.

Implementing an iBATIS DAO in Spring

With the configuration complete, we need to implement the DAO in Spring. This is done by changing the SimpleJdbcTemplate we used for JDBC to the iBATIS SqlMapClientTemplate located in the org.springframework.orm.ibatis package. This is where Spring really shines. The only code we change is in the implementation of the DAO. No other code in Spring changes to support adding iBATIS to persist the database. Listing 8-17 shows the DAO implementation.

Listing 8-17. *The DAO Implementation for iBATIS*

```
package com.af.core.dao.ibatis;

import java.util.List;
import org.springframework.orm.ibatis.SqlMapClientTemplate;
import com.af.core.dao.EcommerceDao;
import com.af.core.domain.Product;

public class EcommerceDaoImpl implements EcommerceDao
{
      private SqlMapClientTemplate sqlMapClientTemplate;

      public void setSqlMapClientTemplate(SqlMapClientTemplate sqlMapClientTemplate)
      {
            this.sqlMapClientTemplate = sqlMapClientTemplate;
      }

      public List<Product> getProducts()
      {
            return sqlMapClientTemplate.queryForList("getProducts");
      }
      public int insertProduct(Product product)
      {
          return
            ((Integer)sqlMapClientTemplate.insert("insertProduct",
            product)).intValue();
      }

      public int deleteProduct(Product product)
      {
          return
              ((Integer)sqlMapClientTemplate.delete("deleteProduct",
              product.getProductId())).intValue();
      }

      public int updateProduct(Product product)
      {
          return
              ((Integer)sqlMapClientTemplate.update("updateProduct",
              product)).intValue();
      }
}
```

The DAO executes queries through iBATIS by using the sqlMapClientTemplate to do a lookup based on the SQL map ID. As you can see for the method getProducts(), we are using the sqlMapClientTemplate to execute a queryForList(). We pass in the SQL map ID getProducts to execute the query. The result is mapped in the SQL map's resultMap and passed back as a List of Product objects to the DAO. In the insert and update methods, we are passing in a Product domain object to use within the query.

Setting Up the BlazeDS Server for iBATIS

For this solution, I set up a BlazeDS server and named it SpringDataPersistence. The name SpringDataPersistence merely is the BlazeDS folder name renamed in the *<tomcat-install-directory>*/webapps. I copied the compiled Spring source code to the *<tomcat-install-directory>*/webapps/SpringDataPersistence/WEB-INF/classes folder. I then added the following RemoteObject entry to the *<tomcat-install-directory>*/webapps/SpringDataPersistence/WEB-INF/flex/remoting-config.xml file:

```
<?xml version="1.0" encoding="UTF-8"?>
<service id="remoting-service"
    class="flex.messaging.services.RemotingService">

    <adapters>
        <adapter-definition id="java-object" class="flex.messaging.services. ➥
            remoting.adapters.JavaAdapter" default="true"/>
    </adapters>

    <default-channels>
        <channel ref="my-amf"/>
    </default-channels>

    <destination id="ecommerceService">
        <properties>
            <factory>spring</factory>
            <source>ecommerceService</source>
        </properties>
    </destination>
</service>
```

Now that I have an access point via RemoteObject, I can set up the applicationContext.xml file's (see Listing 8-14) location in the server's *<tomcat-install-directory>*/webapps/SpringDataPersistence/WEB-INF/web.xml file:

```
<context-param>
    <param-name>contextConfigLocation</param-name>
    <param-value>/WEB-INF/applicationContext.xml</param-value>
</context-param>
```

To execute this example, we need a simple Flex application that uses a RemoteObject call to get results from the services. This client application will be used for calling the iBATIS server-side implementations with Spring. Listing 8-18 shows the Flex source code for the application.

Listing 8-18. *Flex Application to Execute iBATIS Transactions*

```
<?xml version="1.0" encoding="utf-8"?>
<mx:Application xmlns:mx="http://www.adobe.com/2006/mxml">

    <mx:RemoteObject id="roIbatis"
            destination="ecommerceService"
            endpoint="{roEndpoint}"
            result="resultHandler(event)"
            fault="faultHandler(event)"/>

    <mx:Script>
        <![CDATA[
        import mx.collections.ArrayCollection;
        import mx.rpc.events.ResultEvent;
        import mx.rpc.events.FaultEvent;
        import mx.utils.ObjectUtil;
        import mx.controls.Alert;
        import mx.utils.StringUtil;

        [Bindable]
        private var guestListDP:ArrayCollection =
            new ArrayCollection();

        [Bindable]
        private var roEndpoint:String =
    "http://localhost:8080/SpringDataPersistence/spring/messagebroker/amf

        private function resultHandler(event:ResultEvent):void
        {
            guestListDP = ArrayCollection(event.result);
        }

        private function faultHandler(event:FaultEvent):void
        {
            ta1.text = ObjectUtil.toString(event.fault);
        }
        ]]>
    </mx:Script>

    <mx:Panel title="iBATIS Integration Example"
            paddingLeft="10" paddingRight="10"
            paddingBottom="10" paddingTop="10"
            horizontalAlign="center" width="716" height="579">
```

```
    <mx:Button label="iBATIS: Get Products"
            click="roIbatis.getProducts()"/>
    <mx:DataGrid id="dg" dataProvider="{guestListDP}"
            width="100%" height="100%" />

        <mx:TextArea id="ta1" width="100%" height="100%"/>
    </mx:Panel>
</mx:Application>
```

Thus far, you have seen two ways to persist databases in Spring. Now that you know how to use JDBC and iBATIS, we will take a look at using Hibernate rather than iBATIS.

Using Hibernate 3 with Annotations

As you saw, using iBATIS involves quite a bit of work to define the SQL map. If you do not need to closely manage your SQL statements, Hibernate may be a good solution for you. With Hibernate, you do not need to define SQL maps.

Hibernate is an open source persistence framework that is extremely popular among developers. Unlike iBATIS, Hibernate is a fully operational ORM solution. Hibernate cuts down on the code you need to write, as well as the configuration you need to do.

In this section, we will concentrate on integrating Spring with Hibernate 3 and making the Spring beans transactional with annotations. You can go ahead and download Hibernate 3. From the download page (http://www.hibernate.org/6.html), you will need to get the packages listed in Table 8-3. They contain the JARs you will need to compile and run your Spring/Hibernate 3 integration project with annotations.

Table 8-3. *Required Hibernate 3 Packages*

Package	Required JARs
hibernate-distribution-3.x.GA-dist	hibernate3.jar antlr-2.x.jar commons-collections-3.x.jar dom4j-1.x.jar jta-1.x.jar slf4j-api-1.x.jar slf4j-log4j12-1.x.jar
hibernate-annotations-3.x.GA	hibernate-annotations.jar ejb3-persistence.jar hibernate-commons-annotations-3.x.GA hibernate-commons-annotations.jar
Other JAR files	javassist.jar log4j.jar

> **Note** You will not find `slf4j-log4j12-1.x.jar` in the current Hibernate distribution. It is required, and you can download it from `http://www.slf4j.org/download.html`.

Configuring Spring with Hibernate

You can use Java 5 annotations to tag domain objects with metadata that defines how objects should be persisted in Hibernate. First, you need to configure the `hibApplication.properties` and `applicationContext.xml` files to use Hibernate 3, as shown in Listings 8-19 and 8-20. This is similar to any other ORM configuration to set up the Spring beans and database management.

Listing 8-19. *The hibApplication.properties File for Hibernate 3 and Annotations*

```
# JDBC Connection information
jdbc.driverClassName=com.mysql.jdbc.Driver
jdbc.url=jdbc:mysql://localhost/apress
jdbc.username=af
jdbc.password=af
# Hibernate 3 configuration
hibernate.show_sql=true
hibernate.format_sql=true
hibernate.transaction.factory_class=org.hibernate.transaction.JDBCTransactionFactory
hibernate.dialect=org.hibernate.dialect.MySQLDialect
hibernate.c3p0.min_size=5
hibernate.c3p0.max_size=20
hibernate.c3p0.timeout=1800
hibernate.c3p0.max_statements=50
```

Listing 8-20. *The applicationContext.xml File for Hibernate 3 and Annotations*

```
<?xml version="1.0" encoding="UTF-8"?>
<beans
      xmlns="http://www.springframework.org/schema/beans"
      xmlns:xsi="http://www.w3.org/2001/XMLSchema-instance"
      xmlns:tx="http://www.springframework.org/schema/tx"
      xsi:schemaLocation="http://www.springframework.org/schema/beans
            http://www.springframework.org/schema/beans/spring-beans-2.5.xsd
            http://www.springframework.org/schema/tx
            http://www.springframework.org/schema/tx/spring-tx-2.5.xsd"
      default-lazy-init="true">
```

```xml
<!-- START Load application properties -->
<bean id="propertyConfigurer"
   class="org.springframework.beans.factory.config. ➥
     PropertyPlaceholderConfigurer">
   <property name="location">
         <value>WEB-INF/hibApplication.properties</value>
   </property>
</bean>
<!-- END Load application properties -->

<!-- START HIBERNATE CONFIG -->
<!-- Configure SessionFactory -->
<bean id="sessionFactory" class="org.springframework.orm. ➥
   hibernate3.annotation.AnnotationSessionFactoryBean">
  <property name="annotatedClasses">
        <list>
             <value>com.af.core.domain.ProductH</value>
        </list>
  </property>

  <property name="hibernateProperties">
        <props>
             <prop key="hibernate.show_sql">${hibernate.show_sql}</prop>
             <prop key="hibernate.format_sql">${hibernate.format_sql}</prop>
                <prop key="hibernate.transaction.factory_class">
                  ${hibernate.transaction.factory_class}
                </prop>
                <prop key="hibernate.dialect">${hibernate.dialect}</prop>
                <prop key="hibernate.c3p0.min_size">
                  ${hibernate.c3p0.min_size}
                </prop>
                <prop key="hibernate.c3p0.max_size">
                  ${hibernate.c3p0.max_size}
                </prop>
                <prop key="hibernate.c3p0.timeout">
                  ${hibernate.c3p0.timeout}
                </prop>
                <prop key="hibernate.c3p0.max_statements">
                  ${hibernate.c3p0.max_statements}
                </prop>
                <prop key="hibernate.connection.driver_class">
                  ${jdbc.driverClassName}</prop>
                <prop key="hibernate.connection.url">
                  ${jdbc.url}
                </prop>
```

```
                    <prop key="hibernate.connection.username">
                       ${jdbc.username}
                    </prop>
                    <prop key="hibernate.connection.password">
                       ${jdbc.password}
                    </prop>
             </props>
        </property>
   </bean>

   <!-- enable the configuration of transactional behavior based on annotations -->
   <tx:annotation-driven transaction-manager="txManager"/>

   <bean id="txManager" class="org.springframework.orm.hibernate3. ➥
      HibernateTransactionManager">
      <property name="sessionFactory"><ref local="sessionFactory"/></property>
   </bean>

   <bean class="org.springframework.beans.factory.annotation. ➥
      RequiredAnnotationBeanPostProcessor"/>

   <!-- define data access beans -->
   <bean id="ecommerceDao" class="com.af.core.dao.hibernate.EcommerceDaoImpl">
      <property name="sessionFactory" ref="sessionFactory"/>
   </bean>

   <!-- END HIBERNATE CONFIG -->
   <!-- Config Service -->
   <bean id="ecommerceService" class="com.af.core.services.hibernate. ➥
      EcommerceServiceImpl">
      <property name="ecommerceDao"><ref bean="ecommerceDao"/></property>
   </bean>
</beans>
```

You will need to create a sessionFactory that uses an AnnotationSessionFactoryBean in Spring. This bean is similar to the LocalSessionFactory, except it creates a SessionFactory that uses annotations located in domain objects. In Listing 8-20, you see the definition of sessionFactory, which sets the classes that will be annotated—in this case, the com.af.core. domain.ProductH class. It also pulls in Hibernate properties stored in the hibApplication. properties file (Listing 8-19). These properties hold the database connection parameters, as well as Hibernate parameters such as show_sql, format_sql, and so on.

RequiredAnnotationBeanPostProcessor implements BeanPostProcessor, which enforces required bean properties that have been configured through Spring's annotation type Required. This moves the responsibility of checking for a dependency-injected value to the container. You do not need to code a method to validate all properties that have been set with setters.

For this example, we will make the Spring bean's methods transactional. Notice that we have set the bean txManager to use the Hibernate 3 HibernateTransactionManager, which is set to the sessionFactory. Along with that, there is a <tx:annotation-driven> element that has its transaction-manager property set to use the txManager. With those settings, we can now apply transaction annotations on our Spring beans.

Adding Annotations to the Application

For this Hibernate example, we are adding annotations to the application, as well as making it transactional. This will require some updates to the service layer and changing the DAO's ORM support. Listing 8-21 shows the rewritten domain object for products, called ProductH. It now is annotated with the corresponding product database table attributes. The @Table metadata tag defines the product table name. Each Java variable is also tagged with the @Column metadata to define its name. These tags will act as a SQL map to load the returned table field data to the corresponding domain object variables when the domain object is used as part of the return value.

Listing 8-21. *The ProductH.java Domain Object with Annotations*

```
package com.af.core.domain;

import javax.persistence.Entity;
import javax.persistence.Table;
import javax.persistence.Column;

@Entity
@Table(name="PRODUCT")
public class ProductH implements java.io.Serializable
{
    @Id
    @Column(name="PRODUCTID")
    @GeneratedValue(generator="InvSeq")
    @SequenceGenerator(name="InvSeq",
        sequenceName="group_table_seq01", allocationSize=5)
    private int productID;

    @Column(name="SKU")
    private String SKU;

    @Column(name="PRODUCTNAME")
    private String productName;

    @Column(name="PRODUCTDESCRIPTION")
    private String productDescription;

    @Column(name="SUPPLIERID")
    private int supplierID;
```

```
    @Column(name="CATEGORYID")
    private int categoryID;

    @Column(name="UNITQUANTITY")
    private int unitQuantity;

    @Column(name="UNITPRICE")
    private float unitPrice;

    @Column(name="MSRP")
    private float MSRP;

    @Column(name="AVAILABLESIZE")
    private String availableSize;

    @Column(name="AVAILABLECOLORS")
    private String availableColors;

    @Column(name="SIZE")
    private String size;

    @Column(name="COLOR")
    private String color;

    @Column(name="IMAGE")
    private String image;

    //Getters and Setters ...
}
```

With the domain object set in our project, we will need to add a few annotations to the service and DAO layer in Spring to enable transaction support. To start, add the @Transactional annotation to the EcommerceService and EcommerceServiceImpl classes, as shown in Listings 8-22 and 8-23.

Listing 8-22. *EcommerceService Made Transactional with Annotations (EcommerceService.java)*

```
package com.af.core.services.hibernate;

import com.af.core.domain.ProductH;
import java.util.List;
import org.springframework.transaction.annotation.Transactional;

public interface EcommerceService
{
    @Transactional(readOnly=true)
    List<ProductH> getProducts();
```

```
        @Transactional(readOnly=false)
        ProductH insertProduct(ProductH product);

        @Transactional(readOnly=false)
        void deleteProduct(ProductH product);

        @Transactional(readOnly=false)
        void updateProduct(ProductH product);
}
```

Listing 8-23. *EcommerceServiceImpl Made Transactional with Annotations*
(EcommerceServiceImpl.java)

```
package com.af.core.services.hibernate;

import com.af.core.dao.hibernate.EcommerceDao;
import com.af.core.domain.ProductH;

import java.util.List;
import java.io.Serializable;
import org.springframework.transaction.annotation.Propagation;
import org.springframework.transaction.annotation.Transactional;

@Transactional(propagation=Propagation.SUPPORTS, readOnly=true)
public class EcommerceServiceImpl implements Serializable,
        EcommerceService
{
        // Injected by Spring
        EcommerceDao ecommerceDao;

        public EcommerceDao getEcommerceDao()
        {
                return ecommerceDao;
        }

        public void setEcommerceDao(EcommerceDao ecommerceDao)
        {
                this.ecommerceDao = ecommerceDao;
        }

        // Product
        @Transactional(propagation=Propagation.SUPPORTS, readOnly=true)
        public List<ProductH> getProducts()
        {
        return ecommerceDao.getProducts();
        }
```

```
@Transactional(propagation=Propagation.REQUIRED, readOnly=false)
public ProductH insertProduct(ProductH product)
{
        return ecommerceDao.insertProduct(product);
}
@Transactional(propagation=Propagation.REQUIRED, readOnly=false)
public void deleteProduct(ProductH product)
{
        ecommerceDao.deleteProduct(product);
}
@Transactional(propagation=Propagation.REQUIRED, readOnly=false)
public void updateProduct(ProductH product)
{
        ecommerceDao.updateProduct(product);
}
}
```

Annotating the EcommerceService forces all implementations of the service to be transactional. In the implementation of the service, notice that there is a mix of methods that require transactions and those that are read-only. For transactions that modify the persisted storage, you should set the readOnly attribute to false. Set readOnly to true when you are doing only a read against the persisted storage. You should also set propagation to REQUIRED when you are doing a modification of the data, since it could be corrupted during the transaction. That way, you are guaranteed to get a rollback if there is a failure in the transaction.

Now, we will repeat the same process for the DAO to make it transactional. Listings 8-24 and 8-25 show the updates to the EcommerceDao and EcommerceDaoImpl.

Listing 8-24. *EcommerceDao Made Transactional with Annotations (EcommerceDao.java)*

```
package com.af.core.dao.hibernate;

import java.util.List;
import org.springframework.transaction.annotation.Transactional;
import org.springframework.transaction.annotation.Propagation;

import com.af.core.domain.ProductH;

public interface EcommerceDao
{
        @Transactional(readOnly=true, propagation=Propagation.SUPPORTS)
        List<ProductH> getProducts();

        @Transactional(readOnly=false, propagation=Propagation.REQUIRED)
        ProductH insertProduct(ProductH product);

        @Transactional(readOnly=false, propagation=Propagation.REQUIRED)
        void deleteProduct(ProductH product);
```

```
      @Transactional(readOnly=true, propagation=Propagation. REQUIRED)
      void updateProduct(ProductH product);
}
```

Listing 8-25. *EcommerceDaoImpl Made Transactional with Annotations (EcommerceDaoImpl.java)*

```java
package com.af.core.dao.hibernate;

import java.util.List;

import org.springframework.orm.hibernate3.support.HibernateDaoSupport;
import org.springframework.transaction.annotation.Propagation;
import org.springframework.transaction.annotation.Transactional;

import com.af.core.dao.hibernate.EcommerceDao;
import com.af.core.domain.ProductH;

@Transactional(propagation=Propagation.SUPPORTS, readOnly=true)
public class EcommerceDaoImpl extends HibernateDaoSupport implements EcommerceDao
{
      @Transactional(propagation=Propagation.SUPPORTS, readOnly=true)
      public List<ProductH> getProducts()
      {
            return getHibernateTemplate().find("from Product");
      }
      @Transactional(propagation=Propagation.REQUIRED, readOnly=false)
      public ProductH insertProduct(ProductH product)
      {
            return (ProductH) getHibernateTemplate().merge(product);
      }
      @Transactional(propagation=Propagation.REQUIRED, readOnly=false)
      public void deleteProduct(ProductH product)
      {
            getHibernateTemplate().delete(product);
      }
      @Transactional(propagation=Propagation. REQUIRED, readOnly=false)
      public void updateProduct(ProductH product)
      {
            getHibernateTemplate().delete(product);
      }
}
```

As you can see, we use the same annotations as with the service layer to add transaction support to the DAO and its interface.

Setting Up the BlazeDS Server for Hibernate

I am using the same BlazeDS server for this solution that I set up for the iBATIS example and named SpringDataPersistence. I will reuse the RemoteObject entry in the <tomcat-install-directory>/webapps/SpringDataPersistence/WEB-INF/flex/remoting-config.xml file for Hibernate:

```
<?xml version="1.0" encoding="UTF-8"?>
<service id="remoting-service"
    class="flex.messaging.services.RemotingService">

    <adapters>
        <adapter-definition id="java-object" class="flex.messaging.services. ➥
            remoting.adapters.JavaAdapter" default="true"/>
    </adapters>

    <default-channels>
        <channel ref="my-amf"/>
    </default-channels>

    <destination id="ecommerceService">
      <properties>
        <factory>spring</factory>
        <source>ecommerceService</source>
      </properties>
    </destination>

</service>
```

There are no changes needed for the <tomcat-install-directory>/webapps/SpringDataPersistence/WEB-INF/web.xml file, which indicates the location of the server applicationContext.xml file for the Hibernate application (Listing 8-20):

```
<context-param>
    <param-name>contextConfigLocation</param-name>
    <param-value>/WEB-INF/applicationContext.xml</param-value>
</context-param>
```

To execute this example, we can use the same application as we did with iBATIS (see Listing 8-18). It is pointed to the same BlazeDS server. Since the DAO layer was replaced by a Hibernate implementation, we can call the same endpoint and service method name as in the iBATIS implementation. This is a testament to the ability to plug in a new ORM solution without making many code changes. As you see, there are no changes to the Flex code base to support the different ORM frameworks in this case.

Summary

This chapter covered a lot of ground in regard to Spring and data persistence. We first covered how transaction management plays an integral part for ensuring data consistency. Without transaction management, your data could be left in a corrupted state. Transaction management has managers for JDBC, iBATIS, Hibernate, and most of the popular ORM packages. Transaction management provides a means to build robust software with Spring, which supports programmatic transaction management that calls commit and rollback methods directly.

Spring also supports declarative transaction management through declaring transactions through XML in the application context and through annotations. Declaring transactions can be accomplished with Spring's AOP framework by creating a proxy with the TransactionProxyFactoryBean. We also determined that using annotations is a cleaner way to declare transactions at the class level and the method level. Spring 2.5 provides an AspectJ aspects library that allows you to use @Transactional to manage transactions on methods.

We also took a look at persisting data with JDBC and ORM solutions such as iBATIS and Hibernate. With those solutions, you saw how easy it is to replace a DAO implementation of JDBC or an ORM. Note that you should not mix application logic with the DAO layer. Mixing logic couples your beans together in a way that will not allow you to easily replace a DAO persistence solution.

In the next chapter, you will learn how to secure applications with Spring, Flash, Flex, and web tier security.

CHAPTER 9

■ ■ ■

Security

Trust no one; trust no user-based content. That should be your motto when delivering secure software and systems. It is far better to overprepare for a threat than to do nothing about it in the hope that it will never happen. Flex applications can be accessed from the Internet, of course, which makes them wide open to attacks from nefarious software if they are not secured.

This chapter will dive into three security areas: Flash Player security, Flex security, and Spring Security 2.*x*. We will focus on how Spring Security can provide authentication and authorization for Flex applications, and how BlazeDS plays its part by integrating Flex session context with Spring's context.

The two terms you will become very familiar with are *authentication* and *authorization*. Authentication is the process of processing a username and password against a security system that allows you access to an application when the credentials are validated. Authorization is granted after a user is authenticated by passing groups or roles back to a user interface. Those groups can be applied to the user interface to allow access to content or sections of the application.

Upon completing this chapter, you will have learned how to secure your Flex and Spring applications by integrating the two frameworks.

Flash Player Security

Flash Player runs applications compiled into SWF files. The compiled SWF can consist of Flash or Flex applications, or a combination of both integrated together. These SWF files generally reside on a server and are downloaded to the client workstation when first accessed. Once the SWF file is downloaded to the client workstation, it is displayed and ready for interaction by being executed in the Flash Player.

Flash Player is available across a wide range of platforms, devices, and browsers. From a security point of view, that just means there are more diverse channels of attack and more potential exploits to guard against. You must protect your user data and hosting environments, and ensure that end-user information remains private. Two concepts you need to understand are local vs. network access and cross-domain access.

Note For details on security for specific versions of Flash Player. see the corresponding security PDFs on the Adobe Security Resource Center site (http://www.adobe.com/resources/security).

Local vs. Network Access

A SWF is not limited to running within the context of a web application; it can run from the local file system, a CD, or through a browser. By default, Flash Player has access to local content or network content only. Flash provides tight security controls to prevent a SWF from scanning the local file system or network assets from remote locations. The SWF must be trusted for the content it is trying to access, or Flash Player will not allow the SWF access. This prevents a SWF from becoming a virus or tool to steal personal information from users.

When a SWF accesses local content, it is loaded into the *local-with-file-system* sandbox, which is the default setting. This setting cannot access the network to load other SWF files, send HTTP requests, make external connections, or call a URL, except for getting local files or making a `mailto:` request. What the SWF can do is interact with other local-with-file-system files. One way to start Flash Player is to double-click a SWF directly in your file system, which will execute the SWF and open Flash Player.

On the other hand, if the SWF is running in a *local-with-networking* sandbox, it loses the right to access local content. This prevents a SWF running in a browser from accessing your file system. But it can transmit data over the network or Internet and read data from trusted content providers, such as data services on remote servers.

One other option is to run the SWF in a *local-trusted* sandbox, which grants the SWF both local and network access. It can read and write to servers, communicate with other SWF files, and access the file system locally. You must give the SWF explicit permissions to run in a local-trusted sandbox that includes the following:

- SWFs that run in Flex Builder

- SWFs with trusted permissions to the directory in which they reside, provided by the user

- SWFs trusted by Flash Player

■**Caution** Be very careful running a SWF in a local-trusted sandbox. If you do not know the author of the SWF or what the SWF does, do not allow it to run. The only time you should run a Flex SWF in a local-trusted sandbox is when you are testing your application locally. Generally, I run my Flex applications from a Tomcat server to eliminate any issues that arise from being in a local-trusted sandbox.

In Flex, you can set the sandbox parameter in your compiler options by setting `-use-network` to `true` for a local-with-networking sandbox or `false` for a local-with-file-system sandbox. Be aware that a SWF set to local-with-file-system cannot access another SWF with a different local access setting and vice versa.

Cross-Domain Access

One of the big "gotchas" you will encounter when you deploy a Flex or Flash application across a network, and your SWF needs to communicate with a distributed data source, is a security error due to not having your cross-domain file set up. You will see an error like this:

```
(mx.rpc::Fault)#0
 errorID = 0
  faultCode = "Channel.Security.Error"
  faultDetail = "Destination: DefaultHTTP"
  faultString = "Security error accessing url"
  message = "faultCode:Channel.Security.Error faultString:'Security error accessing
      url' faultDetail:'Destination: DefaultHTTP'"
  name = "Error"
  rootCause = (flash.events::SecurityErrorEvent)#1
    bubbles = false
    cancelable = false
    currentTarget = (flash.net::URLLoader)#2
      bytesLoaded = 0
      bytesTotal = 0
      data = (null)
      dataFormat = "text"
    eventPhase = 2
    target = (flash.net::URLLoader)#2
    text = "Error #2048: Security sandbox violation: Link: cannot load data from
      http://www.distributedDomain.com."
    type = "securityError"
```

This security measure is in effect so a SWF cannot connect or scan for information on domains on which it is not trusted. When a SWF is running on the Internet or a network, it can never access local files.

These restrictions are in place for accessing data sources for domains other than those from which the SWF is loaded. Any content—such as other SWFs, images, audio, and video—can be loaded into the SWF. However, some restrictions apply to accessing the internal aspects of this content, such as not being able to access ActionScript variables and methods, pixel information from images (bitmaps), or sound information from audio files. Neither can you load remote data stored in plain-text or XML files.

Allowing Cross-Domain Access with allowDomain()

To allow access to remote SWFs, you can use the allowDomain() method to grant SWF and HTML files access to methods and variables in the SWF in which you called the allowDomain() method.

If you have two SWF files, domainA.swf and domainB.swf, located on the same domain, you can use cross-scripting to allow communication between the SWFs. *Cross-scripting* is one SWF calling or modifying ActionScript methods or variables in another SWF. The methods and variables must be public for cross-scripting access.

If your two SWFs reside on different domains, they cannot talk to each other. By calling Security.allowDomain("domainB.swf") in domainA.swf, domainA.swf gives domainB.swf permission to call its public methods and variables.

Using Cross-Domain Policy Files

For non–SWF based content, a cross-domain policy file is required for communication to data services. For SWF-based content such as bitmaps, audio, and video, the cross-domain policy file is needed to access different content providers' data with ActionScript. XML and text files are considered data providers, and they require a cross-domain policy file for access; otherwise, the content providers will load and run in Flash Player.

To expose data to SWF files, a `cross-domain.xml` policy file needs to be put on the server that contains data the SWF is trying to access. It does not need to be on the same server that serves the SWF. The cross-domain file is an XML file that defines domains from which a SWF can access data and content. This data and content can be in the form of databases, bitmaps, audio, or video. Any SWF that is served from a domain the server sees as trusted will grant access to its assets on that server.

Flash Player will attempt to load a cross-domain policy file when a SWF tries to access data from another domain. Flash Player is responsible for managing that information to provide a secure sandbox for you to run your compiled SWFs.

The `cross-domain.xml` file resides at the root directory of the web server that is serving the data. With the `cross-domain.xml` file, site owners may configure their server to allow several levels of access to its data. The policies that can be defined are very flexible, allowing sites to be accessible by IP, domain, or subdomain or open to all access points. The following example grants access to SWFs that originate from an IP or domain, and shows how to use a wildcard for access:

```
<?xml version="1.0"?>
<!-- http://www.appfoundation.com/crossdomain.xml -->
<cross-domain-policy>
    <allow-access-from domain="www.appfoundation.com"/>
    <allow-access-from domain="*.appfoundation.com"/>
    <allow-access-from domain="555.555.555.555"/>
</cross-domain-policy>
```

You can also set your cross-domain policy to be open to everyone by setting the wildcard character (*) for the domain. There are a few high-profile sites with public web services that use an open cross-domain policy, such as Amazon, Flickr, Yahoo!, and YouTube. The open policy file would look like this:

```
<?xml version="1.0"?>
<!-- http://www.appfoundation.com/crossdomain.xml -->
<cross-domain-policy>
    <allow-access-from domain="*"/>
</cross-domain-policy>
```

The `<allow-access-from>` tag also provides a `secure` attribute, which defaults to `true`. If your policy is located on a secure HTTPS server, set the secure attribute to `false`:

```
<?xml version="1.0"?>
<!-- http://www.appfoundation.com/crossdomain.xml -->
<cross-domain-policy>
    <allow-access-from domain="*.appfoundation.com" secure="false"/>
</cross-domain-policy>
```

You can also apply security for the domain down to the port level. To configure a port for a domain, you simply add the `to-ports` attribute to the `<allow-access-from>` tag in your XML configuration, like this:

```
<?xml version="1.0"?>
<!-- http://www.appfoundation.com/crossdomain.xml -->
<cross-domain-policy>
    <allow-access-from domain="*.appfoundation.com" to-ports="1234"/>
</cross-domain-policy>
```

Another point of interest is the usage of the `loadPolicyFile()` method to access a nondefault policy file. You can tell Flash Player to use a policy file from a specified URL, as follows:

```
Security.loadPolicyFile("www.appfoundation.com/myDomainPolicy.xml")
```

Permissions granted from this file will apply in the same manner as the default cross-domain policy files. This technique can be used in enterprise architectures where you need to work with multiple domains. For instance, say you are moving from HTTP to HTTPS domains and need access across the network to run your SWF application. Using `loadPolicyFile()` can work around issues where DNS aliasing prevents you from getting the cross-domain policy from the web server.

Flex Security

Security for a Flex application depends on appropriate application programming, as well as on Flash Player itself. You must write your software in a way that implements secure functions to support the application you have built. This means securing your source code, removing sensitive information from your SWF, and making sure that data input is secure in your components.

When writing a Flex application, you should do the following to make it as secure as possible:

- Hide your source code by disabling the `viewSourceURL` property.

- Validate input to your forms and controls.

- Secure your ActionScript.

- Make passwords secure.

- Use `SharedObject` to store nonsensitive persistent data on the user's computer.

You also should understand which MXML tags have security restrictions.

Understanding Security Restrictions Within MXML Tags

MXML tags can trigger operations that require the application to be granted secure access to data or destinations the MXML calls. These operations include calling a URL outside the domain where the application resides, HTTP requesting a URL not served over HTTPS, and attempting to access an asset located in a distributed Flash Player sandbox.

As explained earlier in this chapter, you are required to grant access to your MXML through a `cross-domain.xml` policy file or through the `allowDomain()` method. These actions require security settings in Flash Player. There are also situations that trigger a security check to occur, such as the following:

- Using the `<mx:SWFLoader>` MXML tag

- Using the `<mx:DataSevice>` MXML tag

- Using the messaging tags `<mx:Consumer>` and `<mx:Producer>`

- Writing a class that extends the `Channel` class

- Using Flex communication protocols such as `<mx:HTTPService>`, `<mx:RemoteObject>`, and `<mx:WebService>`

These tags also have several associated base classes built into the Flash API, including `ExternalInterface`, `Loader`, `NetStream`, `SoundMixer`, `URLLoader`, and `URLRequest`.

Disabling the Ability to View Source Code

You can choose to share your source code by using the `viewSourceURL` property in the `<mx:Application>` tag of your application, as follows:

```
<?xml version="1.0" encoding="utf-8"?>
<mx:Application xmlns:mx="http://www.adobe.com/2006/mxml"
    viewSourceURL="srcview/index.html">
</mx:Application>
```

This will create a folder in your Flex application distribution that contains all of the source code for your application. Other developers running your Flex application on a web server can right-click the application and select View Source from the menu that appears. The Flex application will launch a new window with all of the source code available to view. Users can also download the source in the form of a zip file.

This is great for sharing, but be sure to remove the `viewSourceURL` property from your Flex application before it goes to a production site or is made available on the Internet. Otherwise, anyone could get all of your hard work.

Securing Data in SWF Files

Just like conventional web pages, Flash-based applications must handle data responsibly. The SWF must be secure in what information it contains. This is especially important with data, variables, and ActionScript in your SWF.

Since the SWF file is built on an open format, there is a possibility that data compiled within the SWF could be extracted using a SWF decompiler. Granted, this takes some time and effort, but it is quite feasible. Like HTML and JavaScript, SWF files can be read by users, although reading the information is much more difficult, since it is binary rather than plain text.

There are several ways to ensure that you limit the exposure of your sensitive information while making it available in your SWF. To better secure your SWF, you can employ the following techniques, as appropriate:

- Never deliver a SWF with sensitive information loaded into constants. Such data includes usernames, passwords, SQL statements, and any configuration data used for server-side security.

- Never validate a username or password in your Flex or Flash application. Let the server handle those requests. Remember that, for the most part, your Flex application is a data-capture point and should not hold much business logic.

- Be careful how much information you use for comments. Comments can be extracted and used to attack a system or can give revealing hints about how to reverse-engineer your application. Also remove debugging information from your code and all excess code.

- Try to load sensitive information into your SWF at runtime. This information should reside on a server where it is not publicly accessible. Since the data is not part of your SWF, you will have eliminated a potential breach in your security. When transferring data to your SWF, you can use Secure Sockets Layer (SSL) to do so securely. Use SSL whenever possible.

- If you have algorithms that must not be compromised, put them on the server instead of in your ActionScript.

- Be sure your Flex applications are deployed on trusted servers to limit the exposure of the configuration files and other server-side assets needed to run your application.

- If you have images, sound, or video that you do not want shared, do not embed them into your application, because they could be extracted from the SWF.

Validating Input

Validating input entails more than just checking whether a phone number is formatted correctly or if a user needs help based on what was typed in a form field. It is also a way to ensure you are accepting only the data you expect. What if you expect to get an address and instead you get something like `DELETE * from products`? This is called *SQL injection*. You will want a way to filter out SQL commands before the statement is sent to your server and potentially executed. One way to handle SQL injection is to create parameterized queries that do not take plain-text entries. That way, you are never uncritically executing a query sent from a client application.

Many Flex applications take data entry through `TextInput`, `TextArea`, `Text`, or even `DataGrid` components. These controls open up the system to potential attacks. It is up to you to program the inputs so that malicious characters cannot be entered into your application.

One way to reduce the risk of bad data input is to use the Flex validators. These help to specify what can and cannot be typed into an input control. Flex provides several validators, such as `StringValidator`, `PhoneNumberValidator`, `DateValidator`, and `CreditCardValidator`. These provide a more secure means of data capture and should be used when you are building a Flex application exposed to the Internet or for general usage.

In traditional settings, much of the data validation occurs on the server. I am an advocate of keeping your business logic on the server, even though Flex is quite capable of doing all data validation. That being said, there are advantages to allowing Flex to validate data before it is shipped to the server. You do not need to handle errors returned from the server, and by validating data in Flex, you will process fewer transactions on server-side resources. This helps to create a more responsive application, which will please your end users.

Another approach to securing input characters in Flex is to create ActionScript filters to remove potentially harmful characters before they are sent to a server. Characters you will want to strip out are those that have meaning in a programming language or system, such as the following:

- Semicolon (;)

- Apostrophe (')

- Dollar sign ($)

- Quotation mark (")

Flex can also render HTML in controls. Before you save characters in an HTML input control, you should convert the following characters to limit exposure to malicious HTML injection:

- Left and right brackets (< >); translate to &lt and &gt

- Left and right parentheses (( )); translate to &#40 and &#41

- Pound sign (#); translates to &#35

- Ampersand (&); translates to &#38

Note For more information about potentially harmful characters, see "Understanding Malicious Content Mitigation for Web Developers" at http://www.cert.org/tech_tips/malicious_code_mitigation.html.

Securing ActionScript

Within ActionScript, several security management techniques can help manage your Flex applications, as well as help you understand what is happening to your application when someone attempts to misuse it. To get started, let's take a look at how you can use the Logging API to capture and write messages from your application to a target's output location.

Logging API

In Flex, you can use the Logging API to log messages so you can see what your application is doing based on output methods you define. This technique is equivalent to using the global trace() method to output debugging messages for your application. The Logging API consists of three main parts:

Logger: The logger is an interface responsible for sending messages to an active target. Your loggers implement ILogger, which is a layer of abstraction that allows you to use the log class. The loggers you create work under a category, which is an informative string used to define your log messages. You can use categories to effectively filter log information.

Log target: A log target defines where a message should be written. The TraceTarget and MiniDebugTarget targets are already defined in Flex, with TraceTarget the most commonly used. The Logging API is connected to the global trace system through log targets. The trace() method and log targets send log information to the same output locations.

Destination: A destination is simply where a log message is written. This can be a file, the console, or in memory to be displayed in the Flex application. You can configure your destination as you wish. The default destination is the flashlog.txt file.

Log levels are defined in the LogEventLevel class as constants, as shown in Table 9-1. Setting log levels allows you to limit the amount of messages sent to logging destinations. This helps you determine what you need logged to keep your log files manageable when you have moved your application to a production environment.

Table 9-1. *Log Level Constants for the LogEventLevel Class*

Log Level	Description
ALL (0)	Logs all levels of messages.
DEBUG (2)	Logs debugging activities in a Flex application. Setting DEBUG as the logging level will include logging for DEBUG, INFO, WARN, ERROR, and FATAL messages.
INFO (4)	Logs general information including INFO, WARN, ERROR, and FATAL messages.
WARN (6)	Logs a message when the Flex application has a problem. The application can still run with a warning message. This level will include WARN, ERROR, and FATAL messages.
ERROR (8)	Logs an error message when enoountering a problem that renders the Flex application in a state of restricted service. This level of logging includes only ERROR and FATAL messages.
FATAL (1000)	Logs a message when a FATAL error has occurred, rendering the Flex application inoperable.

Debug Output

You may want to hide or suppress debug information from the global trace() method in case a user has the debug version of Flash installed. Flash Player writes all output from trace() statements to a log file on the client. If clients are running the debug version of Flash Player, they could see your output. Be sure to remove all trace() statements and Logging API calls that output debugging information.

Note If you are using the Logging API within your custom components, you will want to set the
LogEventLevel to NONE before you compile your application. That way, you will not output debugging
information from your components to consumers.

Error Management

Error management is as critical in Flex as in any other application. Managing your errors for
login, security, and component-level errors helps you create more robust software that will
better serve your end users.

SecurityError exceptions can be thrown in response to security violations such as the
following:

- Security sandbox violations

- Attempts to access a URL not allowed by the security sandbox

- Port number violations

- Attempts to access a user device that was denied by the user

Flash Player is responsible for dispatching SecurityErrorEvents to notify a Flex application that a violation has occurred. Flex can set listeners for the SecurityErrorEvent to handle
the violation. It can read the event's text property to determine which violation prompted the
event to be dispatched. Listing 9-1 shows adding an event listener to listen for a security violation.

Listing 9-1. *SecurityError Example*

```
<?xml version="1.0"?>
<mx:Application xmlns:mx="http://www.adobe.com/2006/mxml" >

    <mx:Script>
    <![CDATA[
        import flash.events.SecurityErrorEvent;
        import mx.controls.Alert;
        import flash.display.Sprite;
        import flash.net.Socket;

        private var socket:Socket = new Socket();

        private function initApp():void
        {
            socket.addEventListener(SecurityErrorEvent.SECURITY_ERROR,
                securityErrorHandler);
        }
```

```
        private function triggerSecurityError():void
        {
                var host:String = "www.appfoundation.com";

                socket.connect(host, 65536);
        }

        private function securityErrorHandler(event:SecurityErrorEvent):void
        {
                trace("securityErrorHandler: " + event.text);
        }
    ]]>
    </mx:Script>

    <mx:Button label="Do It!" click="triggerSecurityError()"/>

</mx:Application>
```

■**Tip** It is good practice to wrap methods that may trigger a security error with a try/catch block. This will help protect sensitive information, such as a URL or other behind-the-scenes information you don't want users to see.

The sample application tries to make a socket connection to an invalid port number. That is what triggers the SecurityErrorEvent. If there are no listeners defined, Flash Player will show the SecurityErrorEvent text property if the debugger version of Flash is installed. If you run this application through the Flex debugger, you will see a trace message with the following information error:

SecurityError: Error #2003: Invalid socket port number specified.

Password Protection

Any time you create a login panel, you will have a password input box displayed for the user. Using passwords in Flex is no different than using them in other application types. You are using this field to authenticate users based on their credentials against a server-side repository, like Lightweight Directory Access Protocol (LDAP), a database, Resource Access Control Facility (RACF), or Windows NT security. Passwords are never stored locally. They reside in one of these server repositories.

Never use a SharedObject object (discussed in the next section) to store user credentials. The SharedObject method allows you to hold persisted data locally for Flex to consume. Anyone with access to the computer on which you store data in a SharedObject can easily access the plain-text file. I also suggest transporting passwords using SSL or another form of secure protocol.

The main time you will be concerned with a password is when you ask the user to enter it through a text-based control in Flex, such as a TextArea, TextInput, or Text component. To make sure that the field does not display the password text as typed, use the displayAsPassword property on the control and set it to true. This will mask the password with asterisks when a character is typed. Listing 9-2 shows an example of using the displayAsPassword property.

Listing 9-2. *Protecting Passwords Using displayAsPassword*

```
<?xml version="1.0" encoding="utf-8"?>
<mx:Application xmlns:mx="http://www.adobe.com/2006/mxml">

    <mx:Script>
    <![CDATA[
        private function doLogin():void
        {
            // Send the login credentials to a server side authentication
            // server and handle the result
        }
    ]]>
    </mx:Script>

    <mx:Panel title="Password Protection Example"
        paddingLeft="10" paddingRight="10" paddingBottom="10" paddingTop="10"
        horizontalAlign="center" width="506" height="300"
        styleName="blackBackground">
        <mx:VBox id="loginBox"
            backgroundImage="assets/images/LoginScreen.png">
            <mx:Canvas width="370" height="227" styleName="canvasFont">
                <mx:VBox x="50" y="9" verticalGap="-1">
                    <mx:HBox horizontalGap="0" x="26" y="14">
                        <mx:Label text="APPFOUNDATION"
                            styleName="labelFontOrange"/>
                        <mx:Label text="LOG IN"
                            styleName="labelFontWhite"/>
                    </mx:HBox>
                    <mx:TextArea backgroundAlpha="0" wordWrap="true"
                        borderStyle="none"
                        selectable="false" editable="false"
                        text="Enter your username and password below."
                        width="288" height="35"/>
                </mx:VBox>
                <mx:TextInput id="txtUserName" width="278" height="18"
                    enter="doLogin()"
                    y="67" x="52" styleName="loginTextInput"/>
```

```
                        <mx:TextInput id="txtPassword" width="278" height="18"
                            enter="doLogin()"
                            displayAsPassword="true" y="88" x="52"
                            styleName="loginTextInput"/>
                        <mx:VBox width="100%" y="101" horizontalAlign="center">
                            <mx:Text id="boxLoginMessage" />
                            <mx:Label id="lblLoginMsg"
                                    styleName="loginMessageFont"/>
                        </mx:VBox>
                        <mx:Button label="LOG IN" styleName="loginButton"
                            click="doLogin()"
                            x="276" y="128" width="65" height="31"/>
                    </mx:Canvas>
                </mx:VBox>
            </mx:Panel>
</mx:Application>
```

Figure 9-1 shows the simple login screen produced by this example.

Figure 9-1. *Output from masked password in a TextInput control*

The SharedObject Class

The SharedObject class allows you to store persistent data on a user's computer. This data is in a local plain-text file that can be read using the SharedObject.getLocal() method. You can store object data in a SharedObject object simply by creating a new SharedObject, much as you would add object attributes to a value object in Flex.

Listing 9-3 shows an example of a Flex application that takes in notes and stores them locally in a SharedObject defined as Notes.

Listing 9-3. *Local SharedObject Example*

```
<?xml version="1.0" encoding="utf-8"?>
<mx:Application xmlns:mx="http://www.adobe.com/2006/mxml"
      creationComplete="initSharedObject()">

    <mx:Style source="assets/css/style.css"/>

    <mx:Script>
        <![CDATA[
            import mx.controls.Alert;

            public var so:SharedObject;

            private function initSharedObject():void
            {
                so = SharedObject.getLocal("Notes");
                if (so.size > 0)
                    taNotes.text = so.data.notes;
            }
            private function clearNotes(event:MouseEvent):void
            {
                taNotes.text = "";
            }
            private function saveNotes(event:MouseEvent):void
            {
                so.data.notes = taNotes.text;
                so.flush();
            }
            private function deleteSavedNotes(event:MouseEvent):void
            {
                so.clear();
                taNotes.text = "";
            }
        ]]>
    </mx:Script>

    <mx:Panel title="SharedObject Example"
        paddingLeft="10" paddingRight="10" paddingBottom="10" paddingTop="10"
        horizontalAlign="center" width="592" height="377">
        <mx:HBox width="100%" height="100%">
            <mx:VBox>
                <mx:Button id="clearNotesbtn" width="100%"
                    click="clearNotes(event)"
                    label="Clear Notes"/>
```

```
                    <mx:Button id="saveNotesbtn" width="100%"
                            click="saveNotes(event)"
                            label="Save Notes"/>
                    <mx:Button id="deleteNotesbtn" width="100%"
                            click="deleteSavedNotes(event)"
                            label="Delete Notes"/>
                </mx:VBox>
                <mx:TextArea id="taNotes" width="100%" height="100%"/>
            </mx:HBox>
        </mx:Panel>
</mx:Application>
```

In the initialize method of Listing 9-3, SharedObject.getLocal("Notes") is called to create a
SharedObject in memory for Flash Player to use. By adding the object name on the instantiation of the SharedObject, you can retrieve any previously saved data from the local file. In this
case, I am setting the object data to the <mx:TextArea> text property.

You can type anything into the free-form TextArea, as shown in Figure 9-2, and save it to
the local SharedObject by clicking the Save Notes button. This will set the taNotes.text content
to the SharedObject's data property so.data.notes. The next time you start the application, it
will pull the notes from the local SharedObject and display them.

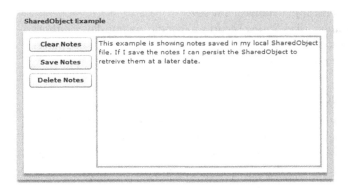

Figure 9-2. *The SharedObject.mxml application*

You also have the option to delete content in the SharedObject by invoking the SharedObject.
clear() method. This will remove any data from your local SharedObject file.

■**Caution** You should be careful what you save in a local SharedObject, since it potentially can be
accessed from other SWFs than the one that saved the data.

Authentication and Authorization for Flex with Spring Security

Spring Security 2.*x* has evolved from the Acegi Security system to become a much easier solution for enterprise security in Spring. Spring Security 2.*x* adds many new features, such as AspectJ pointcut support, namespace configuration syntax for other security systems (LDAP for example), and OpenID integration.

Every application needs to provide secure methods of data transport, business logic access, and secure access. Flex must take all of these security aspects into account when delivering a user interface on the Web or a client's intranet. Spring Security is a robust way of deploying Flex applications that require an enterprise security solution.

To get the latest version of Spring Security, visit `http://springframework.org/download` to download the Spring Security 2.*x* JAR files. The examples in this book use `spring-security-core-2.0.4.jar`, `spring-security-core-tiger-2.0.4.jar`, and `spring-security-taglibs-2.0.4.jar`.

Spring Security offers the ability to integrate authentication and authorization with your Flex applications. You log in a user (authenticate) and apply roles to your Flex applications (authorize). You can create a user profile that is held in your Flex application's context to control what a user sees and doesn't see. By letting the server and client know who users are and what roles they have, you can grant or deny access to business logic and user interface functions. This can be applied to Flex applications of any size.

You can secure a Flex application using Spring Security to handle method-level authorization, URL security, authentication, and user roles for authorization. You can also use BlazeDS to apply security restrictions to RemoteObject destination definitions.

Using Method-Level Security

AspectJ implements join points, pointcuts, advices, and aspect constructs for AOP in Java. In particular, when triggered, pointcuts perform specific actions, such as controlling security role access. To implement method-level security, you can use AspectJ pointcuts to define which objects and methods should be secure and the access level setting.

Listing 9-4 shows an example of the pointcut definitions to secure Spring methods. These global method security definitions are located in a new file called `SecurityContext.xml`. This keeps the security functions separate from those in the `ApplicationContext.xml` file.

Listing 9-4. *The Global Method Security Definition*

```
<security:global-method-security>
    <security:protect-pointcut
        expression="execution(* com.af.core.services.*Service.delete*(..))"
        access="ROLE_ADMIN"/>
    <security:protect-pointcut
        expression="execution(* com.af.core.services.*Service.get*(..))"
        access="ROLE_USER"/>
</security:global-method-security>
```

This example demonstrates how naming conventions can be your friend. For my applications, I end every Spring service name with Service. As you can see in Listing 9-4, I have secured all methods that end with Service in the name. This way, I do not need to deal with every individual service I have created for an application. Within the services, I allow access to delete methods only for a user with the access group of ROLE_ADMIN. All get methods are accessible with the group ROLE_USER. Users who are not in one of the defined groups will not have access to execute the methods owned by the access group.

Securing Flex with Spring Security

To demonstrate how to secure Flex with Spring Security, we will run through an end-to-end example using Spring Security, BlazeDS, and Spring. We will expand the Flex code in Listing 9-2 to authenticate against Spring Security using Spring's in-memory storage. When we build the AF – Client Manager application in the upcoming chapters, we will use Hibernate to persist security credentials from a database.

Setting Up BlazeDS Server

The first task is to add security filters to the web.xml file located on the BlazeDS server, as shown in Listing 9-5.

Listing 9-5. *The web.xml File with Spring Security Filters*

```
<context-param>
      <param-name>contextConfigLocation</param-name>
      <param-value>
            /WEB-INF/applicationContext.xml,
            /WEB-INF/springSecurityContext.xml
       </param-value>
</context-param>

<filter>
      <filter-name>springSecurityFilterChain</filter-name>
      <filter-class>
            org.springframework.web.filter.DelegatingFilterProxy
      </filter-class>
</filter>

<filter-mapping>
      <filter-name>springSecurityFilterChain</filter-name>
      <url-pattern>/*</url-pattern>
</filter-mapping>
```

In the web.xml file, a filter is used to intercept all requests. This filter will listen for security requests to properly process them in a secure container. Also notice that we added the springSecurityContext.xml file as part of the context parameters. This will load both context files when your web server starts.

With that done, we need to configure the security context to actually secure URLs, Spring methods, and Spring in-memory users. All of this will reside in the springSecurityContext.xml file, shown in Listing 9-6.

Listing 9-6. *The springSecurityContext.xml Security Definitions*

```xml
<?xml version="1.0" encoding="UTF-8"?>
<beans xmlns="http://www.springframework.org/schema/beans"
       xmlns:xsi="http://www.w3.org/2001/XMLSchema-instance"
       xmlns:security="http://www.springframework.org/schema/security"
       xsi:schemaLocation="
       http://www.springframework.org/schema/beans
       http://www.springframework.org/schema/beans/spring-beans-2.5.xsd
       http://www.springframework.org/schema/security
       http://www.springframework.org/schema/security/spring-security-2.0.4.xsd">

<security:http auto-config="true">
    <security:intercept-url pattern="index.html" filters="none"/>
    <security:intercept-url pattern="*.swf" filters="none"/>
    <security:intercept-url pattern="*.html" access="ROLE_USER"/>
</security:http>

<security:authentication-provider>
    <security:user-service>
        <security:user name="katiebug" password="test"
                authorities="ROLE_USER, ROLE_ADMIN"/>
        <security:user name="colie" password="test" authorities="ROLE_USER"/>
    </security:user-service>
</security:authentication-provider>

</beans>
```

This security configuration secures URL access and creates the in-memory user credentials we will store for the application. This is also where you would create your method-level security declarations, as explained in the previous section. For this application, we are performing only authentication and authorization in Flex. We will implement method-level security in the AF – Client Manager application.

URL access is controlled by using the <security:http> tag to intercept URL patterns you define. In this case, we are concerned with the index.html (Flex SWF wrapping file), all SWFs, and all HTML files. We did not secure the SWF. The SWF contains our Flex application, and we want everyone to be able to download and use the SWF.

We have also set up a <security:authentication-provider> for our Flex login screen to access. In this case, the in-memory storage will be sufficient for our application. We created two roles for the application users: ROLE_USER and ROLE_ADMIN. These roles will be used for authorization of components in our Flex application.

Since we are going to use Spring Security to authenticate Flex users, we need to create a RemoteObject destination in the /WEB-INF/flex/remoting-config.xml file, as follows:

```
<destination id="securityService">
    <properties>
            <factory>spring</factory>
            <source>securityService</source>
        </properties>
</destination>
```

This gives a destination for Flex to access the `securityService` Spring bean. This application will implement only the `securityService` in Spring, and will not have any other business
logic or services. In your `applicationContext.xml` file, you need to add only the following bean:

```
<bean id="securityService"
    class="com.af.springsecurity.flex.services.SecAuthServiceImpl"/>
```

Setting up Spring Security in BlazeDS takes only a few more steps than you would normally go
through to configure Spring beans. With security implemented on the back end, we can proceed
with creating the Spring security service and the Flex application to consume those services.

Creating the Spring Security Authentication Bean

The Spring bean for authentication is a section of code that you will want to partition into its
own package structure so you can reuse it in other applications. As you work toward creating a
robust security solution with Spring Security, you will want to add features to the core security
classes that you write. This bean will integrate `FlexContext` with Spring Security.

Since we are using in-memory storage for the usernames and passwords, we will not need
a DAO layer for the Spring bean. This bean will consist of a class that implements the
`SecService` interface. The `SecService` interface will expose the `authenticateUser()` method
that accepts a username and password to pass into Spring Security. Listing 9-7 shows the
`SecService` class, and Listing 9-8 shows the `SecServiceImpl` class.

Listing 9-7. *The SecService Class (SecService.java)*

```
package com.af.springsecurity.flex.services;

import com.af.springsecurity.flex.domain.UserProfile;

public interface SecService
{
    public UserProfile authenticateUser(String username, String password);
}
```

Listing 9-8. *The SecServiceImpl Class (SecServiceImpl.java)*

```
package com.af.springsecurity.flex.services;

import com.af.springsecurity.flex.domain.UserProfile;

import flex.messaging.FlexContext;
```

```java
import java.security.Principal;
import java.util.List;
import java.io.Serializable;

import org.springframework.context.ApplicationContext;
import org.springframework.security.Authentication;
import org.springframework.security.AuthenticationManager;
import org.springframework.security.GrantedAuthority;
import org.springframework.security.context.SecurityContextHolder;
import org.springframework.security.providers.UsernamePasswordAuthenticationToken;
import org.springframework.transaction.annotation.Propagation;
import org.springframework.transaction.annotation.Transactional;
import org.springframework.web.context.support.WebApplicationContextUtils;

public class SecServiceImpl implements Serializable, SecService
{
    public UserProfile authenticateUser(String username, String password)
    {
        String name;
        Authentication authentication;
        ApplicationContext context;
        AuthenticationManager authManager;
        UsernamePasswordAuthenticationToken token =
            new UsernamePasswordAuthenticationToken(username,password);
        GrantedAuthority[] authorities;
        int authoritiesCount;
        String[] authorizedGroups;

        context =
    WebApplicationContextUtils.getWebApplicationContext(
        FlexContext.getServletConfig().getServletContext());

        authManager = (AuthenticationManager)context.getBean(
            "_authenticationManager");

        authentication = authManager.authenticate(token);

        SecurityContextHolder.getContext().setAuthentication(authentication);

        authorities =
    SecurityContextHolder.getContext().getAuthentication().getAuthorities();

        authoritiesCount = authorities.length;

        authorizedGroups = new String[authoritiesCount];
```

```
        for (int counter = 0; counter < authoritiesCount ; counter++)
        {
                authorizedGroups[counter] = authorities[counter].getAuthority();
        }

        name =
    SecurityContextHolder.getContext().getAuthentication().getName();

        return new UserProfile(authorizedGroups,name);
    }
}
```

▦ Note The SecService bean is derived from Jettro Coenradie's examples at http://www.adobe.com/
devnet/flex/articles/flex_security.html and http://www.gridshore.nl. Be sure to check
out more of his articles from those two web sites.

The SecService bean is responsible for authenticating user credentials against Spring
Security stored in memory. Once the user is authenticated, the group roles are pulled from
memory and sent back to Flex. FlexContext is used to access Spring's application context
through Spring's ServletContext class. We also register an AuthenticationManager bean in an
application context called _authenticationManager. Notice that there is no reference to the
_authenticationManager bean in Listing 9-8. This bean is managed by Spring Security when
you use the security namespace. It is an underlying bean available in the security namespace,
and it is automatically registered for you to use.

You will also want to create a token to hold in context based on the username and password using the UsernamePasswordAuthenticationToken class. This token is passed into the
authenticate() method managed by the _authenticationManager bean we created and is persisted
in session for future use.

The last point of interest is the result of the authorization attempt. If the user is authenticated, authorization groups will be packaged and sent back to the Flex client. In this case, a
UserProfile domain object containing the username and groups is created and sent back. This
domain object actually contains more attributes than we are populating. As you can see in
Listing 9-9, we are using only two of the attributes through a public constructor. When this
domain object is populated from a database, it will have a full set of user profile data to represent
the Flex principal. This domain object is mapped in Flex with a similar UserProfile value object.

Listing 9-9. *The UserProfile Domain Object*

```
package com.af.springsecurity.flex.domain;

import java.io.Serializable;
```

```
public class UserProfile implements Serializable
{
        int objectIdentifier;
        private String username;
        String userFirstName;
        String userMiddleName;
        String userLastName;
        String organizationID;
        String creationDate;
        String lastUpdateDate;
        private String[] groups;

        public UserProfile(String[] groups, String username)
        {
                this.groups = groups;
                this.username = username;
        }

        // Getters and Setters
}
```

Creating the Flex Application to Authenticate and Authorize Users

Earlier, in Listing 9-2, we built a login screen that protected the password in Flex. To expand on that example, we need to use that component to authenticate the user with Spring Security. We will also use this opportunity to apply the granted user groups to authorize components in the Flex application based on whether the user is an administrator. This technique can be used to secure access rights for users of enterprise Flex applications.

Listing 9-10 shows the Flex Spring Security application, and Listing 9-11 shows the user profile.

Listing 9-10. *The Flex SpringSecurity Application (SpringSecurity.mxml)*

```
<?xml version="1.0" encoding="utf-8"?>
<mx:Application xmlns:mx="http://www.adobe.com/2006/mxml">

        <mx:Script>
        <![CDATA[
                import com.af.security.vo.UserProfile;
                import mx.rpc.events.ResultEvent;
                import mx.rpc.events.FaultEvent;
                import mx.controls.Alert;

                private var userProfile:UserProfile = new UserProfile();
```

```
        private function doLogin():void
        {
              securityService.authenticateUser(txtUserName.text,
                                                      txtPassword.text);
        }
        private function authorizationResultHandler (event:ResultEvent):void
        {
              userProfile.groups = event.result.groups as Array;
              userProfile.userIsAdmin();
        }
        private function authorizationFaultHandler(event:FaultEvent):void
        {
              Alert.show(event.fault.toString());
        }
  ]]>
  </mx:Script>


<mx:RemoteObject id="securityService" destination="securityService"
     endpoint="http://localhost:8080/blazeds/messagebroker/amf"
     fault="authorizationFaultHandler(event)"
     result=" authorizationResultHandler (event)">
  </mx:RemoteObject>


<mx:Panel title="Spring Security Example"
        paddingLeft="10" paddingRight="10" paddingBottom="10" paddingTop="10"
        horizontalAlign="center" width="506" height="300"
      styleName="blackBackground" label="horizontal">
        <mx:HBox width="100%" height="100%">
              <mx:VBox id="loginBox"
                    backgroundImage="assets/images/LoginScreen.png">
                    <mx:Canvas width="370" height="227" styleName="canvasFont">
                          <mx:VBox x="50" y="9" verticalGap="-1">
                                <mx:HBox horizontalGap="0" x="26" y="14">
                                      <mx:Label text="APPFOUNDATION"
                                            styleName="labelFontOrange"/>
                                      <mx:Label text="LOG IN"
                                            styleName="labelFontWhite"/>
                                </mx:HBox>
                                <mx:TextArea backgroundAlpha="0" wordWrap="true"
                                      borderStyle="none"
                                      selectable="false" editable="false"
                                      text="Enter your username and password
                                      below." width="288" height="35"/>
                          </mx:VBox>
```

```
                                  <mx:TextInput id="txtUserName" width="278"
                                       height="18" enter="doLogin()"
                                        y="67" x="52" styleName="loginTextInput"/>
                                  <mx:TextInput id="txtPassword" width="278"
                                       height="18" enter="doLogin()"
                                       displayAsPassword="true" y="88" x="52"
                                       styleName="loginTextInput"/>
                                  <mx:VBox width="100%" y="101"
                                       horizontalAlign="center">
                                       <mx:Text id="boxLoginMessage" />
                                       <mx:Label id="lblLoginMsg"
                                            styleName="loginMessageFont"/>
                                  </mx:VBox>
                                  <mx:Button label="LOG IN" styleName="loginButton"
                                       click="doLogin()"
                                       x="276" y="128" width="65" height="31"/>
                            </mx:Canvas>
                      </mx:VBox>
                      <mx:VBox borderStyle="solid" visible="{userProfile.isAdmin}"
                            showEffect="Dissolve" >
                            <mx:Image source="assets/images/KaitBug.png" />
                            <mx:Label text="Authorized"/>
                      </mx:VBox>
                </mx:HBox>
           </mx:Panel>
</mx:Application>
```

Listing 9-11. *The User Profile (UserProfile.as)*

```
package com.af.security.vo
{
     import mx.collections.ArrayCollection;

     [Bindable]
     [RemoteClass(alias="com.af.springsecurity.domain.UserProfile")]

     public class UserProfile
     {
          public var groups:Array;
          public var username:String;
          public var isAdmin:Boolean = false;
```

```
public function userIsAdmin():void
{
    for (var i:String in groups)
    {
        if (groups[i] == "ROLE_ADMIN")
        {
            isAdmin = true;
        }
    }
}
public function addUserGroup(group:String):void
{
    groups.push(group);
}
```

This is another component that you will want to separate from your main Flex code and add to your component library. You can reskin the login screen for any application you build. For this example, we are building an all-in-one application to authenticate users against Spring Security.

When you first run this application, you will not see the image in the top right of the main panel. You will see the image only after you are authorized to access that content. Currently, the only user who can see the content is katiebug (one of my daughter's many nicknames). She has admin rights for this application. When a user is authorized through the RemoteObject call to the securityService destination, the results arrive in the handleAuthenticatePrincipal result handler. The result handler sets the authorized groups to the userProfile.groups Array and performs a check to see if the user is an administrator. If an error is returned from the server, the authorizationFaultHandler is called, and the error message is displayed in the client. In this example, we also set an endpoint to a local Tomcat web server that contains the compiled Spring services and BlazeDS server. That way, we can run our application remotely from the web server container.

The UserProfile value object contains the username and groups Array necessary to apply authorization for the application. This value object will eventually be created in a singleton model to be accessed by the entire application to manage authorized content.

To run this application, you will need the commons-logging.jar and backport-utils-concurrent.jar files. Running the Flex application will allow you to attempt to authorize user credentials against Spring Security, as shown in Figure 9-3. By using the username katiebug and password test, the user is granted the ROLE_ADMIN and ROLE_USER roles. With ROLE_ADMIN, Flex will allow access to the image content.

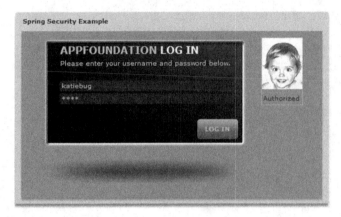

Figure 9-3. *Output from authenticating a user with ROLE_ADMIN*

Although this example only uses an image, you can see how this technique can be employed to handle authorized content such as data-entry components, financial data in a dashboard, or access to sensitive data loaded into List and DataGrid controls.

Summary

In this chapter, you have seen that Flex and Spring security play a critical role in building robust software that protects your client's sensitive data. You learned how to secure Flex applications and how to secure the Spring service layer by implementing authentication in Spring that returns authorization groups to Flex for use in the user interface.

There are times that you may want to secure URLs or methods with Spring's context. This is to prevent unauthorized access to those controls. This also relieves the user interface from building in security logic to handle which methods a user can and cannot call on the server, which is a good practice.

Flash Player offers quite robust security to prevent a SWF from scanning networks or local directories on your computer for information. Flash Player relies on a cross-domain policy file to grant access to resources outside the domain in which the SWF is running. This is one of the major issues that many people new to Flex and Flash run into when building a distributed system. The issue usually does not manifest itself until you move to a model office or production environment. Run those applications from a web server, rather than locally, to expose as many cross-domain issues as you can. Running the application directly in Flex Builder runs the application in a local-trusted sandbox, which bypasses most security and will give you a false sense of trust, as you'll find when you move to production, which will run the application in a local-with-networking sandbox.

In this chapter's coverage, Flex security was divided into two categories. The first was integrating Flex with Spring Security through authorization and applying authentication in the Flex application. The second was to build secure applications in Flex by securing your application through removing viewSourceURL, avoiding sensitive information in debug statements, validating input, managing errors, protecting passwords, and using shared objects that store persistent data on a user's computer.

So far, this book has focused on giving you the means to build Flex and Spring applications that are integrated to provide an end-to-end enterprise solution for delivering robust software to fit business needs of major organizations. In the next chapter, we will move on to the second focus of this book: building the AF – Client Manager application. Chapter 10 will bring all aspects of the enterprise development process together with the definition and starting points of building a large-scale RIA with Spring integration.

CHAPTER 10

■ ■ ■

Flex, Spring, Cairngorm, Hibernate: Bringing It All Together

So far, we have focused on individual aspects of Flex and Spring by defining many integration points involving security, ORM solutions, project definition, and database connectivity. Much of programming reflects one of my favorite analogies: crawl, walk, then run. You learn the individual pieces, then begin to put them together, and in the end, you have a complete software solution. What better way to learn the complete solution than to build one from scratch?

The remainder of this book will involve taking what you have learned and building an enterprise Flex application on Spring. I will be sharing what went into building the AF – Client Manager application in detail, so you will have a complete understanding of large-scale RIA development.

I know that if you wanted to learn a single platform or single language, you would not be reading this book. You are reading it to find out how to integrate Flex with Spring and its solid architecture. For Flex, we will use Cairngorm as the developer framework to deliver the user interface. In Spring, a DAO will be integrated with a service implementation.

In Chapter 2, we defined the project work breakdown structure. This chapter will define the three projects that we need to support Flex and Spring development. I will describe everything you need to develop the application, including the SWCs, JARs, and RIA artifacts. RIA artifacts are located in a common repository where any Flex application modules—such as reusable components, local images, local shared CSS, and compiled modules—can access them.

To get started, we will refine the project's business needs and how to deliver those needs with Flex and Spring.

AF – Client Manager Project Definition

Before we set up our environment, we need to define the project business objectives for AF – Client Manager. From a technical standpoint, this project will be built with the following technology stack: Flex, Cairngorm, Spring, Spring BlazeDS Integration, Spring Security, BlazeDS, Hibernate, Tomcat, and MySQL. Each of these layers will play a role in configuration and have architectural implications across all integration points of the stack. We have covered most of these issues in the previous chapters. Now we are bringing all the technology together. Our aim is to build the application so that each component of the architecture is secure, properly integrated, and robust.

Note To properly scale this application, you would run it across multiple application servers by either sharing web sessions across servers or by implementing a load balancer that applies a sticky bit to keep you routed to the server to which you initially connect.

Project Business Need

Most middle- to large-sized companies need a way to manage client accounts, projects, and financials with an integrated software package. One purpose of the AF – Client Manager is to deliver those core management functions. Another purpose of this application involves building an RIA that can serve as a product, as well as contributing to our company's showcase of RIAs.

This application will be responsible for running day-to-day operations for client management. In time, it will act as a client portal for use in a collaborative environment, easing the burden of project documentation and speeding up communication.

The main goal of the AF – Client Manager project is to provide a robust, web-based solution to client management. The application will be accessible from anywhere that has a live connection to the Internet. It will be hosted on a public domain, so you will have access within corporate firewalls.

Functional Overview

We need to divide the application functionality into workable units. In keeping with object-oriented principles, we want the objects to correspond in name and function as close as possible to real-life objects. This helps us divide the function points into human-readable components for developers to work with. This usually requires developers and architects to work together to deliver the object model. The final object model includes the following objects:

- Documents
- Client
- ClientContacts
- ClientLinks
- ContentUpload
- Invoices
- InvoiceDetails
- Issues
- Media
- PDFGeneration
- Projects
- ProjectRisks

- ProjectTasks

- UserProfile

This list includes objects that relate directly to the database tables, as well as two function-ality pieces: ContentUpload and PDFGeneration. Each of these will drive data manipulation between Flex, Spring, and MySQL.

Each object will be replicated as a value object in Flex and a domain object in Spring. Figure 10-1 illustrates the relationships in the object model.

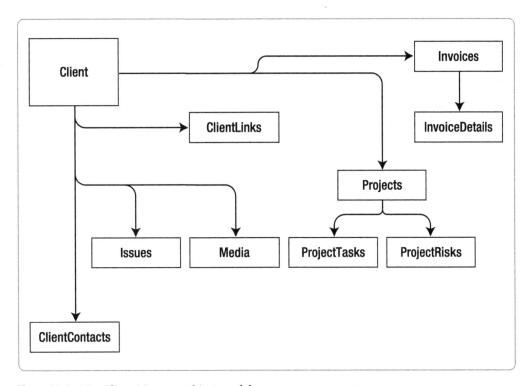

Figure 10-1. *AF – Client Manager object model*

Now let's take a closer look at each object and its properties. One item to note across all of these objects is the assocobjectID property, which is used to store the parent-child relationship between objects. This property is used to reference object lists or individual objects based on the client object.

Documents Object

The Documents object will hold all Microsoft Word, PDF, and Microsoft Excel file descriptions. These files will be uploaded and stored on the server's file system. A corresponding entry will use this object's properties to store the object and relationship to its parent. Table 10-1 lists the Documents object's properties.

Table 10-1. *Documents Object Properties*

Property	Description
objectidentifier	The primary key for the object
assocobjectID	A key used to link this object to a parent object; will hold the primary key of the parent object
fileName	The file name hosted without the location; the location will be a configuration parameter
fileType	The three-character file extension
creationDate	The time and date the file was uploaded

Client Object

The Client object will contain information needed to lay out client information. This object will be the parent to all other objects in the system. This application is based on a client as the center of the object model. Table 10-2 lists the Client object's properties.

Table 10-2. *Client Object Properties*

Property	Description
objectidentifier	The primary key for the object
assocobjectID	A key used to link this object to a parent object; will hold the primary key of the parent object
clientName	The client's name
clientID	The numerical representation of the client to be used for invoices and in other objects
phone	The primary phone number to contact the business or organization
link	The primary web site for the client
image	A field that will hold the name of a company logo that has been uploaded to the system
description	A field that will contain a business description for the client
notes	A field that will hold client annotations based on conversations or meetings
addressLine1	Primary address location
addressLine2	Secondary address location
city	The city where this business is located
state	The state where the business is located
zip	The postal code where the business is located

ClientContacts Object

The ClientContacts object keeps track of any contacts attached to the primary client. Its properties are listed in Table 10-3.

Table 10-3. *ClientContacts Object Properties*

Property	Description
objectidentifier	The primary key for the object
assocobjectID	A key used to link this object to a parent object; will hold the primary key of the parent object
contactName	The contact's name
responsibility	A reference field to define which action this contact helps with, such as gatekeeper
phoneWork	The work phone number for the contact
phoneCell	The cell phone number for the contact
email	The contact's e-mail address
jobTitle	The contact's job title

ClientLinks Object

The ClientLinks object is used to hold alternative links that are important to store. Some clients have multiple web sites or very deep sites that need to be referenced. Table 10-4 lists the ClientLinks object's properties.

Table 10-4. *ClientLinks Object Properties*

Property	Description
objectidentifier	The primary key for the object
assocobjectID	A key used to link this object to a parent object; will hold the primary key of the parent object
linkName	A definition or name for the link to better understand what the link references
url	The fully qualified URL to web content

Invoice Object

Invoices will be tied to individual clients to bill them periodically. The information in the invoice will allow for financial tracking by client. Table 10-5 lists the Invoice object's properties.

Table 10-5. *Invoice Object Properties*

Property	Description
objectidentifier	The primary key for the object
assocobjectID	A key used to link this object to a parent object; will hold the primary key of the parent object
clientNumber	The numerical reference to the client
clientName	The name of the client to be invoiced
clientAddress	The address of the client to be invoiced
clientPhone	The phone number of the client to be invoiced
invoiceDate	The date the invoice was created
invoiceNumber	The unique number to reference the invoice
toBePaidUntil	The date to bill through for recurring invoices
comments	Free-form comment to make notes to the client
percentDiscount	The percent of discount of price of services to the client

InvoiceDetails Object

The InvoiceDetails object will always be owned by an Invoice parent object. It will hold the details of the units of work the make up the pricing in the invoice. Table 10-6 lists the InvoiceDetails object's properties.

Table 10-6. *InvoiceDetails Object Properties*

Property	Description
objectidentifier	The primary key for the object
assocobjectID	A key used to link this object to a parent object; will hold the primary key of the parent object
detail	A description of the unit of work in the invoice
quantity	The multiplying factor for a unit of work
unitPrice	How much a unit of work costs

Issues Object

Issues will be owned by clients and projects. The Issues object will hold and track information that needs to be resolved for a client. Its properties are listed in Table 10-7.

Table 10-7. *Issues Object Properties*

Property	Description
objectidentifier	The primary key for the object
assocobjectID	A key used to link this object to a parent object; will hold the primary key of the parent object
issue	A title for the issue
openDate	When the issue was entered into the system
issueStatus	The status of the issue, which will drive visual cues in the user interface
issueDescription	A free-form field to contain detailed information regarding the issue and action plan to resolve it

Media Object

The Media object will hold client-based content, which can include media uploaded to the system, such as images and movies. Table 10-8 lists the Media object's properties.

Table 10-8. *Media Object Properties*

Property	Description
objectidentifier	The primary key for the object
assocobjectID	A key used to link this object to a parent object; will hold the primary key of the parent object
creationDate	When the media was uploaded to the server
mediaName	A title to define the media object
mediaDescription	A free-form field to contain a description of the media object
media	The name of the file that has been uploaded to the system

Projects Object

The `Project` object will hold the main project tasks and scope for client projects. Table 10-9 lists the `Project` object's properties.

Table 10-9. *Project Object Properties*

Property	Description
objectidentifier	The primary key for the object
assocobjectID	A key used to link this object to a parent object; will hold the primary key of the parent object
projectName	The name of the project
startDate	The planned start date for the project
endDate	The planned completion date for the project
projectSpace	The industry segment or organization department to which the project belongs
projectStatus	The project status indicator to denote if the project is on track
projectNotes	A free-form field to enter notes for the project
projectScope	A free-form field to define the units of work for the project at a descriptive level
projectBusinessNeed	A free-form field to define the business need for the client—the reason for doing the project
projectProcessFlow	The logical flow of the entire project

ProjectRisks Object

The `ProjectRisks` object will hold the risks defined by project managers for client projects. Its properties are listed in Table 10-10.

Table 10-10. *ProjectRisks Object Properties*

Property	Description
objectidentifier	The primary key for the object
assocobjectID	A key used to link this object to a parent object; will hold the primary key of the parent object
risk	The title or name of the identified project risk
openDate	When the risk was entered into the system
riskStatus	The status of the risk, which will drive visual cues in the user interface
riskDescription	A free-form field to contain detailed information regarding the risk and action plan to resolve it

ProjectTasks Object

The ProjectTasks object is a listing of high-level tasks and milestones that need to be tracked for the selected client project. Its properties are listed in Table 10-11.

Table 10-11. *ProjectTasks Object Properties*

Property	Description
objectidentifier	The primary key for the object
assocobjectID	A key used to link this object to a parent object; will hold the primary key of the parent object
taskName	The defined name for a task or milestone
owner	The developer or organizational unit that owns the task or milestone
progress	The percentage of completion of the task or milestone
projectName	The owning project's name
taskStatus	The status of the task or milestone, which will drive visual cues in the user interface
taskDescription	A free-form field to contain detailed information regarding the task or milestone
startDate	The planned start date for the task or milestone
endDate	The planned completion date for the task or milestone

UserProfile Object

The UserProfile object contains user information that is stored on the client after authentication. It does not contain any password content. Table 10-12 lists the UserProfile object's properties.

Table 10-12. *UserProfile Object Properties*

Property	Description
objectidentifier	The primary key for the object
assocobjectID	A key used to link this object to a parent object; will hold the primary key of the parent object
userName	The user ID that is used for authentication
userFirstName	The user's first name
userMiddleName	The user's middle name
userLastName	The user's last name
creationDate	The date the user was entered into the system
lastUpdateDate	The date the user was last updated
groups	The authorization groups associated with the user

Now we have defined the core objects that will represent data structures throughout our application. These objects will help Flex visualize data returned from our Spring services. They will also be a mapping for the application data structures from Flex to Spring to the database tables.

Development Projects: Flex, Flex Library, and Spring

For the AF – Client Manager application, we need three main projects to support development:

- A Flex project is required to build the user interface and handle user gestures throughout the application.

- The Flex Library project will be used to keep any custom components we create as a result of building the application. We will identify those components during the building of the Flex modules. That way, we can reuse those components in future applications.

- We need a Spring project to maintain all of our Spring code. This project will be the main driver to build the entire application for deployment to a production server. This project will not be an all-in-one unit, as you usually see with a Flex and BlazeDS installation. We will separate out the server and services from the Flex source. This will require us to define endpoints for all RemoteObject calls to the server and work with a cross-domain file.

We'll start with the Flex project.

Flex Project: AF – Client Manager

If you have Flex Builder, you can simply create a new project there. If not, you will need to set up your directory structure to support building the application via Ant. Either way will work with the Ant script supplied in this book's appendix. You can create your Flex project in Eclipse as a generic project to be built by Ant using the Flex SDK, but cannot debug Flex projects.

Here are the project details for the Flex portion of the AF – Client Manager:

Project name: af_ClientManager

Project type: Flex

Required libraries: Cairngorm.swc (http://opensource.adobe.com/wiki/display/ cairngorm/Downloads) and af_lib.swc (from our Flex Library project compile)

As noted, for this project, we will use Cairngorm as the development framework, which will help to organize the application for better maintainability. You do not need the enterprise version of Cairngorm for this project.

For the Flex project, you will need to create the directory structure defined in Figure 10-2.

Figure 10-2. *Flex AF – Client Manager project directory structure*

Flex Library Project: af_lib

The idea behind a Flex library is to create a well-structured collection of Flex components. These components can extend existing Flex components or be created entirely from scratch.

In Chapter 4, we created two custom Flex classes, `CustomDateChooser` and `RoundedGradientBorder`, and put them in a Flex Library project. We will use these classes throughout the AF – Client Manager application. If you have not created a Flex Library project, now is the time to do so, and move the classes from Chapter 4 into the library. If you have Flex Builder, you can create a new Flex Library project. Be sure to add the project name and specify `src` for the source directory. If not, you can create a general project in Eclipse with the directory structure shown in Figure 10-3.

Here are the details for the Flex Library project:

Project name: `af_lib`

Project type: Flex Library

Figure 10-3. *The af_lib project package structure*

Spring Project: af_Central

The Spring project will serve multiple functions. First, it will be the repository for all of our Spring source code. Second, it will act as the driving project to build the entire application.

The project will contain all of the libraries to deploy BlazeDS as well as Spring, Spring Security, Spring BlazeDS Integration, and Hibernate 3 with annotations.

The af_Central project is a centralized data service portfolio of reusable services that extend data functions served by a BlazeDS server running on Tomcat. Connectivity to the service layer is achieved using Spring's application context to wire Spring beans that Flex can consume via RemoteObject calls through the Spring BlazeDS Integration (SBI) server.

Here are the details for the Spring project:

Project name: af_Central

Project type: Java with Spring, SBI, Spring Security, Hibernate 3 with annotations, BlazeDS

Required libraries: See Table 10-13

Table 10-13 lists all of the libraries used for the af_Central project to compile Java code. These JAR files need to be located in the libs directory and deployed to a Tomcat or other web server with BlazeDS in its WEB-INF/lib directory.

Table 10-13. *Required Libraries for af_Central*

Owner	JAR File
BlazeDS (turnkey installation)	
	flex-messaging-common.jar
	flex-messaging-core.jar
	flex-messaging-opt.jar
	flex-messaging-proxy.jar
	flex-messaging-remoting.jar
	backport-util-concurrent.jar
	cfgatewayadapter.jar
	commons-httpclient-3.0.1.jar
	commons-codec-1.3.jar
	commons-logging.jar
	concurrent.jar
	xalan.jar
Hibernate 3 (JAR files located in the zip distribution)	
	hibernate3.jar
	antlr-2.7.6.jar
	commons-collections-3.1.jar

Table 10-13. *Required Libraries for af_Central*

Owner	JAR File
	dom4j-1.6.1.jar
	jta-1.1.jar
	javaassist-3.4.GA.jar
	slf4j-api-1.5.2.jar
	slf4j-log4j12-1.5.2.jar
Hibernate Annotations (JAR files located in the zip distribution)	
	ejb3-persistence.jar
	hibernate-annotations.jar
	hibernate-commons-annotations.jar
Servlet container (JAR is from your web server)	
	servlet-api.jar
Logging (JAR located in the Spring with dependencies zip file)	
	log4j-1.2.15.jar
Spring and Spring MVC	
	spring_2.5.x.jar
	spring-beans.jar
	spring-context.jar
	spring-context-support.jar
	spring-core.jar
	spring-tx.jar
	spring-web.jar
	spring-webmvc.jar
Spring BlazeDS Integration	
	org.springframework.flex-1.x.jar
Spring Security (JAR files located in the Security distribution zip file)	
	spring-security-core-2.0.4.jar
	spring-security-core-tiger-2.0.4.jar

As you can see, this project has many JAR files that could cause a problem if missing. Most of these libraries are runtime libraries that are loaded when the application is started in Tomcat. I wanted to give you a complete list of what is required so you can check that nothing is missing when you build and deploy your project. You can see how the Spring project is defined in Figure 10-4.

Figure 10-4. *The af_Central package structure*

In Eclipse, create a new Java project and name it af_Central. You should be using jdk1.5 or later to compile all of the source code in this project. Remove the src folder during the project-creation process by selecting "Remove source folder 'src' from build path" on the Source tab. Create a new source folder called AppFoundation, which will contain all project source code and build components for BlazeDS. The last change is to modify the default output folder to reflect af_Central/AppFoundation/WebRoot/WEB-INF/classes so all built source code from Eclipse will be zipped into a WAR file for deployment by Ant.

For BlazeDS, you will find the JARs listed in Table 10-13 by deploying the blazeds.war to Tomcat or another web server. You will want to download the latest BlazeDS turnkey version available from http://opensource.adobe.com/wiki/display/blazeds/Downloads. You will also want to download the latest SBI release from http://www.springsource.org/download.

We have covered most of what is needed for our application. Now, it's time to put it all in one place.

Spring Configuration for Flex

Setting up the server side for Flex to consume Spring services will require the installation of Tomcat (see the instructions for installing Tomcat in this book's appendix). Then follow these steps to configure a new Spring project:

1. Download the Spring Framework from `http://www.springframework.org/download`.

2. Copy the `spring.jar` file that you downloaded to the `AppFoundation/WebRoot/WEB-INF/lib` directory in the `af_Central` project, which contains the BlazeDS server, and add it to the Java Build Path in the project properties. In the `root/libs` directory for the project, you should keep only the files needed for compilation, not those for deployment. That way, you are not maintaining multiple locations for JAR libraries.

3. Modify the `web.xml` file on the `af_Central` BlazeDS server and add the security `listener`, `filter`, `filter-mapping`, and `context-param` definitions, as follows:

```
<listener>
    <listener-class>
        org.springframework.web.context.ContextLoaderListener
    </listener-class>
</listener>

<filter>
    <filter-name>springSecurityFilterChain</filter-name>
    <filter-class>
        org.springframework.web.filter.DelegatingFilterProxy
    </filter-class>
</filter>

<filter-mapping>
    <filter-name>springSecurityFilterChain</filter-name>
    <url-pattern>/*</url-pattern>
</filter-mapping>

<context-param>
    <param-name>contextConfigLocation</param-name>
        <param-value>
            /WEB-INF/springSecurityContext.xml
        </param-value>
</context-param>
```

4. In the Spring project in Eclipse, register the SBI front controller in `AppFoundation/WebRoot/WEB-INF/flex/services-config.xml`:

```
    <servlet>
        <servlet-name>Spring MVC Dispatcher Servlet</servlet-name>
        <servlet-class>org.springframework.web.servlet.DispatcherServlet
        </servlet-class>
        <init-param>
            <param-name>contextConfigLocation</param-name>
            <param-value>/WEB-INF/applicationContext.xml</param-value>
        </init-param>
        <load-on-startup>1</load-on-startup>
    </servlet>
```

After adding those configuration items to the web.xml file, it should look similar to
Listing 10-1.

Listing 10-1. *The web.xml Configuration for Spring Security and SBI Server*

```
<?xml version="1.0" encoding="UTF-8"?>

<!DOCTYPE web-app PUBLIC "-//Sun Microsystems, Inc.// ➡
DTD Web Application 2.3//EN" ➡
"http://java.sun.com/dtd/web-app_2_3.dtd">

<web-app>
    <display-name>AF Central WS</display-name>
    <description>AF Central WS</description>

    <!-- Http Flex Session attribute and binding listener support -->
    <listener>
        <listener-class>flex.messaging.HttpFlexSession</listener-class>
    </listener>

    <!-- The front controller of this Spring Web application,
    responsible for handling all application requests -->
    <servlet>
        <servlet-name>Spring MVC Dispatcher Servlet</servlet-name>
        <servlet-class>org.springframework.web.servlet.DispatcherServlet
        </servlet-class>
        <init-param>
            <param-name>contextConfigLocation</param-name>
            <param-value>/WEB-INF/applicationContext.xml</param-value>
        </init-param>
        <load-on-startup>1</load-on-startup>
    </servlet>
```

```xml
<!-- Map all *.spring requests to the DispatcherServlet for handling -->
<servlet-mapping>
    <servlet-name>Spring MVC Dispatcher Servlet</servlet-name>
    <url-pattern>/spring/*</url-pattern>
</servlet-mapping>

<welcome-file-list>
    <welcome-file>index.htm</welcome-file>
</welcome-file-list>

<listener>
    <listener-class>
        org.springframework.web.context.ContextLoaderListener
    </listener-class>
</listener>

<filter>
    <filter-name>springSecurityFilterChain</filter-name>
    <filter-class>
        org.springframework.web.filter.DelegatingFilterProxy
    </filter-class>
</filter>

<filter-mapping>
    <filter-name>springSecurityFilterChain</filter-name>
    <url-pattern>/*</url-pattern>
</filter-mapping>

<context-param>
    <param-name>contextConfigLocation</param-name>
        <param-value>
            /WEB-INF/springSecurityContext.xml
        </param-value>
</context-param>
</web-app>
```

With that done, you are ready to wire your Spring beans in the application context. We will do that in Chapter 12, when we create the Spring beans. For now, we are ready to start writing code for the Spring portion of the project.

We are going to use the security modules you saw in Chapter 9 in the AF – Client Manager application. The springSecurityContext.xml file referenced is the same one we created in Chapter 9, repeated here as Listing 10-2.

Listing 10-2. *The springSecurityContext.xml File*

```xml
<?xml version="1.0" encoding="UTF-8"?>
<beans xmlns="http://www.springframework.org/schema/beans"
xmlns:xsi="http://www.w3.org/2001/XMLSchema-instance"
xmlns:security="http://www.springframework.org/schema/security"
xsi:schemaLocation="
http://www.springframework.org/schema/beans
http://www.springframework.org/schema/beans/spring-beans-2.5.xsd
http://www.springframework.org/schema/security
http://www.springframework.org/schema/security/spring-security-2.0.xsd">

<security:http auto-config="true">
    <security:intercept-url pattern="index.html" filters="none"/>
    <security:intercept-url pattern="*.swf" filters="none"/>
    <security:intercept-url pattern="*.html" access="ROLE_USER"/>
</security:http>

<security:authentication-provider>
    <security:user-service>
        <security:user name="katiebug" password="test"
            authorities="ROLE_USER, ROLE_ADMIN"/>
        <security:user name="colie" password="test"
            authorities="ROLE_USER"/>
    </security:user-service>
</security:authentication-provider>

</beans>
```

Hibernate Configuration for Spring

As you learned in Chapter 8, Hibernate offers a robust solution for ORM integration in Spring. For the AF – Client Manager application, we will use Hibernate 3 with annotations to deliver the payload to and from our database. To make this happen, we need to configure applicationContext.xml to implement Hibernate, annotated classes, and transaction management.

Listing 10-3 shows the hibApplication.properties file, which is located with the applicationContext.xml file in *<tomcat-install-directory>*/webapps/af_Central/WEB-INF>. It contains Hibernate setup properties and database connection information. Listing 10-4 is a complete listing of what is needed in the applicationContext.xml file for Hibernate configuration.

Listing 10-3. *The hibApplication.properties File*

```
# JDBC Connection information
jdbc.driverClassName=com.mysql.jdbc.Driver
jdbc.url=jdbc:mysql://localhost/apress
jdbc.username=af
```

```
jdbc.password=afpass
# Hibernate 3 configuration
hibernate.show_sql=true
hibernate.format_sql=true
hibernate.transaction.factory_class=org.hibernate.transaction.JDBCTransactionFactory
hibernate.dialect=org.hibernate.dialect.MySQLDialect
hibernate.c3p0.min_size=5
hibernate.c3p0.max_size=20
hibernate.c3p0.timeout=1800
hibernate.c3p0.max_statements=50
```

Listing 10-4. *The applicationContext.xml File Using Hibernate 3 with Annotations and Transaction Management*

```xml
<?xml version="1.0" encoding="UTF-8"?>
<beans
      xmlns="http://www.springframework.org/schema/beans"
      xmlns:xsi="http://www.w3.org/2001/XMLSchema-instance"
      xmlns:tx="http://www.springframework.org/schema/tx"
      xsi:schemaLocation="http://www.springframework.org/schema/beans
            http://www.springframework.org/schema/beans/spring-beans-2.0.xsd
            http://www.springframework.org/schema/tx
            http://www.springframework.org/schema/tx/spring-tx-2.0.xsd"
      default-lazy-init="true">

   <!-- START Load application properties -->
   <bean id="propertyConfigurer"
    class="org.springframework.beans.factory.config.PropertyPlaceholderConfigurer">
      <property name="location">
         <value>WEB-INF/hibApplication.properties</value>
      </property>
   </bean>
   <!-- END Load application properties -->

   <!-- START HIBERNATE CONFIG -->
   <!-- Configure SessionFactory -->
   <bean id="sessionFactory" class= ➥
      "org.springframework.orm.hibernate3.annotation.AnnotationSessionFactoryBean">
      <property name="annotatedClasses">
         <list>
            <!-- Add annotated domain objects here-->
         </list>
      </property>
```

```xml
        <property name="hibernateProperties">
            <props>
                <prop key="hibernate.show_sql">${hibernate.show_sql}</prop>
                <prop key="hibernate.format_sql">${hibernate.format_sql}</prop>
                    <prop key="hibernate.transaction.factory_class">
                        ${hibernate.transaction.factory_class}
                    </prop>
                    <prop key="hibernate.dialect">${hibernate.dialect}</prop>
                    <prop key="hibernate.c3p0.min_size">
                        ${hibernate.c3p0.min_size}
                    </prop>
                    <prop key="hibernate.c3p0.max_size">
                        ${hibernate.c3p0.max_size}
                    </prop>
                    <prop key="hibernate.c3p0.timeout">
                        ${hibernate.c3p0.timeout}
                    </prop>
                    <prop key="hibernate.c3p0.max_statements">
                        ${hibernate.c3p0.max_statements}
                    </prop>
                    <prop key="hibernate.connection.driver_class">
                        ${jdbc.driverClassName}
                    </prop>
                    <prop key="hibernate.connection.url">${jdbc.url}</prop>
                    <prop key="hibernate.connection.username">
                        ${jdbc.username}
                    </prop>
                    <prop key="hibernate.connection.password">
                        ${jdbc.password}
                    </prop>
            </props>
        </property>
    </bean>

    <!-- enable the configuration of transactional behavior based on annotations -->
    <tx:annotation-driven transaction-manager="txManager"/>

    <bean id="txManager"
        class="org.springframework.orm.hibernate3.HibernateTransactionManager">
        <property name="sessionFactory"><ref local="sessionFactory"/></property>
    </bean>

    <bean class="org.springframework.beans.factory.annotation. ➥
        RequiredAnnotationBeanPostProcessor"/>


<!-- END HIBERNATE CONFIG -->
```

```
<!-- Define data access beans -->

<!-- Add Services -->
```

```
</beans>
```

In Listing 10-4, I highlighted configuration sections where you will define annotated domain objects, DAOs, and Spring beans.

With Hibernate configured and ready for beans to be added to the file, we can move forward to starting the Flex project by wiring all of the components together.

Cairngorm Configuration for Flex

We have already defined the Flex project directory structure and downloaded the Cairngorm library. With the folders in place, we can start building the required Cairngorm classes needed to support data transport for the application. Even though we have not defined the service layer in Spring, we can create the core classes that are needed for Cairngorm, as well as the value objects we defined earlier in this chapter.

For large-scale Flex applications, I create a skeleton framework for the application by defining all components needed based on the wireframes. Setting up Cairngorm is quite simple and should be done when creating the skeleton for the application. We have already added the Cairngorm.swc to the project build path and are ready to define the layers needed for the project.

Value Objects

As you've learned, value objects are used in Flex to map to object data from Spring domain objects. A value object is nothing more than a class implementation of a custom data type built in ActionScript that contains properties to support data visualization in views.

Earlier in this chapter, we discussed the objects to be used in the AF – Client Manager application. You will need to create a value object that reflects the properties for those definitions as part of this process. Listing 10-5 shows the ClientVO.as file. Before the class definition, notice a bindable RemoteClass metadata tag definition to the corresponding Spring domain object. This maps the value object to the Spring domain object.

Listing 10-5. *The ClientVO.as Value Object*

```
package com.af.clientmanager.model.vo
{
    [Bindable]
    [RemoteClass(alias="com.af.core.domain.Client")]

    public class ClientVO
    {
        public var objectIdentifier:Number;
        public var assocobjectID:Number;
        public var clientName:String;
```

```
            public var clientID:int;
            public var link:String;
            public var description:String;
            public var notes:String;
            public var phone:String;
            public var addressLine1:String;
            public var addressLine2:String;
            public var city:String;
            public var state:String;
            public var zip:String;
        }
    }
```

Cairngorm Delegates

Our application has four main service layers: security, projects, clients, and dashboard. Security will be wrapped into an af_lib component to completely separate all security control into that component. The application only needs to know how to handle basic security errors and a returned user profile object. The delegates we create here will eventually house all of the methods that relate to Spring bean operations. Listings 10-6, 10-7, and 10-8 show the three delegates we need for this project.

Listing 10-6. *The Client Delegate (ClientDelegate.as)*

```
package com.af.clientmanager.business
{
    import com.adobe.cairngorm.business.ServiceLocator;
    import com.af.model.vo.*;

    import mx.rpc.AsyncToken;
    import mx.rpc.IResponder;

    public class ClientDelegate
    {
        private var responder : IResponder;
        private var service : Object;

        public function ClientDelegate( responder : IResponder )
        {
            this.service = ServiceLocator.getInstance().getService(
                "clientService" );
            this.responder = responder;
        }
```

```
            // Method calls...
            public function insertClient(clientVO : ClientVO ): void
            {
                    var call:AsyncToken = service.insertLoreCategory(ClientVO);
                    call.addResponder( responder );
            }
        }
}
```

Listing 10-7. *The Dashboard Delegate (DashboardDelegate.as)*

```
package com.af.clientmanager.business
{
      import com.adobe.cairngorm.business.ServiceLocator;
      import com.af.model.vo.*;

      import mx.rpc.AsyncToken;
      import mx.rpc.IResponder;

      public class DashboardDelegate
      {
            private var responder : IResponder;
            private var service : Object;

            public function DashboardDelegate( responder : IResponder )
            {
                    this.service = ServiceLocator.getInstance().getService(
                        "dashboardService" );
                    this.responder = responder;
            }

            // Method calls...
      }
}
```

Listing 10-8. *The Project Delegate (ProjectDelegate.as)*

```
package com.af.clientmanager.business
{
      import com.adobe.cairngorm.business.ServiceLocator;
      import com.af.model.vo.*;

      import mx.rpc.AsyncToken;
      import mx.rpc.IResponder;
```

```
public class ProjectDelegate
{
    private var responder : IResponder;
    private var service : Object;

    public function ProjectDelegate( responder : IResponder )
    {
        this.service = ServiceLocator.getInstance().getService(
            "projectService" );
        this.responder = responder;
    }

    // Method calls...
}
}
```

Model Locator

The ModelLocator in Cairngorm serves as a singleton class responsible for holding stateful application information and data returned from data sources. These stateful global classes are accessible from any components in the application that access an instance of the model. This allows you to hold data on the model and bind views to the data. If the data is updated, the view is updated automatically using data binding. You may also elect to create submodels for large applications. When you need to partition your application into major functional points, submodels will help you keep track of what the data belongs to or the origin of the data. You can see the base definition of the AF – Client Manager's ModelLocator class in Listing 10-9.

Listing 10-9. *The AF – Client Manager Model Locator (ModelLocator.as)*

```
package com.af.clientmanager.model
{
    import com.adobe.cairngorm.model.ModelLocator;

    [Bindable]
    public class ModelLocator implements com.adobe.cairngorm.model.ModelLocator
    {
        private static var modelLocator :
          com.af.clientmanager.model.ModelLocator;

        public static function getInstance() :
          com.af.clientmanager.model.ModelLocator
        {
            if ( modelLocator == null )
                modelLocator = new com.af.clientmanager.model.ModelLocator();

            return modelLocator;
        }
```

```
        public function ModelLocator()
        {
                if (com.af.clientmanager.model.ModelLocator.modelLocator != null)
                    throw new Error( "Only one ModelLocator instance should " +
                        "be instantiated" );
        }

        // Add all global constants, variables, and submodels here
        public const SERVICE_ENDPOINT =
            "http://localhost:8080/af_Central/spring/messagebroker/amf";
    }
}
```

Services Definition Class

The services class is a Cairngorm ServiceLocator component that defines all endpoints for RemoteObject calls to the Spring service layer. Since we are planning to have a separate service layer from the Flex project (with a different web context in Tomcat), we need to define an endpoint on the RemoteObjects. The endpoint tag takes the fully qualified URL of the location the AMF gateway is running on our BlazeDS server, such as the following:

http://localhost:8080/af_Central/spring/messagebroker/amf.

In Listing 10-10, you can see that I moved the endpoint to the model under a constant named SERVICE_ENDPOINT. That way, I can make a change in only one place to modify my RemoteObject endpoints.

Listing 10-10. *The Services.mxml File with RemoteObject Endpoints*

```
<?xml version="1.0" encoding="utf-8"?>
<cairngorm:ServiceLocator
      xmlns:mx="http://www.adobe.com/2006/mxml"
      xmlns:cairngorm="com.adobe.cairngorm.business.*">

      <mx:Script>
            <![CDATA[
            import com.af.clientmanager.model.ModelLocator;

            [Bindable]
            public var model : ModelLocator = ModelLocator.getInstance();
            ]]>
      </mx:Script>

      <mx:RemoteObject endpoint="{model.SERVICE_ENDPOINT}"
          id="clientService"
          destination="clientService"
          showBusyCursor="true">
      </mx:RemoteObject>
```

```
    <mx:RemoteObject endpoint="{model.SERVICE_ENDPOINT}"
        id="dashboardService"
        destination="dashboardService"
        showBusyCursor="true">
    </mx:RemoteObject>

    <mx:RemoteObject endpoint="{model.SERVICE_ENDPOINT}"
        id="projectService"
        destination="projectService"
        showBusyCursor="true">
    </mx:RemoteObject>

</cairngorm:ServiceLocator>
```

Controller Class Definition

The controller class in Cairngorm will map events to commands. Flex is an event-driven framework, and Cairngorm extends the base event. Every database interaction will require an event and command to execute a transaction based on a user gesture in Flex. The command is responsible for processing the result or fault and moving the data to the appropriate model for a view to be updated. The code in Listing 10-11 sets the main controller for the application that is a singleton class.

Listing 10-11. *The Main Controller Class (MainController.as)*

```
package com.af.clientmanager.control
{
    import com.adobe.cairngorm.control.FrontController;
    import com.af.clientmanager.control.commands.events.*;

    public class MainController extends FrontController
    {

        public function MainController():void
        {
            addCommand(GerClientsEvent.EVENT_GET_CLIENT,
              GetClientCommand );
            addCommand(DeleteClientEvent.EVENT_DELETE_CLIENT,
              DeleteClientCommand );

            // Add all command-to-event mappings here...
        }
    }
}
```

Service Locator and Front Controller in the Flex Application

In the root MXML component that contains the `<mx:Application>` tag, we need to set the `Services` and `MainController` instances. These will be loaded into memory when the Flex application is started and will set listeners for service and `CairngormEvent` calls. Listing 10-12 shows the two instances created in the main application.

Listing 10-12. *The af_ClientManager.mxml File*

```xml
<?xml version="1.0" encoding="utf-8"?>
<mx:Application xmlns:mx="http://www.adobe.com/2006/mxml"
     pageTitle="AF Client Manager"
     layout="absolute"
     xmlns:view="com.af.view.*"
     xmlns:services="com.af.clientmanager.services.*"
     xmlns:control="com.af.clientmanager.control.*">

     <mx:Style source="assets/css/style.css"/>

     <!-- ===================================================================== -->
     <!-- the ServiceLocator where we specify the remote services -->
     <services:Services id="services"/>

     <!-- the FrontController, containing Commands-to-Event mappings -->
     <control:MainController id="mainController" />
     <!-- ===================================================================== -->

</mx:Application>
```

Summary

This chapter is the starting point for our project development of the AF – Client Manager application. There are many concerns you need to take into account when building a large-scale application, including security, project deployment, multiple developers, and development frameworks.

In this chapter, we defined the business needs for this project, as well as the objects we will build in the application, such as objects for client, projects, and issues. These objects will be implemented in both Flex and Spring. They will be created as value objects in Flex and domain objects in Spring, and they will fully support the data mappings from the database tables we will define in the next chapter.

With the objects defined, we next created three projects to support development. The Flex Library project will store custom reusable components for Flex to use. The Flex project is the user interface for the AF – Client Manager. The Spring project will serve several purposes. We called the Spring project `af_Central` because it will act as a centralized data services platform that includes our Spring beans, Spring Security, and BlazeDS. The Flex project will implement endpoints on the RemoteObjects that point to the `af_Central` AMF gateway. That way, we can separate the user interface from our server layer and distribute it over multiple servers if needed for scalability.

Within the separate applications, we went through the initialization of the Spring, Hibernate, and Cairngorm configuration. We created starting places for each of the configurations that will be added to as we build the application.

The next chapter will expand on the object model we defined and translate it into a database schema. From the database schema, we will build the tables to support our application and implement security to support the Spring Security modules we have created.

CHAPTER 11

■ ■ ■

Building the Database

Almost any application needs a way to get and display data. This is especially true for RIAs. One of the first stages of application design is to define the database schema and business objects. For the AF – Client Manager application, we have already defined the objects the application will use to manage data (in the previous chapter). Now we need to define and build a persistent storage location for that data.

This chapter introduces the database schema we will use for the AF – ClientManager RIA. It also provides some basic principles to follow when designing a relational database to support large-scale RIAs. For this application, we will use MySQL as the database provider, although the database design created in this chapter can be used with other databases. The general practice for this book is to keep all solutions open source (and free), and MySQL fits well with that approach. If you have a commercial application to roll out, you can easily transfer the database schema and SQL commands to a commercial database solution such as Oracle or Microsoft SQL Server.

Database design is an activity in which experience is particularly important, and the relational schema I will present here draws heavily on my own practical experience. It embodies a design that I have used with very large online transaction processing (OLTP) databases when data integrity and scalability were essential.

Database Design Overview

The primary goal of database design is to build a scalable and robust solution that is never a bottleneck for a system. The architecture needs to support heavy server workloads, handle the required user base, and provide a stable data management solution. Performance and reliability are also important features for any database.

Much of scaling a database solution depends on the size of your user base. In the case of the AF – Client Manager application, we are not going to be supporting 200,000 users. The number of users will depend very much on the size of the user organization. So we do not need to consider hosting the database across multiple servers. We can even host the database on the same computer as the web server, if necessary. Over time, the database could get quite large, so we will build a database schema that can expand with the data.

Database Terminology

Before we get into specifics of database design, let's review the definitions of a few terms:

Database: A database is a collection of related data that can be persisted from an outside source. The database can be very complex, holding millions of rows of data, or as simple as just a few users in a secure data set.

Table: Tables are made up of columns and rows, similar to a spreadsheet. The columns are given unique names to define data elements.

Keys: Keys are unique indicators that point to a row or rows of data. A *primary key* is a unique identifier that can identify a single row in a table. A *foreign key* is a key in a table that can identify a row in another table. The primary-to-foreign key connection is the foundation of a relational database.

Next, let's look at some good practices that apply to all relational database design endeavors.

Database Design Tips

Building tables using a solid approach can help alleviate the stress of delivering data across multiple tables. Here are some guidelines for good database design:

- Remove redundant data in tables. Break out common objects like addresses and phone numbers.

- Columns should not represent data sets like invoice1, invoice2, and so on. That is the purpose of rows.

- Be careful about using the AUTO_INCREMENT attribute for a table. In our example, we will need to create a unique generation scheme for objectIdentifier values, so we always have unique numbers for each table's primary keys.

- Keep the storage requirements as small as possible to reduce disk space consumption.

- Identify frequent queries to properly tune the database.

- Keep naming conventions in mind when creating your tables. (Table names are case-sensitive; column names are not.)

- When you first install the database, you will have an initial user of root. Set the password, and then rename the user.

- Let Tomcat or your application server control database pooling where appropriate.

- Lock down the database install directory by allowing access only by a special user on the operating system. That way, your data files are protected from an administrator or another user accidentally corrupting them.

- Keep media objects like files and movies out of the database. It is better to just store pointers to the media located on the file system.

Of course, before you begin to design your database, you first need to choose a database solution. As noted earlier, for the AF – Client Manager application, we will be using MySQL.

MySQL Database Overview

Before we start executing CREATE TABLE statements for the tables, you need to understand the functionality of MySQL that is important for developing RIAs. For this book, I am using MySQL Community Server, which is free to download from http://dev.mysql.com/downloads. For MySQL installation instructions, see this book's appendix.

■ **Note** We are only going to scratch the surface of MySQL in this chapter. For more details, refer to a book devoted to MySQL. Apress (http://www.apress.com) offers a series of books on MySQL, ranging from beginner tutorials to definitive guides. A good place to start is *The Definitive Guide to MySQL 5, Third Edition* by Michael Kofler (Apress, 2005).

Types of Tables in MySQL

When you create a table in MySQL, you can specify its type (using the ENGINE = directive). If you do not specify the table type, MySQL will choose for you based on the configuration of the default table type.

For building RIAs, three table types are of interest:

HEAP: HEAP tables are used when a temporary table is created in MySQL. They can also be used when the table size will fit in physical memory on the database server and there are few updates.

MyISAM: MyISAM tables are most suitable when disk space and read efficiency are high priorities. Database speed is mostly limited by the underlying hardware—in particular, the amount of random access memory (RAM). MyISAM is generally the default storage engine for MySQL.

InnoDB: InnoDB tables offer database transactions, row-level locking, foreign key constraints, and crash recovery. If you have an application that requires transactions, greater database security, or many concurrent users making changes, consider setting your tables to the InnoDB type.

For the AF – Client Manager application, we will set all tables to the InnoDB type to take advantage of the advanced features it offers.

Data Types in MySQL

Part of building tables in any database is defining the data type for each column. Choosing the column data types determines the type of information that can be stored. Table 11-1 summarizes the data types MySQL supports.

Table 11-1. *MySQL Data Types*

Type	Data Type	Description
CHAR()	Text	Fixed character set, 0–255
VARCHAR()	Text	Variable character set, 0–255
TINYTEXT	Text	String maximum of 255 characters
TEXT	Text	String maximum of 65,535 characters
BLOB	Text	String maximum of 65,535 characters
MEDIUMTEXT	Text	String maximum of 16,777,215 characters
MEDIUMBLOB	Text	String maximum of 16,777,215 characters
LONGTEXT	Text	String maximum of 4,294,967,295 characters
LONGBLOB	Text	String maximum of 4,294,967,295 characters
TINYINT()	Number	–128 to 127 normal 0 to 255 unsigned
SMALLINT()	Number	–32,768 to 32,767 normal 0 to 65,535 unsigned
MEDIUMINT()	Number	–8,388,608 to 8,388,607 normal 0 to 16,777,215 unsigned
INT()	Number	–2,147,483,648 to 2,147,483,647 normal 0 to 4,294,967,295 unsigned
BIGINT()	Number	–9,223,372,036,854,775,808 to 9,223,372,036,854,775,807 normal 0 to 18,446,744,073,709,551,615 unsigned
FLOAT	Number	Small number with decimal point
DOUBLE(,)	Number	Large number with decimal point
DECIMAL(,)	Number	DOUBLE stored in a string with a fixed decimal point
DATE	Date	Formatted date, *YYYY-MM-DD*
DATETIME	Date	Formatted date and time, *YYYY-MM-DD HH:MM:SS*
TIMESTAMP	Date	Formatted date and time, *YYYYMMDDHHMMSS*
TIME	Date	Formatted time, *HH:MM:SS*
ENUM()	Misc	Enumerated column with defined values
SET	Misc	Each column can have more than one defined value

Hierarchy Storage

There are many situations where you need to retain a hierarchy to display in a user interface. Flex has tree views that we will use in the AF – Client Manager application to keep project tasks in line. To make this happen using an ArrayCollection in Flex, we will need to retain row indicators that identify parent-child relationships.

A good way to manage hierarchies in the database is by keeping a parent identifier in the table that is responsible for a hierarchy. Table 11-2 is a representation of a database table that keeps track of programming language hierarchies.

Table 11-2. *The programming_lang Table Structure*

objectIdentifier	languageName	nodeID
1	All Languages	0
2	Flex	1
3	ActionScript	2
4	MXML	2
5	Spring	1
6	ORM	5
7	Hibernate	6
8	iBATIS	6

As you can see, the programming_lang table defines parent-child relationships through the nodeID. The nodeID is simply the objectIdentifier of the parent object. When we get this list back from the database, we can upload it into a tree structure based on the order and relationships of the objectIdentifier to nodeID.

For this to work properly, you will need to order your query by nodeID to allow for efficient loading of data in the Flex client, as follows:

```
SELECT * from programming_lang ORDER BY nodeID;
```

After you get the results of the previous query and load them into a Flex component, you should expect to see a view like the following:

```
All Languages
    Flex
    ActionScript
        MXML
    Spring
        ORM
            Hibernate
            iBATIS
```

There is no need for your Flex client to be ordering data from a database query result.

AF – Client Manager Database Schema Design

Now it's time to complete the database schema for the AF – Client Manager application, and then focus on building the tables to hold data for the application.

The data model will be agnostic to the actual database software you choose. This is important, because it means that you can port the data model to any solution you prefer.

AF – Client Manager Data Model

The AF – Client Manager data model is shown in Figure 11-1. It is a relational model that uses `objectIdentifier-to-assocobjectID` links to associate data with the proper owning object. Every table will have an `objectIdentifier` as the primary key to the object. For all deletions and updates, the `objectIdentifier` will be used to manipulate the associated data. I have been using this database solution in application design since 2000, and it has proven itself to be quite scalable and a good way to keep object relations intact across your database.

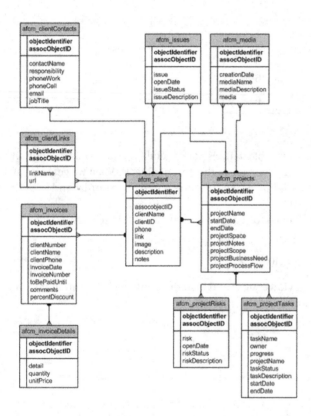

Figure 11-1. *The AF – Client Manager data model*

You can also use the relationships to create cascading deletes from the system when a base object is removed. For example, in the AF – Client Manager application, the client table will be the controlling object. It will own contacts, projects, and invoices. You can allow the system to enact a deletion on all contacts, projects, and invoices owned by the Client object when a client is deleted from the system. The object relationships will allow you to build that type of cascading delete for your system.

The center of this data model is the Client object. This is important from a design perspective, since the Client object will own most of the data in the system. That being the case, the Flex user interface will be required to pass client objectIdentifier values into Projects, Invoices, ClientLinks, ClientContacts, Issues, and Media objects to manipulate those data elements in the system. Two other children of client can own data: projects and invoices. The supplemental tables for invoices and projects will be used to display lists within the owning objects in Flex. When these objects are queried, we will return the parent with a list as part of the main object, such as a return of invoices with an array of invoiceDetails in it.

The database schema is designed with expansion in mind, taking into account that the application may grow with new functionality. The design allows you to partition data objects into groups like clients, projects, and invoices. The partitioning opens up an opportunity for future data integration through object relationships. In the future, clients may not be the only owners of projects or invoices.

AF – Client Manager Database Table Creation

I have explained the business reasons for creating the AF – Client Manager application and how it will allow you to track detailed information about your clients to better serve their business needs. We have decided the client will be at the center of the database relationships between objects. MySQL has been chosen for this project. Now we need to execute the CREATE statements to build the tables for the application.

You have a couple of options for creating the tables, depending on how you like to work. You can use the command-line interface to execute CREATE statements, or use MySQL Administrator if you prefer a GUI.

Using the Command-Line Interface

MySQL supports basic command-line interfaces for SQL editing. You can open your favorite command-line interface, such as Cygwin or Windows cmd.exe. You can add MySQL to your system PATH by setting the install location's bin directory in your PATH, as follows:

```
PATH = C:\Program Files\MySQL\MySQL Server 5.0\bin
```

This will allow you to open your command-line editor and use the MySQL binary to execute database commands.

To log in to your MySQL database, execute the following command:

```
mysql -u username -p
```

Once you log in, you will have access to a SQL editor to create tables. You can also execute other basic SQL statements, such as INSERT, UPDATE, DELETE, and SELECT. I have already created a table called products under the apress schema. Let's execute a DESCRIBE statement to see the table layout:

```
mysql> describe apress.products;
```

Figure 11-2 shows the results.

```
+--------------------+--------------------+------+-----+---------+----------------+
| Field              | Type               | Null | Key | Default | Extra          |
+--------------------+--------------------+------+-----+---------+----------------+
| ProductID          | int(11)            | NO   | PRI | NULL    | auto_increment |
| SKU                | varchar(45)        | YES  |     | NULL    |                |
| ProductName        | varchar(45)        | YES  |     | NULL    |                |
| ProductDescription | varchar(250)       | YES  |     | NULL    |                |
| SupplierID         | int(11)            | YES  |     | NULL    |                |
| CategoryID         | int(10) unsigned   | YES  |     | NULL    |                |
| UnitQuantity       | int(10) unsigned   | YES  |     | NULL    |                |
| UnitPrice          | float              | YES  |     | NULL    |                |
| MSRP               | float              | YES  |     | NULL    |                |
| AvailableSize      | varchar(45)        | YES  |     | NULL    |                |
| AvailableColors    | varchar(150)       | YES  |     | NULL    |                |
| Size               | varchar(45)        | YES  |     | NULL    |                |
| Color              | varchar(45)        | YES  |     | NULL    |                |
| Image              | varchar(45)        | YES  |     | NULL    |                |
+--------------------+--------------------+------+-----+---------+----------------+
14 rows in set (0.00 sec)
```

Figure 11-2. *Results from executing the DESCRIBE command on the MySQL products table*

The other option for managing the database is to use the free tools provided by MySQL.

Using the MySQL Administrator Tool

If you are not a command-line guru, you will be very interested in the MySQL GUI tools. MySQL provides MySQL Administrator, MySQL Query Browser, and MySQL Migration Toolkit. I generally use MySQL Administrator to manage tables for the databases I build.

You can download the tools from the MySQL web site (http://dev.mysql.com/downloads/gui-tools/5.0.html). The installation is quite simple; see this book's appendix for instructions.

Once you have MySQL Administrator installed, start it and enter your user credentials. Figure 11-3 shows the interface for editing and creating tables. This is the edit view for a products table I have already created under the apress schema. There is also a button to create a new table, so that you can use the same interface to key in your columns and set the table options.

As noted, you can use MySQL Administrator or the command line to create your tables. It is up to you to decide which works best for you and which is more productive.

Now we are ready to execute the CREATE statements for the AF – Client Manager tables.

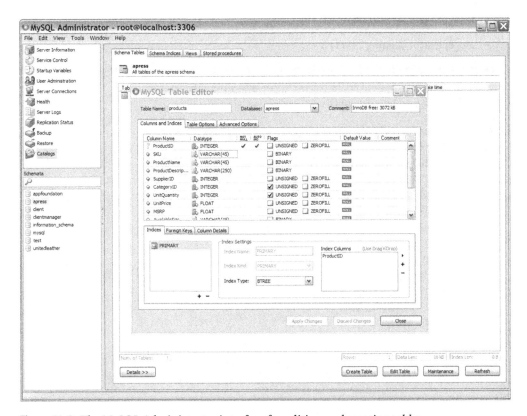

Figure 11-3. *The MySQL Administrator interface for editing and creating tables*

Creating the AF – Client Manager Tables

The AF – Client Manager has many objects that we need to place in persistent storage to support the Flex data visualization in the user interface. In the apress schema, create the following tables using the statements shown in their corresponding listings:

- afcm_client (Listing 11-1)

- afcm_clientContacts (Listing 11-2)

- afcm_clientLinks (Listing 11-3)

- afcm_invoices (Listing 11-4)

- afcm_invoiceDetails (Listing 11-5)

- afcm_issues (Listing 11-6)

- afcm_media (Listing 11-7)

- afcm_projects (Listing 11-8)

- afcm_projectRisks (Listing 11-9)

- afcm_projectTasks (Listing 11-10)

- sec_operator (Listing 11-11)

- sec_oper_access_groups (Listing 11-12)

Listing 11-1. *The afcm_client Table*

```
CREATE TABLE `apress`.`afcm_client` (
  `objectIdentifier` BIGINT NOT NULL,
  `assocobjectID` BIGINT NOT NULL,
  `clientName` VARCHAR(120),
  `clientID` INTEGER UNSIGNED,
  `link` VARCHAR(120),
  `image` VARCHAR(45),
  `description` TEXT,
  `notes` TEXT,
  `phone` VARCHAR(45),
  `addressLine1` VARCHAR(120),
  `addressLine2` VARCHAR(120),
  `city` VARCHAR(120),
  `state` VARCHAR(20),
  `zip` VARCHAR(10),
  PRIMARY KEY(`objectIdentifier`)
)
ENGINE = InnoDB;
```

Listing 11-2. *The afcm_clientContacts Table*

```
CREATE TABLE `apress`.`afcm_clientContacts` (
  `objectIdentifier` BIGINT NOT NULL,
  `assocobjectID` BIGINT UNSIGNED NOT NULL,
  `contactName` VARCHAR(120),
  `responsibility` VARCHAR(45),
  `email` VARCHAR(45),
  `jobTitle` VARCHAR(45),
  `phoneWork` VARCHAR(45),
  `phoneCell` VARCHAR(45),
  `addressLine1` VARCHAR(120),
  `addressLine2` VARCHAR(120),
  `city` VARCHAR(120),
  `state` VARCHAR(20),
  `zip` VARCHAR(10),

  PRIMARY KEY(`objectIdentifier`)
)
ENGINE = InnoDB;
```

Listing 11-3. *The afcm_clientLinks Table*

```
CREATE TABLE `apress`.`afcm_clientLinks` (
  `objectIdentifier` BIGINT NOT NULL,
  `assocobjectID` BIGINT UNSIGNED NOT NULL,
  `linkName` VARCHAR(45),
  `url` VARCHAR(120),
  PRIMARY KEY(`objectIdentifier`)
)
ENGINE = InnoDB;
```

Listing 11-4. *The afcm_invoices Table*

```
CREATE TABLE `apress`.`afcm_invoices` (
  `objectIdentifier` BIGINT NOT NULL,
  `assocobjectID` BIGINT UNSIGNED NOT NULL,
  `clientNumber` VARCHAR(25),
  `clientName` VARCHAR(120),
  `invoiceDate` DATETIME,
  `invoiceNumber` VARCHAR(25),
  `toBePaidUntil` DATETIME,
  `comments` TEXT,
  `percentDiscount` FLOAT,
  PRIMARY KEY(`objectIdentifier`)
)
ENGINE = InnoDB;
```

Listing 11-5. *The afcm_invoiceDetails Table*

```
CREATE TABLE `apress`.`afcm_invoiceDetails` (
  `objectIdentifier` BIGINT NOT NULL,
  `assocobjectID` BIGINT NOT NULL,
  `detail` TEXT,
  `quantity` TINYINT,
  `unitPrice` FLOAT,
  PRIMARY KEY(`objectIdentifier`)
)
ENGINE = InnoDB;
```

Listing 11-6. *The afcm_issues Table*

```
CREATE TABLE `apress`.`afcm_issues` (
  `objectIdentifier` BIGINT NOT NULL,
  `assocobjectID` BIGINT NOT NULL,
  `issue` TEXT,
  `openDate` DATETIME,
  `issueStatus` CHAR,
  `issueDescription` TEXT,
```

```
    PRIMARY KEY(`objectIdentifier`)
)
ENGINE = InnoDB;
```

Listing 11-7. *The afcm_media Table*

```
CREATE TABLE `apress`.`afcm_media` (
  `objectIdentifier` BIGINT NOT NULL,
  `assocobjectID` BIGINT NOT NULL,
  `creationDate` DATETIME,
  `mediaName` VARCHAR(120),
  `mediaDescription` TEXT,
  PRIMARY KEY(`objectIdentifier`)
)
ENGINE = InnoDB;
```

Listing 11-8. *The afcm_projects Table*

```
CREATE TABLE `apress`.`afcm_projects` (
  `objectIdentifier` BIGINT NOT NULL,
  `assocobjectID` BIGINT NOT NULL,
  `projectName` VARCHAR(120),
  `startDate` DATETIME,
  `endDate` DATETIME,
  `projectSpace` VARCHAR(120),
  `projectNotes` TEXT,
  `projectScope` TEXT,
  `projectBusinessNeed` TEXT,
  `projectProcessFlow` TEXT,
  PRIMARY KEY(`objectIdentifier`)
)
ENGINE = InnoDB;
```

Listing 11-9. *The afcm_projectRisks Table*

```
CREATE TABLE `apress`.`afcm_projectRisks` (
  `objectIdentifier` BIGINT NOT NULL,
  `assocobjectID` BIGINT NOT NULL,
  `risk` TEXT,
  `openDate` DATETIME,
  `closeDate` DATETIME,
  `riskStatus` VARCHAR(25),
  `riskDescription` TEXT,
  PRIMARY KEY(`objectIdentifier`)
)
ENGINE = InnoDB;
```

Listing 11-10. *The afcm_projectTasks Table*

```
CREATE TABLE `apress`.`afcm_projectTasks` (
  `objectIdentifier` BIGINT NOT NULL,
  `assocobjectID` BIGINT NOT NULL,
  `taskName` VARCHAR(120),
  `owner` VARCHAR(120),
  `progress` VARCHAR(10),
  `projectName` VARCHAR(120),
  `taskStatus` VARCHAR(45),
  `taskDescription` TEXT,
  `startDate` DATETIME,
  `endDate` DATETIME,
  PRIMARY KEY(`objectIdentifier`)
)
ENGINE = InnoDB;
```

Listing 11-11. *The sec_operator Table*

```
CREATE TABLE `apress`.`sec_operator` (
  `objectIdentifier` BIGINT NOT NULL,
  `operatorID` VARCHAR(8) NOT NULL,
  `password` VARCHAR(20),
  `enabled` BOOLEAN,
  PRIMARY KEY(`objectIdentifier`)
)
ENGINE = InnoDB;
```

Listing 11-12. *The sec_oper_access_groups Table*

```
CREATE TABLE `apress`.`sec_oper_access_groups` (
  `objectIdentifier` BIGINT NOT NULL,
  `assocobjectID` BIGINT NOT NULL,
  `groupName` VARCHAR(40),
  `groupDescription` TEXT,
  `creationDate` DATETIME,
  PRIMARY KEY(`objectIdentifier`)
)
ENGINE = InnoDB;
```

That concludes the creation of all tables needed for the AF – Client Manager application. I added the sec_operator and sec_oper_access_groups tables so you can create a DAO implementation to authenticate against the MySQL database if needed. Remember that we are using the security solution we created in Chapter 9 for the AF – Client Manager application.

Summary

This chapter introduced MySQL as the database solution for the AF – Client Manager application. You learned about three types of tables in MySQL; HEAP, MyISAM, and InnoDB. InnoDB was chosen to represent data for the AF – Client Manager application to take advantage of its features, which include database transactions, row-level locking, foreign key constraints, and crash recovery.

We discussed the different data types MySQL offers. These are important to understand so we can properly map data from MySQL, to Spring, and finally to Flex.

We also took a look at design tips for your database. These tips apply to general database design.

If you are building trees or tabbed lists in Flex, you will eventually need to store a hierarchy. In this chapter, you learned how to store a simple hierarchy in a database table that can be used in Flex to display parent-child relationships.

Aside from learning some of the basics of MySQL and database design, you investigated the AF – Client Manager schema design. It is based on relationships between the main object, client, and child objects in the system. To create a relationship between objects, the `objectIdentifier` of the parent object is stored in a child object's `assocobjectID`. For example, this would create a contract between a client and its invoices. In this schema, each object has a unique `objectIdentifier`.

We also covered different ways to create and manage your tables. I strongly recommend using the free MySQL Administrator. It gives you a visual way of managing your databases. If you like using command-line tools, then you have that option as well.

In the next chapter, we will define and build the Spring services for the AF – Client Manager application.

■ ■ ■

## CHAPTER 12

Building the Spring Services

In this chapter, you will learn how to implement and structure Spring for a real-world application. We will build the AF – Client Manager's back-end services in Spring using Hibernate to persist a MySQL database. The Spring services will be configured to accept Remoting calls from the Flex client.

Spring Security will be implemented to authenticate and authorize users of the Flex client. It will be based on the security solution created in Chapter 9. Authorization groups will allow you to lock down functionality in the Flex client, preventing those who do not have administrative privileges from entering data where they do not have access.

You will also learn about application development in Spring that provides a solid base for RIAs. The architecture and practices used in this part of the AF – Client Manager project have been developed over several years of iterations to simplify the Spring architecture. The simplification of the architecture leads to quicker times to market for RIAs, with a robust Spring service layer for data access.

You will see how to make the Spring DAO layer transactional to protect data from becoming corrupted in a real-world application. This involves using annotations in Hibernate to map results directly to domain objects that are accessed by the DAO and service layers.

Upon finishing this chapter, you will have a solid foundation for building large-scale Spring service back ends to support your RIAs.

Spring Architecture and Service Definition

The main architecture component for the AF – Client Manager application is the `af_Central` Spring project, which is a centralized data service portfolio of reusable services that run within BlazeDS. It mainly handles the data input and output for the entire system.

Figure 12-1 shows the entire application stack from Flex to the MySQL database. This is a fairly typical three-tier architecture to support the functions of the application.

The BlazeDS server has quite a bit of responsibility for the system. BlazeDS will be running inside a Tomcat container. It will contain all of the Spring components and will load the Spring application context to properly wire the Spring beans. The Spring BlazeDS Integration (SBI) implementation will expose the Spring service layer to Flex, so Flex can make RemoteObject calls to Spring.

Spring Security, combined with the security objects in the `af_Central` application, will control access to the system. The components in this layer work together to grant access to only users entering valid credentials. Spring Security will return any errors related to security faults and return granted rights to user groups if they are authorized. In addition to controlling access rights to the system, Spring Security will secure methods in the Spring beans.

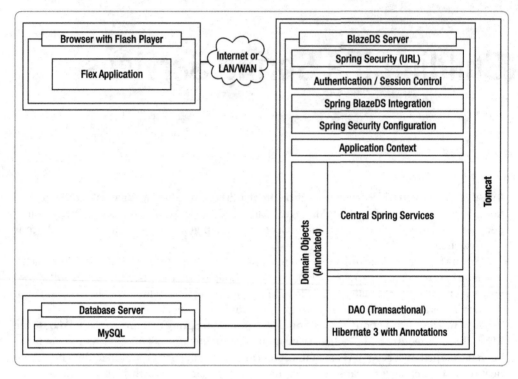

Figure 12-1. *The AF – Client Manager systems architecture*

The business logic for the system will be contained in the Spring beans. No logic will be present in the Flex application, except for form-based validation and data validation.

The data for the system is stored in a MySQL database, which we built in Chapter 11. The database access will be abstracted away through Hibernate. The domain objects that are shared through the Spring beans will be annotated to allow Hibernate to use them directly as a data-mapping solution, instead of manually mapping every SQL result.

With the architecture defined, we can now identify the services that will be supported by af_Central. These services are listed in Table 12-1.

Table 12-1. *Services Supported by af_Central*

Service	Description
secService	Manages authentication and authorization calls from the Flex application. It will return to Flex a userProfile domain object that does not contain the user's password.
clientService	Contains methods for the Client, ClientContacts, and ClientLinks objects. The Client object is at the center of the relationship model and will be used throughout the Flex application to manipulate child data owned by client.
invoiceService	Handles invoices and invoice details.

Table 12-1. *Services Supported by af_Central*

Service	Description
mediaService	Handles all media by storing pointers to files on the server's file system.
projectService	Manages access to projects. This service will control project risks and project tasks that are tied to individual client projects.

Spring BlazeDS Integration Configuration

The SBI project from SpringSource, introduced in Chapter 6, is a core component required to integrate Flex with Spring. To give Flex access to Spring, you need to configure a BlazeDS server to use SBI. Refer to the "Integrating Flex and Spring with Spring BlazeDS Integration" section in Chapter 6 for the steps for setting up SBI.

Spring Remote Services for Flex

Each Spring service provides a piece of functionality that is commonly needed. The Spring services will have different levels of granularity that represent pieces of the business the application is supporting, such as clients, projects, and invoices.

Most services are treated as a black box by developers. This is an appropriate technique if you do not care how the service was put together, and are only concerned with how to access it. In this case, we are programming the service as well as the user interface. Therefore, we need to understand how each service interacts in the architecture and how it provides data to the RIA.

Service consolidation is a key to successful service design. The idea is to create groups of business functionality that logically fit into individual packages. For example, consider the business requirements to build the Client, ClientLinks, and ClientContacts objects. Each of these objects could have a service defined individually. Instead, these three Spring beans will be consolidated into one service. The ClientService will contain all methods to support functionality, including clients, client contacts, and client links. This approach allows you to make logical groupings to reuse your services with other applications, so they can be leveraged by multiple user interfaces and mobile devices.

Before we jump in and create our services, we need to code the domain objects based on the database tables we created. I generally start design by building the database tables before any of the Spring or Flex objects. That way. I can normalize the data and avoid needing to change a bunch of objects in my Spring and Flex source code. Generally, most architects take a bottom-up approach to designing data structures.

Domain Objects

Among the fundamental components of the Spring architecture that we are using for this application are domain objects. They represent data structures that are written in Java to hold information that is shared throughout the Spring layers. Domain objects, in the case of the af_Central application, are populated by query returns through Hibernate. The domain objects are replicated as value objects in Flex.

We need to define the following domain objects to support the Spring services:

- `Client.java` (Listing 12-1)

- `ClientContacts.java` (Listing 12-2)

- `ClientLinks.java` (Listing 12-3)

- `InvoiceDetails.java` (Listing 12-4)

- `Invoices.java` (Listing 12-5)

- `Issues.java` (Listing 12-6)

- `Media.java` (Listing 12-7)

- `ProjectRisks.java` (Listing 12-8)

- `Projects.java` (Listing 12-9)

- `ProjectTasks.java` (Listing 12-10)

Each of these domain objects reside in the `com.af.core.domain` package.

The Java classes will be annotated to allow Hibernate to properly map table results to the domain objects. Note the `@Entry` and `@Table` annotations at the top of the domain object definitions. `@Table` is set at the class level to define to which table the domain object is to be mapped. `@Entity` defines the bean as a persistent POJO class, or an entity bean. The `@Id` simply identifies the location of the attributes to be annotated. The last piece of interest is the `@Column` annotation, which defines the column name that maps from the database table to the local variable.

Listing 12-1 includes the getters and setters for the `Client.java` domain object; they are omitted from the other listings for brevity.

Tip You can generate getters and setters in Eclipse by defining your public variables in the domain object and selecting the Source ➤ Generate Getters and Setters menu option.

Listing 12-1. *The Client.java Domain Object*

```
package com.af.core.domain;

import javax.persistence.*;

@Entity
@Table(name="AFCM_CLIENT")

public class Client implements java.io.Serializable
{
        static final long serialVersionUID = 1L;
```

```java
@Id
@Column(name="OBJECTIDENTIFIER")
private long objectIdentifier;

@Column(name="ASSOCOBJECTID")
private long assocobjectID;

@Column(name="CLIENTNAME")
private String clientName;

@Column(name="LINK")
private String link;

@Column(name="DESCRIPTION")
private String description;

@Column(name="NOTES")
private String notes;

@Column(name="PHONE")
private String phone;

@Column(name="ADDRESSLINE1")
private String addressLine1;

@Column(name="ADDRESSLINE2")
private String addressLine2;

@Column(name="CITY")
private String city;

@Column(name="STATE")
private String state;

 @Column(name="ZIPCODE")
private int zipCode;

public Client() {}

public long getObjectIdentifier() {
    return objectIdentifier;
}
public void setObjectIdentifier(long objectIdentifier) {
    this.objectIdentifier = objectIdentifier;
}
public long getAssocobjectID() {
    return assocobjectID;
}
```

```java
    public void setAssocobjectID(long assocobjectID) {
        this.assocobjectID = assocobjectID;
    }
    public String getClientName() {
        return clientName;
    }
    public void setClientName(String clientName) {
        this.clientName = clientName;
    }
    public String getLink() {
        return link;
    }
    public void setLink(String link) {
        this.link = link;
    }
    public String getDescription() {
        return description;
    }
    public void setDescription(String description) {
        this.description = description;
    }
    public String getNotes() {
        return notes;
    }
    public void setNotes(String notes) {
        this.notes = notes;
    }
    public String getPhone() {
        return phone;
    }
    public void setPhone(String phone) {
        this.phone = phone;
    }
    public String getAddressLine1() {
        return addressLine1;
    }
    public void setAddressLine1(String addressLine1) {
        this.addressLine1 = addressLine1;
    }
    public String getAddressLine2() {
        return addressLine2;
    }
    public void setAddressLine2(String addressLine2) {
        this.addressLine2 = addressLine2;
    }
    public String getCity() {
        return city;
    }
```

```java
        public void setCity(String city) {
            this.city = city;
        }
        public String getState() {
            return state;
        }
        public void setState(String state) {
            this.state = state;
        }
        public int getZip() {
            return zipCode;
        }
        public void setZip(int zipCode) {
            this.zipCode = zipCode;
        }
}
```

Listing 12-2. *The ClientContacts.java Domain Object*

```java
package com.af.core.domain;

import javax.persistence.*;

@Entity
@Table(name="AFCM_CLIENTCONTACTS")

public class ClientContacts implements java.io.Serializable
{
        static final long serialVersionUID = 2L;

        @Id
        @Column(name="OBJECTIDENTIFIER")
        private long objectIdentifier;

        @Column(name="ASSOCOBJECTID")
        private long assocobjectID;

        @Column(name="CONTACTNAME")
        private String contactName;

        @Column(name="RESPONSIBILITY")
        private String responsibility;

        @Column(name="EMAIL")
        private int email;
```

```java
        @Column(name="JOBTITLE")
        private int jobTitle;

        @Column(name="PHONEWORK")
        private String phoneWork;

        @Column(name="PHONECELL")
        private String phoneCell;

        @Column(name="ADDRESSLINE1")
        private String addressLine1;

        @Column(name="ADDRESSLINE2")
        private String addressLine2;

        @Column(name="CITY")
        private String city;

        @Column(name="STATE")
        private String state;

        @Column(name="ZIPCODE")
        private int zipCode;

        public ClientContacts() {}

        // Getters and setters...
}
```

Listing 12-3. *The ClienLinkst.java Domain Object*

```java
package com.af.core.domain;

import javax.persistence.*;

@Entity
@Table(name="AFCM_CLIENTLINKS")

public class ClientLinks implements java.io.Serializable
{
        static final long serialVersionUID = 3L;

        @Id
        @Column(name="OBJECTIDENTIFIER")
        private long objectIdentifier;
```

```java
        @Column(name="ASSOCOBJECTID")
        private long assocobjectID;

        @Column(name="LINKNAME")
        private String linkName;

        @Column(name="URL")
        private String url;

        public ClientLinks() {}

    // Getters and setters...
}
```

Listing 12-4. *The InvoiceDetails.java Domain Object*

```java
package com.af.core.domain;

import javax.persistence.*;

@Entity
@Table(name="AFCM_INVOICEDETAILS")

public class InvoiceDetails implements java.io.Serializable
{
        static final long serialVersionUID = 4L;

        @Id
        @Column(name="OBJECTIDENTIFIER")
        private long objectIdentifier;

        @Column(name="ASSOCOBJECTID")
        private long assocobjectID;

        @Column(name="DETAIL")
        private String detail;

        @Column(name="QUANTITY")
        private int quantity;

        @Column(name="UNITPRICE")
        private Float unitPrice;

        public InvoiceDetails() {}

        // Getters and setters...
}
```

Listing 12-5. *The Invoices.java Domain Object*

```java
package com.af.core.domain;

import java.sql.Date;

import javax.persistence.*;

@Entity
@Table(name="AFCM_INVOICES")

public class Invoices implements java.io.Serializable
{
        static final long serialVersionUID = 5L;

        @Id
        @Column(name="OBJECTIDENTIFIER")
        private long objectIdentifier;

        @Column(name="ASSOCOBJECTID")
        private long assocobjectID;

        @Column(name="CLIENTNUMBER")
        private String clientNumber;

        @Column(name="CLIENTNAME")
        private String clientName;

        @Column(name="INVOICEDATE")
        private Date invoiceDate;

        @Column(name="INVOICENUMBER")
        private String invoiceNumber;

        @Column(name="TOBEPAIDUNTIL")
        private Date toBePaidUntil;

        @Column(name="COMMENTS")
        private String comments;

        @Column(name="PERCENTDISCOUNT")
        private Float percentDiscount;

    public Invoices() {}

        // Getters and setters...
}
```

Listing 12-6. *The Issues.java Domain Object*

```java
package com.af.core.domain;

import java.sql.Date;

import javax.persistence.*;

@Entity
@Table(name="AFCM_ISSUES")

public class Issues implements java.io.Serializable
{
    static final long serialVersionUID = 6L;

    @Id
    @Column(name="OBJECTIDENTIFIER")
    private long objectIdentifier;

    @Column(name="ASSOCOBJECTID")
    private long assocobjectID;

    @Column(name="ISSUE")
    private String issue;

    @Column(name="OPENDATE")
    private Date openDate;

    @Column(name="CLOSEDATE")
    private Date closeDate;

    @Column(name="ISSUESTATUS")
    private String issueStatus;

    @Column(name="ISSUEDESCRIPTION")
    private String issueDescription;

    public Issues() {}

    // Getters and setters...
}
```

Listing 12-7. *The Media.java Domain Object*

```java
package com.af.core.domain;

import java.sql.Date;
```

```
import javax.persistence.*;

@Entity
@Table(name="AFCM_MEDIA")

public class Media implements java.io.Serializable
{
        static final long serialVersionUID = 7L;

        @Id
        @Column(name="OBJECTIDENTIFIER")
        private long objectIdentifier;

        @Column(name="ASSOCOBJECTID")
        private long assocobjectID;

        @Column(name="CREATIONDATE")
        private Date creationDate;

        @Column(name="MEDIANAME")
        private String mediaName;

        @Column(name="MEDIADESCRIPTION")
        private String mediaDescription;

        public Media() {}

        // Getters and setters...
}
```

Listing 12-8. *The Client.java Domain Object*

```
package com.af.core.domain;

import java.sql.Date;

import javax.persistence.*;

@Entity
@Table(name="AFCM_PROJECTRISKS")

public class ProjectRisks implements java.io.Serializable
{
        static final long serialVersionUID = 8L;

        @Id
        @Column(name="OBJECTIDENTIFIER")
        private long objectIdentifier;
```

```
        @Column(name="ASSOCOBJECTID")
        private long assocobjectID;

        @Column(name="RISK")
        private String risk;

        @Column(name="OPENDATE")
        private Date openDate;

        @Column(name="CLOSEDATE")
        private Date closeDate;

        @Column(name="RISKSTATUS")
        private String riskStatus;

        @Column(name="RISKDESCRIPTION")
        private String riskDescription;

        public ProjectRisks() {}

        // Getters and setters...
}
```

Listing 12-9. *The Projects.java Domain Object*

```
package com.af.core.domain;

import java.sql.Date;

import javax.persistence.*;

@Entity
@Table(name="AFCM_PROJECTS")

public class Projects implements java.io.Serializable
{
        static final long serialVersionUID = 9L;

        @Id
        @Column(name="OBJECTIDENTIFIER")
        private long objectIdentifier;

        @Column(name="ASSOCOBJECTID")
        private long assocobjectID;

        @Column(name="PROJECTNAME")
        private String projectName;
```

```
        @Column(name="STARTDATE")
        private Date startDate;

        @Column(name="ENDDATE")
        private Date endDate;

        @Column(name="PROJECTSPACE")
        private String projectSpace;

        @Column(name="PROJECTNOTES")
        private String projectNotes;

        @Column(name="PROJECTSCOPE")
        private String projectScope;

        @Column(name="PROJECTBUSINESSNEED")
        private String projectBusinessNeed;

        @Column(name="PROJECTPROCESSFLOW")
        private String projectProcessFlow;

        public Projects() {}

        // Getters and setters...
}
```

Listing 12-10. *The ProjectTasks.java Domain Object*

```
package com.af.core.domain;

import java.sql.Date;

import javax.persistence.*;

@Entity
@Table(name="AFCM_PROJECTTASKS")

public class ProjectTasks implements java.io.Serializable
{
        static final long serialVersionUID = 10L;

        @Id
        @Column(name="OBJECTIDENTIFIER")
        private long objectIdentifier;

        @Column(name="ASSOCOBJECTID")
        private long assocobjectID;
```

```
    @Column(name="TASKNAME")
    private String taskName;

    @Column(name="OWNER")
    private String owner;

    @Column(name="PROGRESS")
    private String progress;

    @Column(name="PROJECTNAME")
    private String projectName;

    @Column(name="TASKSTATUS")
    private String taskStatus;

    @Column(name="TASKDESCRIPTION")
    private String taskDescription;

    @Column(name="STARTDATE")
    private Date startDate;

    @Column(name="ENDDATE")
    private Date endDate;

    public ProjectTasks() {}

    // Getters and setters...
}
```

Spring Service Layer

The service layer in Spring is exposed to external access from Flex through SBI's Spring-managed MessageBrokerFactoryBean class and is wired in the application context. Each component in the service layer contains an interface that implements a Spring bean. These beans vary in the business functionality they contain.

The implementation classes also inject data into the DAO layer. The DAO for each service is defined with getters and setters within the class. Each method call uses the DAO definition to access methods in the DAO layer. The methods in this layer mimic the return types from the DAO layer.

As mentioned earlier, we will group the services logically. We will create client, invoice, media, and project services. All of these services are located in the com.af.core.services package.

The Client Service

The client service contains methods for Clients, ClientContacts, and ClientLinks. Each of those definitions has supporting domain objects. The client service is defined in Listings 12-11 and 12-12.

Listing 12-11. *ClientService.java*

```java
package com.af.core.services;

import com.af.core.domain.Client;
import com.af.core.domain.ClientContacts;
import com.af.core.domain.ClientLinks;

import java.util.List;

public interface ClientService
{
    // Clients
    List<Client> getClients();

    void insertClient(Client client);

    void deleteClient(Client client);

    void updateClient(Client client);

    // Client Contacts
    List<ClientContacts> getClientContacts();

    void insertClientContact(ClientContacts clientContact);

    void deleteClientContact(ClientContacts clientContact);

    void updateClientContact(ClientContacts clientContact);

    // Client Links
    List<ClientLinks> getClientLinks();

    void insertClientLink(ClientLinks clientLink);

    void deleteClientLink(ClientLinks clientLink);

    void updateClientLink(ClientLinks clientLink);
}
```

Listing 12-12. *ClientServicesImpl.java*

```java
package com.af.core.services;

import com.af.core.dao.ClientDao;
import com.af.core.domain.Client;
import com.af.core.domain.ClientContacts;
import com.af.core.domain.ClientLinks;
```

```java
import java.util.List;
import java.io.Serializable;

public class ClientServiceImpl implements Serializable, ClientService
{
      // injected by Spring
      ClientDao clientDao;

      public ClientDao getClientDao() {
            return clientDao;
      }

      public void setClientDao(ClientDao clientDao) {
            this.clientDao = clientDao;
      }

      // Clients
      public List<Client> getClients() {
            return clientDao.getClients();
      }
      public void insertClient(Client client) {
            clientDao.insertClient(client);
      }
      public void deleteClient(Client client) {
            clientDao.deleteClient(client);
      }
      public void updateClient(Client client)  {
            clientDao.updateClient(client);
      }

      // ClientContacts
      public List<ClientContacts> getClientContacts() {
            return clientDao.getClientContacts();
      }
      public void insertClientContact(ClientContacts clientContact) {
            clientDao.insertClientContact(clientContact);
      }
      public void deleteClientContact(ClientContacts clientContact) {
      clientDao.deleteClientContact(clientContact);
      }
      public void updateClientContact(ClientContacts clientContact)  {
            clientDao.updateClientContact(clientContact);
      }

      // ClientLinks
      public List<ClientLinks> getClientLinks() {
            return clientDao.getClientLinks();
      }
```

```java
        public void insertClientLink(ClientLinks clientLinks) {
            clientDao.insertClientLink(clientLinks);
        }
        public void deleteClientLink(ClientLinks clientLinks) {
            clientDao.deleteClientLink(clientLinks);
        }
        public void updateClientLink(ClientLinks clientLinks) {
            clientDao.updateClientLink(clientLinks);
        }
}
```

Invoice Service

Invoices, with full details, will be served from the invoice service. Information from this service will be used to chart client progress in sales on the AF – Client Manager dashboard component. Listings 12-13 and 12-14 show this service.

Listing 12-13. *InvoiceService.java*

```java
package com.af.core.services;

import java.util.List;

import com.af.core.domain.InvoiceDetails;
import com.af.core.domain.Invoices;

public interface InvoiceService
{
    // Invoices
    List<Invoices> getInvoices();

    void insertInvoice(Invoices invoices);

    void deleteInvoice(Invoices invoices);

    void updateInvoice(Invoices invoices);

    // Invoice Details
    List<InvoiceDetails> getInvoiceDetails();

    void insertInvoiceDetail(InvoiceDetails invoiceDetails);

    void deleteInvoiceDetail(InvoiceDetails invoiceDetails);

    void updateInvoiceDetail(InvoiceDetails invoiceDetails);
}
```

Listing 12-14. *InvoiceServiceImpl.java*

```java
package com.af.core.services;

import com.af.core.dao.InvoiceDao;
import com.af.core.domain.InvoiceDetails;
import com.af.core.domain.Invoices;

import java.util.List;
import java.io.Serializable;

public class InvoiceServiceImpl implements Serializable, InvoiceService
{
      // injected by Spring
      InvoiceDao invoiceDao;

      public InvoiceDao getInvoiceDao() {
            return invoiceDao;
      }

      public void setInvoiceDao(InvoiceDao invoiceDao) {
            this.invoiceDao = invoiceDao;
      }

      // Invoices
      public List<Invoices> getInvoices() {
            return invoiceDao.getInvoices();
      }
      public void insertInvoice(Invoices invoices) {
            invoiceDao.insertInvoice(invoices);
      }
      public void deleteInvoice(Invoices invoices) {
            invoiceDao.deleteInvoice(invoices);
      }
      public void updateInvoice(Invoices invoices)  {
            invoiceDao.updateInvoice(invoices);
      }

      // Invoice Details
      public List<InvoiceDetails> getInvoiceDetails() {
            return invoiceDao.getInvoiceDetails();
      }
      public void insertInvoiceDetail(InvoiceDetails invoiceDetails) {
            invoiceDao.insertInvoiceDetail(invoiceDetails);
      }
      public void deleteInvoiceDetail(InvoiceDetails invoiceDetails) {
            invoiceDao.deleteInvoiceDetail(invoiceDetails);
      }
```

```
    public void updateInvoiceDetail(InvoiceDetails invoiceDetails)  {
        invoiceDao.updateInvoiceDetail(invoiceDetails);
    }
}
```

Media Service

The media service, detailed in Listings 12-15 and 12-16, maintains file locations for audio, video, and documents for the entire system. It acts as a pointer to media located on the file system. (We do not want to store binary files in the database due to potential performance issues.)

Listing 12-15. *MediaService.java*

```
package com.af.core.services;

import java.util.List;

import com.af.core.domain.Media;

public interface MediaService
{
    // Media
    List<Media> getMedia();

    void insertMedia(Media media);

    void deleteMedia(Media media);

    void updateMedia(Media media);
}
```

Listing 12-16. *MediaServiceImpl.java*

```
package com.af.core.services;

import com.af.core.dao.MediaDao;
import com.af.core.domain.Media;

import java.util.List;
import java.io.Serializable;

public class MediaServiceImpl implements Serializable, MediaService
{
    // injected by Spring
    MediaDao mediaDao;
```

```java
    public MediaDao getMediaDao() {
        return mediaDao;
    }

    public void setMediaDao(MediaDao mediaDao) {
        this.mediaDao = mediaDao;
    }

    // Media
    public List<Media> getMedia() {
        return mediaDao.getMedia();
    }
    public void insertMedia(Media media) {
        mediaDao.insertMedia(media);
    }
    public void deleteMedia(Media media) {
        mediaDao.deleteMedia(media);
    }
    public void updateMedia(Media media)  {
        mediaDao.updateMedia(media);
    }
}
```

Project Service

The project service is a major component of the application. It will control all aspects of project management from a data perspective. The main Projects domain object will be tied to the parent Client object. Listings 12-17 and 12-18 show this service.

Listing 12-17. *ProjectService.java*

```java
package com.af.core.services;

import com.af.core.domain.Issues;
import com.af.core.domain.ProjectRisks;
import com.af.core.domain.Projects;
import com.af.core.domain.ProjectTasks;

import java.util.List;

public interface ProjectService
{
    // Projects
    List<Projects> getProjects();

    void insertProject(Projects project);
```

```
        void deleteProject(Projects project);

        void updateProject(Projects project);

        // Project Tasks
        List<ProjectTasks> getProjectTasks();

        void insertProjectTask(ProjectTasks projectTasks);

        void deleteProjectTask(ProjectTasks projectTasks);

        void updateProjectTask(ProjectTasks projectTasks);

        // Project Risks
        List<ProjectRisks> getProjectRisks();

        void insertProjectRisk(ProjectRisks projectRisk);

        void deleteProjectRisk(ProjectRisks projectRisk);

        void updateProjectRisk(ProjectRisks projectRisk);

        // Issues
        List<Issues> getIssues();

        void insertIssue(Issues issue);

        void deleteIssue(Issues issue);

        void updateIssue(Issues issue);
    }
```

Listing 12-18. *ProjectServiceImpl.java*

```
package com.af.core.services;

import com.af.core.dao.ProjectDao;
import com.af.core.domain.Issues;
import com.af.core.domain.ProjectRisks;
import com.af.core.domain.ProjectTasks;
import com.af.core.domain.Projects;

import java.util.List;
import java.io.Serializable;
```

```java
public class ProjectServiceImpl implements Serializable, ProjectService
{
      // injected by Spring
      ProjectDao projectDao;

      public ProjectDao getProjectDao() {
            return projectDao;
      }

      public void setProjectDao(ProjectDao projectDao) {
            this.projectDao = projectDao;
      }

      // Projects
      public List<Projects> getProjects() {
            return projectDao.getProjects();
      }
      public void insertProject(Projects project) {
            projectDao.insertProject(project);
      }
      public void deleteProject(Projects project) {
            projectDao.deleteProject(project);
      }
      public void updateProject(Projects project)  {
            projectDao.updateProject(project);
      }

      // Project Tasks
      public List<ProjectTasks> getProjectTasks() {
            return projectDao.getProjectTasks();
      }
      public void insertProjectTask(ProjectTasks projectTask) {
            projectDao.insertProjectTask(projectTask);
      }
      public void deleteProjectTask(ProjectTasks projectTask) {
            projectDao.deleteProjectTask(projectTask);
      }
      public void updateProjectTask(ProjectTasks projectTask)  {
            projectDao.updateProjectTask(projectTask);
      }

      // Project Risks
      public List<ProjectRisks> getProjectRisks() {
            return projectDao.getProjectRisks();
      }
      public void insertProjectRisk(ProjectRisks projectRisk) {
            projectDao.insertProjectRisk(projectRisk);
      }
```

```
    public void deleteProjectRisk(ProjectRisks projectRisk) {
        projectDao.deleteProjectRisk(projectRisk);
    }
    public void updateProjectRisk(ProjectRisks projectRisk)  {
        projectDao.updateProjectRisk(projectRisk);
    }


    // Issues
    public List<Issues> getIssues() {
        return projectDao.getIssues();
    }
    public void insertIssue(Issues issue) {
        projectDao.insertIssue(issue);
    }
    public void deleteIssue(Issues issue) {
        projectDao.deleteIssue(issue);
    }
    public void updateIssue(Issues issue)  {
        projectDao.updateIssue(issue);
    }
}
```

DAO Implementation with Hibernate 3

The DAO layer is responsible for accessing the database to perform CRUD operations (create, read, update, and delete Java objects). To simplify the JDBC functions and integrate with the MySQL database, we're using Hibernate as the ORM framework. Hibernate, combined with transaction management, will secure the DAO methods to protect data from corruption if an error occurs during a transaction. Hibernate will map results from the database back to the annotated domain objects.

In the domain objects, we set the @Table attribute to the actual table name the query will use to map the database table columns to the annotated domain object. For example, to return a list of Client objects to Flex, you will need to state the domain object you wish to map the result to in the getHibernateTemplate().find("from DomainObjectName") method. The following code snippet from ClientDaoImpl shows how to set the mapping object in the query:

```
    public List<Client> getClients(){
        return getHibernateTemplate().find("from Client ");
    }
```

The insert methods include a call to generate a unique objectIdentifier for the object passed into the method. We are not using the database auto-increment capability because that would place duplicate objectIdentifiers throughout the object model. Since we are using objectIdentifiers of parent objects by placing them into the assocobjectID property of child objects, we need to create a unique number for each object. The utility class shown in Listing 12-19 takes the system time in milliseconds based on current system time. The NewObjectIdentifier() method returns a large number that is hard to duplicate, even when performing large amounts of transactions per second. To make the ID a little more robust, it's created as a singleton, and we check the last three digits. If they match, we get a new system time to ensure uniqueness.

Listing 12-19. *The AFObjID Utility*

```
package com.af.common.util;

import java.util.Date;

public class AFObjID
{
     // Singleton instance
     private static AFObjID myInstance;

     public static int varianceID = 0;
     private static long previousTime = 0;
     private static int currentTime = 0;

     private AFObjID(){}

     public static AFObjID getInstance()
     {
          if (myInstance == null)
               myInstance = new AFObjID();

          return myInstance;
     }

     public static long NewObjectIdentifier()
     {
          Date    aTime = new Date();
          int     i;
          long newObjectID;
          long baseID;
          long  systemTime;
          String  calculatedID;

          // Get system time
          systemTime = aTime.getTime();
```

```
                // Adjust currentTime
                // Check if seconds have not changed to not create a duplicate ID.
                if (999 < currentTime)
                {
                    while (systemTime <= previousTime)
                    {
                        aTime = new Date();
                        systemTime = aTime.getTime();
                    }
                    currentTime = 0;
                }

                i = currentTime++;

                // Result in base seconds with identifier appended
                baseID = systemTime;
                calculatedID = String.valueOf(baseID) +
                  String.valueOf(((varianceID * 1000) + i));

                newObjectID = Long.valueOf(calculatedID).longValue();
                return newObjectID;
        }
}
```

The read functions return a list of objects to Flex using the getHibernateTemplate().
find("tableName") method to query the database. Updates use the merge("domain object")
method on getHibernateTemplate() to update data in the database. The final database access
control is the delete("domain object") method, which will take an input object and search the
database to delete it based on the primary key.

We have already defined and created the service layer. Now we need to create all of the
DAOs to support the service calls. The DAOs match the services in granularity and handle all
interaction with the database. The following DAOs are required for the AF – Client Manager
application:

- Client DAO (Listings 12-20 and 12-21)

- Invoice DAO (Listings 12-22 and 12-23)

- Media DAO (Listings 12-24 and 12-25)

- Project DAO (Listings 12-26 and 12-27)

There are stored in the com.af.core.dao package.

Listing 12-20. *ClientDao.java*

```
package com.af.core.dao;

import java.util.List;
import org.springframework.transaction.annotation.Transactional;
```

```java
import org.springframework.transaction.annotation.Propagation;

import com.af.core.domain.Client;
import com.af.core.domain.ClientContacts;
import com.af.core.domain.ClientLinks;

public interface ClientDao
{
    // Clients
    @Transactional(readOnly=true, propagation=Propagation.SUPPORTS)
    List<Client> getClients();

    @Transactional(readOnly=false, propagation=Propagation.REQUIRED)
    Client insertClient(Client client);

    @Transactional(readOnly=false, propagation=Propagation.REQUIRED)
    void deleteClient(Client client);

    @Transactional(readOnly=true, propagation=Propagation.REQUIRED)
    void updateClient(Client client);

    // ClientContacts
    @Transactional(readOnly=true, propagation=Propagation.SUPPORTS)
    List<ClientContacts> getClientContacts();

    @Transactional(readOnly=false, propagation=Propagation.REQUIRED)
    ClientContacts insertClientContact(ClientContacts clientContacts);

    @Transactional(readOnly=false, propagation=Propagation.REQUIRED)
    void deleteClientContact(ClientContacts clientContacts);

    @Transactional(readOnly=true, propagation=Propagation.REQUIRED)
    void updateClientContact(ClientContacts clientContacts);

    // ClientLinks
    @Transactional(readOnly=true, propagation=Propagation.SUPPORTS)
    List<ClientLinks> getClientLinks();

    @Transactional(readOnly=false, propagation=Propagation.REQUIRED)
    ClientLinks insertClientLink(ClientLinks clientLinks);

    @Transactional(readOnly=false, propagation=Propagation.REQUIRED)
    void deleteClientLink(ClientLinks clientLinks);

    @Transactional(readOnly=true, propagation=Propagation.REQUIRED)
    void updateClientLink(ClientLinks clientLinks);
}
```

Listing 12-21. *ClientDaoImpl.java*

```java
package com.af.core.dao.hibernate;

import java.util.List;

import org.springframework.orm.hibernate3.support.HibernateDaoSupport;
import org.springframework.transaction.annotation.Propagation;
import org.springframework.transaction.annotation.Transactional;

import com.af.common.util.AFObjID;
import com.af.core.dao.ClientDao;
import com.af.core.domain.Client;
import com.af.core.domain.ClientContacts;
import com.af.core.domain.ClientLinks;

@Transactional(propagation=Propagation.SUPPORTS, readOnly=true)
public class ClientDaoImpl extends HibernateDaoSupport implements ClientDao
{
    AFObjID aSingleton = AFObjID.getInstance();

    // Clients
    @Transactional(propagation=Propagation.SUPPORTS, readOnly=true)
    public List<Client> getClients(){
        return getHibernateTemplate().find("from Client ");
    }

    @Transactional(propagation=Propagation.REQUIRED, readOnly=false)
    public Client insertClient(Client client){
        client.setObjectIdentifier(aSingleton.NewObjectIdentifier());
        return (Client) getHibernateTemplate().merge(client);
    }

    @Transactional(propagation=Propagation.REQUIRED, readOnly=false)
    public void deleteClient(Client client){
        getHibernateTemplate().delete(client);
    }

    @Transactional(propagation=Propagation.REQUIRED, readOnly=false)
    public void updateClient(Client client){
        getHibernateTemplate().merge(client);
    }

    // ClientContacts
    @Transactional(propagation=Propagation.SUPPORTS, readOnly=true)
    public List<ClientContacts> getClientContacts(){
        return getHibernateTemplate().find("from ClientContacts ");
    }
```

```java
@Transactional(propagation=Propagation.REQUIRED, readOnly=false)
public ClientContacts insertClientContact(ClientContacts clientContact){
    clientContact.setObjectIdentifier(aSingleton.NewObjectIdentifier());
    return (ClientContacts) getHibernateTemplate().merge(clientContact);
}

@Transactional(propagation=Propagation.REQUIRED, readOnly=false)
public void deleteClientContact(ClientContacts clientContact){
    getHibernateTemplate().delete(clientContact);
}

@Transactional(propagation=Propagation.REQUIRED, readOnly=false)
public void updateClientContact(ClientContacts clientContact){
    getHibernateTemplate().delete(clientContact);
}

// ClientLinks
@Transactional(propagation=Propagation.SUPPORTS, readOnly=true)
public List<ClientLinks> getClientLinks(){
    return getHibernateTemplate().find("from ClientLinks ");
}

@Transactional(propagation=Propagation.REQUIRED, readOnly=false)
public ClientLinks insertClientLink(ClientLinks clientLinks){
    clientLinks.setObjectIdentifier(aSingleton.NewObjectIdentifier());
    return (ClientLinks) getHibernateTemplate().merge(clientLinks);
}

@Transactional(propagation=Propagation.REQUIRED, readOnly=false)
public void deleteClientLink(ClientLinks clientLinks){
    getHibernateTemplate().delete(clientLinks);
}

@Transactional(propagation=Propagation.REQUIRED, readOnly=false)
public void updateClientLink(ClientLinks clientLinks){
    getHibernateTemplate().delete(clientLinks);
}
}
```

Listing 12-22. *InvoiceDao.java*

```java
package com.af.core.dao;

import java.util.List;
import org.springframework.transaction.annotation.Transactional;
import org.springframework.transaction.annotation.Propagation;
```

```java
import com.af.core.domain.InvoiceDetails;
import com.af.core.domain.Invoices;

public interface InvoiceDao
{
    // Invoices
    @Transactional(readOnly=true, propagation=Propagation.SUPPORTS)
    List<Invoices> getInvoices();

    @Transactional(readOnly=false, propagation=Propagation.REQUIRED)
    Invoices insertInvoice(Invoices invoices);

    @Transactional(readOnly=false, propagation=Propagation.REQUIRED)
    void deleteInvoice(Invoices invoices);

    @Transactional(readOnly=true, propagation=Propagation.REQUIRED)
    void updateInvoice(Invoices invoices);

    // Invoice Detail
    @Transactional(readOnly=true, propagation=Propagation.SUPPORTS)
    List<InvoiceDetails> getInvoiceDetails();

    @Transactional(readOnly=false, propagation=Propagation.REQUIRED)
    InvoiceDetails insertInvoiceDetail(InvoiceDetails invoiceDetails);

    @Transactional(readOnly=false, propagation=Propagation.REQUIRED)
    void deleteInvoiceDetail(InvoiceDetails invoiceDetails);

    @Transactional(readOnly=true, propagation=Propagation.REQUIRED)
    void updateInvoiceDetail(InvoiceDetails invoiceDetails);
}
```

Listing 12-23. *InvoiceDaoImpl.java*

```java
package com.af.core.dao.hibernate;

import java.util.List;

import org.springframework.orm.hibernate3.support.HibernateDaoSupport;
import org.springframework.transaction.annotation.Propagation;
import org.springframework.transaction.annotation.Transactional;

import com.af.common.util.AFObjID;
import com.af.core.dao.InvoiceDao;
import com.af.core.domain.InvoiceDetails;
import com.af.core.domain.Invoices;
```

```
@Transactional(propagation=Propagation.SUPPORTS, readOnly=true)
public class InvoiceDaoImpl extends HibernateDaoSupport implements InvoiceDao
{
      AFObjID aSingleton = AFObjID.getInstance();

      // Invoices
      @Transactional(propagation=Propagation.SUPPORTS, readOnly=true)
      public List<Invoices> getInvoices(){
            return getHibernateTemplate().find("from Invoices");
      }

      @Transactional(propagation=Propagation.REQUIRED, readOnly=false)
      public Invoices insertInvoice(Invoices invoices){
            invoices.setObjectIdentifier(aSingleton.NewObjectIdentifier());
            return (Invoices) getHibernateTemplate().merge(invoices);
      }

      @Transactional(propagation=Propagation.REQUIRED, readOnly=false)
      public void deleteInvoice(Invoices invoices){
            getHibernateTemplate().delete(invoices);
      }

      @Transactional(propagation=Propagation.REQUIRED, readOnly=false)
      public void updateInvoice(Invoices invoices){
            getHibernateTemplate().delete(invoices);
      }

      // Invoice Detail
      @Transactional(propagation=Propagation.SUPPORTS, readOnly=true)
      public List<InvoiceDetails> getInvoiceDetails(){
            return getHibernateTemplate().find("from InvoiceDetails");
      }

      @Transactional(propagation=Propagation.REQUIRED, readOnly=false)
      public InvoiceDetails insertInvoiceDetail(InvoiceDetails invoiceDetails){
            invoiceDetails.setObjectIdentifier(aSingleton.NewObjectIdentifier());
            return (InvoiceDetails) getHibernateTemplate().merge(invoiceDetails);
      }

      @Transactional(propagation=Propagation.REQUIRED, readOnly=false)
      public void deleteInvoiceDetail(InvoiceDetails invoiceDetails){
            getHibernateTemplate().delete(invoiceDetails);
      }
```

```
        @Transactional(propagation=Propagation.REQUIRED, readOnly=false)
        public void updateInvoiceDetail(InvoiceDetails invoiceDetails){
                getHibernateTemplate().delete(invoiceDetails);
        }
}
```

Listing 12-24. *MediaDao.java*

```
package com.af.core.dao;

import java.util.List;
import org.springframework.transaction.annotation.Transactional;
import org.springframework.transaction.annotation.Propagation;

import com.af.core.domain.Media;

public interface MediaDao
{
    // Media
    @Transactional(readOnly=true, propagation=Propagation.SUPPORTS)
    List<Media> getMedia();

    @Transactional(readOnly=false, propagation=Propagation.REQUIRED)
    Media insertMedia(Media media);

    @Transactional(readOnly=false, propagation=Propagation.REQUIRED)
    void deleteMedia(Media media);

    @Transactional(readOnly=true, propagation=Propagation.REQUIRED)
    void updateMedia(Media media);
}
```

Listing 12-25. *MediaDaoImpl.java*

```
package com.af.core.dao.hibernate;

import java.util.List;

import org.springframework.orm.hibernate3.support.HibernateDaoSupport;
import org.springframework.transaction.annotation.Propagation;
import org.springframework.transaction.annotation.Transactional;

import com.af.common.util.AFObjID;
import com.af.core.dao.MediaDao;
import com.af.core.domain.Media;
```

```java
@Transactional(propagation=Propagation.SUPPORTS, readOnly=true)
public class MediaDaoImpl extends HibernateDaoSupport implements MediaDao
{
      AFObjID aSingleton = AFObjID.getInstance();

      // Media
      @Transactional(propagation=Propagation.SUPPORTS, readOnly=true)
      public List<Media> getMedia(){
            return getHibernateTemplate().find("from Media");
      }

      @Transactional(propagation=Propagation.REQUIRED, readOnly=false)
      public Media insertMedia(Media media){
            media.setObjectIdentifier(aSingleton.NewObjectIdentifier());
            return (Media) getHibernateTemplate().merge(media);
      }

      @Transactional(propagation=Propagation.REQUIRED, readOnly=false)
      public void deleteMedia(Media media){
            getHibernateTemplate().delete(media);
      }

      @Transactional(propagation=Propagation.REQUIRED, readOnly=false)
      public void updateMedia(Media media){
            getHibernateTemplate().delete(media);
      }
}
```

Listing 12-26. *ProjectDao.java*

```java
package com.af.core.dao;

import java.util.List;
import org.springframework.transaction.annotation.Transactional;
import org.springframework.transaction.annotation.Propagation;

import com.af.core.domain.Issues;
import com.af.core.domain.ProjectRisks;
import com.af.core.domain.ProjectTasks;
import com.af.core.domain.Projects;

public interface ProjectDao
{
      // Projects
      @Transactional(readOnly=true, propagation=Propagation.SUPPORTS)
      List<Projects> getProjects();
```

```java
@Transactional(readOnly=false, propagation=Propagation.REQUIRED)
Projects insertProject(Projects project);

@Transactional(readOnly=false, propagation=Propagation.REQUIRED)
void deleteProject(Projects project);

@Transactional(readOnly=true, propagation=Propagation.REQUIRED)
void updateProject(Projects project);

// Project Tasks
@Transactional(readOnly=true, propagation=Propagation.SUPPORTS)
List<ProjectTasks> getProjectTasks();

@Transactional(readOnly=false, propagation=Propagation.REQUIRED)
ProjectTasks insertProjectTask(ProjectTasks projectTasks);

@Transactional(readOnly=false, propagation=Propagation.REQUIRED)
void deleteProjectTask(ProjectTasks projectTasks);

@Transactional(readOnly=true, propagation=Propagation.REQUIRED)
void updateProjectTask(ProjectTasks projectTasks);

// Project Risks
@Transactional(readOnly=true, propagation=Propagation.SUPPORTS)
List<ProjectRisks> getProjectRisks();

@Transactional(readOnly=false, propagation=Propagation.REQUIRED)
ProjectRisks insertProjectRisk(ProjectRisks projectRisks);

@Transactional(readOnly=false, propagation=Propagation.REQUIRED)
void deleteProjectRisk(ProjectRisks projectRisks);

@Transactional(readOnly=true, propagation=Propagation.REQUIRED)
void updateProjectRisk(ProjectRisks projectRisks);

// Issues
@Transactional(readOnly=true, propagation=Propagation.SUPPORTS)
List<Issues> getIssues();

@Transactional(readOnly=false, propagation=Propagation.REQUIRED)
Issues insertIssue(Issues issue);

@Transactional(readOnly=false, propagation=Propagation.REQUIRED)
void deleteIssue(Issues issue);

@Transactional(readOnly=true, propagation=Propagation.REQUIRED)
void updateIssue(Issues issue);
}
```

Listing 12-27. *ProjectDaoImpl.java*

```java
package com.af.core.dao.hibernate;

import java.util.List;

import org.springframework.orm.hibernate3.support.HibernateDaoSupport;
import org.springframework.transaction.annotation.Propagation;
import org.springframework.transaction.annotation.Transactional;

import com.af.common.util.AFObjID;
import com.af.core.dao.ProjectDao;
import com.af.core.domain.Issues;
import com.af.core.domain.ProjectRisks;
import com.af.core.domain.ProjectTasks;
import com.af.core.domain.Projects;

@Transactional(propagation=Propagation.SUPPORTS, readOnly=true)
public class ProjectDaoImpl extends HibernateDaoSupport implements ProjectDao
{
    AFObjID aSingleton = AFObjID.getInstance();

    // Projects
    @Transactional(propagation=Propagation.SUPPORTS, readOnly=true)
    public List<Projects> getProjects(){
        return getHibernateTemplate().find("from Projects");
    }

    @Transactional(propagation=Propagation.REQUIRED, readOnly=false)
    public Projects insertProject(Projects project){
        project.setObjectIdentifier(aSingleton.NewObjectIdentifier());
        return (Projects) getHibernateTemplate().merge(project);
    }

    @Transactional(propagation=Propagation.REQUIRED, readOnly=false)
    public void deleteProject(Projects project){
        getHibernateTemplate().delete(project);
    }

    @Transactional(propagation=Propagation.REQUIRED, readOnly=false)
    public void updateProject(Projects project){
        getHibernateTemplate().delete(project);
    }
```

```java
// Project Tasks
@Transactional(propagation=Propagation.SUPPORTS, readOnly=true)
public List<ProjectTasks> getProjectTasks(){
     return getHibernateTemplate().find("from ProjectTasks");
}


@Transactional(propagation=Propagation.REQUIRED, readOnly=false)
public ProjectTasks insertProjectTask(ProjectTasks projectTasks){
     projectTasks.setObjectIdentifier(aSingleton.NewObjectIdentifier());
     return (ProjectTasks) getHibernateTemplate().merge(projectTasks);
}


@Transactional(propagation=Propagation.REQUIRED, readOnly=false)
public void deleteProjectTask(ProjectTasks projectTasks){
     getHibernateTemplate().delete(projectTasks);
}


@Transactional(propagation=Propagation.REQUIRED, readOnly=false)
public void updateProjectTask(ProjectTasks projectTasks){
     getHibernateTemplate().delete(projectTasks);
}

// Project Risks
@Transactional(propagation=Propagation.SUPPORTS, readOnly=true)
public List<ProjectRisks> getProjectRisks(){
     return getHibernateTemplate().find("from ProjectRisks");
}


@Transactional(propagation=Propagation.REQUIRED, readOnly=false)
public ProjectRisks insertProjectRisk(ProjectRisks projectRisks){
     projectRisks.setObjectIdentifier(aSingleton.NewObjectIdentifier());
     return (ProjectRisks) getHibernateTemplate().merge(projectRisks);
}


@Transactional(propagation=Propagation.REQUIRED, readOnly=false)
public void deleteProjectRisk(ProjectRisks projectRisks){
     getHibernateTemplate().delete(projectRisks);
}


@Transactional(propagation=Propagation.REQUIRED, readOnly=false)
public void updateProjectRisk(ProjectRisks projectRisks){
     getHibernateTemplate().delete(projectRisks);
}
```

```
    // Issues
    @Transactional(propagation=Propagation.SUPPORTS, readOnly=true)
    public List<Issues> getIssues(){
        return getHibernateTemplate().find("from Issues");
    }

    @Transactional(propagation=Propagation.REQUIRED, readOnly=false)
    public Issues insertIssue(Issues issue){
        return (Issues) getHibernateTemplate().merge(issue);
    }

    @Transactional(propagation=Propagation.REQUIRED, readOnly=false)
    public void deleteIssue(Issues issue){
        getHibernateTemplate().delete(issue);
    }

    @Transactional(propagation=Propagation.REQUIRED, readOnly=false)
    public void updateIssue(Issues issue){
        getHibernateTemplate().delete(issue);
    }
}
```

Registration of Spring Beans

The AF – Client Manager application requires a few advanced techniques, including transaction management, annotations, and Hibernate inclusion. I have tried to create an environment that is easy to repeat by breaking down each piece of the architecture individually. My goal is to allow those techniques to be quickly deployed so you can focus on the business logic more than the configuration of the Spring beans.

Setting Up the Application Context

To set up your application context to support the services, DAOs, Hibernate, transaction management, annotations, and database connectivity, you need to configure the following in the applicationContext.xml file:

- Loading of the Hibernate property file

- A session factory for annotated classes and reading Hibernate properties

- Transaction managers

- DAOs and services

Loading the Hibernate Property File

The Hibernate property file contains JDBC information to connect to the MySQL database, including the driver class name, URL, username, and password. It also contains Hibernate-specific information for debugging and footprint tags, as shown in Listing 12-28.

Listing 12-28. *The hibApplication.properties File*

```
#  Application Properties
path.webinf=webapps/af_Central/WEB-INF
# JDBC Connection information
jdbc.driverClassName=com.mysql.jdbc.Driver
jdbc.url=jdbc:mysql://localhost/apress
jdbc.username=af
jdbc.password=afpass
# Hibernate
hibernate.show_sql=true
hibernate.format_sql=true
hibernate.transaction.factory_class=org.hibernate.transaction.JDBCTransactionFactory
hibernate.dialect=org.hibernate.dialect.MySQLDialect
hibernate.c3p0.min_size=5
hibernate.c3p0.max_size=20
hibernate.c3p0.timeout=1800
hibernate.c3p0.max_statements=50
```

Loading the file in the application context is done by adding a `PropertyPlaceHolderConfigurer` bean to the `applicationContext.xml` file. The `PropertyPlaceHolderConfigurer` sets a property for a file location that holds the information that Hibernate will use at runtime, as follows:

```
<!-- START Load application properties -->
<bean id="propertyConfigurer"
    class="org.springframework.beans.factory.config.PropertyPlaceholderConfigurer">
    <property name="location">
        <value>WEB-INF/hibApplication.properties</value>
    </property>
</bean>
<!-- END Load application properties -->
```

Creating the Session Factory

The session factory part of the application context is responsible for creating an `AnnotationSessionFactoryBean` to define all `annotatedClasses` and `hibernateProperties` properties. Every domain object that has annotations needs to be defined as an annotated class so it can be mapped to from the data call results.

The `hibernateProperties` property takes what is loaded from the external `hibApplication.properties` file (see Listing 12-28) we loaded in the `applicationContext.xml` file. This is one way to simplify configuration for Hibernate, as this file can get extremely large when many beans are defined.

```xml
<bean id="sessionFactory" class="org.springframework.orm.hibernate3.annotation. ➡
    AnnotationSessionFactoryBean">
        <property name="annotatedClasses">
            <list>
                    <value>com.af.core.domain.Client</value>
                    <value>com.af.core.domain.ClientContacts</value>
                    <value>com.af.core.domain.ClientLinks</value>
                    <value>com.af.core.domain.InvoiceDetails</value>
                    <value>com.af.core.domain.Invoices</value>
                    <value>com.af.core.domain.Issues</value>
                    <value>com.af.core.domain.Media</value>
                    <value>com.af.core.domain.ProjectRisks</value>
                    <value>com.af.core.domain.Projects</value>
                    <value>com.af.core.domain.ProjectTasks</value>
            </list>
        </property>

        <property name="hibernateProperties">
            <props>
                    <prop key="hibernate.show_sql">
                        ${hibernate.show_sql}
                    </prop>
                    <prop key="hibernate.format_sql">
                        ${hibernate.format_sql}
                    </prop>
                    <prop key="hibernate.transaction.factory_class">
                        ${hibernate.transaction.factory_class}
                </prop>
                    <prop key="hibernate.dialect">
                        ${hibernate.dialect}
                    </prop>
                    <prop key="hibernate.c3p0.min_size">
                        ${hibernate.c3p0.min_size}
                    </prop>
                    <prop key="hibernate.c3p0.max_size">
                        ${hibernate.c3p0.max_size}
                    </prop>
                    <prop key="hibernate.c3p0.timeout">
                        ${hibernate.c3p0.timeout}
                    </prop>
                    <prop key="hibernate.c3p0.max_statements">
                        ${hibernate.c3p0.max_statements}
                    </prop>
                    <prop key="hibernate.connection.driver_class">
                        ${jdbc.driverClassName}
                    </prop>
```

```
                    <prop key="hibernate.connection.url">
                        ${jdbc.url}
                    </prop>
                    <prop key="hibernate.connection.username">
                        ${jdbc.username}
                    </prop>
                    <prop key="hibernate.connection.password">
                        ${jdbc.password}
                     </prop>
                </props>
            </property>
    </bean>
```

Configuring Transaction Managers

This application is required to be transactional as well as using annotations to allow for method-level transaction definition. Adding the following configuration elements to the applicationContext.xml file will enable the use of transactions based on annotations within Spring beans:

```
<tx:annotation-driven transaction-manager="txManager"/>

<bean id="txManager" class="org.springframework.orm.hibernate3. ➥
    HibernateTransactionManager">
        <property name="sessionFactory"><ref local="sessionFactory"/></property>
</bean>

<bean class="org.springframework.beans.factory.annotation.➥
    RequiredAnnotationBeanPostProcessor"/>
```

Configuring the DAOs and Services

Setting up the DAOs and Spring service beans is nothing new by this point in the book. We need to add all the wiring for the beans next. Each of the DAOs references the session factory that defines the database connectivity parameters and the annotated domain objects for data mapping.

The service configuration sets a reference to the appropriate DAO so the service can inject data into the DAO layer.

```
<!-- START DAO CONFIG -->
<bean id="clientDao" class="com.af.core.dao.hibernate.ClientDaoImpl">
        <property name="sessionFactory" ref="sessionFactory"/>
</bean>

<bean id="invoiceDao" class="com.af.core.dao.hibernate.InvoiceDaoImpl">
        <property name="sessionFactory" ref="sessionFactory"/>
</bean>
```

```xml
<bean id="mediaDao" class="com.af.core.dao.hibernate.MediaDaoImpl">
    <property name="sessionFactory" ref="sessionFactory"/>
</bean>

<bean id="projectDao" class="com.af.core.dao.hibernate.ProjectDaoImpl">
    <property name="sessionFactory" ref="sessionFactory"/>
</bean>

<bean id="secDao" class="com.af.security.dao.hibernate.SecDaoImpl">
    <property name="sessionFactory" ref="sessionFactory"/>
</bean>
<!-- END DAO CONFIG -->

<!-- START SERVICE CONFIG -->
<bean id="clientService" class="com.af.core.services.ClientServiceImpl">
    <property name="clientDao"><ref bean="clientDao"/></property>
</bean>

<bean id="invoiceService" class="com.af.core.services.InvoiceServiceImpl">
    <property name="invoiceDao"><ref bean="invoiceDao"/></property>
</bean>

<bean id="mediaService" class="com.af.core.services.MediaServiceImpl">
    <property name="mediaDao"><ref bean="mediaDao"/></property>
</bean>

<bean id="projectService" class="com.af.core.services.ProjectServiceImpl">
    <property name="projectDao"><ref bean="projectDao"/></property>
</bean>

<bean id="secService" class="com.af.security.services.SecServiceImpl">
    <property name="secDao"><ref bean="secDao"/></property>
</bean>
<!-- END SERVICE CONFIG -->
```

Putting It All Together

To give you the full picture of the applicationContext.xml file for the AF – Client Manager application, Listing 12-29 shows the complete code.

Listing 12-29. *The AF – Client Manager applicationContext.xml File*

```xml
<?xml version="1.0" encoding="UTF-8"?>
<beans
    xmlns="http://www.springframework.org/schema/beans"
    xmlns:xsi="http://www.w3.org/2001/XMLSchema-instance"
    xmlns:tx="http://www.springframework.org/schema/tx"
```

```xml
    xsi:schemaLocation="http://www.springframework.org/schema/beans
    http://www.springframework.org/schema/beans/spring-beans-2.0.xsd
    http://www.springframework.org/schema/tx
    http://www.springframework.org/schema/tx/spring-tx-2.0.xsd"
    default-lazy-init="true">

<!-- START Load application properties -->
<bean id="propertyConfigurer"
  class="org.springframework.beans.factory.config. ➥
     PropertyPlaceholderConfigurer">
  <property name="location">
     <value>WEB-INF/hibApplication.properties</value>
  </property>
</bean>
<!-- END Load application properties -->

<!-- START HIBERNATE CONFIG -->
<!-- Configure SessionFactory -->
<bean id="sessionFactory" class="org.springframework.orm.hibernate3. ➥
    annotation.AnnotationSessionFactoryBean">
  <property name="annotatedClasses">
      <list>
            <value>com.af.core.domain.Client</value>
            <value>com.af.core.domain.ClientContacts</value>
            <value>com.af.core.domain.ClientLinks</value>
            <value>com.af.core.domain.InvoiceDetails</value>
            <value>com.af.core.domain.Invoices</value>
            <value>com.af.core.domain.Issues</value>
            <value>com.af.core.domain.Media</value>
            <value>com.af.core.domain.ProjectRisks</value>
            <value>com.af.core.domain.Projects</value>
            <value>com.af.core.domain.ProjectTasks</value>
      </list>
  </property>

  <property name="hibernateProperties">
      <props>
            <prop key="hibernate.show_sql">
               ${hibernate.show_sql}
            </prop>
            <prop key="hibernate.format_sql">
               ${hibernate.format_sql}
            </prop>
            <prop key="hibernate.transaction.factory_class">
               ${hibernate.transaction.factory_class}
            </prop>
```

```xml
                    <prop key="hibernate.dialect">
                        ${hibernate.dialect}
                    </prop>
                    <prop key="hibernate.c3p0.min_size">
                        ${hibernate.c3p0.min_size}
                    </prop>
                    <prop key="hibernate.c3p0.max_size">
                        ${hibernate.c3p0.max_size}
                    </prop>
                    <prop key="hibernate.c3p0.timeout">
                        ${hibernate.c3p0.timeout}
                  </prop>
                    <prop key="hibernate.c3p0.max_statements">
                        ${hibernate.c3p0.max_statements}
                    </prop>
                    <prop key="hibernate.connection.driver_class">
                        ${jdbc.driverClassName}
                    </prop>
                    <prop key="hibernate.connection.url">
                        ${jdbc.url}
                    </prop>
                    <prop key="hibernate.connection.username">
                        ${jdbc.username}
                    </prop>
                    <prop key="hibernate.connection.password">
                        ${jdbc.password}
                    </prop>
                </props>
        </property>
</bean>

<!-- enable the configuration of transactional behavior based on annotations -->
<tx:annotation-driven transaction-manager="txManager"/>

<bean id="txManager" class="org.springframework.orm.hibernate3. ➥
    HibernateTransactionManager">
    <property name="sessionFactory"><ref local="sessionFactory"/></property>
</bean>

<bean class="org.springframework.beans.factory.annotation.➥
    RequiredAnnotationBeanPostProcessor"/>
<!-- END HIBERNATE CONFIG -->

<!-- START DAO CONFIG -->
<bean id="clientDao" class="com.af.core.dao.hibernate.ClientDaoImpl">
    <property name="sessionFactory" ref="sessionFactory"/>
</bean>
```

```xml
    <bean id="invoiceDao" class="com.af.core.dao.hibernate.InvoiceDaoImpl">
      <property name="sessionFactory" ref="sessionFactory"/>
    </bean>

    <bean id="mediaDao" class="com.af.core.dao.hibernate.MediaDaoImpl">
      <property name="sessionFactory" ref="sessionFactory"/>
    </bean>

    <bean id="projectDao" class="com.af.core.dao.hibernate.ProjectDaoImpl">
      <property name="sessionFactory" ref="sessionFactory"/>
    </bean>

    <bean id="secDao" class="com.af.springsecurity.dao.hibernate.SecDaoImpl">
      <property name="sessionFactory" ref="sessionFactory"/>
    </bean>
    <!-- END DAO CONFIG -->

    <!-- START SERVICE CONFIG -->
    <bean id="clientService" class="com.af.core.services.ClientServiceImpl">
      <property name="clientDao"><ref bean="clientDao"/></property>
    </bean>

    <bean id="invoiceService" class="com.af.core.services.InvoiceServiceImpl">
      <property name="invoiceDao"><ref bean="invoiceDao"/></property>
    </bean>

    <bean id="mediaService" class="com.af.core.services.MediaServiceImpl">
      <property name="mediaDao"><ref bean="mediaDao"/></property>
    </bean>

    <bean id="projectService" class="com.af.core.services.ProjectServiceImpl">
      <property name="projectDao"><ref bean="projectDao"/></property>
    </bean>

    <bean id="secService" class="com.af.springsecurity.services.SecServiceImpl">
      <property name="secDao"><ref bean="secDao"/></property>
    </bean>
    <!-- END SERVICE CONFIG -->
</beans>
```

Setting Up Security

Security for this application will be provided by Spring Security integrated with BlazeDS. Security roles will be held in a security context file. You can change this solution to call an external security package, if necessary.

We'll use the security implementation we created in Chapter 9 for the AF – Client Manager application, to reduce complexity of adding another architecture component to the application.

You will need to follow the security configuration steps starting with Listing 9-5 in Chapter 9. The beans defined in this section match the secService and secDao definitions in the applicationContext.xml file.

Summary

We began this chapter by defining the Spring server-side architecture for the AF – Client Manager application. The af_Central project is a combination of all Spring beans running within a BlazeDS server. It was all merged in one location to separate the services from the Flex source code. This is done to let you distribute the application tiers across multiple hardware layers.

Next, we covered the Spring service definitions, which group the business functionality in the services. For example, the ClientService contains the Client, ClientContacts, and ClientLinks objects. Each of those objects has the basic CRUD methods. Logically, it makes sense to group common service functions in one service.

Then we walked through the creation of all domain objects for the application in conjunction with the creation of the Spring services. After coding the services, we created the DAO layer with Hibernate. Both the services and DAO beans have an interface and an implementation for the bean. We registered the beans in the applicationContext.xml file, which contains wiring for service beans, DAO beans, and Hibernate configuration.

This concludes the creation of the back-end Spring services for Flex. In the next chapter, you will see how to code the Flex user interface to consume the Spring services.

CHAPTER 13

∎∎∎

Building the Flex
User Interface

This chapter covers building the Flex portion of the AF – Client Manager application, starting with the client management module. You will learn how to get and display data from the Spring services defined in the previous chapter. You will also see the benefits of using the Cairngorm development framework to deliver the transport architecture for the Flex application. Cairngorm will be the integration point for the back-end services from Flex.

MVC is the common design pattern used throughout the user interface during development. You will see how it is implemented with Cairngorm to decouple data from the views. The controllers in Cairngorm will bind events to commands in the architecture to receive results and faults.

After finishing this chapter, you will be able to build Flex applications with the existing Spring application developed in the previous chapter. This will give you the complete road map for success with integrating Flex on Spring.

Flex Architecture and Component Definition

Back in Chapter 7, we examined the Cairngorm architecture and how the components are executed in Flex. You have seen how the transport architecture is wired. Now we need to take a stab at creating a component model for the application.

Creating a component model for the application should be part of your design process. This is done after the wireframes are complete so you have pictures from which to derive your components. You can also do a rapid prototype to demonstrate application functionality to a client. You can do this without a live data source by using local XML files read into your application via HTTPService calls.

The purpose of the component model is to name the components for your application and build the skeleton for each view before coding any application logic into the application. Notice that I did not say business logic. That is because you should retain all business logic within your Spring business logic layer. Think of it this way: if you are planning to use your business logic to support Flex and mobile devices, you don't want to re-create business logic in the Flex application and mobile device pages.

Creating the component model is an important part of Flex design. It provides a visualization of what needs to be coded by developers and allows developers to easily define components for the application. Usually, for large-scale projects, multiple developers are involved. In Flex development, you want lines drawn in the sand to allow for modular development. These lines are nothing more than the functional components of the application. Defining the components also will allow you to determine which components are reusable.

After creating the component model, the next step is to take this model and code the application skeleton. At the end of this process, you will have a completely wired set of component shells in a working application. This allows you to work through flow issues before you get deep into writing the actual code for the individual components. The "clean version" of the application is easier to debug, since there are not as many issues that could be masking work flow problems.

Once you have the application wired, you can decide on major animations and transitions. You can implement those effects before you deal with the transport of data through Cairngorm, and build those effects while you set up the transport layer.

AF – Client Manager Component Model and Directory Structure

We completed the application design and produced the wireframes for the AF – Client Manager application back in Chapter 2. Now we will model the application components and wire the application together, so you can see how your application will flow and where you can start building effect transitions between screens.

Figure 13-1 shows the component model for the AF – Client Manager application.

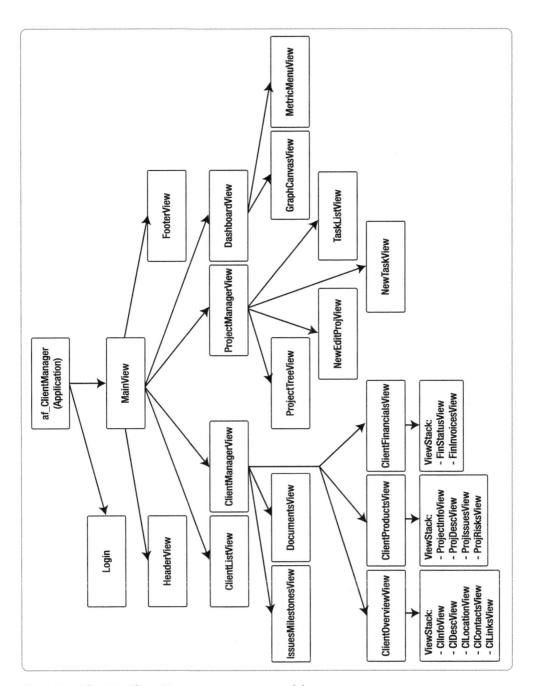

Figure 13-1. *The AF – Client Manager component model*

The first step is to create the directory structure based on the component model. It should look similar to Figure 13-2.

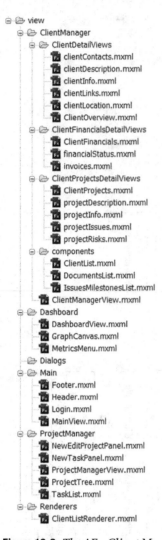

Figure 13-2. *The AF – Client Manager view directory structure*

The AF – Client Manager Model

In Chapter 10, we set up the Cairngorm configuration for Flex by creating the base classes for the delegates, model locator, services, and controller. We also instantiated the controller and services as singletons in the `<mx:Application>` MXML. To properly wire the application, we need to use the model for binding `<mx:ViewStack selectedIndex="{model.MainViewStackState}">`, as shown in Listing 13-1. We also need to build the base value object for the client object, as shown in Listing 13-2.

Listing 13-1. *ModelLocator.mxml*

```
package com.af.clientmanager.model
{
    import com.adobe.cairngorm.model.ModelLocator;
    import com.af.clientmanager.model.vo.*;

    import mx.collections.ArrayCollection;

    [Bindable]
    public class ModelLocator implements com.adobe.cairngorm.model.ModelLocator
    {
        private static var modelLocator :
            com.af.clientmanager.model.ModelLocator;

        public static function getInstance() :
            com.af.clientmanager.model.ModelLocator
        {
            if ( modelLocator == null )
                modelLocator = new com.af.clientmanager.model.ModelLocator();

                return modelLocator;
        }

            public function ModelLocator()
            {
                if(
com.af.clientmanager.model.ModelLocator.modelLocator !=
                    null )
                    throw new Error( "Only one ModelLocator" +
                        "instance should be instantiated" );
            }
            public const SERVICE_ENDPOINT:String =
        "http://localhost:8080/af_Central/spring/messagebroker/amf";
            public const YAHOO_APP_ID:String = "YOUR YAHOO APP ID";
            public const UPLOAD_URL:String = "";
            public const DIRECTORY_NAME:String = "af_Central";

            //Global Menu Constants
            public const CLIENT_MANAGER:int = 0;
            public const PROJECT_ADMIN:int = 1;
            public const DASHBOARD:int = 2;
            public var MainViewStackState:int = 0;
```

```
                    // Data Providers
                    public var clientsDP:ArrayCollection = new ArrayCollection();
                    public var contactsDP:ArrayCollection = new ArrayCollection();
                    public var issuesDP:ArrayCollection = new ArrayCollection();
                    public var documentsDP:ArrayCollection = new ArrayCollection();

                    public var selectedClient:ClientVO = new ClientVO;
                    public var selectedContact:ClientContactsVO = new ClientContactsVO;
            }
    }
```

Listing 13-2. *ClientVO.as*

```
package com.af.clientmanager.model.vo
{
        [Bindable]
        [RemoteClass(alias="com.af.core.domain.Client")]

        public class ClientVO
        {
                public var objectIdentifier:Number;
                public var assocobjectID:Number;
                public var clientName:String;
                public var clientID:int;
                public var link:String;
                public var description:String;
                public var notes:String;
                public var phone:String;
                public var addressLine1:String;
                public var addressLine2:String;
                public var city:String;
                public var state:String;
                public var zip:String;
        }
}
```

A ViewStack in Flex provides a container that allows you to switch between views based on the SelectedChild or SelectedIndex of its children.

With the basis of the transport layer built earlier, we can focus on the application wiring.

AF – Client Manager Application Wiring

For every Flex application I build for a client, I work through the component model to wire together the application. We'll do that now for the AF – Client Manager, focusing on some key views.

> **Note** Stringing together the application is work that can be done in conjunction with the designers, before any skinning or styling is done.

Application View

We'll start with the top of the component model: af_ClientManager.mxml. This contains the <mx:Application> tag shown in Listing 13-3. You can find the style sheet (CSS) for the application in Listing 13-29, at the end of the chapter. For the application, we will be using the login code from Listing 9-10 in Chapter 9. You can find the full login code with the rest of this book's downloadable code (available from the book's details page at http://www.apress.com).

Listing 13-3. *af_ClientManager.mxml*

```
<?xml version="1.0" encoding="utf-8"?>
<mx:Application xmlns:mx="http://www.adobe.com/2006/mxml"
     pageTitle="AF Client Manager"
     layout="absolute"
     xmlns:view="com.af.view.*"
     xmlns:services="com.af.clientmanager.services.*"
     xmlns:control="com.af.clientmanager.control.*"
     xmlns:Main="com.af.clientmanager.view.Main.*"
     xmlns:model="com.af.clientmanager.model.*"
     initialize="initApp()" >

     <mx:Style source="assets/css/style.css"/>

     <mx:Script>
          <![CDATA[
          import mx.events.ListEvent;
          import mx.controls.Alert;

          private function initApp():void
          {
               // Currently set to applicationView to bypass
               // the login process.
               vsAppLevel.selectedChild = applicationView;
          }
          public function loginSuccess():void
          {
               vsAppLevel.selectedChild = applicationView;
          }
          ]]>
     </mx:Script>
```

```
<!-- ====================================================================== -->
<!-- the ServiceLocator where we specify the remote services -->
<services:Services id="services"/>

<!-- the FrontController, containing Commands-to-Event mappings -->
<control:MainController id="mainController" />
<!-- ====================================================================== -->

<mx:Fade id="fadeInApp" alphaFrom="0" alphaTo="1" duration="500" />

<mx:VBox width="100%" height="100%" backgroundAlpha=".88"
      verticalScrollPolicy="off" horizontalScrollPolicy="off"
      verticalAlign="top" horizontalAlign="center">
    <mx:ViewStack id="vsAppLevel" width="100%" height="100%" paddingTop="0"
          creationPolicy="all">
        <mx:Canvas id="loginView" showEffect="Fade" hideEffect="Fade">
            <Main:Login width="100%" height="100%" />
        </mx:Canvas>
        <mx:VBox width="100%" height="100%"
            id="applicationView" backgroundAlpha="0"
                verticalScrollPolicy="off"
                horizontalScrollPolicy="off"
                paddingTop="0"
                verticalAlign="top" horizontalAlign="center"
                showEffect="Fade" hideEffect="Fade">
            <mx:VBox width="985" height="735"
                paddingTop="0" verticalGap="0"
                verticalScrollPolicy="off"
                horizontalScrollPolicy="off"
                borderStyle="solid" borderThickness="2"
                backgroundColor="#FFFFFF"
                backgroundAlpha=".75">

                    <Main:Header backgroundColor="red" />

                     <mx:VBox width="100%" height="100%">
                          <Main:MainView />
                     </mx:VBox>

                     <Main:Footer backgroundColor="blue"/>

                </mx:VBox>
            </mx:VBox>
        </mx:ViewStack>
    </mx:VBox>
</mx:Application>
```

Listing 13-3 contains several items of interest. This is the root level of our application, since it includes the <mx:Application> tag. In the <mx:Script> block, notice the init() function. This is where you can set preselections for a ViewStack or make Cairngorm calls, if necessary. The ViewStack controls which part of the application can be seen. It also contains the application header, main view, and footer.

In the root component of the application, you should not have any logic other than to set the ViewStack in the application. In this case, we are showing the login view first. Upon successful authentication, the user will be taken to the main application view.

■Note You might notice that I've set colors directly in the component definition. I do this so I can clearly define the component height and width and see how they fit together when I run the application. Those backgroundColor definitions will be deleted when I start to build the application layers. All styles will be moved to CSS, and will never be represented in MXML. This is the only level at which I will define the application height and width (which is 985 by 735). Try not to set static height and width throughout your application, or you will regret it when it changes, and you need to dig through your application to modify sizes. Use percentages in your components unless you need an exact size.

The footer is trivial and will have no function other than to display company information. The header will have navigation components that change the view state of the application. Listings 13-4 and 13-5 show the header and footer MXML components.

Listing 13-4. *Header.mxml (com.af.clientmanager.view.Main)*

```
<?xml version="1.0" encoding="utf-8"?>
<mx:Canvas xmlns:mx="http://www.adobe.com/2006/mxml"
       width="100%" height="75">

    <mx:Script>
        <![CDATA[
        import com.af.clientmanager.view. ➥
            dialogs.DeleteClientConfirmationDialog;
        import mx.managers.PopUpManager;
        import com.af.clientmanager.control. ➥
            commands.events.DeleteClientEvent;
        import com.af.clientmanager.control. ➥
            commands.events.InsertClientEvent;
        import mx.events.ItemClickEvent;
        import com.af.clientmanager.model.vo.ClientVO;
        import com.adobe.cairngorm. ➥
            control.CairngormEventDispatcher;
        import com.af.clientmanager.control. ➥
            commands.events.UpdateClientEvent;
        import mx.controls.Alert;
        import com.af.clientmanager.model.ModelLocator;
```

```
        [Bindable]
        public var model : ModelLocator =
            ModelLocator.getInstance();

        private function clearClientDetails():void
        {
                // remove all information from
                // the panels after pop-up
                model.selectedClient = new ClientVO();
        }
        private function saveClient():void
        {
                if(model.selectedClient.objectIdentifier > 0)
    CairngormEventDispatcher.getInstance().dispatchEvent(new
        UpdateClientEvent(model.selectedClient));
                else
                {
    CairngormEventDispatcher.getInstance().dispatchEvent(new
        InsertClientEvent(model.selectedClient));
                }
        }
        private function deleteClient():void
        {
                // Don't try to delete unless a client is selected
                if(model.selectedClient.objectIdentifier > 0)
                {
                    var pop1:DeleteClientConfirmationDialog =
                        DeleteClientConfirmationDialog(
                    PopUpManager.createPopUp(this,
                        DeleteClientConfirmationDialog, true));
                    pop1.confirmationMessageTitle =
                        "Delete Confirmation";
                    pop1.confirmationMessageBody =
                        "Are you sure you want to delete:   " +
                        model.selectedClient.clientName;

                    PopUpManager.centerPopUp(pop1);
                }
        }
        private function ➡
            functionsBBClick(event:ItemClickEvent):void
        {
                switch (event.index)
                {
                    case 0:
                        clearClientDetails();
                        break;
```

```
                        case 1:
                                saveClient();
                                break;
                        case 2:
                                deleteClient();
                                break;
                    }
            }
        private function ➥
            componentsBBClick(event:ItemClickEvent):void
            {
                switch (event.index)
                {
                        case 0:
                                model.MainViewStackState=
                                    model.CLIENT_MANAGER;
                                break;
                        case 1:
                                model.MainViewStackState=
                                    model.PROJECT_ADMIN;
                                break;
                        case 2:
                                model.MainViewStackState=
                                    model.DASHBOARD;
                                 break;
                    }
            }
    </mx:Script>

    <mx:HBox width="100%" height="100%">
    <mx:Image  width="190" height="74"/>
    <mx:VBox width="100%" height="100%" verticalAlign="bottom">
    <mx:HBox width="100%">
            <mx:Button label="N" click="clearClientDetails()"/>
            <mx:Button label="S" click="saveClient()"/>
            <mx:Button label="D" click="deleteClient()"/>

            <mx:Spacer width="100%" />
            <mx:Button label="Client Manager"
                click="{model.MainViewStackState=model.CLIENT_MANAGER}"/>
            <mx:Button label="Project Administrator"
                click="{model.MainViewStackState=model.PROJECT_ADMIN}"/>
            <mx:Button label="Dashboard"
                    click="{model.MainViewStackState=model.DASHBOARD}"/>
            </mx:HBox>
            </mx:VBox>
        </mx:HBox>
</mx:Canvas>
```

Listing 13-5. *Footer.mxml (com.af.clientmanager.view.Main)*

```
<?xml version="1.0" encoding="utf-8"?>
<mx:Canvas xmlns:mx="http://www.adobe.com/2006/mxml"
     width="100%" height="25">

    <mx:Label text="Footer" fontSize="16" color="white" fontWeight="bold" />

</mx:Canvas>
```

Once the application view is complete, we can move on to the main view.

Main View

The MainView component holds the major aspects of the application and drives which part of the application is visible based on its ViewStack state. Listing 13-6 shows MainView.mxml.

Listing 13-6. *MainView.mxml (com.af.clientmanager.view.Main)*

```
<?xml version="1.0" encoding="utf-8"?>
<mx:Canvas xmlns:mx="http://www.adobe.com/2006/mxml"
     width="100%" height="100%"
     backgroundColor="#888888"
     xmlns:ClientDetailViews=
         "com.af.clientmanager.view.ClientManager. ➥
         ClientDetailViews.*"
     xmlns:ClientFinancialsDetailViews=
         "com.af.clientmanager.view.ClientManager. ➥
         ClientFinancialsDetailViews.*"
     xmlns:ClientProjectsDetailViews=
         "com.af.clientmanager.view.ClientManager. ➥
         ClientProjectsDetailViews.*"
     xmlns:components="com.af.clientmanager.view. ➥
         ClientManager.components.*"
     xmlns:ClientManager="com.af.clientmanager.view. ➥
         ClientManager.*"
     xmlns:ProjectManager="com.af.clientmanager.view. ➥
         ProjectManager.*"
     xmlns:Dashboard="com.af.clientmanager.view.Dashboard.*">

    <mx:Script>
        <![CDATA[
        import com.af.clientmanager.model.ModelLocator;

         [Bindable]
        public var model : ModelLocator =
           ModelLocator.getInstance();
        ]]>
    </mx:Script>
```

```
        <mx:HBox width="100%" height="100%">
            <components:ClientList />
            <mx:ViewStack id="vsMain" width="100%" height="100%"
                    paddingTop="0"
                    creationPolicy="all"
                    selectedIndex="{model.MainViewStackState}">
                <mx:Canvas id="clientManagerView"
                    showEffect="Fade" hideEffect="Fade">
                        <ClientManager:ClientManagerView />
                </mx:Canvas>
                <mx:Canvas id="projectManagerView"
                    showEffect="Fade" hideEffect="Fade">
                        <ProjectManager:ProjectManagerView />
                </mx:Canvas>
                <mx:Canvas id="dashboardView" showEffect="Fade"
                    hideEffect="Fade">
                        <Dashboard:DashboardView />
                </mx:Canvas>
            </mx:ViewStack>
        </mx:HBox>
</mx:Canvas>
```

The main view contains several namespace definitions. Those alias definitions will grant you access to use components in their locations. This view contains and maintains ClientList, ClientManagerView, ProjectManagerView, and DashboardView.

Note that in the naming conventions, anything with View in its name is a top-level container for multiple components. The components within those views will not have View in their names, as they are children of a view.

As I said, the main view controls what is seen. The ViewStack is bound to the model. MainViewStackState variable, which allows you to execute a user gesture elsewhere in the application that will change the view.

Client Manager View

Another view of interest is the client manager view. Listing 13-7 shows ClientManagerView.mxml.

Listing 13-7. *ClientManagerView.mxml (com.af.clientmanager.view)*

```
<?xml version="1.0" encoding="utf-8"?>
<mx:VBox xmlns:mx="http://www.adobe.com/2006/mxml"
    width="100%" height="100%"
    xmlns:ClientDetailViews="com.af.clientmanager.view. ➥
        ClientManager.ClientDetailViews.*"
    xmlns:ClientProjectsDetailViews="com.af.clientmanager.view. ➥
        ClientManager.ClientProjectsDetailViews.*"
    xmlns:ClientFinancialsDetailViews="com.af.clientmanager. ➥
        view.ClientManager.ClientFinancialsDetailViews.*"
    xmlns:components="com.af.clientmanager.view. ➥
        ClientManager.components.*">
```

```
            <mx:VBox width="100%" height="100%">
                <mx:HBox>
                    <mx:Button label="Overview"
                        click="{vsAppLevel.selectedChild=
                        clientOverview}"/>
                    <mx:Button label="Projects"
                        click="{vsAppLevel.selectedChild=
                        clientProjects}"/>
                    <mx:Button label="Financials"
                        click="{vsAppLevel.selectedChild=
                        clientFinancials}"/>
                </mx:HBox>
                <mx:ViewStack id="vsAppLevel" width="100%" height="100%"
                        paddingTop="0"
                        creationPolicy="all">
                    <mx:Canvas id="clientOverview"
                        showEffect="Fade" hideEffect="Fade">
                          <ClientDetailViews:ClientOverview />
                    </mx:Canvas>
                    <mx:Canvas id="clientProjects"
                        showEffect="Fade" hideEffect="Fade">
                          <ClientProjectsDetailViews:ClientProjects />
                    </mx:Canvas>
                    <mx:Canvas id="clientFinancials"
                        showEffect="Fade" hideEffect="Fade">
                          <ClientFinancialsDetailViews:ClientFinancials />
                    </mx:Canvas>
                </mx:ViewStack>
                <mx:HBox width="100%" height="40%">
                        <components:IssuesMilestonesList />
                        <components:DocumentsList />
                </mx:HBox>
            </mx:VBox>
    </mx:VBox>
</mx:VBox>
```

The client manager view contains all content pertinent to the client functionality. It will display client details, projects, and financials. You will also have a listing of client issues and documents visible at all times when working in the client management section of the application.

Client Overview

The last piece of the application we will inspect here is ClientOverview.mxml. That is about as deep as we can go to fully string together the application. Listing 13-8 shows the navigation component ready to receive individual components to display client detail data.

Listing 13-8. *ClientOverview.mxml (com.af.clientmanager.view.ClientManager.ClientDetailViews)*

```xml
<?xml version="1.0" encoding="utf-8"?>
<mx:Canvas xmlns:mx=http://www.adobe.com/2006/mxml
    xmlns:ClientDetailViews=
    "com.af.clientmanager.view.ClientManager.ClientDetailViews.*"
    width="100%" height="100%" >

    <mx:TabNavigator borderStyle="solid" width="100%" height="100%">
        <mx:VBox label="General Information"
            width="100%" height="100%">
            <ClientDetailViews:clientInfo />
        </mx:VBox>

        <mx:VBox label="Description" width="100%" height="100%">
            <ClientDetailViews:clientDescription />
        </mx:VBox>

        <mx:VBox label="Location" width="100%" height="100%">
            <ClientDetailViews:clientLocation />
        </mx:VBox>

        <mx:VBox label="Contacts" width="100%" height="100%">
            <ClientDetailViews:clientContacts />
        </mx:VBox>

        <mx:VBox label="Links" width="100%" height="100%">
            <ClientDetailViews:clientLinks />
        </mx:VBox>
    </mx:TabNavigator>
</mx:Canvas>
```

A TabNavigator in Flex is another example of a container that switches content based on which tab is selected. These containers are nice to use when you need to divide up data for a major business component of the application (Client in this case).

The same coding has been done for the remainder of the component model. Now we can implement the application logic, skinning, and Cairngorm data calls. Before we do that, take a look at the application at its current state, as shown in Figure 13-3. It looks very much like something a clown built, but it also clearly defines the component mix for the application. This is the "before" look. For the "after" look, see Figure 13-6 later in this chapter.

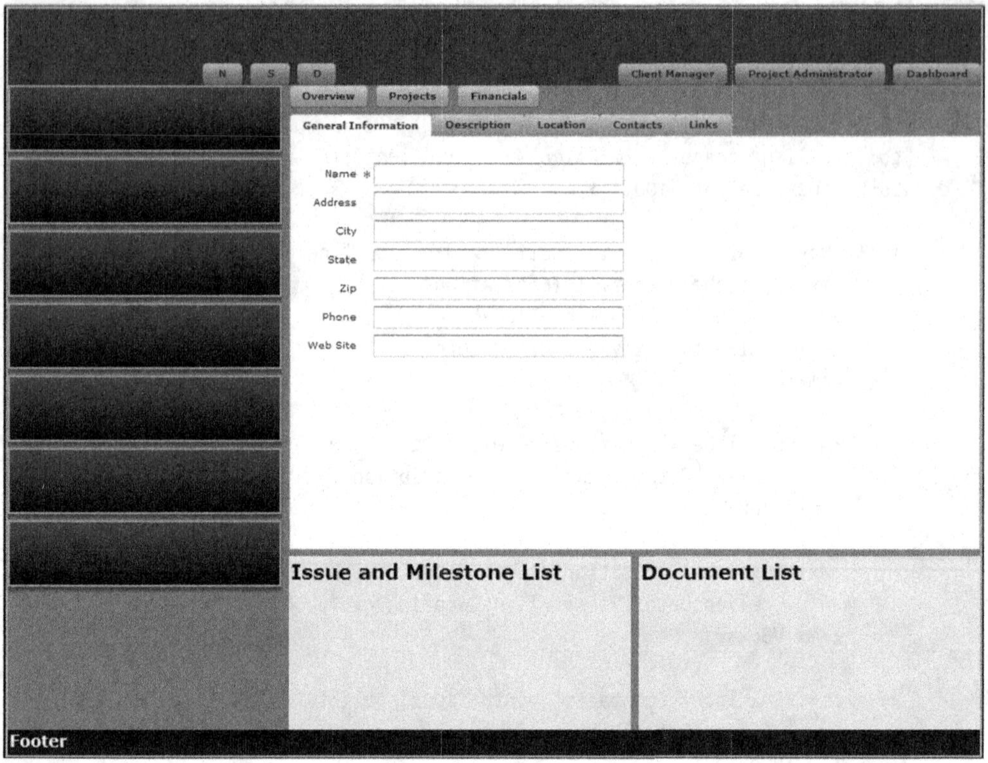

Figure 13-3. *AF – Client Manager strung together*

Keep in mind that what we have now is simply a combination of placeholders and base components, along with the navigation. You will need to remove all style definitions and place them in a style sheet (CSS) as you progress with building the application. For this to be complete, you will need to shell out the following Flex components:

- com.af.clientmanager.view.ClientManager.components.ClientList

- com.af.clientmanager.view.Dashboard.DashboardView

- com.af.clientmanager.view.Dashboard.GraphCanvas

- com.af.clientmanager.view.Dashboard.MetricsMenu

- com.af.clientmanager.view.ClientProjectsDetailViews.ClientProjects

- com.af.clientmanager.view.ClientFinancialsDetailViews.ClientFinancials

- com.af.clientmanager.view.ClientManager.components.IssuesMilestonesList

- com.af.clientmanager.view.ClientManager.components.DocumentsList

- com.af.clientmanager.view.ProjectManager.ProjectManagerView

With the wiring done, we can move on to defining the RemoteObject destinations, so we can start building the remainder of the application.

Flex RemoteObject Configuration

To communicate with the Spring services, you will need to configure a transport protocol in Flex to call those services. The Spring services have been built to return a binary object to Flex. For Flex to call those services, a RemoteObject definition needs to be added to the Cairngorm ServiceLocator. This definition needs to specify a destination that matches the destination running in context in af_Central with BlazeDS. Listing 13-9 shows the RemoteObjects needed to pull data for the AF – Client Manager application.

Listing 13-9. *Services.mxml (com.af.clientmanager.services)*

```
<?xml version="1.0" encoding="utf-8"?>
<cairngorm:ServiceLocator
     xmlns:mx="http://www.adobe.com/2006/mxml"
     xmlns:cairngorm="com.adobe.cairngorm.business.*">

     <mx:Script>
          <![CDATA[
          import com.af.clientmanager.model.ModelLocator;

           [Bindable]
          public var model : ModelLocator =
             ModelLocator.getInstance();
          ]]>
     </mx:Script>

     <mx:RemoteObject endpoint="{model.SERVICE_ENDPOINT}"
          id="clientService"
          destination="clientService"
          showBusyCursor="true">
     </mx:RemoteObject>

     <mx:RemoteObject endpoint="{model.SERVICE_ENDPOINT}"
          id="invoiceService"
          destination="invoiceService"
          showBusyCursor="true">
     </mx:RemoteObject>

     <mx:RemoteObject endpoint="{model.SERVICE_ENDPOINT}"
          id="mediaService"
          destination="mediaService"
          showBusyCursor="true">
     </mx:RemoteObject>
```

```
<mx:RemoteObject endpoint="{model.SERVICE_ENDPOINT}"
       id="projectService"
       destination="projectService"
       showBusyCursor="true">
</mx:RemoteObject>

<mx:RemoteObject endpoint="{model.SERVICE_ENDPOINT}"
       id="secService"
       destination="secService"
       showBusyCursor="true">
</mx:RemoteObject>
```

```
</cairngorm:ServiceLocator>
```

Notice that each service has an endpoint that points to the af_Central AMF gateway running locally on a Tomcat web server. It is stored as a constant on the model, so we need to change it in only one place when this application is moved to a production environment.

```
public const SERVICE_ENDPOINT=
"http://localhost:8080/af_Central/spring/messagebroker/amf";
```

The other counterpart to the ServiceLocator is the destination found in the SERVICE_ ENDPOINT. The destination is defined in the applicationContext.xml file, since we are using Spring Blaze Integration (SBI) to expose service beans for Flex Remoting (which we set up in Chapter 6). The destinations in the Services.mxml definitions match the exposed service beans in applicationContext.xml:

```
<bean id="clientService"
   class="org.springframework.flex.messaging. ➥
   remoting.FlexRemotingServiceExporter">
   <property name="messageBroker"
      ref="mySpringManagedMessageBroker"/>
   <property name="service" ref="clientServiceBean"/>
</bean>

<bean id="projectService"
   class="org.springframework.flex.messaging. ➥
   remoting.FlexRemotingServiceExporter">
   <property name="messageBroker"
      ref="mySpringManagedMessageBroker"/>
   <property name="service" ref="projectServiceBean"/>
</bean>

<bean id="invoiceService"
   class="org.springframework.flex.messaging. ➥
   remoting.FlexRemotingServiceExporter">
   <property name="messageBroker"
      ref="mySpringManagedMessageBroker"/>
   <property name="service" ref="invoiceServiceBean"/>
</bean>
```

```
<bean id="mediaService"
   class="org.springframework.flex.messaging. ➥
   remoting.FlexRemotingServiceExporter">
    <property name="messageBroker"
       ref="mySpringManagedMessageBroker"/>
    <property name="service" ref="mediaServiceBean"/>
</bean>

<bean id="secService"
   class="org.springframework.flex.messaging. ➥
   remoting.FlexRemotingServiceExporter">
    <property name="messageBroker"
       ref="mySpringManagedMessageBroker"/>
    <property name="service" ref="secServiceBean"/>
</bean>
```

As noted, for the AF – Client Manager application, we are using SBI to handle communication between Flex and Spring. If we were using `SpringFactory` instead to expose Spring beans for Remoting, we would set our RemoteObject destinations in the `remoting-config.xml` file, as in the following example:

```
<destination id="secService">
    <properties>
        <factory>spring</factory>
        <source>secService</source>
    </properties>
</destination>

<destination id="clientService">
    <properties>
        <factory>spring</factory>
        <source>clientService</source>
    </properties>
</destination>
```

If you compare the `destination` tag on the RemoteObject to the `id` on the `remoting-config.xml` destinations, you will notice they match. This is how the service is located and a method can be called from Flex. The factory definition for Spring wires the destination service in the `remoting-config.xml` file to Spring's `WebApplicationContext`.

Flex Component Construction Using Cairngorm

We're ready to tackle the main portion of the Flex development work. We have configured the BlazeDS server, MySQL database, and Spring beans, and have built the Spring services. Flex is ready to consume those services with the help of Cairngorm to facilitate the transport of data. We have strung together the entire application and need to populate it with data and application logic to visualize the data. To get started, we will build the main client views that will manage our client's data through the main CRUD calls for the `Client` object.

Coding the Flex Transport Layer

To enable Flex to make calls to the Spring services, we need to create commands to support method calls exposed by Spring. Each command in Cairngorm needs a corresponding event. Flex is an event-based framework, and Cairngorm's Event wraps the base Flex Event class. Listings 13-10 through 13-17 show the four commands with events needed to support getting, deleting, inserting, and updating clients.

Listing 13-10. *DeleteClientEvent.as*

```
package com.af.clientmanager.control.commands.events
{
    import com.adobe.cairngorm.control.CairngormEvent;
    import com.af.clientmanager.control.MainController;
    import com.af.clientmanager.model.vo.ClientVO;

    public class DeleteClientEvent extends CairngormEvent
    {
        public static const EVENT_DELETE_CLIENT:String =
            "event_delete_client";
        public var clientVO : ClientVO;

        public function DeleteClientEvent( clientVO : ClientVO )
        {
            super(EVENT_DELETE_CLIENT );
            this.clientVO = clientVO;
        }
    }
}
```

Listing 13-11. *DeleteClientCommand.as*

```
package com.af.clientmanager.control.commands
{
    import com.adobe.cairngorm.commands.Command;
    import com.adobe.cairngorm.control.CairngormEvent;
    import com.af.clientmanager.business.ClientDelegate;
    import com.af.clientmanager.control.commands.events. ➥
        DeleteClientEvent;
    import com.af.clientmanager.model.ModelLocator;

    import mx.controls.Alert;
    import mx.rpc.IResponder;
    import mx.rpc.events.FaultEvent;
    import mx.rpc.events.ResultEvent;
```

```
public class DeleteClientCommand implements Command, IResponder
{
      private var model : ModelLocator =
         ModelLocator.getInstance();

      public function execute( event : CairngormEvent ) : void
      {
            var delegate : ClientDelegate = new ClientDelegate(
               this );
            var deleteClientEvent : DeleteClientEvent =
               DeleteClientEvent( event );
            delegate.deleteClient( deleteClientEvent.clientVO );
      }

      public function result( data:Object ) : void
      {
            var event:ResultEvent = data as ResultEvent;

            var arrLength:int = model.clientsDP.length;

            // Business logic to remove client
            // from the model ArrayCollection
            for(var i:int =0; i < arrLength; i++)
            {
                  if(model.selectedClient.objectIdentifier ==
                     model.clientsDP[i].objectIdentifier)
                  {
                        model.clientsDP.removeItemAt(i);
                        break;
                  }
            }
      }

      public function fault(event:Object):void
      {
            var faultEvt:FaultEvent = event as FaultEvent;
            Alert.show("ERROR: " + event.toString());
      }
   }
}
```

Listing 13-12. *GetClientsEvent.as*

```
package com.af.clientmanager.control.commands.events
{
    import com.adobe.cairngorm.control.CairngormEvent;
    import com.af.clientmanager.control.MainController;

    public class GetClientsEvent extends CairngormEvent
    {
        public static const EVENT_GET_CLIENTS:String =
            "event_get_clients";
        public function GetClientsEvent():void
        {
            super(EVENT_GET_CLIENTS);
        }
    }
}
```

Listing 13-13. *GetClientsCommand.as*

```
package com.af.clientmanager.control.commands
{
    import com.adobe.cairngorm.commands.ICommand;
    import com.adobe.cairngorm.control.CairngormEvent;
    import com.af.clientmanager.business.ClientDelegate;
    import com.af.clientmanager.control.commands.events. ➥
        GetClientsEvent;
    import com.af.clientmanager.model.ModelLocator;

    import mx.collections.ArrayCollection;
    import mx.controls.Alert;
    import mx.rpc.IResponder;
    import mx.rpc.events.FaultEvent;

    public class GetClientsCommand  implements ICommand, IResponder
    {
        private var model:ModelLocator =
            ModelLocator.getInstance();
        public function execute(event:CairngormEvent):void
        {
            var getClientsEvent:GetClientsEvent =
                GetClientsEvent(event);
            var delegate : ClientDelegate = new ClientDelegate(
                this );
            delegate.getClients();
        }
```

```
            public function result(data:Object):void
            {
                    model.clientsDP = ArrayCollection(data.result);
            }

            public function fault(event:Object):void
            {
                    var faultEvt:FaultEvent = event as FaultEvent;
                    Alert.show("ERROR: " + event.toString());
            }
        }
}
```

Listing 13-14. *InsertClientEvent.as*

```
package com.af.clientmanager.control.commands.events
{
      import com.adobe.cairngorm.control.CairngormEvent;
      import com.af.clientmanager.control.MainController;
      import com.af.clientmanager.model.vo.ClientVO;

      public class InsertClientEvent extends CairngormEvent
      {
          public static const EVENT_INSERT_CLIENT:String =
             "event_insert_client";
          public var clientVO : ClientVO;

          public function InsertClientEvent( clientVO : ClientVO )
          {
                super(EVENT_INSERT_CLIENT );
                this.clientVO = clientVO;
          }
      }
}
```

Listing 13-15. *InsertClientCommand.as*

```
package com.af.clientmanager.control.commands
{
      import com.adobe.cairngorm.commands.Command;
      import com.adobe.cairngorm.control.CairngormEvent;
      import com.af.clientmanager.business.ClientDelegate;
      import com.af.clientmanager.control.commands.events. ➥
         InsertClientEvent;
      import com.af.clientmanager.model.ModelLocator;
      import com.af.clientmanager.model.vo.ClientVO;
```

```
        import mx.controls.Alert;
        import mx.rpc.IResponder;
        import mx.rpc.events.FaultEvent;
        import mx.rpc.events.ResultEvent;

        public class InsertClientCommand implements Command, IResponder
        {
              private var model : ModelLocator =
                 ModelLocator.getInstance();

              public function execute( event : CairngormEvent ) : void
              {
                    var delegate : ClientDelegate = new ClientDelegate(
                       this );
                    var insertClientEvent : InsertClientEvent =
                       InsertClientEvent( event );
                    delegate.insertClient( insertClientEvent.clientVO );
              }

              public function result( data:Object ) : void
              {
                    var event:ResultEvent = data as ResultEvent;
                    model.clientsDP.addItem(ClientVO(data));
              }

              public function fault(event:Object):void
              {
                    var faultEvt:FaultEvent = event as FaultEvent;
                    Alert.show("ERROR: " + event.toString());
              }
        }
}
```

Listing 13-16. *UpdateClientEvent.as*

```
package com.af.clientmanager.control.commands.events
{
        import com.adobe.cairngorm.control.CairngormEvent;
        import com.af.clientmanager.control.MainController;
        import com.af.clientmanager.model.vo.ClientVO;

        public class UpdateClientEvent extends CairngormEvent
        {
              public static const EVENT_UPDATE_CLIENT:String =
                 "event_update_client";
              public var clientVO : ClientVO;
```

```
        public function UpdateClientEvent( clientVO : ClientVO )
        {
              super( EVENT_UPDATE_CLIENT );
              this.clientVO = clientVO;
        }
    }
}
```

Listing 13-17. *UpdateClientCommand.as*

```
package com.af.clientmanager.control.commands
{
    import com.adobe.cairngorm.commands.Command;
    import com.adobe.cairngorm.control.CairngormEvent;
    import com.af.clientmanager.business.ClientDelegate;
    import com.af.clientmanager.control.commands.events. ➥
        UpdateClientEvent;
    import com.af.clientmanager.model.ModelLocator;
    import com.af.clientmanager.model.vo.ClientVO;

    import mx.controls.Alert;
    import mx.rpc.IResponder;
    import mx.rpc.events.FaultEvent;
    import mx.rpc.events.ResultEvent;

    public class UpdateClientCommand implements Command, IResponder
    {
        private var model : ModelLocator =
           ModelLocator.getInstance();

        public function execute( event : CairngormEvent ) : void
        {
              var delegate : ClientDelegate = new ClientDelegate(
                 this );
              var updateClientEvent : UpdateClientEvent =
                 UpdateClientEvent( event );
              delegate.updateClient( updateClientEvent.clientVO );
        }

        public function result( data:Object ) : void
        {
              var event:ResultEvent = data as ResultEvent;
        }
```

```
public function fault( event:Object ) : void
{
        var faultEvt:FaultEvent = event as FaultEvent;
        Alert.show("ERROR: " + event.toString());
}
    }
}
```

A set of commands and events need to be completed for the contact CRUD actions as well. You can use the preceding listings as a starting point to create those commands, as they will be very similar.

Each of the commands we just coded has a specific job. The execute method is called to interface with the delegate. The delegate is responsible for making the actual method call to the Spring service. When a result or fault is returned, the IResponder implemented by the command class will handle the return. The result methods in the commands are responsible for modifying data state for the application. They will provide different functionality based on which view needs to display, as determined by the result. For example, the result of the GetClientsCommand is a list of clients that will be displayed in the main view of the client management application. The result of the call is placed in the model in which the clientsDP ArrayCollection is bound to by the ClientList component.

```
model.clientsDP = ArrayCollection(data.result);
```

With data binding to objects in the model, any change to the object in the model will be reflected in the component that is bound to it.

To allow a command to be executed, you will need to update the MainController class to map events to commands, as shown in Listing 13-18.

Listing 13-18. *MainController.as*

```
package com.af.clientmanager.control
{
        import com.adobe.cairngorm.control.FrontController;
        import com.af.clientmanager.control.commands.*;
        import com.af.clientmanager.control.commands.events.*;

        public class MainController extends FrontController
        {
                public function MainController():void
                {
                    // Client
                    addCommand(GetClientsEvent.EVENT_GET_CLIENTS,
                      GetClientsCommand );
                    addCommand(InsertClientEvent.EVENT_INSERT_CLIENT,
                      InsertClientCommand );
                    addCommand(DeleteClientEvent.EVENT_DELETE_CLIENT,
                      DeleteClientCommand );
```

```
            addCommand(UpdateClientEvent.EVENT_UPDATE_CLIENT,
              UpdateClientCommand );
        }
    }
}
```

The controller in Cairngorm serves two main purposes:

- It accesses the event constants on the events themselves that are used to identify Cairngorm events in the framework.

- It maps the event constants to a corresponding command. Notice that the events in Listings 13-10 through 13-17 call the events on the controller. The controller is listening for those event types to be dispatched, and will call a mapped command when it catches the event.

The commands reference delegates that represent method stubs for each Spring service. Each Spring service has a delegate defined in Cairngorm. This is done to keep the layers in sync for maintainability purposes. You can see the client methods available in Spring through the ClientDelegate in Listing 13-19.

Listing 13-19. *ClientDelegate.as*

```
package com.af.clientmanager.business
{
    import com.adobe.cairngorm.business.ServiceLocator;
    import com.af.clientmanager.model.vo.ClientContactsVO;
    import com.af.clientmanager.model.vo.ClientLinksVO;
    import com.af.clientmanager.model.vo.ClientVO;

    import mx.controls.Alert;
    import mx.rpc.AsyncToken;
    import mx.rpc.IResponder;

    public class ClientDelegate
    {
        private var responder : IResponder;
        private var service : Object;

        public function ClientDelegate( responder : IResponder )
        {
            this.service =
                ServiceLocator.getInstance().getService(
                "clientService" );
            this.responder = responder;
        }
```

```
// Client
public function getClients(): void
{
     var call:AsyncToken = service.getClients();
     call.addResponder( responder );
}

public function insertClient(clientVO : ClientVO): void
{
     var call:AsyncToken =
        service.insertClient(clientVO);
     call.addResponder( responder );
}

public function deleteClient(clientVO : ClientVO): void
{
     var call:AsyncToken =
        service.deleteClient(clientVO);
     call.addResponder( responder );
}

public function updateClient(clientVO : ClientVO): void
{
     var call:AsyncToken =
        service.updateClient(clientVO);
     call.addResponder( responder );
}

// Client Contacts
public function getClientContacts(key:Number): void
{
     var call:AsyncToken =
        service.getClientContacts(key);
     call.addResponder( responder );
}

public function insertClientContact(
   clientContactVO : ClientContactsVO): void
{
     var call:AsyncToken =
        service.insertClientContact(clientContactVO);
     call.addResponder( responder );
}
```

```
        public function deleteClientContact(
           clientContactVO : ClientContactsVO): void
        {
            var call:AsyncToken =
               service.deleteClientContact(clientContactVO);
            call.addResponder( responder );
        }

        public function updateClientContact(
           clientContactVO : ClientContactsVO): void
        {
            var call:AsyncToken =
               service.updateClientContact(clientContactVO);
            call.addResponder( responder );
        }
    }
}
```

With the transport layer created for client management, we can move on to coding the Flex components that will leverage this layer.

Coding the Flex Components

Now the application is starting to come together. The last parts we need to code are the actual views to display data. As you get the hang of building your Spring services and Cairngorm classes, you will see that at this point, you will have built roughly 40% of your application. I generally spend more time building the view than the services, due to the detail that can go into skinning and styling an application. Not only that, but you can get very creative with how you animate components to display data.

Keep in mind that you are building an RIA, not a flat HTML web page. If you have a Flash programming background, you will understand how to apply dynamic data visualization to Flex. I try to give my applications a perception of depth, as well as designing their behavior and look. That way, I get something a little different from many of the stale-looking applications seen on the Web today. With that being said, let's move into coding the client views.

Figure 13-4 shows the original wireframe for the main client view. This wireframe shows several components we will need to complete to bring this view to life.

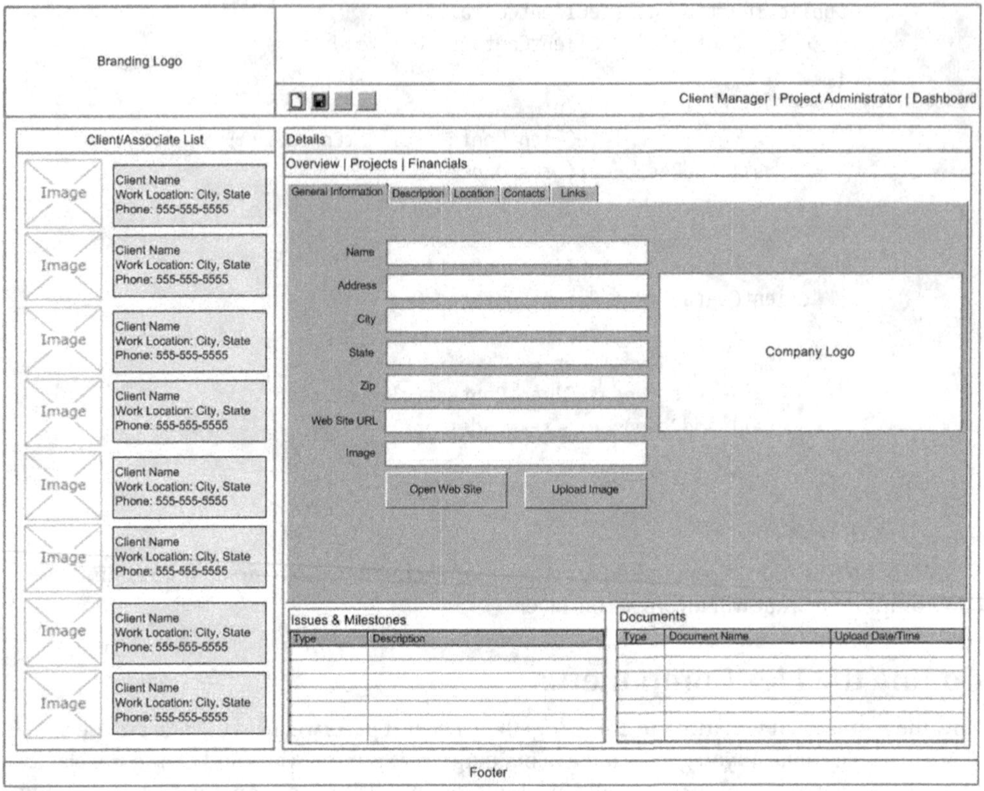

Figure 13-4. *Client view wireframe*

Coding the Client List

The client list is the first component we will tackle. It is a list of client information containing an uploaded company logo, client name, client location, and client phone number. Listings 13-20 and 13-21 show the coding required to implement this list.

Listing 13-20. *ClientList.mxml (com.af.clientmanager.view.ClientManager.components)*

```
<?xml version="1.0" encoding="utf-8"?>
<mx:Canvas xmlns:mx="http://www.adobe.com/2006/mxml"
     height="100%"
     xmlns:Renderers="com.af.clientmanager.view.Renderers.*"
     creationComplete="initComp()">

     <mx:Script>
          <![CDATA[
          import com.adobe.cairngorm.control. ➥
             CairngormEventDispatcher;
```

```
            import com.af.clientmanager.control.commands.events. ➥
               GetClientsEvent;
            import com.af.clientmanager.model.ModelLocator;

            [Bindable]
            private var model:ModelLocator =
               ModelLocator.getInstance();

            private function initComp():void
            {
               CairngormEventDispatcher.getInstance().dispatchEvent(
                   new GetClientsEvent());
            }
            ]]>
      </mx:Script>

      <mx:VBox width="278" height="100%">
            <mx:Repeater id="rp" dataProvider="{model.clientsDP}">
                  <Renderers:ClientListRenderer clientData="{rp.currentItem}"/>
            </mx:Repeater>
      </mx:VBox>
</mx:Canvas>
```

Listing 13-21. *ClientListRenderer.mxml (com.af.clientmanager.view.Renderers)*

```
<mx:Canvas xmlns:mx="http://www.adobe.com/2006/mxml"
      showEffect="Fade"
      width="100%" height="65"
      creationComplete="setText()">

      <mx:Script>
            <![CDATA[
            import com.af.clientmanager.model.vo.ClientVO;
            import mx.effects.Fade;
            import mx.effects.Blur;
            import mx.effects.Parallel;
            import mx.effects.Move;
            import mx.core.IUIComponent;
            import mx.managers.DragManager;
            import mx.core.UIComponent;
            import mx.core.DragSource;
            import mx.controls.Alert;
            import com.af.clientmanager.model.ModelLocator;
```

```
        [Bindable]
        public var model : ModelLocator =
           ModelLocator.getInstance();

        // This object is populated with the data
        // passed in from the controlling control
        [Bindable]
        public var clientData:Object;

        private function setText():void
        {
            clName.text = clientData.clientName;
            clAddress.text = clientData.city + "," +
               clientData.state;
            clPhone.text = clientData.phone;
            MoveItem();
        }
        public function MoveItem():void
        {
            var parallel:Parallel = new Parallel();
            parallel.target = clientItem;

            var blur:Blur = new Blur();
            blur.blurXFrom = 5;
            blur.blurXTo = 0;
            blur.blurYFrom = 5;
            blur.blurYTo = 0;

            var move:Move = new Move();
            move.target = this;
            move.xFrom = -1000;
            move.xTo = 0;
            move.play();

            parallel.addChild(blur);
            parallel.addChild(move);
            parallel.play();
        }
        private function setSelectedItem():void
        {
            model.selectedClient = ClientVO(this.clientData);
            this.dispatchEvent(new Event("changeAddressEvent",
               true)); // Bubble to parent
        }
        ]]>
    </mx:Script>
```

```
    <mx:HBox id="clientItem" styleName="WeatherPanel"
        width="100%" height="65"
        useHandCursor="true" mouseChildren="false"
        buttonMode="true" click="setSelectedItem()">
            <mx:Image source="{clientData.image}" />
            <mx:VBox width="100%" verticalGap="0"
                horizontalScrollPolicy="off"
                verticalScrollPolicy="off">
                    <mx:Label id="clName" styleName="clientListFont"/>
                    <mx:Label id="clAddress"
                        styleName="clientListFont"/>
                    <mx:Label id="clPhone" styleName="clientListFont"/>
            </mx:VBox>
    </mx:HBox>
</mx:Canvas>
```

To populate the client list with data, we first need to trigger a Cairngorm event to tell the Spring service that Flex wants client data. This is done by executing the following line of code (highlighted in Listing 13-20):

```
CairngormEventDispatcher.getInstance().dispatchEvent(new GetClientsEvent());
```

This is triggered in the initComp() method that is called in the creationComplete tag for the Canvas. The CairngormEventDispatcher will execute any event in the Cairngorm framework that is defined by the controller to handle data, or it can be used to trigger other actions in your Flex application, such as state changes. In this case, Cairngorm executes a GetClientsEvent that maps to the GetClientsCommand. This command executes a call to the business delegate ClientDelegate.getClients(). The getClients() method does not take any parameters and will return a list of client objects to the result() method in the command. The result() method then assigns the list to an ArrayCollection on the model, which is bound to from the client list Repeater.dataProvider. The data assignment will cause the Repeater to be populated with the new list of clients.

The nice thing about using a Repeater to build the client list is that it takes a list of data and repeats it in a custom item renderer. Using this technique in Flex allows you to create some dynamic content displays that fit the tone of the application. You also have the ability to easily add effects to the control's display. In the custom renderer, there is a Parallel effect that uses the Blur and Move effects to animate each list item. The client, issue, and document list will remain static on this screen while viewing clients. The information, description, location, contacts, and links will change based on the TabNavigator view. The issue and document lists are shown in Listings 13-22 and 13-23.

Listing 13-22. *IssuesMilestonesList.mxml (com.af.clientmanager.view.ClientManager.components)*

```
<?xml version="1.0" encoding="utf-8"?>
<mx:Canvas xmlns:mx="http://www.adobe.com/2006/mxml"
    width="100%" height="100%"
    styleName="panelSkin">
```

```
<mx:Script>
      <![CDATA[
      import com.af.clientmanager.model.ModelLocator;

      [Bindable]
      public var model : ModelLocator =
         ModelLocator.getInstance();
      ]]>
</mx:Script>

<mx:Label text="Issues &amp; Milestones"
      styleName="heading"
      y="6" x="9"/>

<mx:VBox width="100%" height="100%"
      paddingBottom="10" paddingLeft="10" paddingRight="10"
      y="34">
      <mx:DataGrid width="100%" height="100%"
            dataProvider="{model.issuesDP}"
            y="49">
            <mx:columns>
                  <mx:DataGridColumn dataField="issueStatus"
                     headerText="Status" />
                  <mx:DataGridColumn
                     dataField="issueDescription"
                     headerText="Description"/>
            </mx:columns>
      </mx:DataGrid>
</mx:VBox>
</mx:Canvas>
```

Listing 13-23. *DocumentsList.mxml (com.af.clientmanager.view.ClientManager.components)*

```
<?xml version="1.0" encoding="utf-8"?>
<mx:Canvas xmlns:mx="http://www.adobe.com/2006/mxml"
      width="100%" height="100%"
      styleName="panelSkin">

<mx:Script>
      <![CDATA[
      import com.af.clientmanager.model.ModelLocator;

      [Bindable]
      public var model : ModelLocator =
         ModelLocator.getInstance();
      ]]>
</mx:Script>
```

```
        <mx:Label text="Documents"
              styleName="heading"
              y="6" x="9"/>

        <mx:VBox width="100%" height="100%"
              paddingBottom="10" paddingLeft="10" paddingRight="10"
              y="34">
              <mx:DataGrid width="100%" height="100%"
                  dataProvider="{model.issuesDP}">
                      <mx:columns>
                              <mx:DataGridColumn dataField="mediaType"
                                  headerText="Type" />
                              <mx:DataGridColumn dataField="mediaName"
                                  headerText="Document Name"/>
                              <mx:DataGridColumn dataField="creationDate"
                                  headerText="Upload Date"/>
                      </mx:columns>
              </mx:DataGrid>
        </mx:VBox>
</mx:Canvas>
```

The two list components shown in Listings 13-22 and 13-23 are DataGrid components with dataProviders that reference ArrayCollection collections loaded on the model. Within the DataGrid tags, columns are defined to show only portions of the objects contained in the list. If you do not supply a series of columns, the DataGrid will be populated with the attributes of the entire object that is part of the dataProvider.

Coding the Client Overview

The client overview has several components that make up the contents of a TabNavigator that controls which part of the client details is visible. The first component is clientInfo.mxml, which contains the main information tied to a client, including name, address, phone, and web site. Listing 13-24 shows <mx:Binding> tags that bind form elements to the selected client. If you make a change to the form items, the changes are automatically stored in the selectedClient ClientVO on the model. This makes updating or deleting information easy, since a CairngormEventDispatcher can dispatch an event and add the selectedClient to the call from the model.

Listing 13-24. *clientInfo.mxml (com.af.clientmanager.view.ClientManager.ClientDetailViews)*

```
<?xml version="1.0" encoding="utf-8"?>
<mx:HBox xmlns:mx="http://www.adobe.com/2006/mxml"
      width="100%" height="100%">

      <mx:Script>
              <![CDATA[
              import com.af.clientmanager.model.ModelLocator;
```

```
        [Bindable]
        public var model : ModelLocator =
          ModelLocator.getInstance();

        private function openWebSite(URL:String):void
        {
              var u:URLRequest = new URLRequest(URL);
              navigateToURL(u,"_blank");
        }
        ]]>
</mx:Script>

<mx:Binding source="tiName.text"
    destination="model.selectedClient.clientName"/>
<mx:Binding source="tiAddress.text"
    destination="model.selectedClient.addressLine1"/>
<mx:Binding source="tiCity.text"
    destination="model.selectedClient.city"/>
<mx:Binding source="tiState.text"
    destination="model.selectedClient.state"/>
<mx:Binding source="tiZip.text"
    destination="model.selectedClient.zip"/>
<mx:Binding source="tiPhone.text"
    destination="model.selectedClient.phone"/>
<mx:Binding source="tiLink.text"
    destination="model.selectedClient.link"/>

<mx:PhoneNumberValidator
      source="{tiPhone}"
      property="text" />

<mx:Form>
      <mx:FormItem label="Name" required="true">
            <mx:TextInput id="tiName" width="250" height="30"
                text="{model.selectedClient.clientName}"/>
      </mx:FormItem>
      <mx:FormItem label="Address">
            <mx:TextInput id="tiAddress" width="250"
                text="{model.selectedClient.addressLine1}" />
      </mx:FormItem>
      <mx:FormItem label="City">
            <mx:TextInput id="tiCity" width="250"
                text="{model.selectedClient.city}" />
      </mx:FormItem>
```

```
                    <mx:FormItem label="State">
                          <mx:TextInput id="tiState" width="250"
                              text="{model.selectedClient.state}" />
                    </mx:FormItem>
                    <mx:FormItem label="Zip">
                          <mx:TextInput id="tiZip" width="250"
                              text="{model.selectedClient.zip}" />
                    </mx:FormItem>
                    <mx:FormItem label="Phone">
                          <mx:TextInput id="tiPhone" width="250"
                              text="{model.selectedClient.phone}" />
                    </mx:FormItem>
                    <mx:FormItem label="Web Site">
                          <mx:TextInput id="tiLink" width="250"
                              text="{model.selectedClient.link}" />
                    </mx:FormItem>
                    <mx:FormItem paddingTop="8">
                          <mx:HBox>
                              <mx:Button label="Open Web Site"
                               click="openWebSite(model.selectedClient.link)"/>
                              <mx:Button label="Upload Image"
                               width="100"/>
                          </mx:HBox>
                    </mx:FormItem>
              </mx:Form>
              <mx:VBox width="100%" height="100%" paddingTop="15">
                    <mx:VBox styleName="frame" minHeight="200" minWidth="300"
                          paddingBottom="3" paddingLeft="3"
                          paddingRight="3" paddingTop="3">
                    <mx:Image id="img" y="14" width="200"
                          complete="img.visible=true"/>
                 </mx:VBox>
              </mx:VBox>
        </mx:HBox>
```

Part of the Client object is the client description. This is a free-form text element that allows you to keep notes on this client. It is implemented as a TextArea in Flex, as shown in Listing 13-25. Notice in the clientDescription component that the TextArea text property is bound to the selectedClient.description on the model.

Listing 13-25. *clientDescription.mxml (com.af.clientmanager.view.ClientManager. ClientDetailViews)*

```
<?xml version="1.0" encoding="utf-8"?>
<mx:VBox xmlns:mx="http://www.adobe.com/2006/mxml"
     width="100%" height="100%"
     paddingBottom="5" paddingLeft="5"
     paddingRight="5" paddingTop="5">
```

```
<mx:Script>
    <![CDATA[
    import com.af.clientmanager.model.ModelLocator;

    [Bindable]
    public var model : ModelLocator =
        ModelLocator.getInstance();
    ]]>
</mx:Script>

<mx:Binding source="rteDesc.text"
    destination="model.selectedClient.description"/>

<mx:TextArea id="rteDesc" width="100%" height="100%"
    text="{model.selectedClient.description}" />
</mx:VBox>
```

The client contacts component, shown in Listing 13-26, is a little more detailed, due to the level of information we are going to display. The contact list is built in a similar fashion to the client list, which used a custom renderer in a Repeater to display the data. Along with the pertinent contact information, we are also displaying an image that is tied to the selected contact from the contact list.

Listing 13-26. *clientContacts.mxml (com.af.clientmanager.view.ClientManager.ClientDetailViews)*

```
<?xml version="1.0" encoding="utf-8"?>
<mx:VBox xmlns:mx="http://www.adobe.com/2006/mxml"
    width="100%" height="100%"
    paddingBottom="5" paddingLeft="5" paddingRight="5" paddingTop="5"
    xmlns:Renderers="com.af.clientmanager.view.Renderers.*">

    <mx:Script>
    <![CDATA[
        import mx.managers.PopUpManager;
        import com.af.clientmanager.view.Dialogs. ➡
            DeleteContactConfirmationDialog;
        import com.af.clientmanager.model.vo.ClientContactsVO;
        import com.af.clientmanager.control.commands.events.*;
        import com.af.clientmanager.model.ModelLocator;

        import com.adobe.cairngorm.control. ➡
            CairngormEventDispatcher;

        [Bindable]
        private var model:ModelLocator =
            ModelLocator.getInstance();
```

```
[Embed(source="/assets/packs/cleanSkin/icon_contactDefaultImage.png")]
[Bindable]
public var imgCls:Class;

private function insertContact():void
{
     var contact:ClientContactsVO = new ClientContactsVO;
     // Set the client to contact relationship
     contact.assocobjectID =
        model.selectedClient.objectIdentifier;
     contact.contactName = tiName.text;
     contact.jobTitle = tiTitle.text;
     contact.phoneWork = tiPhoneWork.text;
     contact.phoneCell = tiPhoneCell.text;
     contact.email = tiEmail.text;
     contact.responsibility = tiResponsibility.text;

    CairngormEventDispatcher.getInstance().dispatchEvent(
        new InsertClientContactEvent(contact));
}
private function updateContact():void
{
   CairngormEventDispatcher.getInstance().dispatchEvent(
       new UpdateClientContactEvent(
       ClientContactsVO(model.selectedContact)));
}
private function deleteContact():void
{
     // Don't try to delete unless a client is selected
     if(model.selectedContact.objectIdentifier > 0)
     {
          var pop1:DeleteContactConfirmationDialog =
             DeleteContactConfirmationDialog(
             PopUpManager.createPopUp(this,
             DeleteContactConfirmationDialog, true));
          pop1.confirmationMessageTitle =
             "Delete Confirmation";
          pop1.confirmationMessageBody =
             "Are you sure you want to delete:  " +
             model.selectedContact.contactName;

          PopUpManager.centerPopUp(pop1);
     }
}
```

```
        private function imageError():void
        {
                contactImage.source=imgCls;
        }
        ]]>
</mx:Script>

<mx:Binding source="tiName.text"
   destination="model.selectedContact.contactName"/>
<mx:Binding source="tiTitle.text"
   destination="model.selectedContact.jobTitle"/>
<mx:Binding source="tiPhoneWork.text"
   destination="model.selectedContact.phoneWork"/>
<mx:Binding source="tiPhoneCell.text"
   destination="model.selectedContact.phoneCell"/>
<mx:Binding source="tiEmail.text"
   destination="model.selectedContact.email"/>
<mx:Binding source="tiResponsibility.text"
   destination="model.selectedContact.responsibility"/>

<mx:EmailValidator
   source="{tiEmail}"
   property="text"/>

<mx:PhoneNumberValidator
    source="{tiPhoneWork}"
    property="text" />

<mx:PhoneNumberValidator
    source="{tiPhoneCell}"
    property="text" />

<mx:HBox width="100%" height="100%">
     <mx:VBox width="40%" height="100%" styleName="frame"
        horizontalAlign="center" verticalAlign="middle"
        paddingTop="10">
           <mx:Label text="Contact List" styleName="heading" />
           <mx:List id="contactList" width="100%" height="100%"
              dataProvider="{model.contactsDP}"
              labelField="contactName"
              change="{model.selectedContact=
              ClientContactsVO(contactList.selectedItem)}"/>
     </mx:VBox>
```

```
<mx:VBox width="20%" height="100%">
     <mx:HBox>
          <mx:Button label="Add" width="75"
             click="insertContact()"/>
          <mx:Button label="Update" width="75"
             click="updateContact()"/>
          <mx:Button label="Delete" width="75"
             click="deleteContact()"/>
     </mx:HBox>
     <mx:VBox styleName="frame"
        paddingBottom="3" paddingLeft="3"
        paddingRight="3" paddingTop="3">
          <mx:Image id="contactImage"
             width="100%" height="100%"
             ioError="imageError()" source="{imgCls}"/>
     </mx:VBox>
     <mx:Button label="Upload Image" />
</mx:VBox>
<mx:VBox width="80%" height="100%">
     <mx:Form width="100%">
          <mx:FormItem label="Name" required="false">
            <mx:TextInput id="tiName"
              text="{model.selectedContact.contactName}"
              width="250"/>
          </mx:FormItem>

          <mx:FormItem label="Title" required="false">
               <mx:HBox>
                    <mx:TextInput id="tiTitle"
                 text="{model.selectedContact.jobTitle}"
                          width="250"/>
               </mx:HBox>
          </mx:FormItem>

          <mx:FormItem label="Work" required="false">
               <mx:HBox>
                    <mx:TextInput id="tiPhoneWork"
                 text="{model.selectedContact.phoneWork}"
                          width="250"/>
               </mx:HBox>
          </mx:FormItem>
```

```
                        <mx:FormItem label="Cell" required="false">
                            <mx:HBox>
                                    <mx:TextInput id="tiPhoneCell"
                                text="{model.selectedContact.phoneCell}"
                                            width="250"/>
                            </mx:HBox>
                        </mx:FormItem>

                        <mx:FormItem label="Email" required="false">
                            <mx:HBox>
                                    <mx:TextInput id="tiEmail"
                                text="{model.selectedContact.email}"
                                        width="250"/>
                            </mx:HBox>
                        </mx:FormItem>
                </mx:Form>
            </mx:VBox>
        </mx:HBox>
        <mx:HBox width="100%" height="20%">
            <mx:Label text="Notes:" styleName="heading" />
            <mx:TextArea id="tiResponsibility"
                text="{model.selectedContact.responsibility}"
                width="100%" height="100%" />
        </mx:HBox>
</mx:VBox>
```

In Listing 13-26, notice the use of VBox and HBox to lay out the component. The benefit of using those two containers for layout control is that if this component needs to be scalable in the future, it is ready to go. If you use a Canvas with static x and y locations for positioning, you will need to make changes to support scaling. If you are having issues with the size of your SWF, you can use a Canvas to cut down on the bytes used to create the VBox and HBox containers. This is rarely an issue though.

Upon clicking the Delete button for a selected client, you do not want to directly execute a delete call to the database for that object. I created a dialog box that forces the user to confirm before triggering the actual Cairngorm delete event. In Listing 13-27, you can see when the user clicks Yes, a DeleteClientContact event is triggered to process the contact deletion.

Listing 13-27. *DeleteContactConfirmationDialog.mxml*

```
<?xml version="1.0" encoding="utf-8"?>
<mx:Canvas xmlns:mx="http://www.adobe.com/2006/mxml"
    xmlns:*="*"
    width="0" height="0"
    verticalScrollPolicy="off"
    horizontalScrollPolicy="off"
    creationComplete="initComp();">
```

```
<mx:Script>
    <![CDATA[
    import com.af.clientmanager.control.commands.events. ➥
        DeleteClientEvent;
    import com.adobe.cairngorm.control.CairngormEvent;
    import mx.effects.Blur;
    import mx.effects.Fade;
    import mx.effects.Move;
    import mx.effects.Parallel;
    import mx.effects.Resize;
    import mx.effects.easing.*;
    import mx.events.EffectEvent;
    import mx.controls.Alert;
    import mx.managers.PopUpManager;
    import com.adobe.cairngorm.control. ➥
        CairngormEventDispatcher;
    import com.af.clientmanager.model.ModelLocator;

    [Bindable]
    public var model : ModelLocator =
        ModelLocator.getInstance();

    [Bindable] public var confirmationMessageTitle: String;
    [Bindable] public var confirmationMessageBody: String;

    public function initComp():void
    {
        this.width = 0;
        this.height = 0;

        var parallel:Parallel = new Parallel();
        parallel.target = this;

        var resize:Resize = new Resize();
        resize.target = this;
        resize.widthTo = mainCanvas.width;
        resize.heightTo = mainCanvas.height;

        var move:Move = new Move();
        move.xFrom = this.stage.width/2;
        move.yFrom = this.stage.height/2;
        move.xTo = this.stage.width/2 - mainCanvas.width/2;
        move.yTo = this.stage.height/2 -
            mainCanvas.height/2;
```

```
            var fade:Fade = new Fade();
            fade.alphaFrom = 0;
            fade.alphaTo = 1;

            var blur:Blur = new Blur();
            blur.blurXFrom = 30;
            blur.blurYFrom = 30;
            blur.blurXTo = 0;
            blur.blurYTo = 0;

            parallel.addChild(resize);
            parallel.addChild(move);
            parallel.addChild(fade);
            parallel.addChild(blur);

            resize.easingFunction =
                mx.effects.easing.Circular.easeInOut;
            move.easingFunction =
                mx.effects.easing.Circular.easeInOut;
            fade.easingFunction =
                mx.effects.easing.Circular.easeInOut;

            parallel.duration = 600;
            parallel.play();
            parallel.addEventListener(EffectEvent.EFFECT_END,
                effectEndHandler);

            container.visible = false;
    }
    public function effectEndHandler(event:EffectEvent):void
    {
            container.visible = true;
    }
    private function closeDialog():void
    {
            var parallel:Parallel = new Parallel();
            parallel.target = this;

            var fade:Fade = new Fade();
            fade.alphaFrom = 1;
            fade.alphaTo = 0;

            parallel.addChild(fade);

            fade.easingFunction =
                mx.effects.easing.Circular.easeInOut;
```

```
                  parallel.duration = 400;
                  parallel.play();
                  parallel.addEventListener(EffectEvent.EFFECT_END,
                     closeDialogFinal);

         }
         private function closeDialogFinal(event:EffectEvent):void
         {
               PopUpManager.removePopUp(this);
         }
         public function
         HeaderMouseDownHandler(event:MouseEvent):void
         {
               this.startDrag(false);
         }
         public function
         HeaderMouseUpHandler(event:MouseEvent):void
         {
               this.stopDrag();
         }

         private function yesClicked():void
         {
              CairngormEventDispatcher.getInstance().dispatchEvent(
                 new DeleteClientEvent(model.selectedClient));
              closeDialog();
         }
         ]]>
</mx:Script>

<mx:Canvas id="mainCanvas" width="386" height="196"
   verticalScrollPolicy="off" horizontalScrollPolicy="off"
   styleName="panelSkin">
      <mx:VBox width="100%" height="100%" id="container"
         verticalScrollPolicy="off" horizontalScrollPolicy="off"
         paddingLeft="10" paddingRight="10"
         paddingBottom="10" paddingTop="5"
         verticalGap="0">
            <mx:Canvas width="100%" height="15%"
               verticalScrollPolicy="off"
               horizontalScrollPolicy="off"
               mouseDown="HeaderMouseDownHandler(event);"
               mouseUp="HeaderMouseUpHandler(event);"
               mouseChildren="false" buttonMode="true"
               useHandCursor="true">
                  <mx:Image id="iconImage"
```

```
                source="@Embed('/assets/images/icon_redXwarning.png')"/>
                        <mx:Text text="{confirmationMessageTitle}"
                            width="90%" height="100%" x="25" y="3"
                            styleName="heading"/>
                </mx:Canvas>
                <mx:Spacer height="3" />
                <mx:HBox width="100%" height="80%"
                    verticalScrollPolicy="off"
                    horizontalScrollPolicy="off"
                    horizontalAlign="center" verticalAlign="middle">
                        <mx:Text id="txtMessageBody"
                            text="{confirmationMessageBody}"/>
                </mx:HBox>

                <mx:HBox width="100%" height="5%"
                    verticalScrollPolicy="off"
                    horizontalScrollPolicy="off">
                        <mx:Spacer width="90%" />
                        <mx:Button label="Yes" height="20" width="80"
                            click="yesClicked()"/>
                        <mx:Button label="No" height="20" width="80"
                            click="closeDialog()"/>
                </mx:HBox>
            </mx:VBox>
        </mx:Canvas>
</mx:Canvas>
```

The last piece of the client overview that we will code in this chapter is the client location using the Yahoo! Maps web services API. You will need to download the Yahoo! Maps SWC to use Yahoo! Maps. You will also need to register for a Yahoo! application ID. This can be done by going to `https://developer.yahoo.com/wsregapp/` and logging in to the Yahoo! Developer Network if you have a Yahoo! ID. Once you log in, you will need to fill out the forms to get your Yahoo! application ID. You can get the Yahoo! Maps SWC, as well as information about building Flex applications with Yahoo! Maps integration, at `http://developer.yahoo.com/maps/flash/flexGettingStarted.html`.

Tip You can also use the Google Maps API, which is a similar to embedding Yahoo! Maps into your Flex applications. For more information about the Google Maps API for Flash, see `http://code.google.com/apis/maps/documentation/flash/intro.html`.

For the client overview, we are passing the client's address information to the Yahoo! Maps API to get the map through its web services. Listing 13-28 uses the base open source code from `http://developer.yahoo.com/flash/maps/using.html`.

Listing 13-28. *The Yahoo! Maps API Component: clientLocation.mxml*

```
<?xml version="1.0" encoding="utf-8"?>
<!--
    Copyright (c) 2008 Yahoo! Inc.  All rights reserved.
    The copyrights embodied in the content of this file are
    licensed under the BSD (revised) open source license
-->
<mx:Canvas xmlns:mx="http://www.adobe.com/2006/mxml"
      width="100%" height="100%"
      creationComplete="handleCreationComplete()">

    <mx:Script>
        <![CDATA[
        import mx.core.Application;
        import mx.controls.Alert;
        import mx.events.ResizeEvent;

        // import maps classes.
        import com.yahoo.maps.api.YahooMap;
        import com.yahoo.maps.api.YahooMapEvent;
        import com.yahoo.maps.api.core.location.Address;
        import com.yahoo.maps.webservices.geocoder.GeocoderResult;
        import com.yahoo.maps.webservices.geocoder.events. ➥
            GeocoderEvent; ;

        import com.af.clientmanager.model.ModelLocator;

        [Bindable]
        public var model : ModelLocator =
            ModelLocator.getInstance();

        private var _yahooMap:YahooMap;
        private var _address:Address;

        public function set changeAddress(value:String):void
        {
            address = new
                Address(model.selectedClient.addressLine1 + " " +
            model.selectedClient.city + "," +
            model.selectedClient.state);
            handleCreationComplete();
        }
```

```
private function handleCreationComplete():void
{
    // This examples uses an application id passed into
    // the app via FlashVars.
    // Get your own from the Yahoo! Developer Network
    // @ http://developer.yahoo.com/wsregapp/
    var appid:String = model.YAHOO_APP_ID;

    // Create a new YahooMap object.
    _yahooMap = new YahooMap();

    // List for the MAP_INITIALIZE event from YahooMap
    _yahooMap.addEventListener(
        YahooMapEvent.MAP_INITIALIZE,
        handleMapInitialize);

    // Initialize the map, passing the app-id,
    // width and height.
    _yahooMap.init(appid,mapContainer.width,
        mapContainer.height);

    mapContainer.addChild(_yahooMap);
    mapContainer.addEventListener(ResizeEvent.RESIZE,
        handleContainerResize);

    _yahooMap.addPanControl();
    _yahooMap.addZoomWidget();
    _yahooMap.addTypeWidget();
}

private function
handleMapInitialize(event:YahooMapEvent):void
{
    // Creating a new address object, passing our
    // address string as the single parameter.
    _address = new
        Address(model.selectedClient.addressLine1 + " "
        + model.selectedClient.city + "," +
        model.selectedClient.state);

    // Listen for the GEOCODER_SUCCESS event dispatched
    // when the data comes back from the webservice.
    _address.addEventListener(
        GeocoderEvent.GEOCODER_SUCCESS,
        handleGeocodeSuccess);
```

```
                    // Send the geocode request.
                    _address.geocode();
            }

            private function
            handleGeocodeSuccess(event:GeocoderEvent):void
            {
                    // Retrieve the first result returned by the
                    // geocoder.
                    var result:GeocoderResult =
                        address.geocoderResultSet.firstResult;

                    // Then we&apos;ll get the zoom level and center
                    //lat and lon to position the map on.
                    _yahooMap.zoomLevel = result.zoomLevel;
                    _yahooMap.centerLatLon = result.latlon;
            }

            private function
            handleContainerResize(event:ResizeEvent):void
            {
                    // Set the size of the map based on its
                    // container's size.
                    _yahooMap.setSize(mapContainer.width,
                    mapContainer.height);
            }
            ]]>
    </mx:Script>

    <mx:Binding source="lblAddr.text" destination="changeAddress"/>

    <mx:VBox width="100%" height="100%"
        paddingBottom="5" paddingLeft="5"
        paddingRight="5" paddingTop="5">
            <mx:Label id="lblAddr"
                text="{model.selectedClient.addressLine1}
                {model.selectedClient.city},
                {model.selectedClient.state}"/>
            <mx:UIComponent id="mapContainer"
                width="100%" height="100%"/>
    </mx:VBox>
</mx:Canvas>
```

Now we have coded and implemented the client overview for the application. You can apply the same techniques to coding the other major components of the application, including the client projects, client financials, project administrator, and dashboard views. The source code for these components is available with the rest of the downloadable code for this book.

Skinning and Styling the Application

With the main components in place, it's time to apply skins and styling to the application. This part of the application design is usually handled by a graphic designer in the form of assets such as images, SWFs, or color palettes to use for component fills.

We discussed the policy of keeping your style tags out of your Flex source code so you can easily reskin your applications in Chapter 4. The main reason is to help maintain your application. By putting all of the styles in the application source code, you create maintenance nightmares in large applications. To avoid problems, you should use CSS to skin and style your applications.

The AF – Client Manager is a combination of graphical skinning and programmatic styles. Styles for the application include font sizes, font colors, and background alphas. Skinning, on the other hand, is a little more complex, since I chose to change the base skins for Button, TabNavigator, and TextInput by overriding skins in those components. To do this, I used the 9-slice scaling technique to apply scaled graphics to Flex components.

Using 9-Slice Scaling for Component Skins

The 9-slice scaling technique slices an image file into nine slices that scale when the size of the component that displays the image changes. Using this technique, you can specify which part of the image you want to scale in CSS.

You can define the properties for scaling when you apply the skin in CSS. These can be applied to Flex component tags such as borderSkin, skin, overSkin, and so on. This gives you a dynamic way to import skins for your applications.

Figure 13-5 shows how the application background is sliced into nine sections. The four corners of the image will not scale; only the top, bottom, left, right, and center slices will scale. This is specified in CSS as follows:

```
.applicationSkin {
    backgroundImage: Embed("assets/packs/cleanSkin/application_skin.png",
        scaleGridLeft="15",
        scaleGridRight="975",
        scaleGridTop="60",
        scaleGridBottom="64");
    backgroundSize: "100%";
}
```

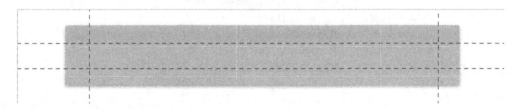

Figure 13-5. *Using 9-slice scaling on an image*

This is the main application skin for the application. It is actually 985 in width and 159 in height. The application is set to scale 100% width by 100% height, based on the size of the display space in the browser. Using 9-slice scaling allows me to use images smaller than the display space and scale them to the larger size. This technique also allows for quick reskinning of the application by switching to a new graphic pack for all skins.

Creating the AF – Client Manager Style Sheet

Listing 13-29 shows the style sheet for the AF – Client Manager application, which handles its skinnng and styling. Notice the custom styles that start with a dot (.). They are used throughout the application in the styleName tag on Flex components. You can also see that it sets the fonts used in the application, which are MyriadWebPro. You will need to define a location for the font files under the assets folder in your project. As you can see in the CSS, I have an /assets/ fonts directory from which I reference the font files.

Listing 13-29. *AF – Client Manager CSS*

```
@font-face
{
     src: url("assets/fonts/MyriadWebPro.ttf");
     font-family: main;
     font-style: normal;
     font-weight: normal;
}


@font-face
{
     src: url("assets/fonts/MyriadWebPro-Bold.ttf");
     font-family: main;
     font-style: normal;
     font-weight: bold;
}
/* Font Styles */
.heading
{
     color:#666666;
     font-family: main;
     font-size: 14pt;
     font-weight: bold;
}


.clientListFont
{
     color:#CCCCCC;
     font-family: main;
     font-size: 13pt;
     font-weight: bold;
}
```

```
.appHeading
{
    color:#222222;
    font-family: main;
    font-size: 20pt;
}
/* End Font Styles */

Application {
    padding-top:0;
    padding-bottom:0;
    padding-left:0;
    padding-right:0;
    vertical-gap:0;
    theme-color: #919191;
    font-family: main;
    color: #333333;
    font-size: 11;
    background-color: #FFFFFF;
}
.frame
{
    background-image:Embed("assets/packs/cleanSkin/frame_skin.png",
        scaleGridLeft="10",
        scaleGridRight="430",
        scaleGridTop="60",
        scaleGridBottom="64");
    background-size: "100%";
}
.frameContainerSkin
{
    background-image:
        Embed("assets/packs/cleanSkin/frame_container_skin.png",
        scaleGridLeft="10",
        scaleGridRight="430",
        scaleGridTop="60",
        scaleGridBottom="64");
    background-size: "100%";
}
 .borderStyleforContainer
 {
    Border-style: solid;
 }
```

```
.applicationSkin {
    background-image:
        Embed("assets/packs/cleanSkin/application_skin.png",
        scaleGridLeft="10",
        scaleGridRight="975",
        scaleGridTop="58",
        scaleGridBottom="62");
    background-size: "100%";
}
.containerSkin {
    background-image:
        Embed("assets/packs/cleanSkin/container_skin.png",
        scaleGridLeft="15",
        scaleGridRight="970",
        scaleGridTop="58",
        scaleGridBottom="62");
    background-size: "100%";
    border-style: borderStyleforContainer;
}
.tabContainerSkin {
    background-image:
        Embed("assets/packs/cleanSkin/tabcontainer_skin.png",
        scaleGridLeft="10",
        scaleGridRight="430",
        scaleGridTop="60",
        scaleGridBottom="64");
    background-size: "100%";
}
.clientList
{
    border-style: solid;
    border-shickness: 2;
    border-color: #f9f9f9;
    border-skin: ClassReference("com.af.components.graphics. ➡
        RoundedGradientBorder");
    fill-colors: #419af2, #0865c4;
    fill-alphas: 1, 1;
    drop-shadow-enabled: true;
    topCornerRadius: 0;
    bottomCornerRadius: 0;
    corner-radius: 0;
    header-height: 0;
}
```

```
TextInput {
    color:#222222;
    font-family: main;
    font-size: 20pt;
    border-skin: Embed("assets/packs/cleanSkin/textinput_skin.png",
        scaleGridLeft="3",
        scaleGridRight="112",
        scaleGridTop="3",
        scaleGridBottom="26");
    padding-left: 2;
}
Button {
    skin: Embed("assets/packs/cleanSkin/button_skin.png",
        scaleGridLeft="7",
        scaleGridRight="21",
        scaleGridTop="7",
        scaleGridBottom="19");
    over-skin: Embed("assets/packs/cleanSkin/button_over_skin.png",
        scaleGridLeft="7",
        scaleGridRight="21",
        scaleGridTop="7",
        scaleGridBottom="19");
    open-duration: 0;
    close-duration: 0;
    corner-radius: 2;
}
ButtonBar {
    First-button-style-name: firstButton;
    button-style-name: middleButton;
    last-button-style-name: lastButton;
}

.firstButton {
    skin: Embed("assets/packs/cleanSkin/button_bar_first.png",
        scaleGridLeft="7",
        scaleGridRight="25",
        scaleGridTop="7,
        scaleGridBottom="19");
    over-skin:
        Embed("assets/packs/cleanSkin/button_bar_first_over.png",
        scaleGridLeft="7",
        scaleGridRight="25",
        scaleGridTop="7,
        scaleGridBottom="19");
}
```

```
.middleButton {
    skin: Embed("assets/packs/cleanSkin/button_bar_middle.png",
        scaleGridLeft="7",
        scaleGridRight="25",
        scaleGridTop="7,
        scaleGridBottom="19");
    over-skin:
        Embed("assets/packs/cleanSkin/button_bar_middle_over.png",
        scaleGridLeft="7",
        scaleGridRight="25",
        scaleGridTop="7,
        scaleGridBottom="19");
}

.lastButton {
    skin: Embed("assets/packs/cleanSkin/button_bar_last.png",
        scaleGridLeft="7",
        scaleGridRight="25",
        scaleGridTop="7,
        scaleGridBottom="19");
    over-skin:
        Embed("assets/packs/cleanSkin/button_bar_last_over.png",
        scaleGridLeft="7",
        scaleGridRight="25",
        scaleGridTop="7,
        scaleGridBottom="19");
}

TabNavigator {
    border-style: none;
    background-alpha: 0;
    corner-radius: 0;
    tab-style-name: "tabButtonStyleName";
    tab-height: 28;
    padding-top:0;
}

.tabButtonStyleName {
    font-weight:normal;
    text-align:left;
    skin:Embed("assets/packs/cleanSkin/tab_skin.png",
        scaleGridLeft="1",
        scaleGridRight="162",
        scaleGridTop="1",
        scaleGridBottom="20");
```

```
         selected-up-skin:
                Embed("assets/packs/cleanSkin/tab_selected_skin.png",
                scaleGridLeft="1",
                scaleGridRight="162",
                scaleGridTop="1",
                scaleGridBottom="20");
         selected-over-skin:
                Embed("assets/packs/cleanSkin/tab_selected_skin.png",
                scaleGridLeft="1",
                scaleGridRight="162",
                scaleGridTop="1",
                scaleGridBottom="20");
         over-skin:Embed("assets/packs/cleanSkin/tab_over_skin.png",
                scaleGridLeft="1",
                scaleGridRight="162",
                scaleGridTop="1",
                scaleGridBottom="20");
    }


.panelSkin {
     border-skin: Embed("assets/packs/cleanSkin/panel_skin.png",
            scaleGridLeft="10",
            scaleGridRight="274",
            scaleGridTop="40",
        scaleGridBottom="101");
  }
```

In Figure 13-6, you can see the results of the skins and styles applied to the application. Because many of its components have custom styling, the application does not look like an out-of-the box Flex application.

Figure 13-6. *The AF – Client Manager main view*

Figure 13-7 shows the location view with the Yahoo! Maps integration.

Figure 13-7. *The AF – Client Manager location view*

Figure 13-8 shows the contact view of the application. Compare this to the wireframe defined in Chapter 2. Using the techniques covered here, you can implement the designs for the rest of the views defined in Chapter 2.

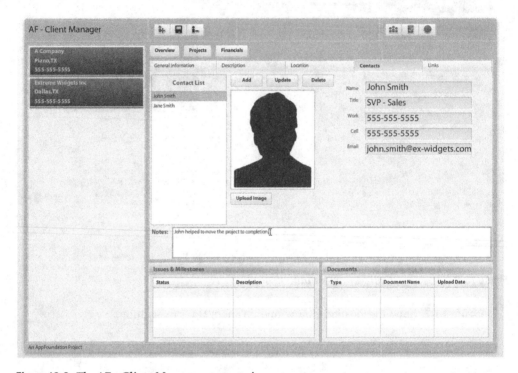

Figure 13-8. *The AF – Client Manager contact view*

You now have a good idea of how to skin the application and the base components needed to build the AF – Client Manager. You can download the full code for the application from this book's detail page at http://www.apress.com.

Touch In

Out of the box, Flex applications are ready for use on touch-screen hardware. I refer to the login process on a touch-screen Flex application as *Touch In.*

The applications I have built that allow Touch In run on the Hewlett-Packard TouchSmart PC. The login process for one application I built had authentication handled by the network behind the scenes, and we needed another way to apply security to the application. Since it was a touch-screen application, we created a keypad that granted users access to the application content when they entered their personal ID number, as shown in Figure 13-9.

Many new applications are moving toward the use of touch-screen technology—on the mobile, surface, and PC platforms. Flex is a great option when building applications for the surface and PC platforms. Figure 13.9 shows an interface that uses Touch In to grant access to application content.

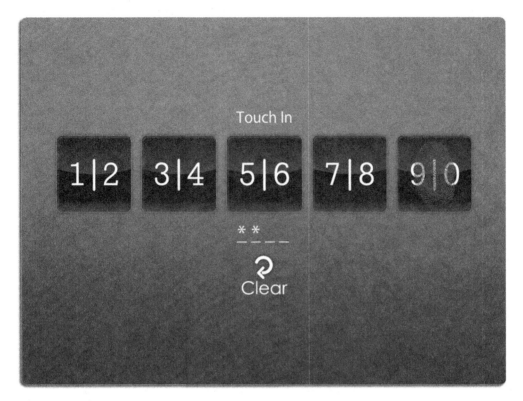

Figure 13-9 *Touch-In interface*

Summary

This chapter capped off the AF – Client Manager project by completing the user interface in Flex. We started by defining a component model, which led us to stringing together the entire application before any application logic or Cairngorm classes were created. Stringing together an application early in the process can result in better effects and transitions, with less rework in the product process. You can also get the application shell written while designers are working on the skinning and styling for the application.

After defining the component model, we handled the RemoteObject configuration that defines the ServiceLocator for Cairngorm. The services must have a destination that corresponds to the IDs of the service definitions on the BlazeDS server. Those destinations grant your application access to methods on Spring beans. The ServiceLocator is an integral part of the transport layer that Cairngorm provides for Flex. You also saw the commands, events, controller, and delegates for each of the Spring services the application calls. With the transport layer in place, we were able to code the Flex component application logic to visualize data returned from Spring services.

In the next chapter, we will move the application to an Adobe Integrated Runtime (AIR) application.

CHAPTER 14

■ ■ ■

Porting the Flex Application to AIR

This chapter provides an introduction to the Adobe Integrated Runtime (AIR) framework for building desktop applications that support using Flash, Flex, HTML, JavaScript, and Ajax. You will be able to leverage your Flex skills to build your AIR applications.

AIR can access back-end Spring services just as Flex does. Unlike Flash and Flex, however, it allows you to access the local file system. This lets you create applications that run on a desktop computer and save files to its hard drive.

In the previous chapters, you coded the AF – Client Manager application. In the Flex project, there was a lot of code written to visualize data. One of our key aims is to reuse all that code in our AIR application. You will see how you can easily port your existing Flex applications to AIR.

Upon finishing this chapter, you will be able to write AIR applications with Flex Builder, as well as use the command line to compile them. You will also be able to distribute, install, and run AIR applications through a single AIR installation file.

What Is AIR?

Adobe AIR is a cross-operating system runtime that enables you to deploy RIAs to the desktop. This in contrast to Flex, which uses the benefits of the Web and desktop applications while running in a web browser. AIR was originally called Apollo, and the first prerelease SDK was made public in March 2007. Version 1.0 of AIR was released in February 2008.

AIR can be used to build RIAs using Adobe Flash, Adobe Flex, Ajax, or HTML. For our purposes, we will focus on Adobe Flex applications running in the AIR framework.

AIR has a familiar programming model, since you code your AIR applications in the same way as code Flex applications: in MXML and ActionScript. You can install AIR applications from a browser or download them for installation like traditional desktop applications. After installation is complete, the application allows updates to be "pushed" to it.

AIR applications are cross-platform, so they can run on different operating systems, including Windows and Mac OS X. Applications can access the local operating system to perform file system operations, drag and drop from the application to the desktop, and issue system notifications. In these ways, AIR can do a lot more than Flex.

So, you may be thinking, why build a Flex application when you could create a fully functional desktop application with AIR instead? The answer is that Flex applications are browser-independent and do not require an installation to a desktop. Additionally, Flash Player has a broader distribution than the AIR environment.

AIR applications can be built using Flex Builder or the Flex SDK. If you have not downloaded and installed the Flex SDK, go ahead and get it from the Adobe Flex Downloads site (http://www.adobe.com/products/flex/flexdownloads/index.html).

Building AIR Applications with the Command Line

Building an AIR application with the command line is a little different than working with Flex. Along with the Flex SDK, you will also need Ant, which can be downloaded from http://ant.apache.org.

With the Flex SDK and Ant installed to your desktop, you need to set the path variables to access the AIR compiler with Ant. Add the following operating system environment variables to your path:

```
C:\apache-ant-1.7.1\bin
C:\Program Files\Adobe\flex_sdk_3\bin
```

Adding those two paths to your environment will give you access to the AIR compiler and Ant build components. AIR will use amxmlc to call mxmlc to compile the application classes, and acompc calls compc to compile library and component classes. As with Flex applications, you will need Java installed on your system to compile AIR applications.

You can specify AIR compilation options either on the command line or within the AIR configuration file air-config.xml, which is used when you run the amxmlc compiler. This file is used to define which AIR libraries you want included in your compile. This is important because the default values in the file will work for getting started with AIR, but you will need to pay more attention to the options for larger-scale projects.

Listing 14-1 demonstrates how to use Ant to build your AIR applications. It is an Ant build script for a basic AIR project using the Flex SDK.

Listing 14-1. *Ant Build Script for a Basic AIR Project*

```xml
<?xml version="1.0" ?>
<project>
    <!-- SDK properties -->
     <!--Your install directory for SDK_HOME may be  -->
     <!--different than the one below -->
    <property name="SDK_HOME" value="C:/Flex3SDK"/>
    <property name="MXMLC.JAR" value="${SDK_HOME}/lib/mxmlc.jar"/>
    <property name="ADL" value="${SDK_HOME}/bin/adl.exe"/>
    <property name="ADT.JAR" value="${SDK_HOME}/lib/adt.jar"/>

    <property name="APP_NAME" value="ExampleApplication"/>
    <property name="APP_ROOT" value="."/>
    <property name="MAIN_SOURCE_FILE" value="${APP_ROOT}/${APP_NAME}.mxml"/>
    <property name="APP_DESCRIPTOR" value="${APP_ROOT}/${APP_NAME}-app.xml"/>
    <property name="AIR_NAME" value="${APP_NAME}.air"/>
    <property name="DEBUG" value="true"/>
```

```
        <property name="STORETYPE" value="pkcs12"/>
        <property name="KEYSTORE" value="ExampleCert.p12"/>

  <target name="compile">
        <java jar="${MXMLC.JAR}" fork="true" failonerror="true">
              <arg value="-debug=${DEBUG}"/>
              <arg value="+flexlib=${SDK_HOME}/frameworks"/>
              <arg value="+configname=air"/>
              <arg value="-file-specs=${MAIN_SOURCE_FILE}"/>
        </java>
  </target>

  <target name="test" depends="compile">
    <target name="test">
        <exec executable="${ADL}">
              <arg value="${APP_DESCRIPTOR}"/>
        </exec>
    </target>
  </target>

  <target name="package" depends="compile">
  <target name="package">
        <java jar="${ADT.JAR}" fork="true" failonerror="true">
              <arg value="-package"/>
              <arg value="-storetype"/>
              <arg value="${STORETYPE}"/>
              <arg value="-keystore"/>
              <arg value="${KEYSTORE}"/>
              <arg value="${AIR_NAME}"/>
              <arg value="${APP_DESCRIPTOR}"/>
              <arg value="${APP_NAME}.swf"/>
              <arg value="*.png"/>
          </java>
    </target>
  </target>
</project>
```

The Ant script in Listing 14-1 performs several tasks that are necessary to compile an AIR project. The first task is to locate the installation of the Flex SDK to give access to the compiler and ADL executable:

```
    <property name="SDK_HOME" value="C:/Flex3SDK"/>
    <property name="MXMLC.JAR" value="${SDK_HOME}/lib/mxmlc.jar"/>
    <property name="ADL" value="${SDK_HOME}/bin/adl.exe"/>
    <property name="ADT.JAR" value="${SDK_HOME}/lib/adt.jar"/>
```

After defining the compiler properties, the script sets the properties that Ant needs to locate the AIR application source file:

```
<property name="APP_NAME" value="ExampleApplication"/>
<property name="APP_ROOT" value="."/>
<property name="MAIN_SOURCE_FILE" value="${APP_ROOT}/${APP_NAME}.mxml"/>
<property name="APP_DESCRIPTOR" value="${APP_ROOT}/${APP_NAME}-app.xml"/>
<property name="AIR_NAME" value="${APP_NAME}.air"/>
<property name="DEBUG" value="true"/>
<property name="STORETYPE" value="pkcs12"/>
<property name="KEYSTORE" value="ExampleCert.p12"/>
```

With the properties for the build set, the compiler needs to be invoked to execute the
mxmlc.jar. In this Java task, you must use the +flexlib parameter when using Java to build the
application. The use of the +configname=air parameter forces mxmlc to load the AIR configuration file during the compile:

```
<target name="compile">
    <java jar="${MXMLC.JAR}" fork="true" failonerror="true">
        <arg value="-debug=${DEBUG}"/>
        <arg value="+flexlib=${SDK_HOME}/frameworks"/>
        <arg value="+configname=air"/>
        <arg value="-file-specs=${MAIN_SOURCE_FILE}"/>
    </java>
</target>
```

To test the application, you can use the AIR Debug Launcher (ADL):

```
<target name="test" depends="compile">
<target name="test">
    <exec executable="${ADL}">
        <arg value="${APP_DESCRIPTOR}"/>
    </exec>
</target>
```

As part of the process to deliver AIR files to desktops, the AIR file needs to be signed using
the AIR Developer Tool (ADT). ADT generates a unique publisher ID that is used to build the
AIR file. If you sign your AIR application, you will want to use the same certificate when you
update your AIR files.

```
<target name="package" depends="compile">
<target name="package">
    <java jar="${ADT.JAR}" fork="true" failonerror="true">
        <arg value="-package"/>
        <arg value="-storetype"/>
        <arg value="${STORETYPE}"/>
        <arg value="-keystore"/>
        <arg value="${KEYSTORE}"/>
        <arg value="${AIR_NAME}"/>
        <arg value="${APP_DESCRIPTOR}"/>
        <arg value="${APP_NAME}.swf"/>
        <arg value="*.png"/>
    </java>
</target>
```

Using the Flex SDK to Create AIR Applications

In case you don't have access to Flex Builder, you can still use the Flex SDK to build AIR applications, as well as Flex applications. The instructions in this section will show you how to create a basic AIR application that will be compiled into a SWF using the Flex SDK. After reading it, you will understand how to compile, test, and package an AIR application using the command-line tools provided in the Flex SDK.

To get started developing an AIR project, you need to create a descriptor file that sets parameters for installing and launching the AIR application. The descriptor in Listing 14-2 shows the basic parameters needed for the application. This file is located at the same level as the main application MXML file.

Listing 14-2. *AIR Descriptor File for af_ClientManager_AIR.xml*

```
<?xml version="1.0" encoding="UTF-8"?>
<application xmlns="http://ns.adobe.com/air/application/1.0">
      <id>af-ClientManager-AIR</id>
      <filename>af_ClientManager_AIR</filename>
      <name>af_ClientManager_AIR</name>
      <version>1.0</version>

      <initialWindow>
            <content>af_ClientManager_AIR.swf</content>
            <visible>true</visible>
            <systemChrome>none</systemChrome>
            <transparent>true</transparent>
            <width>400</width>
            <height>200</height>
      </initialWindow>
</application>
```

The `<id>` tag uniquely identifies the application with the publisher ID. This ID is used for installation as well as application-to-application communication, access to private encrypted storage, and access to private storage. The `<version>` tag is the current version of the application, such as version 1, 1.5.3 or beta 1.4.1. The `<name>` tag is the name of the application that is installed in the AIR application installer. The `<filename>` tag is used as the file name of the application.

Building Your First AIR Application

Like Flex applications, AIR applications can be built with ActionScript or MXML. Flex applications start with a main file that contains the `<mx:Application>` tag to denote the root component of the application. All other components are contained by the root tag. AIR uses the same framework to build a hierarchy, except the root component must contain a `<mx:WindowedApplication>` tag. The `WindowedApplication` provides the controls necessary to contain the application within a window instead of a browser.

To see how to create an AIR application, begin by creating a file named `af_ClientManager_AIR` in your favorite text editor. Add the MXML code shown in Listing 14-3 to the file, which is the root file for the application source. You can use the same CSS from the AF – Client Manager Flex project (discussed in Chapter 13). Also create a Login.mxml component (located in com. af.clientmanager.view.Main), as shown in Listing 14-4, which will be used in the AIR application.

Listing 14-3. *The af_ClientManager_AIR and Login MXML file*

```
<?xml version="1.0" encoding="utf-8"?>
<mx:WindowedApplication
     xmlns:mx="http://www.adobe.com/2006/mxml"
     layout="absolute"
     xmlns:Main="com.af.clientmanager.view.Main.*">

     <mx:Style source="assets/css/style.css"/>

     <mx:VBox id="vsAppLevel" width="100%" height="100%" paddingTop="0"
          creationPolicy="all" verticalAlign="middle" horizontalAlign="center">
          <mx:Canvas id="loginView" showEffect="Fade" hideEffect="Fade">
               <Main:Login />
          </mx:Canvas>
     </mx:VBox>
</mx:WindowedApplication>
```

Listing 14-4. *Login.mxml*

```
<?xml version="1.0" encoding="utf-8"?>
<mx:Canvas xmlns:mx="http://www.adobe.com/2006/mxml" >

     <mx:Script>
     <![CDATA[
          private function doLogin():void
          {
               // Send the login credentials to a
               // server side authentication server
               // and handle the result
          }
     ]]>
     </mx:Script>

     <mx:VBox id="loginBox"
          backgroundImage="assets/images/LoginScreen.png">
          <mx:Canvas width="370" height="227"
             styleName="canvasFont">
               <mx:VBox x="50" y="9" verticalGap="-1">
                    <mx:HBox horizontalGap="0" x="26" y="14">
                         <mx:Label text="APPFOUNDATION"
                             styleName="labelFontOrange"/>
```

```
                        <mx:Label text="LOG IN"
                            styleName="labelFontWhite"/>
                    </mx:HBox>
                    <mx:TextArea backgroundAlpha="0"
                        wordWrap="true" borderStyle="none"
                        selectable="false" editable="false"
                        text="Please enter your username and password below."
                        width="288" height="35"/>
                </mx:VBox>
                <mx:TextInput id="txtUserName" width="278"
                    height="18" enter="doLogin()"
                     y="67" x="52" styleName="loginTextInput"/>
                <mx:TextInput id="txtPassword" width="278"
                    height="18" enter="doLogin()"
                    displayAsPassword="true"
                    y="88" x="52"
                    styleName="loginTextInput"/>
                <mx:VBox width="100%" y="101"
                    horizontalAlign="center">
                <mx:Text id="boxLoginMessage" />
                <mx:Label id="lblLoginMsg"
                    styleName="loginMessageFont"/>
            </mx:VBox>
            <mx:Button label="LOG IN"
                styleName="loginButton" click="doLogin()"
                x="276" y="128" width="65" height="31"/>
            </mx:Canvas>
        </mx:VBox>
</mx:Canvas>
```

This AIR application is very basic. It just displays the login component that we built in Chapter 9. As you can see, we use the same code as with Flex. The programming model is the same as in Flex.

A benefit of using AIR and Flex is that the code you develop for Flex is fully supported in AIR. This is not totally true going from AIR to Flex though, since some of the functionality—such as drag and drop to the desktop and accessing the local file system to update files—is available only in AIR applications.

Compiling and Testing the AIR Application

Compiling the application through the command line is necessary before you can run it with debugging turned on. To compile, you use the amxmlc compiler to generate a binary SWF file. Open a command shell like Cygwin. If you have your path set for amxmlc, then you can navigate to the location of the project on your hard drive and enter the following command:

```
amxmlc af_ClientManager_AIR.mxml
```

Executing `amxmlc` will create the `af_ClientManager.swf`, which is the compiled AIR application that is now ready to be run. To run the application from the command line, you need to use the ADL command to launch the application. The ADL distribution is found in the `bin` directory of the Flex SDK installation. Enter the following command at your prompt:

```
adl af_ClientManager_AIR-app.xml
```

Running the application produces a login screen that was a component created in Flex. As you can see in Figure 14-1, the AIR application is running on the user's desktop, with the desktop showing through the transparent application window. If you minimize the application using the buttons in the top left of the AIR container, it will move it to your taskbar in Windows.

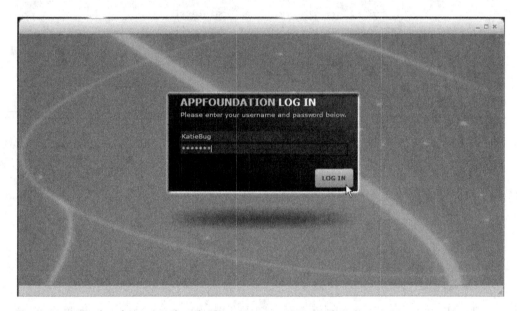

Figure 14-1. *Results of running the af_ClientManager_AIR application*

Building an AIR Installation File

Once you have successfully run and tested your AIR application, you are ready to package it into an AIR installation file using ADT. ADT will package your AIR into an archive that contains the SWF and other application files, ready for distribution to your end users. Before you can run an AIR application on a desktop, you must install the AIR framework on the computer. You can download AIR from `http://labs.adobe.com/downloads/air.html`.

Part of the process to secure your application is to digitally sign all of the AIR installation files using a signed certificate with ADT. You can use a third-party certification generation tool or buy a commercial certification from VeriSign or another vendor.

For the purposes of running and installing this application, you can generate a self-signed certificate. When the application is self-signed, it will display "unknown" for the publisher. This guarantees that the application signature has not been altered since the binary was created, but does not guarantee that the files have not been signed by a malicious party. To prevent this, you should consider having your application files signed by a commercial vendor, if the application is widely available. To self-sign your application with ADT, execute the following command at your prompt:

```
adt –certificate -cn SelfSigned 1024-RSA afCert.pfx yourInitialPassword
```

This command sets the minimum number of parameters to generate a certificate. It sets the key type to 1024-RSA. You could set it to 2048-RSA for a more complex key. It also sets an initial password for the certificate, since ADT will ask for one when creating the installation file.

From here, you are ready to create the AIR installation file by typing the following command:

```
adt -package -storetype pkcs12 -keystore afCert.pfx af_ClientManager.air ➡
af_ClientManager_AIR-app.xml af_ClientManager_AIR.swf
```

When you execute this command, you will be prompted to enter the keystore file password. For this example, it is yourInitialPassword, which was embedded into your signature.

The result of generating an installation file will be the creation of an af_clientManager.air file. This is the AIR package that can be distributed and installed on your users' desktops from a browser or a local download of the package. This works like installing a Windows application from an install executable. You can initialize the installation process by double-clicking the package in the directory where you downloaded it. You can also use a command-line shell to install the package by typing the name of the package at the prompt.

Tip There is much more you can do to secure and deploy your AIR applications. For more information, see http://help.adobe.com/en_US/AIR/1.1/devappsflex/.

I suggest that you visit Adobe at http://www.adobe.com to get a complete understanding of AIR and its distribution possibilities.

Creating an AIR Project with Flex Builder

Writing AIR applications with Flex Builder is not much different than coding a Flex application. The programming models are the same. The differences are in the APIs available to use, such as to provide file system access from AIR applications.

To create an AIR project using Flex Builder, select File ➤ New ➤ Flex Project. That will open the dialog box to create a new Flex project, as shown in Figure 14-2.

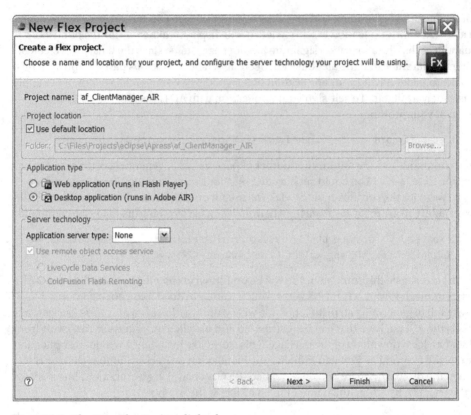

Figure 14-2. *The New Flex Project dialog box*

AIR applications run in Adobe AIR instead of Flash Player, so you need to select "Desktop application (runs in Adobe AIR)" as the application type before moving on. This will create the new Flex project as an AIR project.

Click Next to move to the next step, where you can select the bin directory for your compiled output. Accept the default and click Next once more. Now you will be able to set the source path, as shown in Figure 14-3.

In the Source path tab, you can give your AIR project an application ID that will be compiled into the SWF binary. Once you have your parameters set, click the Finish button to create the new application. This will look very similar to a Flex application, except there will be a different icon displayed at the root level of the project, as shown in Figure 14-4.

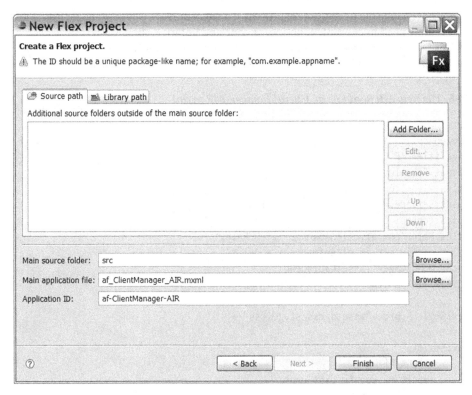

Figure 14-3. *The source path dialog box in Eclipse*

⊞ 🗂 af_ClientManager
⊞ 🗂 af_ClientManager_AIR

Figure 14-4. *AIR and Flex icons in Eclipse projects*

With that done, you are ready to start coding an AIR project using Flex Builder. This is virtually identical to coding an application in Flex. Now, let's move the af_ClientManager Flex project to AIR.

Moving Your Flex Code to AIR

You already have Flex Builder or the Flex SDK installed on your system, as well as Adobe AIR. With these in place, you can migrate the AF – Client Manager application to AIR, package it, and install it on desktops.

Migrating the AF – Client Manager Application

First, create a new AIR application. Either create a new project directory for AIR from the command line or use the Flex Builder wizard to create a new Flex project with desktop application selected as the application type, as explained in the previous sections.

Once you have a new AIR project, you will immediately notice the new application root has the <mx:WindowedApplication> tag as the root tag. Creating an AIR application using Flex

Builder does not change the development process. To move the AF – Client Manager from Flex to AIR, you simply need to copy all of the source code and libraries, such as `Cairngorm.swc`, from the Flex project and paste them into the `src` folder of the new AIR project. Then change the root Flex application file to have the `<mx:WindowedApplication>` tag, as shown in Listing 14-5.

Listing 14-5. *The New AIR Root File af_ClientManager_AIR.mxml*

```
<?xml version="1.0" encoding="utf-8"?>
<mx:WindowedApplication xmlns:mx="http://www.adobe.com/2006/mxml"
      pageTitle="AF Client Manager"
      layout="absolute"
      xmlns:view="com.af.view.*"
      xmlns:services="com.af.clientmanager.services.*"
      xmlns:control="com.af.clientmanager.control.*"
      xmlns:Main="com.af.clientmanager.view.Main.*"
      xmlns:model="com.af.clientmanager.model.*"
      backgroundImage="{AssetLib.appBG}"
      initialize="initApp()" >

      <mx:Style source="assets/css/style.css"/>

      <mx:Script>
            <![CDATA[
            import mx.events.ListEvent;
            import assets.AssetLib;
            import mx.controls.Alert;

            private function initApp():void
            {
                  vsAppLevel.selectedChild = applicationView;
            }
            public function loginSuccess():void
            {
                  vsAppLevel.selectedChild = applicationView;
            }
            ]]>
      </mx:Script>

      <!-- ================================================================== -->
      <!-- the ServiceLocator where we specify the remote services -->
      <services:Services id="services"/>

      <!-- the FrontController, containing Commands-to-Event mappings -->
      <control:MainController id="mainController" />
      <!-- ================================================================== -->

      <mx:Fade id="fadeInApp" alphaFrom="0" alphaTo="1" duration="500" />
```

```
<mx:VBox width="100%" height="100%"
        verticalScrollPolicy="off" horizontalScrollPolicy="off"
        verticalAlign="top" horizontalAlign="center">

        <mx:ViewStack id="vsAppLevel" width="100%" height="100%" paddingTop="0"
                creationPolicy="all">
            <mx:Canvas id="loginView" showEffect="Fade" hideEffect="Fade">
                <Main:Login width="100%" height="100%" />
            </mx:Canvas>
            <mx:VBox width="100%" height="100%" id="applicationView"
                    backgroundAlpha="0"
                    verticalScrollPolicy="off" horizontalScrollPolicy="off"
                    paddingTop="0"
                    verticalAlign="top" horizontalAlign="center"
                    showEffect="Fade" hideEffect="Fade">
                <mx:VBox width="985" height="735"
                        paddingTop="0" verticalGap="0"
                        verticalScrollPolicy="off"
                        horizontalScrollPolicy="off"
                        borderStyle="solid" borderThickness="2">

                    <Main:Header />

                    <mx:VBox width="100%" height="100%">
                        <Main:MainView />
                    </mx:VBox>

                    <Main:Footer />
                </mx:VBox>
            </mx:VBox>
        </mx:ViewStack>
    </mx:VBox>
</mx:WindowedApplication>
```

As you can see, this code ports the entire Flex application into an AIR application container. Now the application will run on the desktop instead of in a browser. That was a painless process, and you have retained 100% of your Flex code—a tremendous productivity boost.

Packaging and Installing the AF – Client Manager AIR Application

Now you are ready to package the application for distribution. You can use the process detailed earlier in this chapter from the command line or use the Flex Builder tools to get this done.

In Flex Builder, select Project ➤ Export Release Build to open the dialog box shown in Figure 14-5. Using the Export Release Build wizard, you can define the build requirements for the AIR application. It is important to notice the name in the "Export to file name" text box, as it will be the package that is seen by a user to download and install.

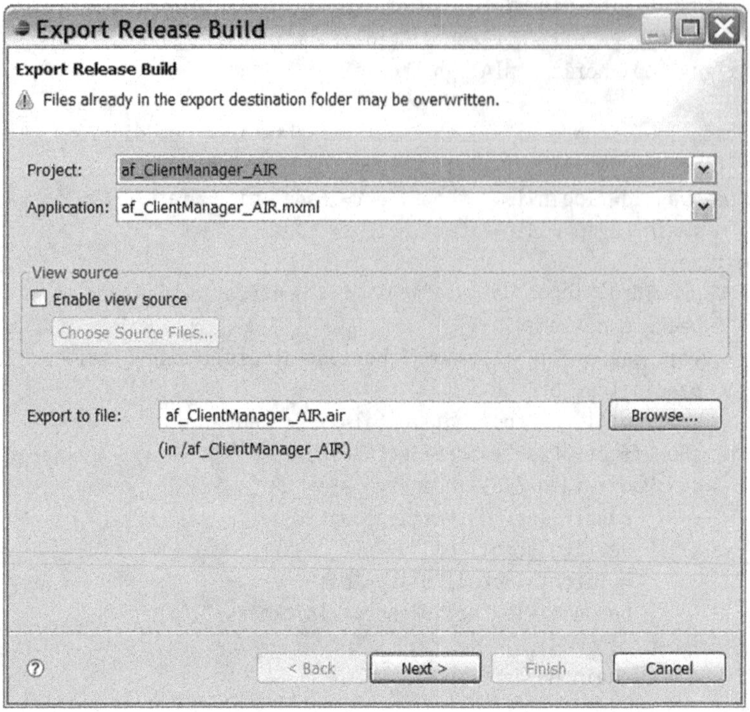

Figure 14-5. *The Export Release Build wizard in Flex Builder*

The next step in the wizard allows you to sign the installation files, as shown in Figure 14-6. You can import a signature from a commercial entity such as VeriSign by clicking the Browse button. If you don't have a digital signature for the application, click the Create button to create a self-signed digital certificate, as shown in Figure 14-7.

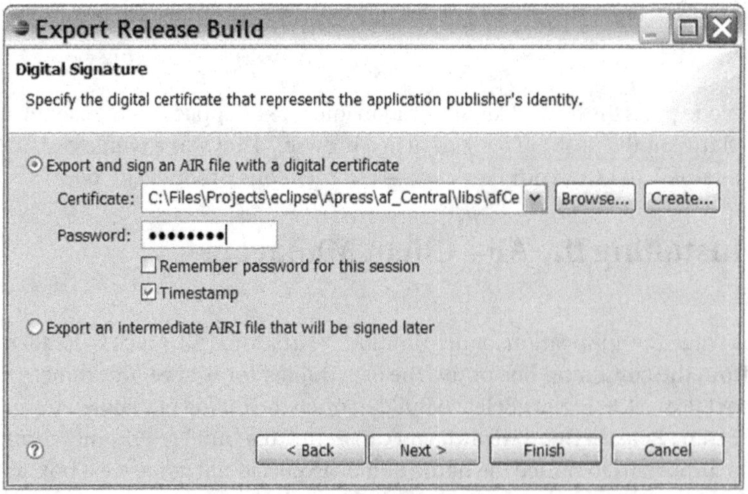

Figure 14-6. *Digital signature configuration*

Figure 14-7. *Creating a self-signed digital certificate*

Click Finish in the Export Release Build wizard. You will now have a newly created af_ClientManager_AIR.air installation binary that is signed and ready to be installed to your (or your users') desktop. Using Flex Builder, you should see the new .air file under the root project folder, as shown in Figure 14-8.

Figure 14-8. *AIR directory structure with new af_ClientManager_AIR.air installation file*

The installation file is now ready for use. You can double-click the file in Eclipse or move it to your desktop for execution. Figure 14-9 shows the first Application Install dialog box that appears. This dialog box shows that this application is self-signed and has unrestricted access to the file system. You should always be aware that an AIR application can access your local system, and install only those applications that are trusted.

Figure 14-9. *Choosing to install the AIR application*

Click the Install button to move to a dialog box that allows you to choose where to install the AIR application, as shown in Figure 14-10.

Figure 14-10. *Choosing where to install the AIR application*

That's it! You have migrated the AF – Client Manager project from Flex to AIR and have it installed on your desktop. If you are using Windows, you can access the AIR application from the Start menu.

To uninstall the AIR application, you can run the install package file again, and you will be presented with an uninstall option.

Summary

This chapter explained how to build AIR applications, as well as how to move your existing Flex application code to an AIR project.

The key point of the chapter is that you can reuse all of your Flex code within your AIR application. All of that hard work is not lost! You also have the same benefits of creating components in Flex or Flash that you can use in AIR.

AIR adds several benefits over Flex. It runs on the desktop and can support offline data storage through the file system to synchronize to a server at a later time. AIR can read and write to persistent storage on your file system, and you can update the application by allowing your users to download new versions using the Updater class.

You can connect to existing Spring services the same way you can with Flex, using a RemoteObject with an endpoint defined that points to the back-end server. This is also a strong benefit of both Flex and AIR development, and the reason we created the af_Central application for Spring services. No reconfiguration was required to point the AIR application to the Spring services.

In this book, we have worked through quite a few concepts that have a broad-reaching impact on how to deliver Flex on Spring. As you now understand, Adobe Flex and Spring provide a huge framework of robust options to deliver small to enterprise-class applications. Flex and Spring work with virtually any architecture, and can scale to meet even the highest demands in regard to user base and transactions per second.

The purpose of this book was to drive home the techniques to deliver RIAs that work hand-in-hand with Spring applications in a straightforward manner that does not cloud the end goal of creating reusable applications. Such applications increase business value and allow you to deliver them in ways that can save you hours of time in application development.

Installing the RIA Tools Platform

Throughout this book, you'll see that several tools are necessary to produce RIAs. These include Apache Tomcat, Eclipse, Flex Builder, MySQL, and Blaze DS. Most of these tools are essential to the development process for RIAs and Spring applications. The only tool that is commercial is Flex Builder, and I present alternative command-line options to create and compile your Flex source code. The other tools are free; most are fully open source.

This appendix describes how to install the tools platform I use to develop RIAs and Spring applications. Of course, it's up to you to decide what you need for developing your own projects. You can replace any of the tools described here with corresponding ones that you prefer. Remember that the goal is to be as efficient as possible when delivering your high-quality applications.

Installing Apache Tomcat

I used Tomcat 5.5.*x* to run the examples in this book. Tomcat 5.5 requires Java 5 or later.

Follow these steps to install Tomcat on your desktop or server:

1. Download Tomcat from `http://tomcat.apache.org/download-55.cgi`.

2. Download the latest version of the Core distribution, in either `.zip` or `tar.gz` format.

3. Extract the archive to your hard drive.

If you download the `.zip` file, you will need to extract its contents to a location of your choice and run the executable `tomcat4w.exe`. This won't install Tomcat as a service. I suggest using the installer if you are setting up a server that needs a service running. If you are installing with the zip distribution, you will not go through the next steps. You will be required to edit the `conf\` `tomcat-users.xml` file to set the admin username and password. The default server runs on port 8080 in both installations.

4. Double-click the installer (`apache-tomcat-5.5.x.exe`).

5. Click Next on the splash screen that comes up in the installer.

6. Click I Agree on the next screen.

7. Choose the components you want to install to your server, as shown in Figure A-1. If you want Tomcat to run as a service, check that box so it will be started automatically when the server boots.

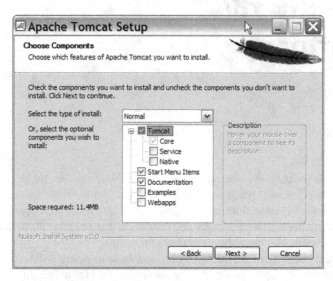

Figure A-1. *Choosing the components to install with Tomcat*

8. Choose an install location on your local file system.

9. Set up the HTTP connection port and administrator login username and password, as shown in Figure A-2.

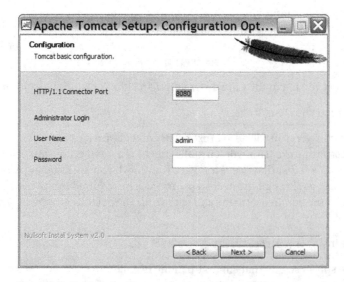

Figure A-2. *Setting the Tomcat basic configuration*

10. Set the path of your Java Virtual Machine (Java 5 or later install location), as shown in Figure A-3.

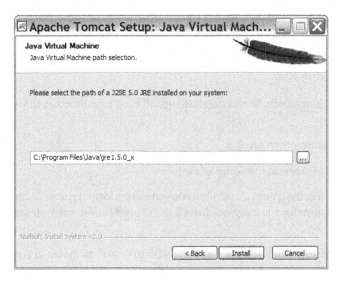

Figure A-3. *Setting the Java Virtual Machine location*

Now you are ready to start hosting web applications on your Tomcat server.

Installing Eclipse

For the examples in this book, I used the Eclipse Classic 3.4.1 distribution. Follow these steps to download and install Eclipse:

1. Download the version of Eclipse for your development platform (Windows, Linux, or Mac OS X) from `http://www.eclipse.org/downloads/`. You may also want to download the Eclipse IDE for Java EE Developers, which comes with web application plug-ins that help with enterprise Java development.

2. Accept the default mirror or choose another that may be faster (based on proximity).

3. Download the distribution and unzip it to your local file system.

4. Find the `eclipse.exe` file and run it.

You can select the default workspace location or create a completely new one to keep your projects categorized.

You are now ready to run Eclipse and start coding away.

Installing MySQL and GUI Tools

For the projects in this book, I used MySQL 5.0 Community Server. MySQL comes with two distributions: the database installation and the GUI Tools to support the database.

Follow these steps to install MySQL:

1. Download MySQL Community Tools for the database server from `http://dev.mysql.com/downloads/mysql/5.0.html`.

2. Extract the MySQL Community Server database installation to a directory of your choice.

3. Double-click the executable to run it.

4. Click Next at the first screen in the Setup wizard.

5. In the next screen, select the type of installation you want to perform: Typical, Complete, or Custom. I chose Custom for the database installation I used for the examples in this book.

6. In the Custom Setup screen, choose the items you wish to install, as shown in Figure A-4. Click Next to continue.

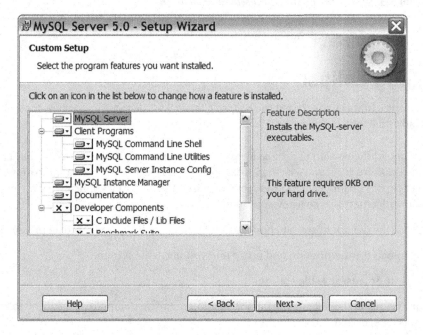

Figure A-4. *MySQL custom setup*

7. The next screen indicates the install directory for MySQL, as shown in Figure A-5. Click the Install button to proceed with the installation.

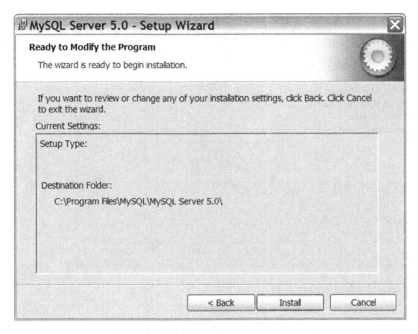

Figure A-5. *MySQL destination folder*

Once the installation is complete, you will be allowed to configure your MySQL server. I accepted the defaults presented by the wizard, and set the root password for the server. This installed MySQL as a service, ready for tables to be built.

To install the GUI Tools for MySQL, download the installer from http://dev.mysql.com/downloads/gui-tools/5.0.html. Then double-click the executable to run it. I accepted the defaults for a custom installation, and installed the MySQL Query Browser and MySQL Administrator, as shown in Figure A-6. These tools are very visual and will help you build and configure your databases quickly.

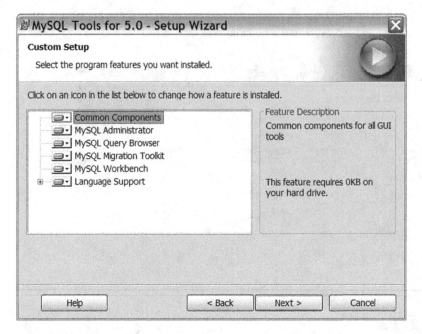

Figure A-6. *MySQL Tools selection*

Installing the Flex Builder Plug-In

Flex Builder can be installed in two fashions: as a stand-alone IDE or as a plug-in to Eclipse. I prefer to install the plug-in to Eclipse, since Eclipse comes with all of the Java development components I need. You must have Eclipse 3.3 or higher installed to use the Flex Builder plug-in.

Follow these steps to install the Flex Builder plug-in for Eclipse:

1. Download the Adobe Flex Builder Eclipse plug-in installation from `http://www.adobe.com/products/flex/flexdownloads/#flex_builder`.

2. Run the executable for Flex Builder by double-clicking it.

3. In the first installer screen, click Next.

4. Accept the license agreement and click Next.

5. You will be presented with a screen to choose your install location, as shown in Figure A-7. Accept the default or choose another location, and then click Next.

Figure A-7. *Flex Builder install folder selection*

6. The next screen asks you to choose an existing Eclipse location, as shown in Figure A-8. The Flex Builder plug-in will be integrated with this Eclipse installation. Click Next to continue.

Figure A-8. *Eclipse folder selection*

7. Click the Install button to install the Flex Builder plug-in.

Installing the Flex SDK

The Flex SDK is required for command-line compiling of your applications. To install the Flex SDK, follow these steps:

1. Download the Flex SDK from `http://www.adobe.com/products/flex/flexdownloads/#flex_builder`.

2. Extract the contents of the Flex SDK zip file to a location of your choice, where you will reference the Flex command-line utilities in the `bin` folder of the Flex SDK installation.

3. You also need access to the Flex compiler, `mxmlc`. Add the operating system environment variable to the path. For example, the following path entry is where I have the Flex SDK installed:

   ```
   Path=C:\Program Files\Adobe\flex_sdk_3\bin
   ```

4. Test that you have access to the Flex compiler. From the command line, type `mxmlc` and press Enter. You should get the following results:

   ```
   C:\mxmlc
   Adobe Flex Compiler (mxmlc)
   Version 3.1.0 build 2710
   Copyright (c) 2004-2007 Adobe Systems, Inc. All rights reserved.

   mxmlc [options] [defaultVar]
   Use 'mxmlc -help' for more information.
   ```

With these steps complete, you can now use the Flex SDK to compile your Flex applications in combination with Ant.

Installing Ant

You can use Ant to compile your Flex application source code. Follow these steps to use Ant for Flex projects:

1. Download Ant from `http://ant.apache.org`.

2. Install Ant by moving the contents of the zip archive to the directory of your choice on your workstation.

3. Add the Ant `bin` directory to your operating systems environment variables in system variables.

   ```
   Path=C:\apache-ant-1.7.1\bin
   ```

4. To check that you have Ant installed correctly with the path set, open a command-line terminal and enter ant. You should see something like this:

```
C:\ant
Buildfile: build.xml does not exist!
Build failed
```

If you get this message, you successfully have Ant installed and ready to build your Flex applications.

Building Flex Applications with Ant

As an alternative to using the commercial Flex Builder application, you can use the Ant script in Listing A-1 to build your Flex applications. The build.xml file needs to be located in the root directory of your Flex project.

Listing A-1. *A build.xml Ant Script to Build Flex Applications*

```xml
<?xml version="1.0" encoding="utf-8"?>
<project name="YourProjectNameHere" basedir=".">
    <property name="FLEX_HOME" value="C:\Program Files\Adobe\flex_sdk_3"/>
    <taskdef resource="flexTasks.tasks" classpath=
        ""${FLEX_HOME}/ant/lib/flasTasks.jar"/>
    <property name="APP_ROOT" value="src"/>
    <property name="OUTPUT_DIR" value="bin" />
    <property name="APP_NAME" value="YourAppNameHere" />

    <target name="init">
        <delete dir="${OUTPUT_DIR}" />
        <mkdir dir="${OUTPUT_DIR}" />
    </target>
    <target name="wrapper">
        <html-wrapper
            title="Flex Ant Compile"
            file="${APP_NAME}.html"
            height="300"
            width="400"
            bgcolor="red"
            application="app"
            swf="${APP_NAME}"
            version-major="9"
            version-minor="0"
            version-revision="0"
            history="true"
            template="express-installation"
            output="${OUTPUT_DIR}"/>
    </target>
```

```xml
    <target name="main" depends="init,wrapper">
        <mxmlc file="${APP_ROOT}/${APP_NAME}.mxml"
            output="${OUTPUT_DIR}/${APP_NAME}.swf"
            keep-generated-actionscript="true">
            <load-config filename="${FLEX_HOME}/frameworks/flex-config.xml"/>
            <source-path path-element="${FLEX_HOME}/frameworks"/>

            <!-- Access to all SWC files in the project libs directory. -->
            <compiler.library-path dir="${FLEX_HOME}/frameworks" append="true">
                <include name="libs" />
                <include name="../bundles/{locale}" />
            </compiler.library-path>
            <compiler.library-path dir="${basedir}" append="true">
                    <include name="libs" />
            </compiler.library-path>
        </mxmlc>
    </target>
    <!-- Perform a clean build -->
    <target name="clean">
        <delete dir="${APP_ROOT}/generated"/>
        <delete>
            <fileset dir="${OUTPUT_DIR}" includes="${APP_NAME}.swf"/>
        </delete>
    </target>
</project>
```

Index

Numbers and Symbols

9-slice scaling, for component skins, 406–407

(pound sign), translating, 248

& (ampersand), translating, 248

() (left and right parentheses), 248

{} (curly braces), using for data binding, 68

* (wildcard character), allowing access to everyone with, 244

@After annotation, using at end of test cycle, 120

@Before annotation, annotating init() method with when testing, 120

@Column annotation, 314

@ContextConfiguration, using when testing, 120

@Entry annotation, at top of domain object definition, 314

@Id annotation, domain object definition, 314

@RunWith annotation, using when testing, 120

@Table annotation, at top of domain object definition, 314

@Test annotation, for tagging a method to execute during unit test, 120

A

ACID, transaction descriptions that make up, 203–204

ActionScript
creating custom components with, 78

in Flex applications, 66–67

mx, 67

securing, 248–255

variable types, 66

ActionScript and MXML, introduction to, 63–67

ActionScript bindings, using for data binding, 71–73

ActionScript BindingUtils class, data binding through, 71–73

ActionScript class,
creating base, 78–79

creating custom <mx:DateChooser> component for, 78–79

ActionScript expressions, data binding through, 70–71

ActionScript filters, securing input characters in Flex with, 248

addCommand() method call, 188

AddContact.as file, for Cairngorm submodel, 186

AddContactCommand.as file, 171–172
Cairngorm command for adding a contact, 191

AddContactEvent.as file, for adding a Cairngorm contact, 189

Adobe AIR, 10

Adobe Exchange, web site address, 147

Adobe Flash Player, 6–7

Adobe Flash Player version penetration numbers, web site address, 6

Adobe Flex. *See* Flex

Adobe Flex Builder. *See* Flex Builder

Adobe Integrated Runtime (AIR). *See* AIR (Adobe Integrated Runtime)

Adobe LiveCycle Data Services (LCDS), included as part of Flex, 10

Adobe Systems, SpringFactory Java class by Jeff Vroom, 144–147

Adobe's Flash Player Player Census page, web site address, 6

ADT. *See* AIR Developer Tool (ADT)

You Need the Companion eBook

Your purchase of this book entitles you to buy the companion PDF-version eBook for only $10. Take the weightless companion with you anywhere.

We believe this Apress title will prove so indispensable that you'll want to carry it with you everywhere, which is why we are offering the companion eBook (in PDF format) for $10 to customers who purchase this book now. Convenient and fully searchable, the PDF version of any content-rich, page-heavy Apress book makes a valuable addition to your programming library. You can easily find and copy code—or perform examples by quickly toggling between instructions and the application. Even simultaneously tackling a donut, diet soda, and complex code becomes simplified with hands-free eBooks!

Once you purchase your book, getting the $10 companion eBook is simple:

❶ Visit **www.apress.com/promo/tendollars/**.

❷ Complete a basic registration form to receive a randomly generated question about this title.

❸ Answer the question correctly in 60 seconds, and you will receive a promotional code to redeem for the $10.00 eBook.

2855 TELEGRAPH AVENUE | SUITE 600 | BERKELEY, CA 94705

Offer valid through 9/09.